2021 AP EXAM FORMAT INFORMATION

The COVID-19 pandemic affected the administration of AP exams in both 2020 and 2021. Although things remain subject to change at any time, it appears we are now on our way back to the traditional AP track. College Board continues to make decisions based on the health and safety of students and educators across the country, so it's a good idea to stay informed of the latest changes to your AP course and exam as the school year progresses.

The big news for the 2021 tests was the introduction of varied testing date and format options. Rather than offering the traditional single test approach, AP exams were administered three times— in early May, late May, and early June—with some subjects having been administered in a digital format in addition to the traditional paper format. Several exams offered different formats for paper- and digital-based exams, and the differences varied by subject. **All exams, however, were full length and covered the full scope of content for each AP course.**

AP World History exam used the following format:

- Exams were offered on paper in early May, and as a digital exam in late May and early June
- The paper and digital versions differed as follows:
  - Section 1A: Both exams contained the typical multiple-choice section
  - Section 1B:
    I. The paper exam contained the typical short answer question (SAQ) section. Students answered 3 SAQs; 2 were required, and students chose the third from 2 options
    II. Students taking the digital exam were given 3 SAQs and needed to answer all 3; test security considerations precluded providing a choice
      a. Question 1 was required, included 1 primary source text, and focused on historical developments or processes between the years 1200 and 2001
      b. Question 2 was required, included 1 map source, and focused on historical developments or processes between the years 1200 and 2001
      c. Question 3 was required, included 1 primary source image, and focused on historical developments or processes between the years 1200 and 2001
- Section 2A: Both exams contained the typical document-based question (DBQ) section.

- ■ Section 2B:
  - • The paper exam contained the typical long essay question (LEQ) section. Students chose 1 LEQ to answer from 3 options.
  - • The digital exam didn't contain a long essay question (LEQ), a question type that was precluded from at-home testing due to security considerations. Instead, it contained a second SAQ section, containing 2 SAQs; and students needed to answer both. Students had 40 minutes—the same time as Section 2B on the paper exam—to answer these 2 SAQs.
  - I. Question 5 was required, included 1 source with a data set (such as a chart, table, or graph), and focused on historical developments or processes between the years 1200 and 2001
  - II. Question 6 was required, included secondary source text, and focused on historical developments or processes between the years 1200 and 2001

In summary, the paper free-response section included 3 SAQs, 1 DBQ, and 1 LEQ with some optionality; the digital free-response section included 3 SAQs, 1 DBQ, and 2 SAQs with no optionality

Is this *5 Steps* guide relevant and up-to-date?

Yes! Everything in this book is reflective of the current course and exam as it was originally designed. The *5 Steps* team strives to keep all information relevant and as up-to-date as possible, both in print and online.

What will happen in May 2022?

Your guess is as good as ours. Whether the AP exams return fully to their original paper format, continue in the 2021 hybrid (paper and online) models, or morph into something entirely new – remains uncertain. However, no matter what College Board will decide for next year - we have you covered! We'll be updating our materials whenever any new information becomes available, and will make every effort to revise our digital resources as quickly as possible.

So, whatever this AP school year may bring, please continue to check in to your *5 Steps* Cross-Platform course at **mheducation.com/5stepsapwh**. We will make every effort to keep the practice tests on the platform reflective of what you'll see on test day.

Most importantly, look for regular updates on the College Board website for the latest information on your course at **apcentral.collegeboard.org**. This will be your best resource for the most up-to-date information on all AP courses.

5 STEPS TO A 5™

AP World History: Modern
2022

Beth Bartolini-Salimbeni
Wendy Petersen

New York Chicago San Francisco Athens London Madrid
Mexico City Milan New Delhi Singapore Sydney Toronto

1 2 3 4 5 6 7 8 9   LHS   26 25 24 23 22 21 (Cross-Platform Prep Course only)
1 2 3 4 5 6 7 8 9   LHS   26 25 24 23 22 21 (Elite Student Edition)

ISBN   978-1-264-26807-8 (Cross-Platform Prep Course only)
MHID   1-264-26807-6

e-ISBN   978-1-264-26808-5 (Cross-Platform Prep Course only)
e-MHID   1-264-26808-4

ISBN   978-1-264-26809-2 (Elite Student Edition)
MHID   1-264-26809-2

e-ISBN   978-1-264-26810-8 (Elite Student Edition)
e-MHID   1-264-26810-6

McGraw Hill, the McGraw Hill logo, *5 Steps to a 5,* and related trade dress are trademarks or registered trademarks of McGraw Hill and/or its affiliates in the United States and other countries and may not be used without written permission. All other trademarks are the property of their respective owners. McGraw Hill is not associated with any product or vendor mentioned in this book.

AP, Advanced Placement Program, and *College Board* are registered trademarks of the College Board, which was not involved in the production of, and does not endorse, this product.

The series editor was Grace Freedson, and the project editor was Del Franz.
Series design by Jane Tenenbaum.

McGraw Hill products are available at special quantity discounts to use as premiums and sales or for use in corporate training programs. To contact a representative, please visit the Contact Us pages at www.mhprofessional.com.

CONTENTS

STEP 5 Build Your Test-Taking Confidence

PREFACE

Welcome to the adventure of Advanced Placement (AP) World History: Modern. Enjoy the challenges of your studies. During the course of the year, you should be prepared to read widely in both your text and readers. Expect to analyze all sorts of primary documents, from text to political cartoons, photographs, paintings, maps, and charts; analytical skills are essential to success on both the multiple-choice and the essay questions. You will write essay after essay as you not only analyze primary documents but also compare issues and analyze continuity and change over time. Along the way, enjoy the fascinating story of humankind and find a little of yourself among the peoples of other societies.

During the 2019–2020 school year AP World History: Modern incorporated changes to the curriculum so that there are now four designated historical periods to cover instead of six: 1200–1450, 1450–1750, 1750–1900, and 1900–present. A new theme—Technology and Innovation—was added so that there are nine instead of five thematic units.

Chapters 1 through 9 in this edition cover background information that may eventually be incorporated into a new AP World History course with a focus on history before 1200 CE. The content on the revised exam, however, covers only the years between 1200 CE and the present. The diagnostic and practice exams reflect this change. These exams are designed to reflect mastery of the historical thinking skills cultivated by any AP history course. Questions that follow each content chapter are designed to help you recall information, though they follow, in general, the AP examination format.

There is one major exception to the new periodization: origins and contributions of major world religions to world history. This material is covered in Chapters 10 and 11. We have left background information in the glossary and in the sections on maps and key individuals. We have included this information with the intent that it may serve as historical context, review, or reference where necessary.

This study guide will ease your passage through the challenges of AP World History: Modern to success on the examination. At first sight, the amount of material in the AP World History: Modern course can appear a bit overwhelming. The goal of this manual is to present that content material and the test-taking skills that will allow you to approach the AP exam with confidence. As a first step, turn now to the Introduction to learn about the five-step study program and how it can help you to organize your preparation.

ACKNOWLEDGMENTS

We wish to thank Grace Freedson and Del Franz for their encouragement and editing, outside readers for their invaluable suggestions, and our families for their extraordinary patience.

—Beth Bartolini-Salimbeni
—Wendy Petersen

BETH BARTOLINI-SALIMBENI holds degrees in history, Spanish, Italian, and comparative literature. A former Fulbright scholar and twice a National Endowment for the Humanities (NEH) fellow, she has taught AP World History, AP European History, and AP Art History at the high school level as well as history and languages at the high school and the university levels, both in the United States and in Italy. Her most recent book is *Italian Grammar for Dummies*. She is currently working on a biography of a nineteenth-century Italian "gentlewoman." In 2014–2015, she was the recipient of the American Association of Italian Teachers Distinguished Service Award (K–12) and the New Mexico Organization of Language Educators Lifetime Achievement Award for her work in Romance languages and cultures.

WENDY PETERSEN earned undergraduate degrees in political science and French before going on to a Master of Arts in political science. Time spent studying in France and England sparked her interest in history, and she began her career teaching world history in southwest Houston in 1997. Since moving to New Mexico in 2000, she has taught a variety of subjects, including French, AP World History, and AP United States Government and Politics. In 2014, she was selected as one of the first teachers to pilot the new Advanced Placement Seminar course, part of the College Board's Advanced Placement Capstone program.

INTRODUCTION: THE FIVE-STEP PROGRAM

Introducing the Five-Step Preparation Program

This book is organized as a five-step program to prepare you for success on the exam. These steps are designed to provide you with vital skills and strategies and the practice that can lead you to that perfect 5. Here are the five steps.

Step 1: Set Up Your Study Program

In this step you'll read a brief overview of the AP World History: Modern exam, including an outline of topics and the approximate percentage of the exam that will test knowledge of each topic. You'll learn:

- Background information about the AP exam
- Reasons for taking the exam
- What to bring to the exam
- Other tips to prepare you for the exam
- How to choose the preparation plan that's right for you
- Timetables for three suggested plans

Step 2: Determine Your Test Readiness

In this step you'll take a diagnostic exam in AP World History: Modern. This pretest should give you an idea of how prepared you are before beginning your study program.

- Go through the diagnostic exam step by step and question by question to build your confidence level.
- Review the correct answers and explanations so that you see what you do and do not yet fully understand.

Step 3: Develop Strategies for Success

In this step you'll learn strategies that will help you do your best on the exam. These strategies cover all four question types: multiple-choice, document-based, continuity and change-over-time, and comparative. This part of your preparation program will help you learn

- how to read multiple-choice questions.
- how to answer multiple-choice questions, including whether or not to guess.
- how to analyze primary documents, including texts, photographs, political cartoons, maps, and charts.
- how to answer the document-based and long essays.
- how to respond to the short-answer questions.

Step 4: Review the Knowledge You Need to Score High

In this step you'll learn or review the material you need to know for the test. This section takes up the bulk of this book. It contains not only summaries of key events and concepts but also vocabulary lists and review questions. The material is organized chronologically. Each unit in this section is followed by a timeline, a list of key comparisons, and a change/continuity chart. The chart will show you at a glance key events and issues in the major world regions. It will also refresh your memory of changes and continuities within each region during the time covered by the unit.

As you review this material, it may be helpful to work with others. Find a study pal or form a small study group, and set a time when you can get together to review.

Step 5: Build Your Test-Taking Confidence

In this step you'll complete your preparation by testing yourself on a full-length practice exam modeled after the actual examination. The test is followed by a discussion of the answers. Be aware that this practice exam is *not* simply a reproduction of questions from actual AP exams, but it mirrors both the material tested and the way in which it is tested.

- Try the strategies provided in Chapter 4 of this book for each type of question on the test.
- Pair up with another student and read and critique each other's essays.
- Take the time not only to check whether or not your answers are correct but also to read the explanation for the correct answers. By doing this, you will review a broad body of concepts in a shorter period of time.

Finally, at the back of this book you'll find additional resources to aid your preparation. These include the following:

- Glossary of terms
- Bibliography for further reading
- List of websites related to the AP World History: Modern exam
- An appendix of selected maps
- An appendix of key individuals

The Graphics Used in This Book

To emphasize particular concepts and strategies, we use several icons throughout this book. An icon in the margin will alert you that you should pay particular attention to the accompanying text. We use these three icons:

The first icon points out a very important concept or fact that you should not pass over.

The second icon calls your attention to a strategy that you may want to try.

The third icon indicates a tip that you might find useful.

STEP 1

Set Up Your Study Program

CHAPTER 1

What You Need to Know About the AP World History: Modern Exam

IN THIS CHAPTER

Summary: Learn background information on the AP program and exam, how exams are graded, what types of questions are asked, what topics are tested, and basic test-taking information.

Key Ideas

✪ Many colleges and universities will give you credit for exam scores of 3 or above.

✪ Multiple-choice questions reflect the amount of course time spent on each of the four AP World History: Modern periods.

✪ The three types of free-response questions are based on the broad course themes and are aligned with course skills.

Background Information

What Is the Advanced Placement Program?

The Advanced Placement (AP) program was begun by the College Board in 1955 to construct standard achievement exams that would allow highly motivated high school students the opportunity to be awarded advanced placement as freshmen in colleges and universities in the United States. Today, there are more than 30 courses and exams with nearly 2 million students taking the annual exams in May.

There are numerous AP courses in the social studies beside World History: Modern, including U.S. History, European History, U.S. Government, Comparative Government, Macroeconomics, Microeconomics, and Psychology. The majority of students who take

AP tests are juniors and seniors; however, some schools offer AP courses to freshmen and sophomores, especially in World History.

Who Writes the AP World History: Modern Exam? Who Corrects the Exams?

Like all AP exams, the World History: Modern exam is written by college and high school instructors of world history. This group is called the AP World History Test Development Committee. The committee constantly evaluates the test, analyzing the test as a whole and on an item-by-item basis. All questions on the World History: Modern exam are field-tested before they actually appear on an AP exam.

A much larger group of college and secondary teachers meets at a central location in early June to correct the exams that were completed by students the previous month. The scoring procedure of each grader (or "reader") during this session is carefully analyzed to ensure that exams are being evaluated on a fair and consistent basis.

How Are Exams Graded?

Sometime in July the grade you receive on your AP exam is reported. You, your high school, and the colleges you listed on your initial application will receive the scores.

There are five possible scores that you may receive on your exam:

- 5 indicates that you are extremely well qualified. This is the highest possible grade.
- 4 indicates that you are well qualified.
- 3 indicates that you are qualified.
- 2 indicates that you are possibly qualified.
- 1 indicates that you are not qualified to receive college credit.

Individual colleges and universities differ in their acceptance of AP exam scores. Most will not consider a score below a 3 on any AP exam. Many highly competitive colleges and universities honor only scores of 5 on AP exams. To find out which universities offer credit, and how much for which score, go to the College Board website: https://apstudent. collegeboard.org/creditandplacement.

Reasons for Taking the Advanced Placement Exam

The higher-order thinking skills that characterize the AP World History: Modern course provide an excellent preparation for college and university studies.
—*College professor*

There are several very practical reasons for enrolling in an AP World History: Modern course and taking the AP World History: Modern exam in May. During the application process colleges look very favorably on students who have challenged themselves by taking Advanced Placement courses. Although few would recommend this, it is possible to take any AP exam without taking a preparatory course for that exam.

Most important, most colleges will reward you for doing well on your AP exams. Although the goal of this manual is to help you achieve a 5, if you get a 3 or better on your AP World History: Modern exam, many colleges will either give you actual credit for a required introductory World History course or allow you to receive elective credit. You should definitely check beforehand with the colleges you are interested in to find out their policy on AP scores and credit; they will vary.

Taking a year of AP World History: Modern (or any AP) course will be a very exacting and challenging experience. If you have the capabilities, allow yourself to be challenged! Many students feel a great personal satisfaction after completing an AP course, regardless of the scores they eventually receive on the actual exam.

What You Need to Know About the AP World History: Modern Exam

The AP World History: Modern exam consists of both multiple-choice and essay questions. The multiple-choice portion is worth 40 percent of the total exam grade, whereas the three essays together count equally for the other 60 percent. Your score on the multiple-choice section is based on the number of questions you answer correctly. There is no "guessing penalty." No points will be deducted for incorrect answers; unanswered questions will be graded as incorrect answers.

Format of the Exam

The following table summarizes the format of the AP World History: Modern exam.

SECTION	TYPE OF QUESTION	NUMBER OF QUESTIONS	TIME	RECOMMENDED TIME	% OF EXAM SCORE
Section I, Part A	Multiple-Choice	55		55 minutes	40%
Section I, Part B	Short-Answer	4: answer questions 1 and 2; choose between questions 3 and 4.	95 minutes	40 minutes	20%
Section II, Part A	Document-Based Question (DBQ)	1	100 minutes	60 minutes	25%
Section II, Part B	Long-Essay	Choose 1 of 3 questions		40 minutes	15%

Multiple-Choice Questions

This section consists of 55 questions. Each question has four possible answers. The questions are arranged in sets of two to four questions per set. Each set begins with a written or visual stimulus. It is recommended that you use 55 minutes of the total 95 minutes you are given for Section I of the exam.

The College Board annually publishes material on the breakdown of questions on the multiple-choice test. However, at press time it was unknown what that breakdown would be.

Short-Answer Questions

The AP exam contains four short-answer questions: you will answer questions 1 and 2, and then choose between questions 3 and 4. Each question will have Parts A and B, and some questions will also contain a Part C. All questions, regardless of the number of parts, are worth the same number of points. At least two of the questions will contain historical texts, maps, drawings, photos, charts, or some other historical item that you must interpret and evaluate. It is recommended that you use 40 minutes of the 95 total minutes you are given for Section I to work on your responses to the short-answer questions.

For DBQs, group your information and then analyze all the details. Find what will actually be useful for your essay. Be clear, concise, and to the point.
—AP student

Essay Questions

During the remaining 100 minutes of the test you will be asked to write two essays: a document-based question (DBQ) and a long-essay question. The essays will be based on the broad themes that form the background of the AP World History: Modern course. According to the College Board description of the AP World History: Modern course, these themes include:

- Human-environmental interaction
  - Disease and its effects on population
  - Migration
  - Settlement patterns
  - Technology
- Cultural development and interaction
  - Religions, belief systems, and philosophies
  - The arts and architecture
- State-building, expansion, and conflict (Governance)
  - Political structures and forms of government
  - Empires
  - Nations and nationalism
  - Revolts and revolutions
  - Regional, transregional, and global organizations and structures
- Creation, growth, and interaction of economic systems
  - Agriculture and pastoralism
  - Trade and commerce
  - Labor systems
  - Industrialization
  - Capitalism and socialism
- Development and change of social structures
  - Gender roles
  - Family and kinship relations
  - Race and ethnicity
  - Social and economic class structures
- Technology and innovation

Also essential to success on the essays is the ability to visualize global patterns and the reactions of societies to global processes. The ability to interpret the context of a document, as well as to analyze point of view, is necessary to compose a satisfactory response to the DBQ.

For further information on the multiple-choice and essay questions, refer to Step 3 of this manual.

Taking the Exam

When you arrive at the exam site, you should have brought the following:

- Several pencils for the multiple-choice questions.
- Several black or blue pens for the essays.
- A traditional, not a smart, watch. Silence any alarms that would go off during the exam period.

- Tissues.
- Your school code.
- Your driver's license and Social Security number.

Leave the following items at home:

- A cell phone or calculator
- Books, a dictionary, study notes, flash cards, highlighters, correction fluid, a ruler, or any other office supplies
- Portable music of any kind; no MP3 players, iPods, or CD players are allowed

Other recommendations:

- Don't study the night before. Arrive at the exam rested.
- Wear comfortable clothing. It's a good idea to layer your clothing so that you are prepared for a variety of temperatures in the exam room.
- Eat a light breakfast and a light lunch on the day of the exam.

CHAPTER 2

How to Plan Your Time

IN THIS CHAPTER

Summary: The right preparation plan for you depends on your study habits, your own strengths and weaknesses, and the amount of time you have to prepare for the test. This chapter recommends some study plans to get you started.

Key Points

✪ Preparing for the exam is important. It helps to have a plan—and stick with it!

✪ You should create a study plan that best suits your situation and prioritize your review based on your strengths and weaknesses.

Three Approaches to Preparing for the AP World History: Modern Exam

It's up to you to decide how you want to use this book to study for the AP World History: Modern exam. This book is designed for flexibility; you can work through it in order or skip around however you want. In fact, no two students who purchase this book will probably use it in exactly the same way.

Your study plan should begin with taking the diagnostic test in Chapter 3. Based on that, you can decide what parts of world history you need to review. The world history content you need for the exam is reviewed in Chapters 14–31. Included in each chapter are test-like multiple-choice questions to help you check your knowledge and practice for the test. You should also include Chapter 4 in your study plan; it contains tips and strategies for each type of question on the exam. Any study plan should culminate with the practice test at the end of the book.

Plan A: The Full-Year Plan (Beginning in Summer)

If you have purchased this book in the summer before your course begins, you can use it to obtain a basic understanding of world history prior to 1200 CE. Your AP course officially starts with that year, but, of course, to understand what's going on in 1200, you'll need some basic knowledge of what's been happening in the world before that date. Chapters 5–13 contain that summary. Include that in your study plan to get up to speed so you can start day one of your course with the background information you need.

A key step in developing your study plan is to take the diagnostic test in the next chapter. This is a practice exam that closely mirrors the actual exam. By taking the diagnostic test, you'll find out exactly what you're up against. You will also see what content you need to review and what skills you need to practice. Identify your weaknesses and focus on these first. Plan to take the diagnostic test in January and the final test in April just before the exam.

Following this plan will allow you to practice your skills and develop your confidence gradually as you go through the AP course. Since you purchased this book in the summer, you'll be able to get the background reading done to begin your course with an understanding of world history prior to 1200. This book is filled with practice exercises; beginning to work through them at the start of the school year maximizes your preparation for the exam. Since you've practiced the whole year, you'll be in peak condition to perform your best on the exam.

The One-Semester Plan

Starting in the middle of the school year should give you ample time to review and prepare for the test. Of course, if you also need to prepare for other AP exams, or if you are super-busy with extracurricular activities, your time will be more limited. You can skip the background reading sections; they are designed to get you up to speed when you start the course.

Regardless of how much time you are able to devote to prepping for the AP World History: Modern exam, you should start by taking the diagnostic test in the next chapter. This will give you an accurate idea of what the test is like. You'll get a sense of how hard the test will be for you, how much time you need to devote to practice, and which types of questions and areas of content you most need to work on. Skip around in this book, focusing on the chapters that deal with the content you find most difficult. Take the final practice test a few days before you take the actual test.

The Six-Week Plan

Okay, maybe you procrastinated a bit too long. But this might not be a problem if you are doing well in your AP World History: Modern class and just need to review areas where you are relatively weak and practice with the types of questions on the exam. In fact, practice with test-like questions is included in most AP World History: Modern classes. So you may be more ready for the exam than you realize.

Start by taking the diagnostic test in the next chapter to find out what the actual test will be like and to identify the content areas and the types of questions that you most need to practice. If you find the diagnostic test difficult, try to devote as much time as possible to the practice questions in the chapters you most need to review. Skip around in this book, focusing first on the content areas where you are weakest. Even if you do well on the diagnostic test, you should take the practice test at the back of this book to practice pacing yourself within the time limits of the exam.

> To review for the World History: Modern AP test, I went over the major concepts and periods in my notes. I also found it helpful to read outside world history books and sources. Also, practice, practice, practice on multiple-choice world history questions, because they are one-half of the AP test. As far as the AP essay section, DBQ practice all year was great preparation.
> —AP student

When to Take the Practice Exams

You should take the diagnostic test in Chapter 3 mid-year or whenever you begin your test preparation. It will show you what the exam is like and, based on your performance, you can identify your strong points as well as the weaknesses you'll need to focus on. Take the final practice test a week or so before the actual test. The practice tests are perhaps the most important part of this book. Taking them will help you do all of the following:

- Give you practice with all the different types of questions and tasks on the AP World History: Modern exam
- Allow you to measure progress and identify areas you need to focus on in your test preparation
- Allow you to practice pacing yourself within the time limits imposed on the test

Following are some things to remember as you plan your test-prep effort, regardless of when you start and how long you plan to practice:

- Establish a calendar of review and start as early as you can.
- Use your mobile phone to time yourself every time you take a timed test.
- Take advantage of the practice tests in this book. They are your friends.
- Don't stay up the night before the test trying to do some last-minute cramming; this may be counterproductive.

Setting Up a Study Group

One of the most effective strategies in preparing for the AP World History: Modern Exam is to study with other students preparing for the exam; however, not all study groups are equally successful. Here are some important considerations to assist you in the successful planning and implementation of your study group.

Why?

- Take advantage of others' strengths and abilities. Different students will have different insights.
- Lessen the individual workload by delegating specific topics (a time period, an event, an individual) to each member to present to the group.
- Increase your likelihood of following through by making commitments to others.

Get more in-depth with your readings. If you can spark a stronger interest in the subject, it is much less difficult to retain the information. —AP student

Who?

- Keep the group small. Study groups tend to work best when there are relatively few participants, usually somewhere between two and five people. Groups that are too large are less efficient and more easily distracted.
- Consider the composition of the group. Close friends do not necessarily make the best study partners. All members should be committed to the success of the group. Think about students who are interested in the material, are willing to ask questions, and are prepared and well organized for class.
- Consider, too, how much flexibility members have in their schedules. Students with many commitments may have trouble accommodating the study group sessions.

Where?

- Select locations with minimal distractions, where conditions allow for discussions.
- Provide seating that is comfortable, preferably with a table for notes and books.
- Some libraries have specific rooms for this purpose.
- Turn off your cell phones.
- Remember that this is a working group, not a potluck. By all means, bring something to drink or eat if you need to; just don't make socializing the focus of the group.

When?

- Plan for sessions to last two to three hours. Any longer and students will lose focus and be more likely to become distracted. Much shorter, and it will be difficult to cover material with any degree of depth.
- If possible, try to plan study sessions for the same day and time. A regular schedule will help the group remember to meet and make it seem more of a commitment, like a class. It also gives members time to prepare in advance.

How?

- For maximum efficiency, have a defined goal or purpose for each session, and ensure that it is clearly communicated to each member in advance. Assign each member specific tasks or responsibilities before meeting. These could include chapters, eras, or historical themes. By doing so, you increase the participation of all members.
- Consider assigning a member to be the facilitator, responsible for managing the time and keeping members focused.

Commitment and discipline in studying are the most important factors in preparing well for the test. —AP student

STEP **2**

Determine Your Test Readiness

CHAPTER **3**   Take a Diagnostic Exam

CHAPTER 3

Take a Diagnostic Exam

IN THIS CHAPTER

Summary: In the following pages you will find a diagnostic exam that is modeled after the actual AP exam. It is intended to give you an idea of your level of preparation in world history. After you have completed both the multiple-choice and the essay questions, check your multiple-choice answers against the given answers and read over the comments to the possible solutions to the free-response questions.

Adjusted rubrics for the DBQ and long-essay question are available on the AP Central website.

Key Ideas

✪ Practice the kind of multiple-choice and free-response questions you will be asked on the real exam.

✪ Answer questions that approximate the coverage of periods and themes on the real exam.

✪ Check your work against the given answers and the possible solutions to the free-response questions.

✪ Determine your areas of strength and weakness.

✪ Earmark the concepts to which you must give special attention.

AP World History: Modern
Diagnostic Test

Section I

Time: 1 hour, 35 minutes

PART A: MULTIPLE-CHOICE QUESTIONS

Recommended Time for Part A—55 Minutes

Directions: Each of the incomplete statements or questions is followed by four answer choices. Select the answer choice that best answers the question and fill in the corresponding oval on the answer sheet provided.

Questions 1 to 3 refer to the following image, a frieze of a Buddhist couple around a stupa with Corinthian columns on either side, India, c. first century CE.

1. What historical process is best illustrated by this frieze?

   (A) The diffusion of cultural ideas and patterns through military conquest
   (B) The significance of trade in the weakening of class systems
   (C) The use of monumental architecture to strengthen political support
   (D) The spread of religion as a result of trade

2. The combination of Greek culture and Eastern political forms shown in this frieze is illustrative of which of the following periods?

   (A) Punic
   (B) Justinian
   (C) Constantinian
   (D) Hellenistic

3. The adoption of conquered people's ideas, institutions, and traditions by ruling groups is best characterized by which of the following rulers?

   (A) Mohandas Gandhi
   (B) Caesar Augustus
   (C) Alexander the Great
   (D) Chinggis Khan

Questions 4 to 7 refer to the following passage.

At the peak of their power, the domains of the Mongol khans, or rulers, made up a vast realm in which once-hostile peoples lived together in peace and virtually all religions were tolerated. . . . The law code first promulgated by Chinggis Khan ordered human interaction. The result was an important new stage in international contact. From eastern Europe to southern China, merchants and travelers could move across the well-policed Mongol domains without fear for their lives or property. The great swath of Mongol territory that covered or connected most of Europe, Asia, and the Middle East served as a bridge between the civilizations of the Eastern Hemisphere. The caravans and embassies that crossed the Mongol lands transmitted new food, inventions, and ideas from one civilized pool to others and from civilized pools to the nomadic peoples who served as intermediaries. Secure trade routes made for prosperous merchants and wealthy, cosmopolitan cities. They also facilitated the spread of foods [and] inventions . . . a major force for economic and social development and the enhancement of civilized life.

—Robert Guisepi, 1992

4. The legacies or adaptations of legacies from the Mongol empire are varied. Most notably, they include which of the following selections?

   (A) Public libraries
   (B) Universal health care
   (C) The game of chess
   (D) Religious tolerance

5. The Mongol empire used which of the following to integrate its vast, geographically diverse area?

   (A) Emphasis on trade networks
   (B) Expansion of bureaucracy to reinforce dominance
   (C) The use of state-sponsored religion to legitimize the government
   (D) Expansion of an interregional canal system

6. Which of the following was a long-term consequence of the Mongol conquest of Russia in the 1200s?

   (A) Russia was excluded from Western European developments (like the Renaissance).
   (B) Russia benefited by becoming the administrative center of Mongol political activity.
   (C) Islam became the dominant religion of Russia.
   (D) Russia developed a centralized bureaucracy.

7. Which statement most accurately compares the Mongol (post-classical) empire with the Persian (classical) empire?

   (A) Both the Mongols and the Persians allowed conquered peoples to maintain their local traditions and cultures.
   (B) The Mongols invested in building large-scale monuments, whereas the Persians focused on public works.
   (C) Both the Persians and the Mongols improved the social, economic, and legal status of women.
   (D) The Mongols created a new syncretic belief system, but the Persians maintained a traditional monotheistic religion.

Questions 8 to 11 refer to the following passage.

The following is excerpted and adapted from an account by Hulderike Schnirdel, a native of Antwerp, who joined Spaniard Pedro de Mendoza's expedition to South America in 1535. He was present at the founding of Asunción, Paraguay, in 1537, recounted here.

The Citie [Lampere]… had Pits…in the middest whereof pikes were stuck…that we Christians pursuing them…might fall into them. When our Generall John Eyollas, gathering all his Souldiers together, who were not above three hundred, went against their Citie Lampere, they understanding before of our coming, making a stand… with their armie of foure thousand men, furnished with Bowe and Arrowes after their manner, commanded that we should be told, that they would provide us victual and other necessaries, that…we might peaceably return to our companions. But it was neither good for our Generall, nor our selves, that we should consent to their request: For this Nation and Countrie, by reason of the plenty of victual, was also most…commodious for us, especially when in foure whole yeares past, we had not seen a morsell of bread, lively onely with fish and flesh and oftentimes in also great penurie…..[We] commanded to signifie unto them that they should be quiet, and we would become their friends. But they would not….wee discharged our brasse Peeces against them. When they heard and saw so many men fell downe dead, and when neither bullets not Arrowes appeared, but holes onely were seen in their bodies, they…tooke their flight in troopes…to shelter themselves in their Towne….[M]ore that three hundred men, in that amassed feare, fell into the aforesaid pits, which themselves had digged. Afterward comming to their Citie, we assaulted it, they courageously defending themselves, till the third day.

8. Based on the passage, what was the primary motivation for the Europeans to conquer the city of Lampere?

   (A) To spread Christianity among the indigenous peoples
   (B) To increase the power of the Spanish crown
   (C) To gain access to their food and other resources
   (D) To gain local allies to assist in further conquests

9. Which of the following statements is supported by the passage?

   (A) Native American vulnerability to disease was the key factor in Spanish conquests in the Americas.
   (B) Native Americans lacked sufficient numbers to defeat the Spanish conquistadors.
   (C) Native Americans were reluctant to hurt the invaders, as they believed the Spanish were gods.
   (D) The key factor in Spanish conquests in the Americas was superior weaponry.

10. Based on the passage, what can one infer regarding the Native Americans?

   (A) They were extremely aggressive and warlike.
   (B) They had defensive military preparations.
   (C) They were cowardly and weak.
   (D) They were poor and malnourished.

11. Based on your knowledge of history, to which social class would a child of Generall Eyolas and one of the Native American women likely belong?

   (A) Mestizos
   (B) Peninsulares
   (C) Mulattoes
   (D) Creoles (Criollos)

Questions 12 to 14 refer to the following graph.

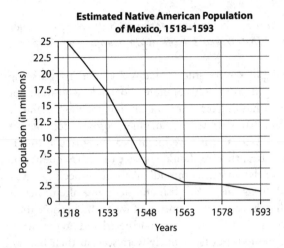

Estimated Native American Population of Mexico, 1518–1593

(C) Importation of new diseases from contact with Europeans

(D) The introduction of slavery into Mexico

13. In the sixteenth century, Europeans were able to conquer and control large numbers of natives in Mexico using which of the following methods?

   (A) Enslaving them
   (B) Placing them on reservations
   (C) Legalizing intermarriage
   (D) Using superior technologies

12. Which best accounts for the change in the Native American population shown in the graph?

   (A) Widespread warfare among the Aztecs and neighboring tribes
   (B) Famine due to poor agricultural practices such as slash-and-burn agriculture

14. Both the encomienda system in colonial Mexico and the manorial system in medieval Europe depended on which of the following ingredients?

   (A) Support from the Catholic Church
   (B) Coercive labor
   (C) An educated merchant class
   (D) A decentralized government

Questions 15 to 17 refer to the following passage.

"Purusa-Sukta"

   Purusa is the lord of the immortals, who grow by means of [ritual] food. When the gods performed a sacrifice with the offering Purusa, spring was its clarified butter, summer the kindling, autumn the oblation.

   It was Purusa, born in the beginning, which they sprinkled on the sacred grass as a sacrifice. It made the beasts of the air, the forest and the village. From that sacrifice completely offered, the mantras [Rig-Veda] and the songs [Samaveda] were born. The sacrificial formulae [Yajurveda] were born from it. From it the horses were born and all that have cutting teeth in both jaws. The cows were born from it, also. From it were born goats and sheep.

   When they divided Purusa, how many ways did they apportion him? What was his mouth? What were his arms? What were his thighs, his feet declared to be? His mouth was the Brahman, his arms were the Rajanaya [Ksatriya], his thighs the Vaisya; from his feet the Sudra was born. Thus, they fashioned the worlds. The gods sacrificed with the sacrifice to the sacrifice. These were the first rites.

—Hymns excerpted and adapted from the *Rig-Veda*, oldest surviving literary work, India, 1500–1000 BCE

15. Which element of the Hindu religion can this passage be used to explain?

   (A) The only requirement for salvation being faith
   (B) The importance of environmental stewardship
   (C) The importance of sacrifice to the gods
   (D) The emphasis on karma, or right actions, to achieve enlightenment

16. Which of the following statements is supported by the information in the passage?

   (A) The caste system was a purely social construct that reflected its time period.
   (B) The caste system was encouraged by regional princes to reinforce social stability.
   (C) The caste system reinforced Indian identity in the face of Muslim invaders.
   (D) The caste system was integral to the Hindu religion, transcending historical eras.

17. Which of the following would best contradict the argument that the caste system imposed rigid economic and social roles on Indian society in the period 600 BCE to 600 CE?

(A) "For there is nothing better for a Kshatriya than a righteous battle."

(B) "The four divisions of human society are created by me [Krishna]."

(C) The person traditionally credited with composing the Mahabarata was born to a fisherwoman.

(D) The Hindu god Shiva is considered to be simultaneously the creator, the preserver, and the destroyer.

Questions 18 to 20 refer to the following passage.

I have, in conformity without resolve, put together some few points concerning the reformation of the Christian estate, with the intent of placing the same before the Christian nobility of the German nation. . . . It is not out of mere arrogance and perversity that I, an individual poor man, have taken upon me to address your lordships. The distress and misery that oppress all the Christian estates, more especially in Germany, have led not only myself, but every one else, to cry aloud and to ask for help. . . . These Romanists have, with great adroitness, drawn three walls around themselves, with which they have hitherto protected themselves, so that no one could reform them, whereby all Christendom has fallen terribly. . . . That the Temporal Power Has no Jurisdiction over the Spirituality . . . That No One May Interpret the Scriptures but the Pope . . . That No One May Call a Council but the Pope. . . . Let us now consider the matters which should be treated in the councils, and with which popes, cardinals, bishops, and all learned men should occupy themselves day and night. . . . It is a distressing and terrible thing to see that the head of Christendom, who boasts of being the vicar of Christ and the successor of St. Peter, lives in a worldly pomp that no king or emperor can equal. What is the use in Christendom of the people called "cardinals"? I will tell you. In Italy and Germany there are many rich convents, endowments, fiefs, and benefices, and as the best way of getting these into the hands of Rome, they created cardinals, and gave them the sees, convents, and prelacies, and thus destroyed the service of God.

—Martin Luther, *Address to the Christian Nobility of the German Nation*

18. In his letter, Martin Luther avoided speaking about which of the following topics?

(A) The wealth of the Church
(B) The power of the clergy
(C) The sale of indulgences
(D) The political nature of the Church

19. Which of the following reformers expressed views similar to those expressed by Martin Luther in his letter?

(A) Ulrich Zwingli
(B) Sir Thomas More
(C) Erasmus
(D) John Wycliffe

20. In response to the criticisms raised by Martin Luther and other Protestant reformers, the Roman Catholic Church made which of the following moves at the Council of Trent?

(A) It accepted the doctrine of predestination.
(B) It rejected saints as intermediaries.
(C) It accepted scriptures in the vernacular.
(D) It rejected salvation based on faith alone.

Questions 21 to 23 refer to the following map, depicting the "Scramble for Africa" that was codified at the Berlin Conference of 1884–1885.

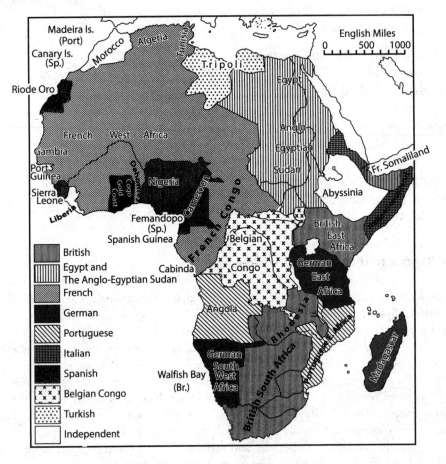

21. The political boundaries shown on the map of Africa reflect which of the following white European beliefs?

(A) Self-determination
(B) Manifest Destiny
(C) Spheres of influence
(D) Racial hierarchies

22. What has changed since this map was drawn?

(A) Political borders have reverted to their traditional ethnic boundaries.
(B) Western economic interests have withdrawn from African affairs.
(C) African nations have successfully adopted stable democratic governments.
(D) African states have gained independence, but arbitrary colonial borders have persisted, resulting in ethnic violence.

23. Which of the following is a direct legacy of the African colonial experience?

(A) A lack of economic infrastructures
(B) A pan-African movement
(C) A resurgence of mercantilism
(D) Incorporation into world market systems

Questions 24 to 27 refer to the following passage.

The city of Ghana consists of two towns. One is inhabited by Muslims and has twelve mosques, salaried imams and muezzins, and jurists and scholars. In the environs are wells with sweet water, from which they drink and with which they grow vegetables. . . . The king's interpreters, the official in charge of his treasury and the majority of his ministers are Muslims. Only royalty may wear sewn clothes. All other people wear robes of cotton, silk, or brocade, according to their means. . . . The king adorns himself like a woman, wearing necklaces round his neck and bracelets on his forearms. . . . He sits . . . in a domed pavilion around which stand ten horses. When people who profess the same religion as the king approach him they fall on their knees and sprinkle dust on their heads, for this is their way of greeting him. As for the Muslims, they greet him only by clapping their hands. [The people's] religion is paganism and the worship of idols. . . . On every donkey-load of salt when it is brought into the country their king levies one golden dinar, and two dinars when it is sent out. From a load of copper the king's due is five mithqals, and from a load of other goods ten mithqals. . . . The nuggets found in all the mines of his country are reserved for the king, only this gold dust being left for the people. But for this the people would accumulate gold until it lost its value. Beyond this country lies another called Malal, the king of which was sincerely attached to Islam, while the common people of his kingdom remained polytheists. Since then their rulers have been given the title of *al-musulmani*.

—*The Book of Routes and Realms*, by Abu Ubaydallah al-Bakri,
eleventh-century Muslim historian and geographer

24. According to the passage, which statement correctly describes the economy of Ghana?

    (A) The king of Ghana's subjects are engaged in salt mining.
    (B) The Ghanians raised cattle for meat and hides.
    (C) The king of Ghana taxed salt and copper imports and exports.
    (D) The Ghanians had a self-sufficient farming economy.

25. What evidence is there in the passage that Ghanians were engaged, directly or indirectly, in trade with Asia?

    (A) They kept horses in their court, which would have come from the Mongols.
    (B) The Ghanian king had adopted the Chinese tradition of the *kow-tow*.
    (C) The king adorned himself with gold and jewels, probably from India.
    (D) The people in his court wore silk robes.

26. What is the most likely explanation for a Muslim being in charge of the Ghanian treasury?

    (A) To facilitate trade with the predominantly Muslim merchants during this era.
    (B) The king of Ghana had recently become a Muslim.
    (C) Merchants and trade were considered taboo in the traditional pagan religion.
    (D) African kings were merely vassals of the Muslim caliphs.

27. Based on the excerpt, which of the following statements correctly describes Islam's influence in Africa during this time period?

    (A) Imams and muezzins ensured that all Africans adhered to Islamic law.
    (B) Some elites converted to Islam, but lower classes kept their traditional beliefs.
    (C) Muslim merchants refused to do business with anyone who was not Muslim.
    (D) African kings required Muslims to conform to pagan customs at court.

Questions 28 to 32 refer to the following map.

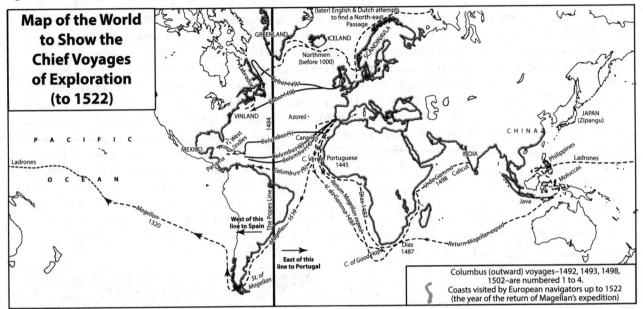

Map of the World to Show the Chief Voyages of Exploration (to 1522)

Columbus (outward) voyages–1492, 1493, 1498, 1502–are numbered 1 to 4.
Coasts visited by European navigators up to 1522 (the year of the return of Magellan's expedition)

28. According to the map, the earliest Atlantic exploration voyages originated in

    (A) Spain.
    (B) Portugal.
    (C) Greenland.
    (D) Scandinavia.

29. Which historical facts can be explained by the information on this map?

    (A) Eventually, the Dutch controlled the spice trade.
    (B) Brazilians today speak Portuguese.
    (C) Canada is divided into English- and French-speaking groups.
    (D) There is a strong Scandinavian community in North America.

30. Zheng He engaged in oceanic exploration for China as early as 1405, well before the Europeans, yet 1450 is frequently used to mark the beginning of this era. Which statement best explains using the later date?

    (A) Zheng He failed to contact other cultures, so he is widely viewed as a failure.
    (B) European influence is the most significant, so beginning with the European voyages makes sense.
    (C) China abandoned exploration early, limiting Chinese impact on a global scale.
    (D) The era is characterized by colonization, and the islands off the East African coast were colonized in 1450.

31. Which part of the world had previously been omitted from transregional trade networks?

    (A) Southeast Asia
    (B) Africa
    (C) Europe
    (D) The Americas

32. Which historical phenomenon resulted from the events depicted on the map?

    (A) Mercantilism
    (B) Nationalism
    (C) Industrialism
    (D) Communism

Questions 33 to 36 refer to the following passages. Both authors were speaking of the French Revolution.

It was the best of times, it was the worst of times, it was the age of wisdom, it was the age of foolishness, it was the epoch of belief, it was the epoch of incredulity, it was the season of Light, it was the season of Darkness, it was the spring of hope, it was the winter of despair, we had everything before us, we had nothing before us, we were all going direct to Heaven, we were all going direct the other way—in short, the period was so far like the present period, that some of its noisiest authorities insisted on its being received, for good or for evil, in the superlative degree of comparison only.

There were a king with a large jaw and a queen with a plain face, on the throne of England; there were a king with a large jaw and a queen with a fair face, on the throne of France. In both countries it was clearer than crystal . . . that things in general were settled for ever.

—*A Tale of Two Cities*, by Charles Dickens

Bliss was it in that dawn to be alive. But to be young was very heaven.

—*The Prelude*, by William Wordsworth

33. Dickens's and Wordsworth's differing views about the French Revolution can be described, respectively, by which of the following adjectives?

(A) Optimistic, encouraged
(B) Understanding, accepting
(C) Cynical, enthusiastic
(D) Sincere, resigned

34. One similarity between the French Revolution and the American Revolution is that both were responses to which of the following?

(A) Transformation of the social class structure
(B) Unfair systems of taxation
(C) New proposed political structures
(D) The privileges and influence of religious leaders

35. Most revolutions produce a strong leading figure; the French Revolution allowed which of the following to assume great power?

(A) King Louis XVI
(B) Robespierre
(C) Jean Lafitte
(D) Lafayette

36. The intellectual foundations of the eighteenth-century political revolutions were based on

(A) the Reformation.
(B) mercantilism.
(C) the Enlightenment.
(D) the Reconquista.

Questions 37 to 39 refer to the following political cartoon showing Woodrow Wilson, published in 1919.

Blowing Bubbles

37. What does the cartoonist intend to suggest in the political cartoon?

   (A) Woodrow Wilson was responsible for the failure of the League of Nations.
   (B) The forces of conflict were too strong for the League of Nations to overcome.
   (C) The League of Nations was too fragile to have lasted long.
   (D) Idealism is necessary to improve the world.

38. Though the League of Nations was short-lived (1919–1946), it set the stage for which of the following?

   (A) NATO
   (B) The United Nations
   (C) The alliance system
   (D) The Marshall Plan

39. Those who argue that the roots of World War II are found in the Treaty of Versailles, which created the League of Nations, point to which of the following?

   (A) The rejection of the League of Nations by the French and the British
   (B) Germany's resentment at having to accept blame for World War I
   (C) Italy's resentment at losing the territory it had won
   (D) The dissolution of the Austro-Hungarian Empire

Questions 40 to 43 refer to the following passage, an account given to a French officer in Algeria in the 1830s by a member of an Arab slave trade caravan.

The Slave Trade

All of you [soldiers], are summoned . . . to hunt the idolatrous Koholanes [a pejorative word for "black Africans"]. . . . The soldiery divided themselves into two companies . . . with orders to attack places without defenses and to carry off the inhabitants as well as seizing all peasants busy cultivating their fields. . . . Whilst waiting for the return of the companies despatched to hunt Negroes, we went every day to the slave market where we bought at the following prices:

A Negro with beard..................10 or 15,000 cowries.

They are not considered as merchandise since one has little chance of preventing them from escaping.

An adult Negress...................10 or 15,000 cowries for the same reasons
An adolescent Negro......................30,000 cowries
A young Negress ....50–60,000 cowries

The price varies according to whether she is more or less beautiful.

A male Negro child.........................45,000 cowries
A female Negro child ....35–40,000 cowries

Finally, our caravan which had set out from Algeria with sixty-four camels and only sixteen persons, was now augmented by four hundred slaves, of whom three hundred were women. . . . It was at this point that suddenly a confused noise of cries and sobs passed from one group of slaves to another and reached our own. . . . Some rolled on the ground, clung to bushes and absolutely refused to walk. . . . They could only be got up with mighty lashes of the whip and by rendering them completely bloody.

40. Which conclusion is supported by the passage?

(A) Africans passively accepted their capture and subsequent enslavement.
(B) North Africans were primarily captured and enslaved by rival African tribes.
(C) Population changes from slavery resulted in North African tribes having more men than women.
(D) Adult male slaves were most highly valued due to their physical strength.

41. What is the most likely destination for the captured slaves in the excerpt?

(A) Elites' homes or harems in the Middle East
(B) Sugar plantations in Brazil
(C) Cotton plantations in North America
(D) Slave armies of the Mughal Empire

42. Which statement best supports the argument that religion played a role in the Arab slave trade?

(A) "Seizing all peasants busy cultivating their fields"
(B) "With orders to attack places without defenses"

(C) "Four hundred slaves, of whom three hundred were women"
(D) "All of you [soldiers], are summoned . . . to hunt the idolatrous Koholanes"

43. How was the Arab trade in Africans different from the Atlantic slave trade?

(A) Unlike Arab slave merchants, those involved in the Atlantic slave trade were motivated by religion.
(B) Slaves taken for the Atlantic slave trade had no prospect of eventual liberty, but slaves taken by Arab merchants did.
(C) Slaves taken for the Atlantic trade were predominantly female; slaves taken by Arab merchants were mostly male.
(D) Slaves taken by Arab merchants were likely to have a shorter life span than those taken for the Atlantic trade.

Questions 44 to 47 refer to the following maps.

The Middle East Before and After World War I Settlements, 1914–1922

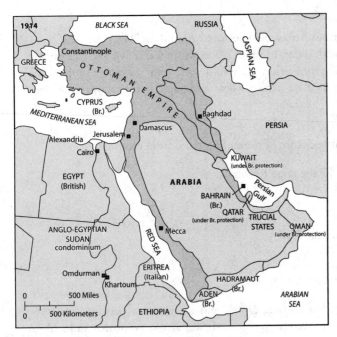

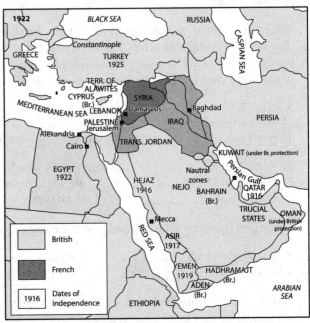

44. The second map shows which of the following?

(A) The encomienda system of colonial influence

(B) The League of Nations' mandate system

(C) Territorial changes from the Berlin Conference

(D) Cold War influence in the Middle East

45. Which twentieth-century principle of government is violated in these maps?

(A) Colonialism

(B) Self-determination

(C) Containment

(D) Mercantilism

46. Which best explains why Great Britain, rather than another country, received control over the territory in Palestine?

(A) The Balfour Declaration

(B) The Zimmerman Telegram

(C) The Berlin Conference

(D) The Non-Aligned Movement

47. What was the impact of the events reflected in these maps?

(A) The Ottoman Empire retaliated.

(B) Italy resented not receiving any territories through this system.

(C) Australia eventually achieved independence.

(D) Kuwait became part of Iraq.

Questions 48 to 51 refer to the following chart, from a speech entitled "Report on Work of Central Committee," given by J. V. Stalin, March 10, 1939.

GROSS PRODUCTION OF GRAIN AND INDUSTRIAL CROPS IN THE U.S.S.R.

	In millions of centners						1938 compared with 1933 (percent)
	1933	1934	1935	1936	1937	1938	
Grain..................	801.0	894.0	901.0	827.3	1,202.9	949.9	118.6
Raw cotton	7.4	11.8	17.2	23.9	25.8	26.9	363.5
Flax fibre	3.3	5.3	5.5	5.8	5.7	5.46	165.5
Sugar beet	109.0	113.6	162.1	108.3	218.6	166.8	153.0
Oil seed	21.5	36.9	43.7	42.3	51.1	46.6	216.7

48. Which statement is supported by the data in the chart?

(A) The Soviets supported grain production at the expense of consumer goods.
(B) All commodities had reduced agricultural output in 1938.
(C) The Soviets had less demand for cotton than for flax fiber.
(D) Over time, the Soviet Union increased production of all reported commodities.

49. What should one consider when evaluating the point of view of these data?

(A) Official government statistics are reliable because they are objective.
(B) Increases in agricultural output were possible only because of German assistance.
(C) Stalin had an incentive to overstate gains for propaganda and political reasons.
(D) Soviet kulaks destroyed crops to protest Soviet policy, making the data invalid.

50. Which of Stalin's policies are most responsible for the information on the chart?

(A) Collectivization
(B) New Economic Plans
(C) Five-Year Plans
(D) The Great Leap Forward

51. What was the effect of Stalin's agricultural policies on the Soviet peasants?

(A) Forced resettlement to Georgia because it had more arable land
(B) Resistance through the destruction of crops and widespread famine
(C) Greater economic stability through the introduction of new types of grain
(D) Improved social status due to their importance to the Soviet economy

Questions 52 to 55 refer to the following passage. It is the Chinese emperor's response to English King George III's diplomatic envoys, who were seeking expanded trading privileges (1793).

Strange and costly objects do not interest me. If I have commanded that the tribute offerings sent by you, O King, are to be accepted, this was solely in consideration for the spirit which prompted you to dispatch them from afar. . . . As your Ambassador can see for himself, we possess all things. I set no value on objects strange or ingenious, and have no use for your country's manufactures. It behooves you, O King, to display even greater devotion and loyalty in future, so that, by perpetual submission to our Throne, you may secure peace and prosperity.

52. According to the passage, what was the Chinese reaction to the British goods?

    (A) Awe at their technological superiority
    (B) Fascination with their strangeness
    (C) Offense at a perceived bribe
    (D) Interpreting them as an act of submission

53. Why were the Chinese not interested in expanding trading rights with Great Britain?

    (A) The Chinese were angry over Britain's interference in their foreign affairs.
    (B) The Chinese had a preexisting exclusive trade agreement with the Dutch.
    (C) They had no interest in the products that Great Britain could provide.
    (D) They were afraid that the British would gain too much influence within China.

54. How did the Chinese restrict foreign trade during the era 1750–1900?

    (A) European merchants were confined to a few cities designated for foreign trade.
    (B) Only the Dutch traded with China; other Europeans had to use them as intermediaries.
    (C) The Chinese imposed extraordinary tariffs on all foreign products.
    (D) They passed laws intended to persecute and harass foreign residents.

55. What was the impact of European demand for Chinese goods?

    (A) The Portuguese increased their international power and prestige.
    (B) The British shifted their focus for trade and colonization to Japan.
    (C) The bulk of the world's silver supply moved to China.
    (D) The British sought control of the Malacca Strait.

GO ON TO PART B

PART B: SHORT-ANSWER QUESTIONS

Recommended Time for Part B—40 minutes

Directions: You need to answer a total of three short-answer questions. You are required to answer Questions 1 and 2, but you may choose to answer either Question 3 or Question 4. The short-answer questions are divided into parts; answer all parts of each of the questions. Each question answered correctly is worth two or three points. Note that short-answer questions are not essay questions—they do not require development and support of a thesis statement.

Question 1 refers to the following passages.

Take up the White Man's burden—
Send forth the best ye breed—
Go bind your sons to exile
To serve your captives' need;
To wait in heavy harness,
On fluttered folk and wild—
Your new-caught, sullen peoples,
Half-devil and half-child. . . .

Take up the White Man's burden—
The savage wars of peace—
Fill full the mouth of Famine
And bid the sickness cease;
And when your goal is nearest
The end for others sought,
Watch sloth and heathen Folly
Bring all your hopes to nought.

—Rudyard Kipling,
"The White Man's Burden," 1899

Pile on the Black Man's Burden.
'Tis nearest at your door;
Why heed long bleeding Cuba,
or dark Hawaii's shore?
Hail ye your fearless armies,
Which menace feeble folks
Who fight with clubs and arrows
and brook your rifle's smoke.
Pile on the Black Man's Burden
His wail with laughter drown
You've sealed the Red Man's problem,
And will take up the Brown,
In vain ye seek to end it,
With bullets, blood or death
Better by far defend it
With honor's holy breath.

—H. T. Johnson,
"The Black Man's Burden":
A Response to Kipling, 1899

1. Answer Parts A and B.

   A. Identify TWO characteristics of the "new imperialism" found in the excerpt from Kipling's poem.
   B. Identify H. T. Johnson's vision of "new imperialism" as expressed in "The Black Man's Burden."

2. Answer Parts A and B.

   A. Explain TWO causes of the Industrial Revolution in Western Europe.
   B. Explain ONE effect of the Industrial Revolution in Western Europe.

Answer EITHER Question 3 OR Question 4.

Question 3 refers to the following quotations.

Study the past if you would define the future.

—Confucius

History is a vast early warning system.

—Norman Cousins

Until lions have their historians, tales of the hunt shall always glorify the hunters.

—African proverb

History is the version of past events that people have decided to agree upon.

—Napoleon Bonaparte

2. Answer Parts A, B, and C.

   A. Explain the idea that Confucius and Norman Cousins share.

   B. Explain how the African proverb accounts for different interpretations of a single historical event.

   C. Explain Bonaparte's view of the purpose of history.

Question 4 refers to the following passage and the artworks.

Art is, at some basic level, personal. People made it, reacted to it, treasured it in ways we can identify with. But art is also intrinsically political, designed to shape a view of the world in empowering ways, ways that write certain people and ideas into the record and leave others out. We need to see art from both perspectives.

—Holland Cotter

"Liberty Leading the People" by Eugène Delacroix (French), 1830

"Third of May 1808," Francisco Goya (Spanish), 1814

4. Answer Parts A, B, and C.

   A. Identify the response of the people
      in Delacroix's artwork to a perceived
      oppressor.
   B. Identify the response of the people in
      Goya's painting to a perceived oppressor.
   C. Explain how these works may be considered
      historical sources.

END OF SECTION I

AP World History: Modern Diagnostic Test

Section II

Time: 100 minutes

PART A: DOCUMENT-BASED QUESTION (DBQ)

Recommended reading time for Part A—15 minutes
Recommended writing time for Part A—45 minutes

Directions: The question is based on the following documents. The documents have been edited and adapted for this exam.

- Read the question carefully.
- Then read all the documents.
- Begin by grouping the documents into categories that reflect their points of view, theme, or intended audience—that is, those that share commonalities.
- Create a thesis that addresses the entire question.
- Analyze the documents that support the thesis. You must use all (or all but one of) the documents.
- Give careful attention to the purpose, point of view, source, and historical context of each document.
- Do NOT list the documents or analyze them one at a time in your essay; they should be incorporated into your argument.
- Bring in historical examples that support your argument.
- Create a persuasive essay that upholds your thesis, connects your argument to the historical context, and draws conclusions.

1. Using the documents and your knowledge of world history, analyze the differing attitudes toward human rights across time and place. Consider the focus and purpose of the documents.

Document 1

> *Source: Translation of the text on the Cyrus Cylinder, 539 BCE*
>
> My vast troops were marching peaceably in Babylon. . . . As for the population of Babylon I soothed their weariness; I freed them from their bonds and made permanent sanctuaries for them. . . . I have enabled all the lands to live in peace.

Document 2

Source: Magna Carta, 1215 CE

JOHN, by the grace of God King of England, Lord of Ireland, Duke of Normandy and Aquitaine, and Count of Anjou. . . . TO ALL FREE MEN OF OUR KINGDOM we have also granted, for us and our heirs for ever, all the liberties written out below. . . . Heirs may be given in marriage, but not to someone of lower social standing. Before a marriage takes place, it shall be made known to the heir's next-of-kin.

At her husband's death, a widow may have her marriage portion and inheritance at once and without trouble. She shall pay nothing for her dower, marriage portion, or any inheritance that she and her husband held jointly on the day of his death. She may remain in her husband's house for forty days after his death, and within this period her dower shall be assigned to her.

No widow shall be compelled to marry, so long as she wishes to remain without a husband. But she must give security that she will not marry without royal consent, if she holds her lands of the Crown, or without the consent of whatever other lord she may hold them of.

Document 3

Source: Recopilación de leyes de las Indias, 1680 (Compilation of laws of the Indies)

Those [Colonists] who should want to make a commitment to building a new settlement in the form and manner already prescribed, be it of more or less than 30 vecinos (freemen). . . .

    Having made the selection of the site where the town is to be built, it must, as already stated, be in an elevated and healthy location; [be] with means of fortification; [have] fertile soil and with plenty of land for farming and pasturage; have fuel, timber, and resources; [have] fresh water, a native population, ease of transport, access and exit; [and be] open to the north wind; and, if on the coast, due consideration should be paid to the quality of the harbor and that the sea does not lie to the south or west; and if possible not near lagoons or marshes in which poisonous animals and polluted air and water breed.

    They [the colonists] shall try as far as possible to have the buildings all of one type for the sake of the beauty of the town. Within the town, a commons shall be delimited, large enough that although the population may experience a rapid expansion, there will always be sufficient space where the people may go to for recreation.

Document 4

Source: French Declaration of the Rights of Man and of the Citizen, 1789

The representatives of the French people, constituted as a National Assembly, and considering that ignorance, neglect, or contempt of the rights of man are the sole causes of public misfortunes and governmental corruption, have resolved to set forth in a solemn declaration the natural, inalienable and sacred rights of man . . . so that by being liable . . . to comparison with the aim of any and all political institutions the acts of the legislative and executive powers may be the more fully respected; and so that by being founded henceforward on simple and incontestable principles the demands of the citizens may always tend toward maintaining the constitution.

1. Men are born and remain free and equal in rights. Social distinctions may be based only on common utility.

2. The purpose of all political association is the preservation of the natural and imprescriptible rights of man. These rights are liberty, property, security, and resistance to oppression.

3. The principle of all sovereignty rests essentially in the nation. No body and no individual may exercise authority which does not emanate expressly from the nation.

4. Liberty consists in the ability to do whatever does not harm another; hence the exercise of the natural rights of each man has no other limits than those which assure to other members of society the enjoyment of the same rights. These limits can only be determined by the law.

5. The law only has the right to prohibit those actions which are injurious to society. No hindrance should be put in the way of anything not prohibited by the law, nor may any one be forced to do what the law does not require.

6. The law is the expression of the general will.

Document 5

Source: United States of America Bill of Rights, 1791

RESOLVED by the Senate and House of Representatives of the United States of America, in Congress assembled, two thirds of both Houses concurring, that the following Articles be proposed to the Legislatures of the several States, as amendments to the Constitution of the United States, all, or any of which Articles, when ratified by three fourths of the said Legislatures, to be valid to all intents and purposes, as part of the said Constitution. . . . **Article the third.** . . . Congress shall make no law respecting an establishment of religion, or prohibiting the free exercise thereof; or abridging the freedom of speech, or of the press; or the right of the people peaceably to assemble, and to petition the Government for a redress of grievances. . . . **Article the sixth.** . . . The right of the people to be secure in their persons, houses, papers, and effects, against unreasonable searches and seizures, shall not be violated, and no Warrants shall issue, but upon probable cause, supported by Oath or affirmation, and particularly describing the place to be searched, and the persons or things to be seized.

Document 6

Source: The Universal Declaration of Human Rights, 1948

Whereas recognition of the inherent dignity and of the equal and inalienable rights of all members of the human family is the foundation of freedom, justice and peace in the world,

Whereas disregard and contempt for human rights have resulted in barbarous acts which have outraged the conscience of mankind, and the advent of a world in which human beings shall enjoy freedom of speech and belief and freedom from fear and want has been proclaimed as the highest aspiration of the common people,

Whereas it is essential, if man is not to be compelled to have recourse, as a last resort, to rebellion against tyranny and oppression, that human rights should be protected by the rule of law,

Whereas it is essential to promote the development of friendly relations between nations,

Whereas the peoples of the United Nations have in the Charter reaffirmed their faith in fundamental human rights, in the dignity and worth of the human person and in the equal rights of men and women and have determined to promote social progress and better standards of life in larger freedom. . . . Therefore, THE GENERAL ASSEMBLY proclaims THIS UNIVERSAL DECLARATION OF HUMAN RIGHTS as a common standard of achievement for all peoples and all nations, to the end that every individual and every organ of society, keeping this Declaration constantly in mind, shall strive by teaching and education to promote respect for these rights and freedoms and by progressive measures, national and international . . .

Document 7

Source: The Cairo Declaration of Human Rights, 1990

The Member States of the Organization of the Islamic Conference, Reaffirming the civilizing and historical role of the Islamic Ummah which Allah made as the best community and which gave humanity a universal and well-balanced civilization, in which harmony is established between hereunder and the hereafter, knowledge is combined with faith, and to fulfill the expectations from this community to guide all humanity which is confused because of different and conflicting beliefs and ideologies and to provide solutions for all chronic problems of this materialistic civilization.

In contribution to the efforts of mankind to assert human rights, to protect man from exploitation and persecution, and to affirm his freedom and right to a dignified life in accordance with the Islamic Shari'ah;

Convinced that mankind which has reached an advanced stage in materialistic science is still, and shall remain, in dire need of faith to support its civilization as well as a self motivating force to guard its rights;

Believing that fundamental rights and freedoms according to Islam are an integral part of the Islamic religion and that no one shall have the right as a matter of principle to abolish them either in whole or in part or to violate or ignore them in as much as they are binding divine commands, which are contained in the Revealed Books of Allah and which were sent through the last of His Prophets to complete the preceding divine messages and that safeguarding those fundamental rights and freedoms is an act of worship whereas the neglect or violation thereof is an abominable sin, and that the safeguarding of those fundamental rights and freedom is an individual responsibility of every person and a collective responsibility of the entire Ummah;

ARTICLE 6:

(a) Woman is equal to man in human dignity, and has her own rights to enjoy as well as duties to perform, and has her own civil entity and financial independence, and the right to retain her name and lineage.

(b) Human beings are born free, and no one has the right to enslave, humiliate, oppress or exploit them, and there can be no subjugation but to Allah the Almighty.

GO ON TO PART B

PART B: LONG-ESSAY QUESTION

Recommended Time for Part B—40 minutes

Directions: Answer ONE of the following questions.

1. Using specific examples, compare the economic causes and effects of the Industrial Revolution in Russia and England.

2. Using specific examples, compare changes in the social hierarchies (class structures) in England and Russia following their respective Industrial Revolutions.

3. Using specific examples, identify and explain the role of women and changes to their status during the English Industrial Revolution.

STOP. END OF SECTION II.

› Answers and Explanations

Section I, Part A: Multiple-Choice

1. **A** The Hellenistic culture combined Greek elements with those from local cultures as Alexander the Great's army conquered the area from North Africa to the Indus valley. Though Greek culture also spread into India through trade in the Bactria region, this image is unrelated to class systems (B). A frieze is not considered monumental sculpture (C). Buddhism is considered a belief system rather than a religion (D).

2. **D** Hellenistic culture involved the blending of Greek and local cultures in the wake of Alexander the Great's conquests of Asia Minor and the Indus valley region. Punic (A) refers to Rome's wars against Carthage; and both Justinian (B) and Constantinian (C) refer to Byzantine emperors.

3. **C** Under Alexander the Great, Greek culture blended with the conquered people's ideas, institutions, and traditions. Gandhi was a twentieth-century Indian nationalist who promoted Indian independence (A); and both Caesar Augustus (B), the first Roman emperor, and Chinggis Khan (D), the first Mongol emperor, retained local customs but did not adopt them personally.

4. **D** The Mongols did not require or force conversion, but encouraged tolerance of all religions. Public libraries (A), universal health care (B), and chess (C) were all characteristic of the golden age of Arab rule.

5. **A** The Mongols, particularly the Golden Horde in Central Asia, used tribute as a method of asserting dominance over the Russian princes (B). The Mongols developed extensive trade networks in Central Asia (A). They did not use religion to reinforce their power (C). The Mongols also did not engage in large-scale public works projects (D).

6. **A** With Russia's conquest by the Mongols, its focus shifted from Western Europe toward the East and Central Asia. Russia was primarily a tributary state (B); it kept its nomadic ways and did not develop trade. The predominant religion in Russia was Orthodox Christianity (C), spread by the Byzantines. When the Mongols converted to Islam, it helped motivate Russia to break free. Russia remained a series of small, disunited principalities (D).

7. **A** Both the Mongols and the Persians left cultural, political, and economic traditions in place, and even some conquered rulers as well. The Mongols typically moved into areas that were already occupied and used the resources that were already in place. Since they were nomadic, building large monuments to glorify themselves was not part of their culture (B). Neither culture is known for promoting equality for women. Both had traditions of harems (C). The Persians were not monotheistic (D); the religion that they were known for developing, Zoroastrianism, had two opposing godlike forces.

8. **C** While you might be familiar with the phrase "God, gold and glory" to describe motives for exploration, the question requires that you confine yourself to the passage. Although the passage mentions Christianity, it is in the context of the pits, not as a motive for conquest. Nor is there discussion of priests or conversions (A). Similarly, though power was a motive for rulers to sponsor exploration, there is nothing in the passage to indicate that these specific soldiers had such desires (B). And finally, though European explorers often exploited rivalries among different native tribes, it was not the main reason the Spanish pursued the city (D). Instead, the passage refers to the fact that the region had "plenty of victual" and that they hadn't had a "morsel of bread" in a long time, indicating they desired its resources.

9. **D** It was the superior weapons, in terms of guns with brass shot, that terrified the Native Americans, who were armed with bows and arrows. Though indigenous Americans ultimately died from European diseases, this is not referenced in the passage (A). Similarly, though the Native Americans did show an initial reluctance to fight the Spanish, offering them assistance if they left, the story about conquistadors being gods

is associated with the Spanish conquest of the Aztecs in Mexico (C). Finally, the passage makes clear that the Spanish only had 300 men, whereas the Native Americans had 4,000 (B).

10. **B** The passage refers to defensive pits that had been dug by the people of Lampere, knowing that the Spanish were coming. Before any fighting occurred, the Native Americans offered to provide food in exchange for a peaceful retreat, which makes (A) incorrect. Although the Native Americans fled from the bullets, they fled to defend their city, which the author indicates they did "courageously," making (C) incorrect. The passage also refers to the food ("victual") in the land, which indicates that the people are probably not malnourished (D).

11. **A** This question requires you to use your knowledge of history and the social classes that developed within the Spanish colonies in the Americas. The mestizo class included those born of European (like Generall Eyollas) and Native American heritage. Peninsulares included only Europeans born in Europe (B). Mulattoes included those of combined African and European heritage (C). Creoles, also called Criollos in some textbooks, included those of exclusively European heritage but born in the Americas.

12. **C** With the arrival of the Europeans came diseases (including smallpox) to which the native peoples had no historical immunity. The Aztecs would have engaged in some warfare, but not enough to lead to such a steep decline (A). Though there was some slash-and-burn agriculture, they primarily used chinampas and terraces (B). Slavery had traditionally been part of Mexican culture, as seen in the Aztec Empire (D). The Europeans used native Mexicans as forced labor, but not until later.

13. **D** The Europeans had guns and steel, against which the Mexicans had no effective defense. Catholicism prohibited the enslavement of Native Americans (A). Reservations were not used in Mexico (B). Intermarriage (C), although legal, could benefit native Mexicans, but would limit Spanish opportunities.

14. **B** The encomienda system entitled Spanish conquerors to control Indian labor, and in return, the Spaniards "civilized and Christianized" natives. Medieval manorialism allowed landholders to give access to, though not ownership of, land to the peasants who worked it. While the Catholic Church approved of and supported both the encomienda and manorial systems, it did not directly involve itself in either (A). The merchant class was separate from the landholding class (C). Although the Spanish central (royal) government supported the encomienda system, there was no effective central government to support manorialism (D).

15. **C** Sacrifice, the source of creation, is mentioned throughout the passage. Salvation through faith (A) is a key element of Protestantism. Though the passage has references to the elements of nature (B), there is no emphasis on stewardship. Karma (D) is not explicitly discussed in the passage.

16. **D** The *Rig-Veda* is a Hindu religious text, and its inclusion of the origins of the caste system make this a feature of their religion. A religious construct is not a social construct (A). This passage does not address social stability (B) or the reaction of Indians to the Muslim presence (C).

17. **C** That a lowborn person could compose a sacred text implies social mobility. Choice (A) supports the argument, since it encourages Kshatriyas to follow their rightful role. Choices (B) and (D) do not address the argument.

18. **C** The sale of indulgences is nowhere mentioned in the excerpt. The wealth of the Church (A) is referred to with the phrase "worldly pomp"; the power of the clergy (B) and the political nature of the Church (D) are both addressed in the discussion of temporal versus spiritual power.

19. **B** Sir Thomas More was executed for refusing to support Protestantism in England. Zwingli (A), Erasmus (C), and Wycliffe (D) were all either precursors or advocates of Protestant reform.

20. **D** The Church reiterated the need for clerical interpretation of scripture and the necessity of good works in order to achieve salvation. Predestination and use of the vernacular (A, C) were both Protestant ideas and thus were

rejected. The Council of Trent continued most Catholic practices, including the use of saints as intermediaries (B).

21. **D** The Europeans clearly ignored or discounted linguistic and ethnic divisions, as well as the wishes and traditions of indigenous cultures, because they considered them unimportant in the "white" scheme of things. Self-determination (A) refers to the idea that indigenous peoples should rule themselves, which was clearly not the case here. Manifest Destiny (B) is a term associated with U.S. westward expansionism. Spheres of influence (C) refers to European economic imperialism in dealings with China.

22. **D** In the post-colonial period, Africa has struggled with ethnic violence among rival groups who were artificially bound together within colonial borders. Most African nations retained their colonial borders (A). Western economic interests (B) have persisted to the present, particularly in the oil and diamond industries. African nations have struggled with political corruption and instability (C).

23. **A** Colonial dominance depended on cash crops and raw materials and did not encourage any development of an artisanal or manufacturing sector. The pan-African movement (B) was limited in duration, scope, and effectiveness. Mercantilism (C) was a historical economic system and isn't really seen today. African nations are not evenly incorporated into world market systems (D). They remain peripheral.

24. **C** The passage refers to the king levying dinars and mithqals on loads of salt and copper. The reference to salt (A) explains that it is imported. Cattle were located in Malal, not in Ghana (B). Ghanians grew vegetables, but the passage indicates that it was enough to be self-sufficient (D).

25. **D** At this time, the most likely source of silk was China. Horses had a centuries-old presence (A) in Africa. There is no reference to touching one's head to the floor (B), and the Muslims simply clap, so while there was a ritual involving kneeling, it was not universal. Gold and jewels (C) were commonly sourced from Africa.

26. **A** Muslims dominated the trade network in Africa in this period. The king who converted was not from Ghana (B), but from Malal. There was a strong tradition of trade in Africa, and the Africans' religion, unlike Islam, did not concern itself with merchants or trade (C). For the most part, African kings (D) remained independent.

27. **B** Because elites often converted for economic reasons, lower classes were allowed to maintain their traditional practices. Many Africans were not Muslim, and so choice (A) is too strong a statement to be accurate. Muslim merchants probably gave more favorable terms to their religious cohorts, but they did not limit their trade only to Muslims (C). According to the passage, Muslims were allowed to greet the king in their own manner (D).

28. **D** The earliest voyages recorded on the map were made by Vikings before 1000 CE. Both Spain and Portugal (A, B) did not explore until the 1400s. Greenland (D) was a Viking destination and not a point of origin.

29. **B** Brazilians speak Portuguese as a result of the line of demarcation established by the Treaty of Tordesillas (the Pope's Line through South America) in 1494. The Dutch (A) are not included on the map. Only English voyages (C) to Canada are listed, and therefore they cannot explain French-speaking Canadians. Although the Vikings did land in North America (D), they did not establish a presence.

30. **C** China abandoned exploration during the Ming Dynasty at the behest of Confucian officials so that the country could focus on protecting its borders. Zheng He in fact contacted many other cultures (A) and brought many exotic animals and products home to China. Choice (B) is an ethnocentric statement and reflects a point of view rather than historical reality. The islands off the East African coast were not colonized by 1450 (D).

31. **D** The Americas had had local, but no transregional, trade. Southeast Asia, Africa, and Europe (A, B, and C) had engaged in several transregional trade networks, including those along the Silk Roads, across the Indian Ocean, and around the Mediterranean.

32. A Mercantilism developed in conjunction with colonies, arising out of exploration. Nationalism is associated with the nineteenth and twentieth centuries (B); industrialism is associated with the eighteenth and nineteenth centuries (C); and communism is a twentieth-century political phenomenon (D).

33. C The only possible description of Wordsworth's reaction is enthusiasm, and thus the other answers (which would make him encouraged [A], accepting [B], or resigned [D]) are unacceptable. **C** also accounts for Dickens's somewhat cynical take, as when he says, "things in general were settled forever."

34. B In France, the heavy tax burden was borne exclusively by the third estate, who could least afford it. In the American colonies, colonists disputed the contention that Parliament had the right to impose taxes on the colonies without colonial representation in Parliament. The American Revolution changed very little with regard to the existing class structure; however, France's class structure changed dramatically (A). Although France wanted to abolish the monarchy, the American colonists kept the ideals of a bicameral legislature, separation of powers, and colonial legislatures, as well as representative government (C). The French Revolution sought to limit the influence of religious leaders, but the American Revolution did not.

35. B Robespierre, called "the Incorruptible," was known initially as the champion of the social revolution that took place in France. Later, in 1794, he was considered a dictator and summarily executed. Louis XVI (A) was the king who was overthrown by the French Revolution. Jean Lafitte (C) was a pirate. Lafayette (D) was known for his participation in the American Revolution, but he was a moderate where the French Revolution was concerned and was eventually exiled from France.

36. C Enlightenment thinkers responded to the social and economic ills that had characterized seventeenth- and eighteenth-century France; they sought to replace the aristocratic old order with a rational, practical, more bourgeois society and government. The Reformation (A) was a sixteenth-century religious movement aimed at reforming the corrupt Catholic Church. Mercantilism (B) was an economic theory that was popular with colonial powers, especially in sixteenth-, seventeenth-, and eighteenth-century Europe. The Reconquista refers to the centuries-long Christian reconquest of Spain from Arab domination.

37. C By comparing the League of Nations to a bubble, the artist implies that it was delicate and could not last. Woodrow Wilson is creating, not destroying, the bubble (A). There is no reference to conflict in the cartoon (B). There is also no reference to the necessity for idealism or the idea that the League of Nations will improve the world (D).

38. B In theory, the United Nations was the successor to the League of Nations. Founded after World War II, it promoted peaceful international relations, acted as an arbiter in international disputes, and called for its member nations to solve sociocultural, economic, and political (humanitarian) problems around the world.

39. B The so-called war guilt clause forced Germany to agree that it was solely responsible for World War I, creating German anger and resentment toward the other European nations at the conference. Both France and Britain joined the League of Nations (A). Italy did not lose territory in World War I, although it did in World War II (C). The Austro-Hungarian Empire's dissolution played no role in the hostilities leading up to World War II (D).

40. C The passage specifies that more women than men were enslaved and that women slaves brought more profit. This would result in tribes with an overpopulation of men. The passage refers to the resistance of slaves (A), and their prices indicate the possibility of escape. The captors in the passage were primarily Arab (B), as indicated by the introduction. Women were more highly valued than men because of their beauty, as indicated in the price lists (D).

41. A Because the slaves were predominantly women and had been captured by Arabs, they were most suited for domestic service or harems. Sugar plantations (B), cotton plantations (C), and armies (D) all favored physical strength, resulting in a preference for males. Arabs did not engage in the Atlantic slave trade, but sold slaves primarily in the Middle East.

42. **D** Specifying that captives were "idolatrous" makes it clear that the slavers were working off a religious premise. Choices A, B, and C all refer to the capture of slaves, not to their ultimate destination or purpose and not to their religious beliefs.

43. **B** According to the end of the excerpt, the North African slaves could look forward to the possibility of freedom. While all slave trade was motivated by profit, the passage indicates that the North Africans rationalized the capture of Africans who were considered idolaters (A). West African slaves were predominantly male; North African slaves were predominantly female (C). Slaves doing plantation work in the Caribbean had a notoriously shorter life span, and most of those slaves came from West Africa (D).

44. **B** The map reflects the distribution of the defeated Central Powers' territories by the League of Nations after World War I. The encomienda system is Latin American (A) and thus is not on the map. The Berlin Conference (C) dealt with all of Africa and included more European nations than simply Britain and France. The Cold War (D) did not play out in the Middle East and would have referred to the Soviets and the United States.

45. **B** Self-determination refers to the right to rule oneself. Colonialism (A) involves a foreign power being either directly or indirectly in control of another nation. Containment (C) refers to the policy of stopping the spread of communism, which was not an issue in the Middle East. Mercantilism (D) was an economic system associated with colonialism and imperialism, whereas the map refers to political administration.

46. **A** The Balfour Declaration indicated that Britain could eventually support a Jewish state, and other countries made no public statement. The Zimmerman Telegram (B), the Berlin Conference (C), and the Non-Aligned Move-

ment (D) do not refer to the Middle East and are therefore incorrect.

47. **B** After World War I, Italy, having joined the Allied Powers after the start of the war, received neither reparations nor territory; therefore, the Italians resented what they perceived to be an unfair division of the spoils of war. The Ottoman Empire was dissolved and never reformed (A); Australia (C) is completely irrelevant to the map; and Kuwait (D) never became part of Iraq.

48. **D** Between 1933 and 1937, according to the chart, production of all the cited commodities increased. Consumer goods (A) are not referred to in the chart. While grain, flax, sugar beets, and oil seed experienced reduced outputs in 1938, cotton production increased (B). The Soviets had more, not less, demand for cotton than for flax fiber (C).

49. **C** Stalin wanted to remain in power and thus had an incentive to produce not just more goods but also positive political propaganda. Official governmental statistics (A) are often notoriously unreliable, designed to maintain or increase support for a government. German assistance is nowhere accounted for in the data at hand (B). Also, it was not until 1939 that Germany and Russia, who had supported opposing sides of those fighting the Spanish Civil War, signed a nonaggression pact. Kulaks (wealthy Russian peasants) had been mostly exterminated by the 1920s (D).

50. **A** Collectivization, or Stalin's plan to create state-run rather than individually held farms, constituted the economic and political planning at the heart of communism. New Economic Plans (B) refer to Lenin; Five-Year Plans (C) refer more to industry than to agriculture; and the Great Leap Forward (D) refers to Mao Zedong's efforts in the late 1950s to recapture the rural peasant base that had made his revolution possible.

51. **B** The peasants under Stalin exerted resistance by destroying crops (and thus his positive data about crop production). Ultimately, collectivization led to repression and the outright slaughter of peasants and to famine. While there was some relocation of peasants during

collectivization, they were not removed en masse to Georgia (A). Rather than seeing increased economic stability, the peasants lost what little economic stability they had had (C). The situation of the peasantry was negatively rather than positively affected by Stalin's economic policies (D).

52. **D** Qianlong, the Qing emperor, makes it clear that he has no use for Great Britain's goods and that only through British submission to the Chinese throne and its stated wishes will there be peace and prosperity. The Chinese reaction to British goods is that while they are perhaps strange and ingenious, they are of no use to a country that has everything (A, B). Rather than perceiving the British manufactured goods as a bribe (C), the Chinese see them as a form of tribute.

53. **C** "We possess all things," writes the Chinese emperor; therefore, anything that the British could produce held no interest for China. While not necessarily angry, the Chinese were very clear that barbarians (including the British) were not allowed to participate in the country's foreign or domestic affairs (A). There was no agreement with the Dutch dealing with exclusive trading privileges with the Chinese. The Dutch followed the practice of working within established Asian trading systems (B). The Chinese pointed out in the letter that no foreigner, or barbarian, was allowed free access to economic, political, or cultural systems (D).

54. **A** European merchants were indeed closely monitored and their movements restricted to specific areas and cities. Likewise, their exchanges with Chinese people were limited. Both the Portuguese and the British (as well as the Dutch) traded with China (B). Products themselves were limited (C), but they did not carry extraordinary tariffs. Laws were intended only to confine and monitor foreign residents (D).

55. **C** Demand for Chinese products was high, but the Chinese had no interest in European goods, preferring instead to be paid in silver. This created a huge demand for silver, driving mining efforts by the Spanish in the Americas. Because the Portuguese did not have the resources to maintain control of the Indian

Ocean trade, their prestige and power declined (A). The British had important colonies in India, and the Japanese also took steps to restrict trade with foreigners (B). The Malacca Strait, though important, was never controlled by the British (D).

Section I, Part B: Short-Answer Questions

1A. You should mention at least two characteristics of the new imperialism (nineteenth century) that are shown in the Kipling work. These may include emigration, settlement, war, and a condescending attitude toward native peoples (who are seen as children who need to be civilized and socialized). There is also an obligation on the part of the colonizer to improve the infrastructure. (2 points possible)

1B. Johnson envisions the new imperialism as something characterized by violence, superior technology on the part of the colonizer, and a sense of the black man's increasing troubles. You need to identify only one of these elements. (1 point possible)

2A. Among the causes of the Industrial Revolution in Western Europe are innovations in agriculture and improved farming methods, the enclosure movement, increase in global trade, demographic shifts from rural to urban, laws that promoted growth in funding for factories, machinery, and transportation. (1.5 points possible)

2B. One effect of the Industrial Revolution in Western Europe could be any of the following: the replacement of cottage industry by centralized and regulated manufacturing; increased production of goods; replacement of women, who returned to traditional domestic roles; societal hierarchy that was determined by wealth instead of by inborn class. (1.5 points possible)

3A. You should recognize that Cousins and Confucius both indicate that to understand the past is to prepare for the future. (1 point possible)

3B. The African proverb makes it clear that history is written by the victors. Women, slaves, peasants, and marginalized and conquered peoples are not given a point of view or are ignored or repressed. (1 point possible)

3C. Bonaparte makes it clear that history can be used to justify the present; that is, the past explains the "why" of current political, economic, or social conditions. (1 point possible)

4A. Key words to identify the people's response in Delacroix's work might include resistance, defiance, rebellion, or aggression. Delacroix mixes allegory and realism to portray his view of the populist French July Revolution of 1830. The dominant and outsized figure of Liberty, symbol of a revolutionary and possibly the model for the U.S. Statue of Liberty, is surrounded by members of the populace: a factory worker, a student or artisan, a rural worker, and a child. (1 point possible)

4B. Key words to identify the response visible in Goya's work are submission, surrender, or resignation; but you might find that both paintings exhibit defiance and interpret the Goya painting as showing the consequences of that defiance. Goya shows his antiwar sentiments in general and Spanish antipathy to being governed by the French in particular. The dehumanized French firing squad confronts an oversized, very human figure. The lantern and central figure's clothing reflect the light of reason (as per the Enlightenment). The firing squad is "inhuman" and shows Goya's distaste for the impersonal killing that characterized the French action.(1 point possible)

4C. Both of these works show the point of view or perspective of two groups: those being depicted in the artworks and those of the artists. Thus, the artwork records, reflects, and refers to historical events and conditions. Art is a commentary, but it can also often be a call to action. (1 point possible)

Section II, Part A: Document-Based Question

The question addresses the evolution of human rights across time and continents. You must sustain a thesis or an argument that explains changes in the idea or scope of human rights. You should take into consideration the following points: Are the human rights documents personal, political, public, or private? Why were the documents created? In other words, what are the focus and purpose of human rights declarations? You should consider the sources of the documents as you analyze them and include outside historical events that may have influenced their creation.

A good response would draw on six or seven of these documents (that is, all or all but one of them) to trace the evolution of human rights, particularly in order to emphasize differences between Eastern and Western perspectives.

You should incorporate analyses of the documents. You may begin by dividing the documents into those that focus on social/socioeconomic, religious, or political points. Since all the documents are "official," or produced by governing bodies, you can make the case that all of them are political. You may also note that some of the documents focus on human rights in a national context (Documents 1 and 3); some focus on the individual (Documents 2, 4, 5, and 7); and some are clearly more global in focus (Documents 6 and 7). There may be some overlap; that is, some documents will fall into more than one category. Simply listing the characteristics of the documents, however, leaves open the question of connections between documents, connections that point out similarities and differences in the focus and purpose of human rights declarations. For example, Document 7 stands out for its emphasis on the ties between religion and human rights; and while it focuses on the individual, it does so within a religious context.

The thesis therefore should address both similarities over time (continuity) and differences in point of view and purpose.

In this question, you are asked to determine what historical events or which historical context would answer the prompt most thoroughly. For example, you might want to point out that the Magna Carta was the king of England's response to pressures from noble landowners who were intent on keeping some of the power they had achieved during the feudal era. This would eventually contribute to the formation of constitutional or parliamentary monarchies and to the expansion of bureaucratic systems involving checks and balances.

Having considered the various points of view, you may want to discuss the nature of human rights concerns—from national (Document 1) to more individual (Documents 4 and 5) to transnational or global (Documents 6 and 7). Clearly the Recopilación (Document 3) reflects the somewhat idealistic (and nationalistic) thoughts governing settlement of the New World in the Age of Exploration and Discovery.

You may consider whether human rights are absolute, as implied in Western (although not Eastern) documents. Or, you may want to make the case that human rights are dependent on situation or location (Document 7). This would lead to an analysis of changes in government—from absolutism to the revolutionary ideal of natural law, or, in other words, from the idea of power residing in the highest earthly authority to its being inherent in human beings.

Finally, because most of the documents refer to law, you could also consider whether human rights are primarily a legal or an ethical-religious-moral concern, again according (always) to the documents. Also, you need to consider the linear chronology of changes, matching those changes to contemporary historical events.

A good response thus will show the connection between theory (of human rights) and action (governmental responses to demands for human rights); and it will both strengthen the original thesis's contentions and demonstrate an ability to extrapolate from documents the nuances of historical thought.

Section II, Part B: Long-Essay Question

A good response may begin with the creation of a verbal Venn diagram, or at least the overlapping section of one, and the laying out of the generally acknowledged causes and effects of the Industrial Revolution. From 1750, population growth and migration created both new markets for goods and a new (primarily urban) labor pool. New technology and inventions (e.g., the steam engine) resulted in more efficient means of transportation, communication, and production of goods. The abolition of slavery in Western Europe and of serfdom in Russia resulted in rural-urban (agricultural to industrial) migration patterns and sustained economies by providing workers.

These elements, in turn, resulted in more specialized labor, a growing middle class that had the income to buy proliferating goods, and a stronger sense of national identity, or nationalism, with this last often replacing traditional mores and even religion, and contributing, along with enhanced means of transportation and communication, to two world wars. Western Europe, and later Russia, embraced a new imperialism in its search for raw materials, and other areas (like Latin America, for example) remained a source for those raw materials as well as for agricultural products. As industry grew, capital and labor provided a general improvement in the standard of living and increased free time for leisure activities (including professional sports, movies and live entertainment, vacations, and travel).

The environmental effects of the Industrial Revolution are both manifold and cumulative: factories and industry have generated air, land, and water pollutants (both in Western Europe and in Russia). The search for raw materials has resulted in deforestation and exhaustion of soils (in Latin America and Africa).

Perhaps the most striking and longest-lasting effect of the Industrial Revolution has been globalization, the integration of economic markets, free trade, and the flow of capital (human and monetary).

Women, migrating with their families from the countryside to the city, found work outside the home in factories and mines. They earned about half of what their male counterparts did, and they were in the forefront of groups seeking more and equal rights.

Scoring: How Did I Do?

As you evaluate how you did on the diagnostic exam, you need to keep several things in mind.

First, look again at the chart from the first chapter of the book. This tells you how much of your score will be determined by each part of the test. The multiple-choice section counts the most, but no one part of the exam will determine your final grade. The following scoring chart reflects the same percentages shown here.

Section	Type of Question	Number of Questions	Time	Recommended Time	% of Exam Score
Section I, Part A	Multiple-Choice	55	95 minutes	55 minutes	40%
Section I, Part B	Short-Answer	Answer 3 questions out of 4.		40 minutes	20%
Section II, Part A	Document-Based Question (DBQ)	1	100 minutes	60 minutes	25%
Section II, Part B	Long-Essay	Choose 1 of 3 questions		40 minutes	15%

The apcentral.collegeboard.com website has specific information about rubrics for the questions. Your teacher should also have this information.

STEP 3

Develop Strategies for Success

CHAPTER 4   Tips for Taking the Exam

Tips for Taking the Exam

IN THIS CHAPTER

Summary: Use these question-answering strategies to raise your AP score.

Key Ideas

✪ If you don't know an answer on a multiple-choice question, try to eliminate one or more answer choices and then guess. There is no penalty for guessing.

✪ Write a solid thesis statement on the DBQ and the long essay.

✪ On the DBQ, use document grouping to analyze the question.

✪ On the DBQ, analyze point of view.

✪ On the long-essay question, analyze the causes and effects of continuity and change and analyze comparisons.

Multiple-Choice Questions

The multiple-choice section of the Advanced Placement World History: Modern examination consists of 55 multiple-choice questions. You will have 1 hour, 35 minutes (95 minutes) to complete the multiple-choice and short-answer sections; it's recommended you spend 55 minutes on the multiple-choice questions. Each multiple-choice question has four answer choices.

The multiple-choice questions require you to analyze the material you have covered in the course. Many of the questions require you to compare among societies, events, or processes, or to indicate how they have changed over time. The questions require you to interpret a written passage, photograph, political cartoon, map, chart, or graph.

The following are some frequently asked questions concerning the multiple-choice section:

1. **If I don't know an answer, should I guess or leave the question unanswered?** There is no guessing penalty on the multiple-choice section. If you do not know an answer, you should select the answer choice that you think is correct. Don't leave any multiple-choice questions unanswered; correct guesses are correct answers.

2. **What strategy should I use to narrow the possible answer choices?** Of the four answer choices found in each question, one is often obviously incorrect. In addition to the correct choice, there is often another answer that is almost correct. Another possibility is that two of the answer choices are correct, but one is a better answer than the other. The best advice is to read the question very carefully to determine exactly what the question is asking, then eliminate the weaker answers until you arrive at the best answer.

3. **Will I be required to know a lot of dates and people to answer the multiple-choice questions?** Some knowledge of specific dates and people will be necessary to answer the multiple-choice questions. For the most part, however, the multiple-choice questions on the Advanced Placement World History: Modern examination ask you to compare societies, issues, or trends within one or more of the eras covered or to analyze how societies, issues, or trends have changed and remained the same over time.

Short-Answer Questions

In Section I, Part B, of the test, you will be given a series of four free-response questions. Each of the questions is divided into two or three parts. You must answer Questions 1 and 2, but you have your choice of answering either Question 3 or 4. These questions account for 20 percent of your score. You will be given 95 minutes to answer Parts A and B of Section I; it's recommended that you spend 40 minutes of that time on the short-answer questions.

Many of the short-answer questions are based upon a stimulus such as a quotation, graph, chart, picture, or map. Other questions in this portion of the exam may ask you to identify and explain examples of a process, an AP World History: Modern theme, or events occurring within a given era. For example, you may be asked to identify and explain the reasons for two types of migration during the twentieth century. Yet another question may require you to read a short summary of an argument and provide examples from world historians to support and refute the argument. You are not required to include a thesis statement in your answers to any of the questions in this portion of the exam. Since you have only 40 minutes to complete this section, you need to read the question and the stimulus, if provided, and then compose an answer that is accurate, brief, and right to the point of the question.

Here are some strategies that will help you succeed on the short-answer questions:

- Read the question stem, paying close attention to the task(s) you are required to address for that question.
- Remember that you must answer three questions in this section, Questions 1 and 2 and then either Question 3 or 4. Remember, too, that you must answer all parts (A, B, and C, if there is a Part C) of each question.

- Remember that the short-answer questions do not require a thesis statement and that taking the time to compose a thesis statement will not add to your score.
- Keep your answers concise and to the point. In other words, just answer the specific questions you are asked.

Document-Based Question

After completing the multiple-choice and short-answer sections, you will have 100 minutes to complete the essays. You will receive a booklet that contains the prompts for both essay questions and a second booklet with lined paper for your responses. You may answer the essay questions in any order. During this portion of the test, you will have to budget your own time; you will not be told at which point you are to move on to the next question.

The suggested time for answering the document-based question is 60 minutes. You should spend approximately 15 minutes reading the documents, 5 minutes in prewriting, and 40 minutes writing your essay. The document-based question usually contains between five and seven documents. Although some of the documents will be text, others may be photographs, drawings, political cartoons, maps, graphs, or charts. In order to successfully answer the DBQ, you need to meet the following requirements:

1. **Write a solid thesis statement.** Do not simply restate the question. Be sure that you take a stand on one side of the topic addressed by the essay prompt and respond to all parts of the question.

2. **Develop and support an organized argument that illustrates relationships among historical evidence such as contradiction, corroboration, and/or qualification.**

3. **Use evidence at least six of the seven documents to support the thesis or a relevant argument.**

4. **Explain the author's point of view, the author's purpose, the historical context, and/or the audience for at least four documents.**

5. **Contextualization:** Situate the author's argument by explaining broader historical events, developments, or processes relevant to the question. This point involves an explanation consisting of a number of sentences or a full paragraph.

6. **Extend your argument by explaining the connections between the argument and ONE of the following:**

   a) A development in a different historical period, situation, era, or geographical area.
   b) A course theme and/or approach to history that is not the focus of the essay (such as political, economic, social, cultural, or intellectual history).
   c) A different discipline or a field of study (such as economics, government, art history, or anthropology).

Long-Essay Question

The long-essay question will test your ability to analyze continuity and change over time and/or to compare a society, event, theme, or process. You have the opportunity to select one of three essays on this part of the exam. The suggested writing time for this essay is 40 minutes, including 5 minutes devoted to prewriting.

The following are the elements that you must address to succeed on the long essay:

1. **Present a thesis that makes a historically defensible claim and responds to all parts of the question.** The thesis must include one or more sentences located in one place, either in the introduction or the conclusion.

2. **Describe similarities AND differences among historical persons, events, developments, or processes.**

3. **Identify and explain the reasons for similarities AND differences among historical persons, events, developments, or processes.** OR, DEPENDING ON THE PROMPT, evaluate the relative significance of historical persons, events, developments, or processes.

4. **Describe causes AND/OR effects of a historical event, development, or process.** AND explain the reasons for the causes AND/OR effects of a historical event, development, or process. If the prompt requires discussion of both causes and effects, responses must address both causes and effects in order to earn both points.

5. **CCOT: Describe historical continuity AND change over time.** Explain the reasons for historical continuity AND change over time.

6. **Describe the ways in which historical development specified in the prompt was different from and similar to developments that preceded AND/OR followed.**

7. **Explain the extent to which the historical development specified in the prompt was different from and similar to developments that preceded AND/OR followed.**

8. **Address the topic of the question with specific examples of relevant evidence.**

9. **Use specific examples of evidence to fully and effectively substantiate the stated thesis or a relevant argument.**

10. **Extend the argument by explaining the connections between the argument and ONE of the following:**

    a) A development in a different historical period, situation, era, or geographical era
    b) A course theme and/or approach to history that is not the focus of the essay (such as political, economic, social, cultural, or intellectual history)
    c) A different discipline or field of inquiry

STEP 4

Review the Knowledge You Need to Score High

- Technological and Environmental Transformations
- Organization and Reorganization of Human Societies
- Regional and Interregional Interactions
- The Global Tapestry and Networks of Exchange
- Land-Based Empires and Trans-Oceanic Interconnections
- Industrialization and Global Integration
- Revolutions and the Consequences of Industrialization
- Revolutions, World Wars, and Depression
- Cold War and the Post-War Balance of Power
- Nationalist Movements
- Accelerating Global Change and Realignments

The World History Environment

IN THIS CHAPTER

Summary: Before we begin to consider the scope of the human story, we must first consider the stage on which the story unfolds: the land and the oceans themselves. The Advanced Placement World History: Modern course divides the globe into a number of regions that include the following: East Asia, Southeast Asia, South Asia, Central Asia, Southwest Asia (the Middle East) and North Africa, sub-Saharan Africa, Eastern Europe, Western Europe, North America, Latin America, and Oceania. The map overleaf illustrates the location of these regions. Keep in mind that political boundaries among nations may vary considerably throughout the different periods of history.

Key Terms

civilization	independent invention
climate	monsoon
cultural diffusion	steppe

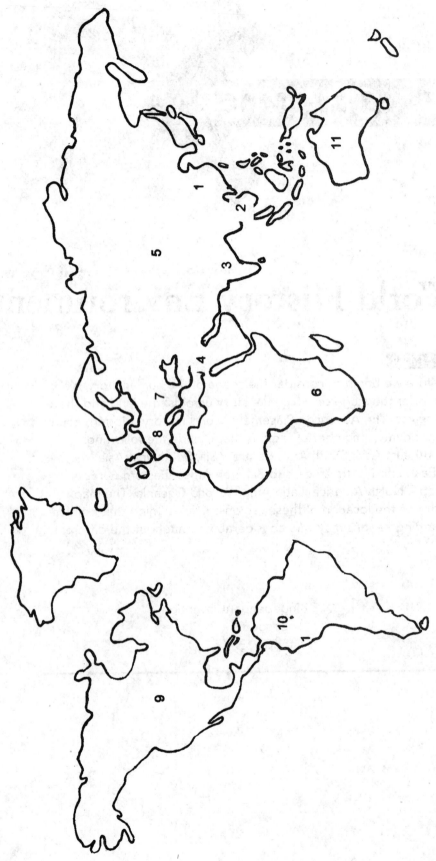

1. East Asia
2. Southeast Asia
3. South Asia
4. Southwest Asia (Middle East) and North Africa
5. Central Asia
6. Sub-Saharan Africa
7. Eastern Europe
8. Western Europe
9. North America
10. Latin America
11. Oceania

Oceans and Seas

The history of the world did not occur in land areas alone; the oceans and seas also have their own stories to tell. Vast migrations of both ancient and modern peoples took place across the waterways of the world; plants, animals, and diseases were exchanged; and competition arose among explorers seeking new lands and merchants pursuing profits. A few points to understand when studying the oceans are:

- The Arctic Ocean, the smallest of the world's oceans, is packed in ice throughout most of the year. Extremely difficult to navigate, it is the location of the famed Northwest Passage sought by early European explorers. The passage is barely usable because of its ice-bound condition.

- The Indian Ocean, the third largest of the oceans, has seen extensive trade since the people of the Harappan civilization sailed through one of its seas, the Arabian Sea, to trade with Sumer. Throughout history the Indian Ocean has seen Malay sailors and Chinese, Muslim, and European traders use the ocean's *monsoon* winds to guide their expeditions through its waters. Africa also was drawn into this trade. Oftentimes, commercial activity in the Indian Ocean produced intense rivalries, especially among the Dutch, Portuguese, and Muslim sailors in the seventeenth century.

- The Atlantic Ocean became the scene of exchange between the Eastern and Western Hemispheres after the voyages of Columbus produced an encounter among European, African, and American peoples. The Caribbean Sea saw the meeting of the three cultures on the sugar plantations of the sixteenth through the eighteenth centuries. The Mediterranean Sea, joined to the Atlantic Ocean, saw the glories of early Middle Eastern and Greco-Roman civilizations. Northern European societies traded in the waters of the North Sea and the Baltic Sea.

- The Pacific Ocean, the world's largest, is dotted with islands that witnessed the ancient voyages of the Polynesian peoples of Oceania. The Bering Sea was the route of the earliest inhabitants of the Americas into those continents. Societies of East and Southeast Asia communicated with one another by means of the Sea of Japan and the South China and East China seas. The Manila galleons of the sixteenth through the nineteenth centuries joined Latin America, the Philippine Islands, and China in trade. World wars saw the use of Pacific islands for strategic purposes.

The following chart illustrates some of the political units and physical features of various world regions.

REGION	EXAMPLES OF MODERN COUNTRIES	MAJOR RIVERS	MAJOR LANDFORMS
East Asia	China, Japan, North Korea, South Korea	Yalu River, Huang He River, Chang Jiang River	Mount Fuji, Gobi Desert, Tibetan Plateau
Southeast Asia	Vietnam, Thailand, Laos, Indonesia, Malaysia	Mekong River, Irawaddy River	Ring of Fire
South Asia	India, Pakistan, Nepal, Bhutan, Bangladesh	Ganges River, Indus River, Brahmaputra River	Himalayas, Hindu Kush, Khyber Pass

continued

REGION	EXAMPLES OF MODERN COUNTRIES	MAJOR RIVERS	MAJOR LANDFORMS
Southwest Asia (Middle East) and North Africa	Egypt, Saudi Arabia, Morocco, Israel, Turkey, Iran, Iraq, Afghanistan	Tigris–Euphrates Rivers, Nile River	Zagros Mountains, Arabian Desert, Sahara Desert
Central Asia	Russia, Mongolia, Kazakhstan	Volga River	Gobi Desert, Lake Baikal, Ural Mountains, steppes
Sub-Saharan Africa	Nigeria, Somalia, Democratic Republic of Congo, Kenya, South Africa	Congo River, Zambezi River, Niger River	Kalahari Desert, tropical rainforests, Great Rift Valley, Mount Kilimanjaro, Lake Victoria
Eastern Europe	Poland, Slovakia, Lithuania, Croatia	Danube River	Caucasus Mountains, Carpathian Mountains
Western Europe	Spain, United Kingdom, Sweden, Italy, Germany, Austria	Rhine River, Rhone River, Elbe River	Alps, Pyrenees Mountains
North America	Canada, United States, Mexico	Mississippi River, Missouri River, St. Lawrence River, Rio Grande River	Rocky Mountains, Canadian Shield, Sierra Madre Mountains
Latin America	Mexico, Cuba, Panama, Brazil, Argentina	Amazon River, Río de la Plata, Paraná	Amazon Rainforest, Andes Mountains, Pampas
Oceania	Australia, New Zealand, Papua New Guinea	Darling River, Murray River	Outback, Great Barrier Reef, Great Dividing Range

Periodization

A unique feature of the Advanced Placement World History: Modern course is its division into four instead of six periods, as previously used.

The four AP World History: Modern periods are:

- Period 1 Regional and Interregional Interactions (c. 1200 CE to c. 1450)
- Period 2 Global Interactions (c. 1450 to c. 1750)
- Period 3 Industrialization and Global Integration (c. 1750 to c. 1900)
- Period 4 Accelerating Global Change and Realignments (c. 1900 to the present)

It is important for you to familiarize yourself with these periods; the ability to compare and contrast societies, events, and trends within periods will be necessary skills to master the multiple-choice questions, as well as the comparative and document-based questions, on the AP examination. You will also need to analyze the impact of interactions among societies. Likewise, a grasp of the changes and continuities (those things that stayed the same) between periods is important to success on the multiple-choice, the continuity and change-over-time, and document-based questions on the exam.

AP World History: Modern Themes

In each of the periods, there are six broad themes that the course emphasizes. These are:

- Human-environmental interaction: disease and its effects on population, migration, settlement patterns, and technology
- Cultural development and interaction: religions, belief systems, and philosophies; science and technology; and the arts and architecture
- Governance, or state-building, expansion, and conflict: political structures and forms of government; empires; nations and nationalism; revolts and revolutions; and regional, transregional, and global organizations and structures
- Creation, growth, and interaction of economic systems: agriculture and pastoralism, trade and commerce, labor systems, industrialization, and capitalism and socialism
- Development and change in social structures: gender roles, family and kinship relations, race and ethnicity, and social and economic class structures
- Technology and innovation

Civilization Versus Society

Another consideration in the AP World History: Modern course is the role of societies as well as civilizations. Historians commonly define a **civilization** as a cultural group that displays five characteristics:

- Advanced cities
- Advanced technology
- Skilled workers
- Complex institutions (examples: government, religion)
- A system of writing or recordkeeping

Not all peoples on the earth live in cultural groups that meet these five criteria. Yet inhabitants of societies (cultural groups that do not satisfy all five characteristics of a civilization) also have made significant contributions to the course of world history. One example is that of the highland people of Papua New Guinea, many of whom lack a written language even today, yet who count among the earliest farmers in the world.

Independent Invention Versus Diffusion

Still another consideration in the Advanced Placement World History: Modern course is the question of whether **cultural diffusion** or **independent invention** is the more significant method of exchange. For example, in the introductory chapters of this study guide, you will read of the spread of agriculture throughout the globe. In this case, it is the task of the historian to investigate where agriculture arose independently, in addition to tracing its diffusion, or spread, through the migration of agricultural peoples. Also, contact of migratory peoples with one another was responsible for the exchange of ideas and technological inventions in addition to the knowledge of agriculture. Patterns of independent invention compared to those of cultural diffusion will remain a thread woven throughout the story of humankind, up to the present.

CHAPTER 6

Development of Agriculture and Technology

IN THIS CHAPTER

Summary: One of the most significant developments in world history was the independent emergence of agriculture, a process that had already taken place in some locations throughout the Eastern Hemisphere by 8000 BCE. The so-called **Agricultural Revolution,** or **Neolithic Revolution,** was in reality more of a slow process following the last great Ice Age and resulting from the warming of global temperatures. The accompanying historical period, known as the **Neolithic Age** (or New Stone Age), was named for its characteristic tools made from stone.

Key Terms

Agricultural Revolution
animism
artifact
foraging
Neolithic Age

Neolithic Revolution
Paleolithic Age
pastoralism, patriarchal
slash-and-burn cultivation
specialization of labor

The Transition from Foraging to Agriculture

At the close of the **Paleolithic Age** (or Old Stone Age), the transition from **foraging** (hunting and gathering) arose as nomadic groups returned to favorite grazing areas year after year. Perhaps some nomadic peoples made an effort to cultivate those crops that they found most appealing; later they may have transplanted seeds from these same favored crops to other areas through which they traveled. Because hunting required greater physical strength, the early cultivation of plants was probably a task left to women, granting them increased importance among agricultural peoples. Women farmers studied the growth patterns of plants, as well as the effect of climate and soil on them. Agricultural development included the domestication of animals as well as the cultivation of crops.

Independent Origins of Agriculture: A Timeline

Key developments in the history of agriculture show the following events in the process:

- Agriculture began sometime after 9000 BCE with the cultivation of grain crops such as wheat and barley in Southwest Asia. Animals such as pigs, cattle, sheep, and goats also were domesticated.
- By 7000 BCE Sudanese Africa and West Africa cultivated root crops such as sorghum and yams.
- Inhabitants of the Yangtze River valley cultivated rice about 6500 BCE.
- About 5500 BCE, people of the Huang He valley began the cultivation of soybeans and millet. They also domesticated chickens and pigs and, later, water buffalo.
- In Southeast Asia, perhaps around 3500 BCE, inhabitants grew root crops such as yams and taro as well as a variety of citrus and other fruits.
- Around 4000 BCE, the peoples of central Mexico cultivated maize, or corn, later adding beans, squash, tomatoes, and peppers.
- The principal crop of the Andean region of South America was potatoes, first cultivated around 3000 BCE. Maize and beans were added later. The only domesticated animals in the Americas were the llama, alpaca, and guinea pig.

(*Note to the student:* The multiple-choice questions on the Advanced Placement examination will not require that you know exact dates. Rather, the dates are given so that you may visualize a pattern of independent invention of agriculture.)

The Spread of Agriculture

After agriculture was established independently in various locations across the globe, the knowledge of crop cultivation spread rapidly. In fact, it was the nature of early agricultural methods that aided the extension of agricultural knowledge. An often-used agricultural method called **slash-and-burn cultivation** involved slashing the bark on trees and later burning the dead ones. The resulting ashes enriched the soil for a number of years. When the soil eventually lost its fertility, however, farmers were forced to move to new territory. By 6000 BCE, agriculture had spread to the eastern Mediterranean basin and the Balkans, reaching Northern Europe about 4000 BCE. These frequent migrations exposed early farmers to new peoples, diffusing both agricultural knowledge and cultural values.

Characteristics of Early Agricultural Societies

Although agriculture required more work than foraging, it had the advantage of producing a more constant and substantial food supply. Consequently, the spread of agriculture not only increased cultural contacts but also allowed for significant population growth.

As populations multiplied, neolithic peoples began to settle in villages. Members of agricultural communities had to cooperate, especially in constructing and maintaining irrigation systems. As villages grew and agriculture continued to supply an abundance, even a surplus, of food, not all villagers were needed as farmers. Some inhabitants began to develop other talents and skills such as the manufacture of pottery, metal tools, textiles, wood products, and jewelry. Others became priests, soldiers, and merchants. Surplus crop production thus allowed a division of labor and, ultimately, the growth of distinct social classes. Two early noteworthy agricultural settlements were:

- Jericho (established around 8000 BCE) in present-day Israel. Here farmers produced wheat and barley, while also trading with neighboring peoples in obsidian and salt. Characteristic of Jericho was a thick wall designed to protect the wealthy settlement against raiders.
- Çatal Hüyük (established around 7000 BCE) in Anatolia (present-day Turkey). Residents of this village left **artifacts** representing a variety of craft products indicating an extensive **specialization of labor**. Artists produced decorative art, which can be seen in frescoes (wall paintings) inside houses and in jewelry. They also traded obsidian with neighboring peoples.

Pastoralism

As agricultural communities arose, **pastoralism** developed in the grasslands of Africa and Eurasia. Pastoralists, or herders, contributed meat and other animal products to the overall food supply, further enlarging neolithic human populations. At times their overgrazing of livestock led to soil erosion and deforestation. Both agricultural and pastoral peoples exchanged food products and technology.

Early Metallurgy

In addition to the development and spread of agriculture, the Neolithic Age witnessed the origins of metallurgy. The first metal that humans learned to use was copper, with which they cast items such as jewelry, weapons, and tools. Later, neolithic humans learned the use of other metals such as gold and bronze (an alloy of copper and tin), giving rise to the term Bronze Age for the later neolithic period. Still later, the knowledge of ironworking was developed independently in Central Asia and sub-Saharan Africa.

Culture of Neolithic Societies

As human populations concentrated in permanent settlements, the specialization of labor as well as trade activity resulted in differing degrees of accumulation of wealth. As time progressed, differences in family wealth manifested themselves in the emergence of social classes.

The inhabitants of early agricultural societies observed their environment in order to further their knowledge of the factors necessary to produce a bountiful harvest. Their knowledge of the seasons in relation to the positions of heavenly bodies led eventually to the development of calendars and of monolithic structures like Stonehenge. Interest in the natural world led neolithic humans to celebrate fertility and the cycles of life. Many agricultural and pastoral societies practiced **animism**, or the belief that divine spirits inhabited natural objects such as rocks and trees. In addition, archeologists have unearthed numerous small, portable figures representing fertility goddesses in the ruins of neolithic villages and of decorative, permanent art, like frescoes and other forms of indoor art.

Beginnings of Cities

As population growth resulted in larger settlements, the agricultural world experienced the rise of cities. Urban areas offered further specialization of labor and more sophisticated technology. New roles emerged as cities required administrators, collectors of taxes and tribute, and religious leaders. Furthermore, women were relegated more to domestic tasks, and patriarchal systems—and gods—caused a shift in gender roles and power structures. Cities also acquired influence over larger territories than villages did and would lead to the establishment of empires.

❯ Rapid Review

The Neolithic Age saw independent origins of agriculture worldwide. As the knowledge of agriculture spread, cultural diffusion marked the ancient world. When crop cultivation produced increasingly larger yields, some farmers specialized in other tasks or crafts. As population concentrations grew increasingly dense, settlements grew into villages and, later, cities. Cities developed a more complex social structure to administer wealth, provide order, and study the meaning of life itself.

❯ Review Questions

1. Answer Parts A and B.

   The Agricultural (or Neolithic) Revolution witnessed the change from hunter-gatherer, foraging societies to those grouped into settlements.

   (A) Identify TWO long-term social or cultural results of the switch to sedentary, non-nomadic populations.

   (B) Identify ONE economic change that accompanied the Neolithic (Agricultural) Revolution.

2. Answer Parts A and B.

   Agriculture was domesticated in different areas at different times.

   (A) Identify TWO examples of independent innovations that resulted in this domestication.

   (B) Identify or explain ONE role of geography in the domestication of agriculture.

Questions 3 to 5 refer to the following images.

3. The major difference between these two pieces of art is best described by which of the following statements?
   (A) The Woman of Willendorf is portable, while the wall painting is applied to a permanent living space.
   (B) The Woman of Willendorf is religious; the wall painting is not.
   (C) The Woman of Willendorf is more symbolic than the wall painting.
   (D) The Woman of Willendorf is patriarchal, while the wall painting is not.

4. The wall painting depicts which advance associated with the Agricultural Revolution?
   (A) Animism
   (B) Trade activity
   (C) Division of labor
   (D) Pastoralism

5. The Woman of Willendorf probably served a specific purpose—as a fertility goddess. Which of the following best describes the purpose the wall painting might have served?
   (A) An interior decorative element
   (B) A merchant's record
   (C) An altar
   (D) A calendar

› Answers and Explanations

1A. The long-term social or cultural results of settlement include a change in the role of women (i.e., their increased importance as cultivators of food supplies and agricultural surplus); division of and specialization of labor, including, for example, farming, metallurgy, and commerce; human migration as a result of soil exploitation, exhaustion, or erosion, resulting in exchanges of knowledge and cultural values; population growth; the development of pastoralism and also the appearance of diseases transmitted from animals to humans; or an increase in decorative artwork. You only need to give TWO examples to answer the question.

1B. Economic changes that the Neolithic (Agricultural) Revolution witnessed could include growth of merchant and artisan classes, inter-settlement trade, and specialization of work.

2A. Independent innovations involved the cultivation of specific crops, compatible with geographic and climatic conditions: wheat and barley in Southwest Asia; root crops in West Africa; rice in China; and corn, beans, squash, tomatoes, and potatoes in Central and South America. Domestication of various animals also varied from region to region. Areas with metal reserves (copper, gold, iron, tin) began production of weapons, tools, and jewelry, independent of one another.

2B. Geography was a principal determinant in which crops could thrive (rice in the Yangtze River valley, citrus fruits in temperate climates). More mountainous regions allowed (or did not allow) for specific crop cultivation as did river valleys, in temperate climates especially.

3. A The size of the Woman of Willendorf allowed her to be carried easily by nomadic peoples. Once settlement became the norm, permanent housing encouraged the application of decorative arts, such as the fresco (wall painting). There is no way to know whether either the Woman of Willendorf or the fresco had religious (B) or symbolic (C) or patriarchal (D) meanings.

4. C Artwork indicates that individuals had the leisure time and the expertise to produce it, or the division of labor characteristic of the era. There is no indication that animism (A), trade (B), or pastoralism (D) is represented in the fresco.

5. A The wall painting covers a bare wall and adds color to an otherwise plain interior. There is no indication that it records merchant (commercial) transactions (B), serves a religious purpose (C), or counts time (D).

CHAPTER 7

Structure of Early Civilizations

IN THIS CHAPTER

Summary: As agricultural villages evolved into cities, some urban areas began to display the characteristics of civilizations (described in Chapter 5). The earliest civilizations in the Eastern Hemisphere arose in Mesopotamia, the Nile, the Indus, and the Huang He valleys; civilizations arose later among the Olmecs in Mesoamerica (Middle America) and the Chavín in the Andes Mountains of South America.

Key Terms

covenant
cuneiform
diaspora
hieroglyphics
jati
Mandate of Heaven
matrilineal
monotheism
oracle bones
patriarchal
pharaoh

polytheism
Quetzalcóatl
Ten Commandments
theocracy
Torah
untouchables
Varna
Vedas
Yahweh
ziggurat

Mesopotamia

The world's earliest civilization arose in the valley of the Tigris and Euphrates rivers in an area the Greeks called Mesopotamia ("Land Between the Rivers"). The cultural achievements of Mesopotamia represented independent innovation, achievements that it passed on to other river valley civilizations in Egypt and, especially, the Indus valley. Around 4000 BCE, the inhabitants of Mesopotamia used bronze and copper. By this time they had already invented the wheel and developed irrigation canals to farm the arid lands of their environment.

About 3500 BCE, a group of invaders called the Sumerians settled in the southernmost portion of Mesopotamia. The Sumerians developed the first example of writing. Called **cuneiform**, it involved pictures pressed into clay using a wedge-shaped stylus. The pictographs initially stood for objects, but later were refined to represent sounds. The Sumerians also developed a number system based on 60 and studied the movement of heavenly bodies. In architecture, the Sumerians expressed the glories of their civilization and of the many gods of nature that they worshipped by building towers called **ziggurats**. They are credited with relating the first epic in world history, *The Epic of Gilgamesh*, which includes a story of a great flood similar to that of the biblical account in Genesis.

The Tigris and Euphrates rivers were noted for their unpredictable and often violent flooding. Irrigation systems to control flooding and channel water for agricultural use required the cooperation of Mesopotamia's settlements. This need promoted the beginnings of government. Early Mesopotamian government was in the form of city-states, with a city government also controlling surrounding territory.

A social structure headed by rulers and elite classes controlled the land, which was farmed by slaves. Slaves could sometimes purchase their freedom. Sumerian families were **patriarchal**, with men dominating family and public life. Men had the authority to sell their wives and children into slavery to pay their debts. By the sixteenth century BCE, Mesopotamian women had begun to wear veils in public. In spite of these restrictions, Mesopotamian women could sometimes gain influence in the courts, serve as priestesses, or act as scribes for the government. Some worked in small businesses.

A lack of natural protective barriers made Mesopotamia vulnerable to invasion by outsiders; most cities in the region constructed defensive walls. Frequent conflicts among local Sumerian kings over water and property rights weakened the city-states. The Sumerian culture later fell to conquest by the Akkadians and the Babylonians, both of whom spread Sumerian culture. The Babylonian king Hammurabi devised a code of laws that regulated daily life and provided harsh "an eye for an eye" punishments for criminal offenses. *The Code of Hammurabi* drew distinctions between social classes and genders, administering less severe punishments to elite classes over commoners and men over women for the same offense. After 900 BCE, Assyrians and Persians dominated Mesopotamia.

Egypt

About 3000 BCE, a second civilization grew up along another river valley, this time the valley of the Nile River in present-day Egypt. In contrast to the unpredictable waters of the Tigris–Euphrates, those of the Nile overflowed once annually, discharging an amount of water that usually varied little from one year to the next. As in Mesopotamia, irrigation projects to channel floodwaters led to the organization of the community and ultimately to the development of political structures. Although several major cities emerged along the Nile, most Egyptian communities were agricultural villages engaged in local trade along the Nile.

The king of Egypt, or **pharaoh**, wielded considerable power. About 2700 BCE, the pharaohs began the construction of huge pyramids that served as tombs for themselves and their families. These tombs were decorated with colorful paintings. Like the Sumerians, the Egyptians were **polytheists**, or worshippers of many gods. Their belief in an afterlife led to the practice of mummification to preserve the bodies of pharaohs and, later, those of members of lower classes.

Egyptian society was composed of a number of defined social classes. Within this social structure, however, commoners could enter government service and rise in social status. Egyptian families were patriarchal, with men dominating households and community life. Among the royalty, however, women sometimes acted as regents for young rulers or as priestesses. Other educated women worked as scribes for the Egyptian government.

The Egyptians did not acquire the use of bronze tools and weapons until long after they had reached Mesopotamia. From the Nubian kingdom of Kush, a site of the independent innovation of ironworking, the Egyptians acquired iron implements.

The Egyptians engaged in some trade with the people of Mesopotamia and later with the kingdom of Kush to the south. Some historians believe that Egyptian picture writing, or **hieroglyphics**, was developed from Sumerian cuneiform as a result of trade contacts with Mesopotamia. Cultural diffusion from Egypt produced a Nubian civilization that incorporated Egyptian pyramids, writing, and religion into its own culture. In addition, the Nubian kingdom of Kush invaded Egypt in the eighth century BCE and ruled the Egyptian people for about a century. Throughout most of its early history, however, surrounding deserts protected Egypt from contact with invading peoples, permitting its civilization to develop its own, unique characteristics.

Indus Valley Civilization

By 2500 BCE, another advanced civilization had emerged along the Indus River in present-day Pakistan. Like the Tigris and Euphrates rivers, the Indus River was noted for its unpredictable and often violent pattern of flooding. Among the urban centers that arose along the Indus were Harappa and Mohenjo-Daro. Streets in both cities were laid out along a precise grid, and houses boasted running water and sewage systems.

Much of what historians know about the Indus valley civilization must come from archeological discoveries, because Harappan writing has yet to be deciphered. Archeological findings of Harappan artifacts in Mesopotamia indicate active trade between the peoples of the Indus valley and Sumer by way of the Persian Gulf. Around 1500 BCE, the Harappan civilization was overtaken by a group of Indo-European peoples called Aryans. The Harappan civilization, which the Aryans conquered, had already declined markedly, perhaps as a result of rivers changing their course or a natural disaster such as an earthquake. The blend of the traditional culture of the Indus valley people and that of the Aryans had a profound effect on the future course of Indian history.

Backgrounds of Classical India

The roots of classical India began during the invasions of the Aryans about 1500 BCE. From their original home in Central Asia, the Aryans brought a tradition of hunting and cattle herding; after their arrival in South Asia, however, they adapted the agricultural methods of native peoples. Aryan iron tools facilitated their success in agriculture.

Although the people of the Harappan civilization of the Indus valley possessed a written language, the Aryans did not. Much of our knowledge of the Aryans comes from their oral epics, called the *Vedas*. The *Vedas* were later written down in the Sanskrit language, which remains a prominent language in India today. The influence of the *Vedas* is evident in the term applied to the early classical period of Indian culture, the Vedic Age (1500 to 500 BCE). The first Aryan epic, the *Rig-Veda,* is a collection of hymns in honor of the

Aryan gods. Other epic literature that shaped Indian culture during the Epic Age (1000 to 600 BCE) includes the *Ramayana*, the *Mahabharata* (considered the greatest epic poem of India), and the *Upanishads*, a collection of religious epic poems.

Aryan Society

Aryan society was based on a village organization composed of families with patriarchal control. Their society was further organized along a class system. When they invaded the Indus valley, the Aryans, who were fair-complexioned compared to the native people they conquered, perceived the people of the Indus valley as inferior. Therefore, they modified the class system with which they were already familiar in their society to define the new relationship between conqueror and conquered. Society was divided into four distinct classes, or *varna*, based on skin color:

- *Kshatriyas*, or warriors and rulers
- *Brahmins*, or priests
- *Vaisyas*, or merchants and farmers
- *Sudras*, or common workers

The first three classes were composed of Aryans, the fourth of the Dravidians, or the native people of India whom the Aryans encountered at the time of their invasion. During the Epic Age, the first two classes reversed in order of importance. At the very bottom of the social structure was a classless group of **untouchables**. Members of this group were involved in occupations perceived as distasteful, such as handling waste products, carrying out the dead, or butchering animals. As the classes became hereditary, they became castes, or rigid social classes that seldom permitted social mobility. Within each caste were numerous subcastes, or *jati*, that further defined Indian society.

The Aryans also introduced to Indian culture their own array of gods and goddesses. Part of their belief system was the veneration of some animals, particularly cattle.

The Shang

The most isolated of the four river valley civilizations was that of the Huang He valley in present-day China. Although the people of the Huang He valley dwelled in a region isolated by deserts, mountains (the Himalayas), and seas, they did engage in some trade with Southwest Asia and South Asia.

The earliest Chinese dynasty that left written records was the Shang dynasty (1766 to 1122 BCE). A key element of the Shang period was the knowledge of bronze metallurgy. This knowledge, which came to China from Southwest Asia by means of Indo-European migrations, strengthened the Shang war machine. Around 1000 BCE, the Shang also became familiar with ironworking. Shang rule was further empowered by the need for central rule to oversee irrigation and flood-control projects along the Huang He River.

During the Shang period, a number of walled cities arose. These urban areas served as cultural, military, and economic centers. Elaborate palaces and tombs were built for Shang rulers.

Examples of early Chinese writing are apparent from a custom of divination using **oracle bones**. When a person sought the advice of the gods on an issue, he or she would visit an oracle, who would scratch the person's question on an animal bone or shell, then heat it. When the oracle bone cracked from the heat, the oracle read the cracks to determine the message from the gods.

Shang society was stratified, with classes of ruling elites, artisans, peasants, and slaves. Families were patriarchal, and the veneration of ancestors was common. The **matrilineal** society that characterized China before the rule of the Shang gradually eroded until women held positions subordinate to those of men.

The Shang dynasty eventually succumbed to the Zhou about 1122 BCE. The Zhou claimed that they overthrew the Shang by the will of the gods, which they termed the "**Mandate of Heaven**." Under the rule of the Zhou, the tradition of central authority that first took root under the Shang continued.

Mesoamerica and Andean South America

Civilizations in the Americas rose later than the river valley civilizations. The civilizations of Mesoamerica and the early societies of the Andes Mountains of South America did not develop in the valleys of major rivers, but rather in a region of smaller rivers and streams near ocean coastlines. Furthermore, the people of the Americas did not know the use of the wheel, nor did they possess large animals to serve as beasts of burden or work animals; the llama of the Andes Mountains was the largest work animal in the Americas from the time of the earliest civilizations until the arrival of the Europeans in the fifteenth century. Human muscle accomplished physical labor in the Americas.

Early Mesoamerican people such as the Olmecs, and later the Maya, constructed lavish pyramids and temples. Like the inhabitants of the river valley civilizations, the people of the Americas were polytheistic, worshipping many gods of nature. Society was stratified, with distinctions among the elite classes of rulers and priests and those of commoners and slaves.

Early Mesoamerican societies provided numerous examples of cultural diffusion. In addition to the transmission of the cultivation of maize, terraced pyramids were commonplace. Regional inhabitants fashioned calendars, the most elaborate being that of the Mayan civilization. The Mayans also had a ball game played on a court. The societies of Mesoamerica also shared the legend of **Quetzalcóatl**, a god who would someday return to rule his people in peace.

In South America, geography and the lack of large pack animals largely prevented communication between the Andean societies and those of Mesoamerica. The cultivation of maize did spread to the Andes, however, while copper metallurgy traveled northward to Mesoamerica. About 900 BCE, the Chavín civilization arose in the Andean highlands of present-day Peru. Characterized by a religion that worshipped gods representing crocodiles, snakes, and jaguars, the Chavín built complex temples to honor their gods. Their civilization was located along trade routes that connected western coastal regions to the Amazon rainforest. For a few centuries, Chavín religious unity and trade connections provided a degree of cultural identity to Andean peoples. The rugged terrain of the Andes, however, prevented a central government from unifying the Andean states.

The Hebrews

Along the eastern coast of the Mediterranean Sea lived the Hebrews, another people who profoundly influenced the course of world history.

The concept of **monotheism**, or the worship of one god, is attributed to the Hebrews, or Jews. The Hebrews traced their origins back to Abraham, who is said to have migrated from Mesopotamia to the land of Canaan on the eastern shores of the Mediterranean about 2000 BCE. In the account recorded in the Bible, the descendants of Abraham migrated to Egypt. They later left Egypt, embarking on a journey called the Exodus under a leader named Moses. In the biblical account, the Exodus was marked by the giving of the **Ten Commandments**, or moral law of the Hebrews. Returning to the land of Canaan, or Palestine, they established a **theocracy**, or a government ruled directly by God.

The heart of Judaism was a **covenant**, or agreement, between God and Abraham in which **Yahweh** would be their god and the Jews would be his people. The history of this covenant relationship became the basis of the **Torah**, or the Hebrew scriptures.

After years of observing the governments of neighboring kingdoms, the Hebrews established the kingdom of Israel about 1000 BCE with its capital at Jerusalem. The kingdom eventually divided into two kingdoms. The northern kingdom of Israel fell to the Assyrians in 722 BCE. Its inhabitants were scattered throughout the far reaches of the Assyrian empire, constituting the first Jewish **diaspora**, or exile. The southern kingdom, called Judah, endured until 586 BCE. Conquered by the Chaldeans (from approximately the same territory as the Babylonian Empire), the people of Judah were carried off into captivity into Babylon. After Cyrus conquered the Chaldeans and allowed the Jews to return to Palestine 70 years later, Palestine remained under Persian rule until it became the province of Judea under the Roman Empire in 63 CE. In 132 CE, after they rebelled against Roman rule, the Jews were spread throughout the Roman Empire in a second diaspora.

› Rapid Review

Beginning with Sumer in Mesopotamia about 3500 BCE, civilization grew along the river valleys of the Tigris–Euphrates, Nile, Indus, and Huang He. These civilizations were characterized by community cooperation necessary to manage irrigation and flood control systems. Later their cooperative efforts were further organized to form the beginnings of political institutions. The knowledge of metallurgy led to the refinement of tools, weapons, and objects of art. Writing systems were developed, and social stratification became apparent. In the Americas, civilizations and societies made notable strides in mathematics, astronomy, and architecture.

› Review Questions

1. Answer Parts A, B, and C.
   (A) Identify and explain one similarity in the religious beliefs or practices of the Egyptians and Sumerians.
   (B) Identify one similarity in the religious beliefs or practices of the Sumerians and the Mesoamericans.
   (C) Identify and explain one way in which the religious beliefs of the Hebrews differed from those of other civilizations.

2. Answer Parts A and B.
   "Women in ancient Mesopotamia were usually subordinate to men."
   (A) Identify TWO pieces of evidence a historian might use to support this conclusion and explain how each supports it.
   (B) Identify ONE piece of evidence that could be used to undermine this argument and explain how it would undermine it.

Questions 3 to 5 refer to the following map. Answer the questions based on the map and your knowledge of world history.

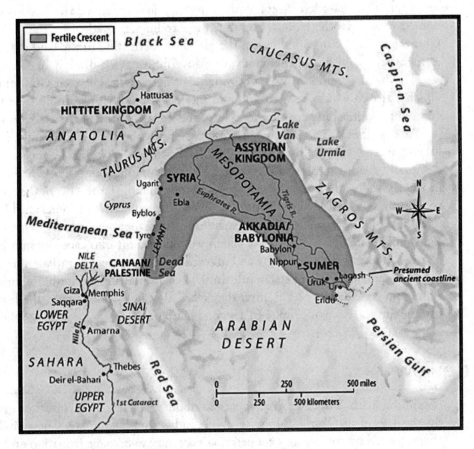

3. What was the most likely form of political organization of this region 5,000 years ago?
   (A) City-states
   (B) A kingdom
   (C) An empire
   (D) Nomadic tribes

4. What was the primary purpose of monumental architecture in this region before 600 BCE?
   (A) Pyramid-shaped tombs for the dead
   (B) Palaces for the ruler and his wives
   (C) Large stone representations of rulers
   (D) Temples to honor the gods

5. Which civilization would most likely have agricultural practices that differed from those of this region before 600 BCE?
   (A) The Egyptians
   (B) The Indus Valley people
   (C) The Mayans
   (D) The Shang Dynasty

› Answers and Explanations

1A. Both Egyptians and Sumerians were polytheistic. Many of their gods also centered on aspects of the natural world. They also both believed in an afterlife, although the Sumerians' version was a bleak netherworld for all the dead.

1B. Both Sumerians and Mesoamericans were polytheistic, with gods that were connected around the natural world (like animals, sky, water features, etc.). Both civilizations built stepped temples (ziggurats in Sumeria) as centers of worship and to honor their gods.

1C. While most other religions of this time were polytheistic, the Hebrews were monotheistic.

2A. A woman in Mesopotamian society could be sold into slavery by her husband to pay his debts. The Code of Hammurabi, a Mesopotamian legal code, had punishments that were less strict for men's infractions than for womens'. The practice of veiling women also began here at this time. All of these practices indicate that a woman's status was less than a man's because she was singled out for harsher treatment, that she did not control her own freedom, and because her actions were more restricted

2B. Nevertheless, women did enjoy some legal protections under the Code of Hammurabi. Mesopotamian women could also serve as priestesses, scribes, or work in small businesses. This demonstrates that women did have autonomy in certain areas, as scribes and priestesses could be influential, and the ability to contribute economically is typically associated with elevated status in world history.

3. **A** The region of Mesopotamia first organized into city-states like Sumer and Ur. Later, kingdoms (B) and empires (C) developed. Although there were nomadic tribes at this time (D), they are not commonly associated with early Mesopotamian civilization and are not typically included when discussing formal political organizational forms, making this a weaker choice.

4. **D** The monumental architecture associated with Mesopotamia at this time are the ziggurats, which were built as temples to honor the gods. The Egyptians built their pyramids as tombs, mostly for pharaohs (A). Large stone representations of rulers, like Ramses II, mostly occurred in Egypt, which is outside the shaded region on the map (C). The most famous palace of the time, built by Nebuchadnezzar in the Neo-Babylonian empire, is slightly out of the period indicated. It was also considered unusual, whereas there are multiple examples of ziggurats in the region, making (B) a weaker answer.

5. **C** The Mayans did not have the wheel, nor did they use metals in tools, nor did they have animals suitable for agricultural work. Thus, their agricultural practices would have been substantially different from the Egyptians (A) and the Shang people (D). Though little evidence of the Indus valley agricultural practices remains, they did have access to animals for work, as well as metal tools, making this a weaker choice (B).

CHAPTER 8

Rise of Classical Civilizations

IN THIS CHAPTER

Summary: Classical civilizations, defined as those that had enduring influence over vast numbers of people, emerged in China, India, and the Mediterranean region. The first of the classical civilizations began in China. Three Chinese **dynasties** made their mark on the values of traditional Chinese civilization—the Zhou, the Qin, and the Han. In India, the rulers of the Gupta dynasty ushered in the golden age of Indian history. The classical Mediterranean civilizations of Greece and Rome developed political, scientific, and philosophical thought that formed the basis of Western civilization.

KEY IDEA

Key Terms

Alexander the Great
aristocracy
Aristotle
artisan
democracy
dynasty
geocentric theory
Hellenistic Age
Indo-Europeans

mystery religion
Pax Romana
polis
sati
Silk Roads
stoicism
Twelve Tables
Zoroastrianism

Classical China

The Zhou

Claiming that they possessed the Mandate of Heaven, or the approval of the gods, the Zhou began to dominate China after the fall of the Shang dynasty. The Mandate of Heaven would be claimed by future Chinese dynasties as a rationalization for their authority to rule. In power from 1029 to 258 BCE, the Zhou:

- Took steps to further centralize the Chinese government.
- Expanded Chinese territory to include the Yangtze River valley. This southern river valley added a fertile rice-growing area to the already rich wheat-producing regions of northern China.
- Produced emperors, calling themselves "Sons of Heaven," who lived lives of luxury.
- Standardized the spoken language.

The Qin

After a period of civil disorder known as the Era of the Warring States, the Zhou were replaced by the Qin dynasty. Under the Qin (221–202 BCE):

- The name of the dynasty, Qin, was applied to the country of China.
- Chinese territory expanded southward as far as northern Vietnam.
- A defensive wall that became the nucleus of the Great Wall was constructed.
- Weights, measures, and coinage were standardized.
- A common written language was standardized.
- The manufacture of silk cloth was encouraged.
- New roads were constructed.

The Han

In 200 BCE, the Qin were replaced by the Han, who ruled until 220 CE. During the rule of the Han dynasty:

- The governmental bureaucracy (ranks of employees) grew stronger.
- Chinese territory expanded into Central Asia, Korea, and Indochina.
- The Chinese civil service exam began.
- Trade along the **Silk Roads** increased.
- A time of peace settled across China.
- Chinese traditions were reinforced through the strengthening of patriarchal society in which the father and other male members of the family were in positions of authority.
- The government oversaw iron production.
- The government sponsored and maintained canals and irrigation systems.
- Society was further stratified, consisting of an elite class (including the educated governmental bureaucracy), peasants and **artisans**, and unskilled laborers (including a small number of slaves).
- Agriculture was improved by the invention of ox-drawn plows and a collar that prevented choking in draft animals.
- Paper was manufactured for the first time.
- Water-powered mills were invented.

Under the Han, the people of China enjoyed a level of culture significantly more advanced than that of other civilizations and societies at that time, a distinction it would maintain until the fifteenth century. So vital were the accomplishments of the Han to Chinese culture that even today the Chinese call themselves the "People of Han."

Classical India

The cultural and social structures of the Vedic and Epic ages formed the basis of the classical civilization of India. Around 600 BCE, northern India was divided into 16 states; one state, Magadha, became prominent. In 327 BCE, **Alexander the Great** of Macedonia reached into the Indian subcontinent as far as the Indus River, where he set up a border state, which he called Bactria. Five years later the Mauryan dynasty was founded by a soldier named Chandragupta, an autocratic ruler who developed a large bureaucracy and a large army in addition to promoting trade and communication. Mauryan rulers were the first to unify most of the Indian subcontinent.

The most prominent of the Mauryan rulers was Ashoka (269–232 BCE), the grandson of Chandragupta. Under Ashoka, all of the Indian subcontinent except for the southern tip came under Mauryan control. Known for the brutality of his conquests, Ashoka later moderated his behavior and values, embracing the tolerance and nonviolence of Buddhism while also respecting the values of Hinduism. Like his grandfather Chandragupta, Ashoka encouraged trade and constructed an extensive system of roads, complete with rest areas for travelers. Along these roads, which connected with the Silk Roads, Ashoka spread the ideas of Buddhism.

Ashoka's influence was insufficient to prevent India from dividing into a number of states once again after his death. Invaders from the northwest, the Kushans, ruled India until 220 CE. Their rule was followed in 320 CE by the Guptas, who ushered in the golden age of Indian history.

Gupta India

In contrast to the Mauryans, the Gupta rulers were Hindus. As a result, during Gupta rule, the caste system and the influence of the Brahmins were reinforced. Because of the strict divisions of the caste system, slavery was not widespread. Although Hinduism was the religion of the ruling dynasty, Buddhism was tolerated and Buddhist monks and nuns spread their influence through urban monasteries. The Gupta style of rule was not as centralized as that of the Mauryan Empire, and local rulers were permitted to maintain authority in their respective territories if they submitted to the ultimate rule of the Guptas. Other accomplishments and features of the Gupta dynasty included:

- High-towered temples in honor of the Hindu gods.
- Lavish wall paintings in caves dedicated to the gods. A key example is the Caves of Ajanta in central India.
- The growth of Sanskrit as the language of the educated.
- The discovery of zero as a placeholder and the development of "Arabic" numerals, the number system used throughout most of the world today. An innovation of Gupta India, Arabic numerals were so called by the Western world because they were carried from India to the West by means of Arabic caravans.
- The development of the decimal system.
- The strengthening of trade, especially between East and Southeast Asia.
- The deterioration in the status of women; society became increasingly patriarchal. Women gradually lost their right to inherit or own property and were married at a younger age. The custom of *sati* was practiced in some parts of India. *Sati* involved the practice of a widow throwing herself on her husband's funeral pyre. The custom was alleged to bestow honor and purity upon the widow.

- Inoculation against smallpox and sterilization during surgery and in the treatment of wounds.
- Knowledge of plastic surgery and the setting of bones.
- Advances in astronomy such as the prediction of eclipses and the identification of planets.
- The classic Hindu temple complete with courtyards, paintings, and sculptures appeared.

The achievements and knowledge of the Gupta remained part of Indian culture long after the decline of their dynasty.

Persia and the Classical World

Before turning to a discussion of classical Mediterranean civilization, it is necessary to discuss one of the cultures that would significantly influence Mediterranean societies: that of the Persians. The Persians (inhabiting a territory approximate to present-day Iran) are counted among the heirs of ancient Mesopotamian civilization. In 550 BCE, the Persian conqueror Cyrus the Great had established an empire that encompassed the northern part of Southwest Asia and a portion of northwestern India. The Persian empire was noted for its tolerance toward the customs of conquered peoples. The Persians introduced a new religion called **Zoroastrianism** that held to a belief in a system of rewards and punishments in the afterlife. They spread the knowledge of iron metallurgy throughout their empire and engaged in an active long-distance trade that linked India, Southwest Asia, and Egypt. The Persian Royal Road, complete with relay stations, was a 1,600-mile highway linking remote portions of the empire. Persian trade contacts with Greece encouraged artistic and philosophical exchange as well.

Classical Civilization in the Mediterranean: Greece

In addition to the role played by the Persians, the culture of a number of societies in the Mediterranean blended to bring about the civilization of Greece. The island of Crete southeast of the Greek mainland was in contact with the Egyptian civilization by the year 2000 BCE. The early Greek civilization, known as Mycenaea, was influenced by that of Crete through contacts with traders in the region. The Greeks were an **Indo-European** people who migrated to the southern portion of the Greek peninsula about 1700 BCE. A second wave of Indo-Europeans called the Dorians invaded about 1100 BCE, destroying the Mycenaean civilization.

About 800 BCE, Phoenician mariners sailed into the Aegean Sea to the east of the Greek mainland. The Phoenicians were largely a seafaring people whose need for accurate recordkeeping in their commercial transactions led them to develop an alphabet of 22 letters representing consonants. The Greeks adapted the Phoenician alphabet, adding symbols for vowel sounds to give the people of the Greek peninsula a common language.

Importance of Geography

Geography was an important determining factor in the course of Greek history. Separated by mountains and hills, the Greek peninsula was left with little available farmland. At the same time, the peninsula's irregular coastline provided relatively easy access to the sea for Greek settlements. Fishing and trading in the waters of the Aegean became another source to increase the supply of food and other products the Greeks could not provide themselves.

The City-State

The rugged terrain also prevented the easy centralization of communities or government. Greek political organization was based on the city-state, or *polis*, consisting of a city and the surrounding countryside, both under the influence of one government. The two most prominent city-states were Sparta and Athens. Sparta's aristocratic government focused on creating a strong military state, which depended upon the labor of slaves. Athens, by contrast, was initially an aristocracy but gradually allowed its inhabitants self-rule. The height of Athenian **democracy** occurred during the rule of the aristocrat Pericles (443 to 429 BCE) and was also considered the golden age of Athens for its achievements in science, philosophy, and the arts. Whereas Sparta's economic life relied on agriculture, the Athenians relied on the sea for their livelihood and engaged in an active trade across the Aegean. The people of Athens, to whom education and artistic expression were important, also depended heavily on slaves. From 500 to 449 BCE, Athens and Sparta joined forces to defeat a series of Persian invasions.

After the Persian Wars, Athens grew from a *polis* to an empire. Its dominant status aroused distrust among other *poleis,* including Sparta. From 431 to 404 BCE, Athens and Sparta and their allies fought each other for dominance in the Peloponnesian Wars. When Athens suffered a devastating plague during the course of the war, the once proud and flourishing *polis* questioned why its gods had allowed such a great tragedy. The weakened Athens saw defeat at the hands of Sparta.

During the eighth century BCE, the population of the Greek city-states increased tremendously, leading the Greeks to seek additional territory. As a result, the Greeks established a number of colonies in Sicily, southern Italy, the eastern Mediterranean, and the Black Sea. These new settlements allowed the Greeks the opportunity to trade grapes and olive oil for products that their rugged terrain could not produce in sufficient quantities, including fish, grain, and honey. Colonies not only served as outlets for population; they also transmitted Greek culture throughout the Mediterranean world.

Culture of Classical Greece

Throughout the classical period, the various Greek city-states, although often rivals, at the same time shared a common culture. Numerous gods and goddesses, who often displayed human characteristics, formed the basis of Greek religion. The Olympic Games, first held in 776 BCE, brought together athletes from across the Greek peninsula to honor their gods. Drama was an integral feature of Greek culture; tragedies explored the relationship between the limitations of humans and the expectations of the gods, whereas comedies often satirized public officials.

Greek philosophy emphasized the power of human reason. The philosopher **Aristotle** wrote on a variety of subjects in politics, arts, and the sciences and became a model of Greek thought by constructing arguments through the use of logic.

Alexander the Great and the Hellenistic Age

When the Greek city-states, or *poleis,* weakened because of their internal conflict in the Peloponnesian War, they captured the attention of Philip, the ruler of the kingdom of Macedon to the north of Greece. When Philip's plans to conquer the Greek *poleis* were cut short by his death, however, his son Alexander stepped in to carry out his father's ambitions. By the time of his death in 323 BCE at the age of 33, Alexander known as "the Great" had conquered not only the Greek *poleis* but also Egypt, Syria, and Palestine as well as Persia. In South Asia, Alexander proceeded as far as the Punjab across the Indus River when his troops refused to proceed any farther.

Throughout the territories he controlled, Alexander established cities, many named Alexandria in his honor. In order to blend the cultures of Persia and Greece, he married a Persian woman and encouraged his officers to do the same. On his death, however, Alexander's empire was divided among his generals. In spite of these divisions, a relative balance of power was maintained among the remnants of Alexander's former empire as the Greek culture served as its unifying force.

The period of Alexander's rule and that of his generals has been termed the **Hellenistic Age**, named after the influence of the Hellenes, as the Greeks called themselves. The Hellenistic Age was characterized by a blend of the cultures of Greece and the Middle East, particularly Persia. Long-distance trade flourished, establishing communications from the Greek homeland to parts of South Asia and North Africa. Hellenistic philosophy sought personal satisfaction and tranquility. The most popular school of Hellenistic philosophy was **stoicism**. Stoicism taught that men and women should use their powers of reason to lead virtuous lives and to assist others. **Mystery religions** taught that believers who followed their practices would be rewarded with a blissful life in the afterworld. The culture of the Hellenistic world would be adopted by another classical Mediterranean culture, that of the Romans. Among the achievements of the Hellenistic world were:

- Euclidean geometry
- Pythagorean Theorem
- Studies of human anatomy and physiology by Galen
- Calculation of the circumference of the earth by Eratosthenes
- Art and architecture flourished, becoming more realistic, even idealistic

In spite of the significant achievements of scientists and mathematicians of the Hellenistic world, one significant error was promoted during the same era. Contrary to the traditions of Southwest Asia, the Hellenistic astronomer Ptolemy expounded a theory of the nature of the universe that placed the earth at its center. His **geocentric theory**, although incorrect, was widely accepted as truth by the West until the scientific revolution of the seventeenth century.

Classical Civilization in the Mediterranean: Rome

The Hellenistic period ended in 146 BCE with the conquest of the Greek peninsula by Rome, although most scholars use the term to refer to the period up until the Roman conquest of Egypt in 31 BCE. Rome began as a kingdom in central Italy about 800 BCE. In 509 BCE, the Roman (Etruscan) monarch was deposed by the **aristocracy**. The resulting Roman republic began a period of expansion in the Mediterranean world. The defeat of the Phoenician city of Carthage in North Africa during the Punic Wars (264–246 BCE) made Rome master of the Mediterranean Sea. The strong military tradition of the Romans led to power struggles among generals. When one of them, Julius Caesar, came to power in 45 BCE, the structures of the Roman republic began to dissolve.

Rome Becomes an Empire

When a conspiracy resulted in the assassination of Julius Caesar in 44 BCE, a period of civil disorder followed, which culminated in 27 BCE with the rule of Octavian, or Augustus Caesar, the grandnephew of Julius Caesar. The period from 27 BCE to 180 CE was known as the *Pax Romana*, or Roman Peace. During this more than 200-year period of peace and prosperity:

- A system of public works, including bridges, aqueducts, and roads, served all parts of the empire. Roman roads and sea lanes connected the Roman Empire with the Silk Roads of Central Asia.
- Highway banditry decreased.
- A common language, Latin, promoted unity within the empire.
- A common coinage facilitated trade.
- Stadiums were constructed to provide entertainment, such as gladiator contests, for Roman citizens.
- Jesus was born in the Roman province of Judea. The new religion of Christianity spread easily, in part because of the Roman roads.

Roman Government

During the days of the Roman republic, government was centered around the Senate, which was composed primarily of members of the aristocracy. The executive resided in two consuls. When crises occurred, the Senate could appoint a dictator who could hold emergency powers for a period of up to six months. During the republic, laws were codified, or written down, in the **Twelve Tables**.

Under the Roman Empire, conquered peoples in various parts of the empire were generally allowed a considerable measure of self-rule unless they rebelled against the authority of the emperor. Many inhabitants in conquered provinces, especially those geographically close to Rome, were granted citizenship.

Roman Law

The most lasting contribution of Rome was its system of laws. From the tradition of the Twelve Tables came a desire to extend Roman standards of justice throughout the empire. Among the legal principles established by the Romans were:

- The concept that a defendant is innocent unless proven guilty by a court of law
- The right of defendants to confront their accusers in a court of law
- The right of judges to set aside laws that were unjust

Roman law served to unite not only the peoples of the vast empire but also left a lasting impact on Western legal tradition.

Roman Culture

Much of the culture of the Romans was adopted from that of the Greeks. The Greek alphabet, a gift of the Phoenicians, was passed on to the Romans, who modified the letters and transmitted the alphabet throughout the various parts of their empire. Many aspects of Greek rational thought, including the works of Aristotle and the philosophical school of Stoicism, became part of Roman life. Greek gods and goddesses, renamed by the Romans, found their way into Roman religious beliefs. Theaters and drama, patterned after their Greek forebears, became popular. Although the Romans were credited with the development of waterproof concrete and of massive arches designed to handle the weight of heavy structures, the architecture of Rome was more a case of cultural diffusion from the Greeks than one of independent invention.

Everyday Life in Greece and Rome

In both classical Mediterranean societies, families were patriarchal, although women in the elite classes of Rome often wielded considerable influence within the family itself. In both Greece and Rome, women sometimes owned property and small businesses. In matters of law, however, women had fewer rights than men. Even Aristotle felt that women should be kept in a subordinate role.

Slavery was commonplace in both Greece and Rome. Aristotle attempted to justify slavery, believing that it was necessary to a thriving society. In some Greek *poleis*, such as Sparta, slaves performed agricultural tasks. In Athens, slaves labored in the silver mines and as household servants. Roman slaves made up as much as one-third of the population. In fact, among the reasons for Roman expansion was the acquisition of slaves from among conquered peoples. Some Roman slaves were used to mine iron and precious metals. Other slaves carried out household duties. Especially prized were educated Greek slaves, who became tutors for the children of Rome's elite class. Slave labor was so widely used by both Greeks and Romans that neither culture found much need for technological advances as labor-saving devices. As a result, the Mediterranean world fell behind the technological level of China and India in the areas of agriculture and manufacturing.

American Civilization

The Maya civilization of the Yucatán Peninsula and present-day Guatemala and Belize reached its height about 300 CE, building on the cultural traditions of the societies of Mesoamerica. Termed the "Greeks of the Americas" because of their exploration of numerous branches of learning, the Maya:

- Developed a system of writing based on pictographs, or glyphs
- Understood the value of zero as a placeholder
- Studied astronomy and predicted eclipses
- Calculated the length of the year within a few seconds of its actual length

The Mayan political organization consisted of small city-states ruled by kings who often fought against one another. Prisoners of war usually ended up as slaves or as sacrifices to the Mayan gods.

To the north of the Mayan homeland, in the Valley of Mexico, the grand and heavily populated city of Teotihuacán featured pyramids, public buildings decorated with murals, and active marketplaces. The city also served as a center of long-distance trade with coastal peoples and Mayans. To the south of Mayan lands, the Mochica people established cities in the central Andes during the first millennium CE. Inhabitants of these cities cooperated to construct irrigation systems. (See Chapter 15 for more detailed information about later American civilizations.)

› Rapid Review

Classical civilizations in China, India, and the Mediterranean forged lasting institutions in their respective regions. China created a complex bureaucracy based on the traditions of family and education. In India, cultural diversity prevailed, while a caste system gradually evolved to rigidly organize this diversity. In the Mediterranean, rational thought and the rule of law prevailed during the dominance of the Greeks followed by the Romans.

› Review Questions

1. Answer Parts A and B.
   (A) The Han Dynasty and the Roman Empire are often compared. Identify TWO shared practices that helped the Han Dynasty and the Roman Empire maintain stability and control of their empires.
   (B) Identify and explain ONE major difference between the two empires.

2. Answer Parts A and B.
   (A) Identify TWO legal or religious systems that were important in maintaining power during the classical era.
   (B) Explain ONE possible difference between Eastern (China, Persia, India) and Western (Greece, Rome) belief or legal systems.

Questions 3 to 5 refer to the following images.

3. Public works such as roads, temples, aqueducts, irrigation systems, or astronomical observatories best served what purpose in classical-era empires?
(A) They kept unemployment down.
(B) They united distant parts of the empire.
(C) They spread and maintained a dominant culture.
(D) They made clear a ruler's achievements.

4. El Castillo was an astrological observatory that enabled the Mayas to perfect which of the following systems?
(A) Ceremonial
(B) Calendrical
(C) Religious
(D) Mathematical

5. Using your knowledge of world history, decide which of the following elements best accounts for a successful empire.
(A) A central government
(B) Specific class divisions
(C) A common religion
(D) Technological prowess

› Answers and Explanations

1A. Shared practices that helped the Han and Roman empires maintain stability and control include organized bureaucracies based on classical ideas and laws; systems of public works, or roads, canals, and aqueducts; delineated social classes and patriarchy; robust trade systems; and emphasis on the family as the central unit of civilization.

1B. One major difference between the empires was the lack of a common language in Han areas of conquest.

2A. During the classical era, Confucianism and its accompanying use of civil service exams made belief and legal systems crucial to maintaining power. The Mandate of Heaven, or approval of the gods, legitimized a ruler's power.

2B. One major difference between Eastern and Western beliefs and legal systems involved the Western traditions of considering a defendant innocent until proven guilty, allowing a judge to declare a law unjust, and in general basing law on secular rather than religious beliefs.

3. **C** Public works spread and maintained aspects of the ruling culture to all corners of an empire. They enabled trade, made agricultural progress feasible and sustainable, and carried ideas from the central government to peripheral areas. They did not necessarily relieve unemployment (A), unite scattered parts of the empire one to another (B), or speak to a ruler's achievements (D), though they did indicate technological prowess.

4. **B** The Mayan calendar resulted from observation of the solar system and remains accurate to this day. El Castillo in fact was built to record aspects of that calendar. It did not serve ceremonial or religious purposes (A, C), and while its mathematical application (D) supported the calendrical system, it did not perfect mathematical systems.

5. **A** Various empires distributed power to regional governing entities; but long-lived extensive empires had a central locus that oversaw most aspects of life—legal systems, education, military and other public service, religion, even language. Class status (B), common religion (C), and technological prowess (D) may all have contributed to sustaining an empire, but individually are not sufficiently decisive.

CHAPTER 9

Interactions in the Late Classical Era

IN THIS CHAPTER

Summary: The classical period came to an end with the weakening and fall of the empires of Rome, Han China, and Gupta India to invaders. The fall of the three great classical empires showed a number of similarities. At the same time, the late classical period featured increased interactions among the classical empires and other peoples of Asia, the Indian Ocean basin, and the Mediterranean world.

Key Terms

Hsiung-nu   Silk Roads
Huns   White Huns
latifundia

Han China

The Han dynasty of China began to decline around 100 CE. Among the causes of its decline were:

- Heavy taxes levied on peasants
- Decline of interest in Confucian intellectual goals
- Poor harvests
- Population decline from epidemic disease
- Social unrest, particularly by students
- Decline in morality
- Weak emperors and the increased influence of army generals

- Unequal land distribution
- Decline in trade
- Pressure from bordering nomadic tribes

As political, economic, and social decay befell Han China, Daoism gained a new popularity. In 184 CE, the Yellow Turbans, a Daoist revolutionary movement, promised a new age of prosperity and security, which would be initiated by magic. Buddhism also spread as Chinese cultural unity was dissolving.

The decay of the Han Empire made it difficult for the Chinese to resist nomadic invaders living along their borders. These invaders, or *Hsiung-nu*, had for decades been raiding Han China, prompting the Chinese to pay them tribute to prevent further invasions. By 220 CE, however, Han China's strength had deteriorated to the point that it could no longer repel a final thrust by the invading Hsiung-nu, who then poured into the empire. The fall of Han China was followed by centuries of disorder and political decentralization until Chinese rulers in the northern part of the country drove out the invaders. In 589 CE, the Sui dynasty ascended to power and continued to establish order in China. In spite of significant threats to Chinese civilization, it did ultimately survive. Confucian tradition endured among the elite classes, and the nomads eventually assimilated into Chinese culture.

Rome

The golden age of Rome—the *Pax Romana*—came to a close with the death of Marcus Aurelius in 180 CE. Historians have noted a number of causes of the decline and fall of Rome, including:

- Ineffective later emperors concerned more with a life of pleasure than a desire to rule wisely
- Influence of army generals
- Decline of trade
- Increasingly high taxes
- Decreased money flow into the empire as conquests of new territory ceased
- Population decline as a result of epidemic disease
- Poor harvests
- Unequal land distribution
- Social and moral decay and lack of interest in the elite classes
- Roman dependence on slave labor
- Recruitment of non-Romans into the Roman army
- Vastness of the empire, rendering it difficult to rule
- Barbarian invasions

Attempts to Save the Roman Empire

As the Roman Empire declined economically, small landowners were frequently forced to sell their land to the owners of large estates, or **latifundia**. The self-sufficiency of the *latifundia* lessened the need for a central authority such as the Roman emperor. Furthermore, the economic self-sufficiency of the estates discouraged trade among the various parts of the empire and neighboring peoples. The decline in trade eventually produced a decline in urban population.

Some emperors tried desperately to save the empire. Diocletian (ruled 284 to 305 CE) imposed stricter control over the empire and declared himself a god. When the Christians refused to worship him, Diocletian heightened persecutions against them. The Emperor Constantine (ruled 312 to 337) established a second capital at Byzantium, which he renamed Constantinople. Converting to Christianity, Constantine allowed the practice of the faith in Rome. Although the Western portion of the empire steadily declined, the eastern portion, centered around Constantinople, continued to thrive and carry on a high volume of long-distance trade.

The last measure that weakened the Western Roman Empire originated in the steppes of Central Asia. In the fifth century CE, the nomadic **Huns** began migrating south and west in search of better pasturelands. The movement of the Huns exerted pressure on Germanic tribes who already lived around the border of the Roman Empire. These tribes, in turn, overran the Roman borders. By 425 CE, several Germanic kingdoms were set up within the empire; by 476 CE, the last Western Roman emperor was replaced by a Germanic ruler from the tribe of the Visigoths.

The eastern portion of the empire did not fall at the same time as the Western empire. One reason for its endurance was that it saw less pressure from invaders. Located on the Bosporus, it was the hub of numerous trade routes and a center of art and architecture. Neighboring empires—most notably the Parthians and, after 227 CE, the Sassanids—served as trade facilitators. Not only did they preserve the Greek culture, but they continued to bring Indian and Chinese goods and cultural trends to the eastern, or Byzantine, empire. The Byzantine Emperor Justinian (ruled 527 to 565 CE) attempted to capture portions of Rome's lost territory. Justinian's efforts were largely in vain, however, as the Western empire increasingly fragmented into self-sufficient estates and tiny Germanic kingdoms. Trade and learning declined, and cities shrank in size. The centralized government of Rome was replaced by rule based on the tribal allegiances of the Germanic invaders.

Gupta India

The fall of Gupta India to invading forces was less devastating than that of Han China or Rome. By 500 CE, Gupta India endured a number of invasions by the **White Huns**, nomadic peoples who may have been related to the Huns whose migrations drove Germanic peoples over the borders of the Roman Empire. Simultaneously, the influence of Gupta rulers was in decline as local princes became more powerful. Until about 600 CE, the nomads drove farther into central India. India fragmented into regional states ruled by the princes, who called themselves Rajput.

Although political decline occurred as a result of invasions, traditional Indian culture continued. Buddhism became less popular, while Hinduism added to its number of followers. Traditional Indian culture met another challenge after 600 CE in the form of the new religion of Islam.

Other Contacts with Classical Civilizations

Although the civilizations of Han China, Gupta India, Greece, and Rome dominated world history during the classical period, other societies and civilizations came into contact with and were influenced by them. Indian merchants drew the people of Southeast Asia into long-distance trade patterns. Contacts between India and Southeast Asia were further broadened by the spread of Buddhism and Hinduism from India to Southeast Asia.

Trade contacts also drew Africa into the classical Mediterranean world. South of Egypt lay the kingdom of Kush. The Kushites had long admired Egyptian culture and adapted their own writing system from Egyptian hieroglyphics. Kush also was a center of the independent invention of iron smelting. About 750 BCE, as Egypt weakened, Kush conquered Egypt. Kush, in turn, was defeated by the Christian kingdom of Axum about 300 CE. Axum and its rival, the kingdom of Ethiopia, traded with parts of the Roman Empire along the eastern Mediterranean. Greek merchants had carried Christianity to Ethiopia in the fourth century CE.

Silk Road Trade

One of the most far-reaching of the contacts between classical civilizations and other societies was the contact of the pastoral nomads of Central Asia with established societies. Central Asian herders often served as trade facilitators along the famed **Silk Roads** that linked trade between China and urban areas in Mesopotamia in the last millennium BCE. During the time of the Roman Empire, the Silk Roads were extended to the Mediterranean world. Named for their most prized trade commodity, the Silk Roads also were noted for the exchange of a variety of other goods between East and West. Nomadic peoples frequently supplied animals to transport goods along the Silk Roads. The Silk Roads served as an artery that transported not only trade goods but also religious beliefs, technology, and disease.

Indian Ocean Trade

The Silk Roads included not only land routes across Central Asia and Europe but also sea lanes in the Indian Ocean. Chinese pottery was traded along with Indian spices and ivory from India and Africa. The Indian Ocean trade network, which included the South China Sea, involved mariners from China, Malaysia, Southeast Asia, and Persia. Sailors used the seasonal monsoon winds to chart their course and carry out voyages that linked sections from East Africa to Southern China.

Trans-Saharan Trade

A third principal trade route in classical times was one across the Sahara. One of the most significant developments in the trade across the Sahara was the use of the camel and the development of the camel saddle. It is possible that the camel arrived in the Sahara from Arabia in the first century BCE. Early Saharan trade patterns included the exchange of salt and palm oil. During the days of the Roman Empire, North Africa also supplied Italy with olives, wheat, and wild animals.

❯ Rapid Review

Although they ultimately fell to nomadic invaders, the classical civilizations of China, India, and the Mediterranean produced traditions that stamped an enduring mark on world cultures. Major world belief systems spread throughout Eurasia. The Silk Roads, Indian Ocean network, and trans-Saharan routes linked the Eastern Hemisphere to the foundations of a global trade network. For more detailed information on trade systems and their effects worldwide, see Chapter 14.

› Review Questions

1. Answer Parts A and B.
   (A) Identify TWO common elements that led to the decline of Han China, Imperial Rome, and Gupta India.
   (B) Identify ONE element that distinguished the fall of Rome from that of Han China and Gupta India.

Questions 2 to 4 refer to the following passage.

. . . trade routes served principally to transfer raw materials, foodstuffs, and luxury goods from areas with surpluses to [areas] where such goods were in short supply… Cities along…trade routes grew rich providing services to merchants and acting as international marketplaces… They also became cultural and artistic centers, where peoples of different ethnic and cultural backgrounds could meet and intermingle… The trade routes were the communications highways of the ancient world. New inventions, religious beliefs, artistic styles, languages, and social customs, as well as goods and raw materials [and even diseases] were transmitted by people moving from one place to another to conduct business.

—Heilbrunn, *Timeline of Art,* 2000

2. Which ONE luxury good that the East sent to the West gave its name to a trade route?
   (A) Camel saddles
   (B) Silk
   (C) Salt
   (D) Spices

3. How did trade routes contribute to urbanization?
   (A) By reducing the need for agricultural products among populations
   (B) By pre-empting and ruining farmlands
   (C) By establishing market centers that provided services for travelers
   (D) By encouraging farmers to move to cities

4. Which of the following best explains the phrase "communications highways" in the passage?
   (A) Roads that allowed development of postal services
   (B) Roads that facilitated cultural contact and exchange
   (C) Roads that permitted businesses to grow
   (D) Roads that allowed the transfer of goods from one place to another

5. Answer Parts A and B.
   (A) Using your knowledge of world history, identify TWO examples of early "globalization," or the political, economic, social, or cultural interdependence or exchanges between different civilizations during the classical age.
   (B) Identify ONE example of syncretism that came about because of early "globalization."

› Answers and Explanations

1A. Of the many reasons for the fall of the Han, Roman, and Gupta empires, one of the most important was overextension, which contributed to the inability of the centralized government to control far-flung lands and the subsequent fragmentation of the empire itself. Other common elements include invasions; unequal distribution of wealth, land, and tax burdens; poor harvests, which led to famine and economic depression; and epidemic disease and subsequent population decline.

1B. While all three empires shared reasons for their decline, only Rome was split in half, with the Emperor Constantine establishing a second capital in Constantinople (today's Istanbul), making it possible for the Eastern Roman Empire to survive another thousand years, until 1453.

2. **B** The Silk Roads served as a conduit not just for silk but for a variety of goods and ideas between Eastern and Western classical civilizations. Other goods included such things as camel saddles (A), salt (C), and spices (D), but none of these left its name on the trade route.

3. **C** Trade routes, with their heavy traffic through frequently barren areas, caused the growth of urban centers that could provide food and housing for traveling merchants. The need for agricultural products (A) rose rather than declined; farmlands (B) frequently increased in value and provided new markets for farmers, thus encouraging farmers to remain in the countryside (D).

4. **B** "Communication" indicates both contact and exchange; and the trade routes, as communication highways, facilitated both. Trade routes certainly contributed to the development of postal services (A) and businesses (C) and allowed goods to be shipped from one place to another (D); but it is the element of exchange that caused "communication" to occur.

5A. The spread of disease—and subsequently of medical practices—is seen as travelers crossed land and sea boundaries. Art forms and symbolism, like the Buddhist statues in Greek dress, occurred as well. Luxuries (silk cloth as a sign of wealth) changed from belonging to just one society.

5B. Early globalization produced varied examples of syncretism, including especially architecture (Asian arched windows and doors in Roman imperial buildings).

Summaries: Technological and Environmental Transformations

Timeline

8000 BCE	First agricultural villages
4000 BCE	First cities
	Beginning of the cultivation of maize in Mesoamerica
3200 BCE	Beginning of Sumerian dominance of Mesopotamia
3000 BCE	Beginning of agriculture in South America
	Beginning of agriculture in New Guinea
3000 BCE to 1000 CE	Indo-European migrations
2600–2500 BCE	Pyramid construction in Egypt
2500–2000 BCE	Height of Harappan society in South Asia
2350 BCE	Beginning of regional empires in Mesopotamia
2200 BCE	Beginning of Chinese dynastic rule
2000 BCE	Beginning of the Bantu migrations
1500 BCE	Beginning of Aryan migrations to South Asia
1500 to 500 BCE	Vedic Age in South Asia
1500 BCE–700 CE	Austronesian migrations
1000–970 BCE	Rule of Hebrew King David
900 BCE	Invention of ironworking in sub-Saharan Africa
800 BCE	Establishment of Greek *poleis*
722 BCE	Assyrian conquest of Israel
586 BCE	New Babylonian (Chaldean) conquest of Judah

Key Comparisons

1. Early agriculture in the Eastern Hemisphere versus the Western Hemisphere
2. Pastoral nomadism versus settled lifestyles
3. Political, economic, and social characteristics of the four river valley civilizations
4. Early civilizations of the Eastern and Western Hemispheres

Change/Continuity Chart

REGION	POLITICAL	ECONOMIC	SOCIAL	CHANGES	CONTINUITIES
East Asia	Dynastic rule Era of the Warring States Mandate of Heaven	Rice, millet Bronze crafts Ironworking	Patriarchal societies Oracle bones Stratified society Urbanization	Irrigation Agriculture Bronze metallurgy	Agriculture
Southeast Asia	Regional kingdoms and empires	Root crops Fruit Trade with South Asia	Villages	Agriculture	Agriculture
Oceania	Regional kingdoms	Foraging	Polytheism Animism Tribal organization	Austronesian migrations	Foraging
Central Asia	Tribal governments	Nomadism Trade facilitators	Indo-European migrations	Trade with settled societies	Pastoral nomadism
South Asia	Community planning Aryan invasions	Grains Sewer systems Trade with Sumer	Urbanization Patriarchal societies *Vedas* Sanskrit	Decline of Harappan civilization Regional empires Aryan society	Agriculture Interest in technological advancement Active trade
Southwest Asia	Mesopotamian city-states Code of Hammurabi Kingdom of Israel Persian Empire	Grains Wheel Cuneiform Trade with Indus valley and Egypt	Urbanization Polytheism Stratified society Slavery Judaism *Epic of Gilgamesh* Phoenician alphabet	Ironworking in Anatolia City-states to empires Conquests of Israel and Judah	Agriculture Irrigation Trade

KEY IDEA

Change/Continuity Chart *(continued)*

REGION	POLITICAL	ECONOMIC	SOCIAL	CHANGES	CONTINUITIES
North Africa	Pharaohs Kingdoms of Egypt and Kush	Barley Trade with Sumer and Persia Ironworking	Urbanization Village life along the Nile Pyramids Hieroglyphics Polytheism Stratified society	Long-distance trade	Regional kingdoms
Sub-Saharan Africa	Tribal government Regional kingdoms	Root crops Trans-Saharan trade	Polytheism Animism Ancestor veneration Slavery	Sub-Saharan trade Bantu migrations	Regional kingdoms Polytheism
Western Europe	Village governments Greek city-states	Cereal agriculture Ironworking	Agricultural villages Olympic Games	Indo-European migrations	Foraging Agriculture
Eastern Europe	Village governments Greek colonization	Cereal agriculture Ironworking	Agricultural villages	Indo-European migrations	Foraging Agriculture
North America	Tribal government	Foraging Nomadism Cultivation of maize	Village organization Polytheism Shamanism	Migration from Asia Agriculture	Village life Nomadism Polytheism Shamanism
Latin America	City-states Regional governments Andean kingdoms	Limited trade Foraging Cultivation of maize	Stratified society Slavery	Agriculture Olmec civilization Chavín culture	Mesoamerican traditions

Organization and Reorganization of Human Societies

Timeline

509 BCE	Establishment of the Roman republic
480–221 BCE	Era of the Warring States in China
336–323 BCE	Rule of Alexander of Macedon (the Great)
330 BCE	Conquest of Achaemenid Empire by Alexander
20 BCE–180 CE	*Pax Romana*
4 BCE–29 CE	Life of Jesus Christ
300–1100 CE	Mayan civilization
Third–first centuries BCE	Spread of Buddhism and Hinduism from South Asia
206 CE–220 CE	Han dynasty
320–550 CE	Gupta dynasty
476 CE	Fall of the Western Roman Empire

Key Comparisons

1. Political, economic, and social characteristics of the empires of Rome, Han China, and Gupta India
2. Exchanges in the Indian Ocean versus those in the Mediterranean Sea
3. The expansion and appeal of Buddhism, Hinduism, and Christianity
4. The origins, philosophies, and goals of Confucianism and Daoism
5. The decline and fall of Han China, Rome, and Gupta India
6. Trans-Saharan versus Silk Roads trade

CHAPTER 10

Origins of World Belief Systems

IN THIS CHAPTER

Summary: The time from 8000 BCE to 600 CE saw the beginnings of many of the world's major belief systems. Both Hinduism and Buddhism originated in India. The philosophies of Confucianism and Daoism profoundly affected traditional Chinese culture. In the Middle East, the Hebrew faith gave the world the concept of **monotheism**, and its offshoots would include Christianity and, later, Islam. Christianity emerged from the Hebrew belief in a **Messiah**, or a savior from sin. Followers of Jesus as the Messiah spread their faith throughout the Roman world. Islam, beginning after the birth of Muhammed in 570 CE, is covered in Chapter 11.

Key Terms

Analects	Messiah
animism	*moksha*
bodhisattvas	New Testament
Brahmin	*nirvana*
dharma	pope
disciple	reincarnation
Edict of Milan	shamanism
filial piety	*yin* and *yang*
karma	

Polytheism

Both nomadic and early agricultural peoples often held to a belief in many gods or goddesses, or polytheism. The ancient river valley civilizations in the Eastern Hemisphere, as well as the early civilizations in the Americas, believed in numerous gods and goddesses representing spirits or objects of nature. The Greeks and Romans also believed in an array of deities who represented natural phenomena but at the same time took on humanlike qualities. Some early peoples practiced a form of polytheism called **animism**, or a belief that gods and goddesses inhabited natural features. Animism was widespread among many societies in Africa and in the Pacific islands of Polynesia. **Shamanism**, a form of animism, expressed a belief in powerful natural spirits that were influenced by shamans, or priests. Shamanism remained a common practice in Central Asia and the Americas.

Hinduism

Hinduism is a belief system that originated in India from the literature, traditions, and class system of the Aryan invaders. In contrast to other world religions, Hinduism did not have a single founder. As a result, the precepts and values of Hinduism developed gradually and embraced a variety of forms of worship. Hinduism took the polytheistic gods of nature that had been central to the worship of the **Brahmins**, or priests, and then changed their character to represent concepts.

According to Hindu belief, everything in the world is part of a divine essence called Brahma. The spirit of Brahma enters gods or different forms of one god. Two forms of the Hindu deity are Vishnu, the preserver, and Shiva, the destroyer. A meaningful life is one that has found union with the divine soul. Hinduism holds that this union is achieved through **reincarnation**, or the concept that after death the soul enters another human or an animal. The person's good or evil deeds in his or her personal life is that person's *karma*. Those who die with good *karma* may be reincarnated into a higher caste, whereas those with evil *karma* might descend to a lower caste or become an animal. If the soul lives a number of good lives, it is united with the soul of Brahma. Upon achieving this unification, or *moksha*, the soul no longer experiences worldly suffering.

Hinduism goes beyond a mystical emphasis to affect the everyday conduct of its followers. The moral law, or **dharma**, serves as a guide to actions in this world. *Dharma* emphasizes that human actions produce consequences and that each person has obligations, or duties, to the family and community.

The Hindu religion reinforced the Indian caste system, offering hope for an improved lifestyle in the next life, especially for members of the lower castes. Those of the upper castes were encouraged by the prospect of achieving *moksha*. Hinduism also extended the Aryan custom of venerating cattle by considering cattle as sacred and forbidding the consumption of beef.

In time, Hinduism became the principal religion of India. Carried by merchants through the waters of the Indian Ocean, Hindu beliefs also spread to Southeast Asia, where they attracted large numbers of followers. During the first century CE, there were already signs of Indian influence in the societies of the islands of the Indian Ocean and in the Malay peninsula. Some rulers in present-day Vietnam and Cambodia adopted the Sanskrit language of India as a form of written communication.

Buddhism

The second major faith to originate in India was Buddhism. In contrast to Hinduism, Buddhism had a founder in an Indian prince named Gautama, born about 563 BCE. Troubled by the suffering in the world, Gautama spent six years fasting and meditating on its cause. After he determined that suffering was the consequence of human desire, he began traveling to spread his beliefs. At this time Gautama became known as "Buddha," or the "enlightened one."

Although later followers would consider Buddha a god, Buddha did not see himself as a deity. Rather, he stressed the existence of a divine essence. Buddhism sought self-control and stressed the equal treatment of peoples from all walks of life. The Buddhist faith, therefore, opposed the caste system.

Buddhism shared with Hinduism the concept of reincarnation but in a different perspective. Buddhist belief held that a series of reincarnations would lead the faithful follower to ever higher levels toward the ultimate goal, which was **nirvana**, or a union with the divine essence.

The popularity of Buddhism emerged from its acceptance of men and women from all ranks of society. At first Buddhism spread through the efforts of monks and nuns who established religious communities in northern India. Located along trade routes, Buddhist monasteries served as lodging for traders, who learned of the teachings of Buddhism through contact with Buddhist monks and nuns. Contact with Hellenistic culture produced the Gandhara Buddhas, a syncretic sculpture combining the symbol of the Buddha with the exaltation of the human body typical of Hellenistic culture. In time, merchants carried the doctrines of Buddhism along the Silk Roads and other trade routes. Initially, Buddhist popularity was strengthened when the Mauryan emperor, Ashoka, adopted its beliefs. The faith, however, did not enjoy a long-term period of popularity in India because of opposition from Hindu Brahmins and the later promotion of Hinduism by Gupta emperors. Buddhism spread along the trade routes to become popular in Southeast Asia and East Asia, especially in Sri Lanka, Japan, Korea, and China. In China, Buddhism blended with Confucianism to reinforce the concept of patriarchal families. As it spread to other locales, Buddhism developed the belief of **bodhisattvas**, which held that, through meditation, ordinary people could reach *nirvana*.

Of the major branches of Buddhism, three stand out: Mahayana, Theravada, and Vajrayana. Mayahana is less doctrinaire and more a guide to living in search of the truth through the use of reason, akin to the scientific method. It appealed to a broad spectrum of people, unlike Theravada, which revolved around practices (meditation, withdrawal from daily life to serve as monks and nuns, for example) rather than around doctrinaire beliefs. The last branch, Vajrayana, which is also called "esoteric Buddhism," popular in Bhutan, Mongolia, and Tibet, emphasizes both practices and beliefs and is associated with the Dalai Lama.

Confucianism

Out of the disorder of the Era of Warring States after the fall of the Zhou dynasty came a number of philosophies designed to create order in China. Among these philosophies was Confucianism, named after its founder, Confucius, or Kúng Fu-tse (551–478 BCE). Confucius believed that the source of good government was in the maintenance of tradition; tradition, in turn, was maintained by personal standards of virtue. These included respect for the patriarchal family (**filial piety**) and veneration of one's ancestors.

Confucius also believed that governmental stability depended on well-educated officials. To this end, he required his followers to study history and literature from the Zhou dynasty to determine the value of these subjects for government officials. Some of the students of Confucius compiled his sayings into the **Analects**, a work that also served to educate the Chinese bureaucracy or government officials. The Han dynasty appreciated Confucian philosophy because it supported order and submission to the government. The civil service examination that developed during the Han dynasty was based on the *Analects* and the course of study developed by Confucius. The Confucian values of veneration of one's ancestors and respect for the patriarchal family, as well as good government staffed by a responsible, well-educated bureaucracy, became basic traditions that defined Chinese culture.

The effects of the spread of Confucianism included relegation of women to decidedly inferior status as compared to that of men. Men were expected to play public and political roles in society; women were expected to stay home and produce the next generation of those capable of carrying out ancestor worship. During the "Golden Age" of Chinese history, that is, during the Tang and Song dynasties, women made some advances, particularly under the reign of the Empress Wu (a unique event in Chinese history) and adopted some of the tenets of Buddhism and Daoism.

Daoism

Another philosophy that developed in response to the Era of Warring States was Daoism. Its founder was Lao-zi (or Lao-tsu), who is believed to have lived during the fifth century BCE. The philosophy adapted traditional Chinese concepts of balance in nature, or *yin* (female, submissive) and *yang* (male, assertive). According to Daoist philosophy, human understanding comes from following "The Way," a life force that exists in nature.

In contrast to the Confucian respect for education and for orderly government, Daoism taught that political involvement and education were unnecessary. Rather, in time, the natural balance of the universe would resolve most problems. Chinese thought and practice gradually blended both Confucianism and Daoism to include a concern for responsibility for the community and time for personal reflection.

Judaism

With origins dating back 4,000 years, Judaism was the first of the three Western monotheistic religions, the other two being Christianity and Islam. Beginning with the covenant that God made with Abraham, in which the Jews were named the Chosen People and promised a holy land, Judaism is grounded in the religious. social, and ethical laws of the Torah, or the first five books of the biblical Old Testament. The Talmud, or oral Torah, consists of rabbinical interpretations and commentary on the Torah.

Unlike other religions, notably Buddhism and Christianity, Judaism was not a missionary religion. It emphasized practice or the following of rules for living over faith and belief. From its inception, Judaism was considered a threat by various rulers. From the Babylonian captivity (c. 607–537 BCE), to the expulsion of all Jews from Spain in 1492, to the founding of the first Jewish ghetto in Venice in 1517, Jews were persecuted, and segregated, from dominant, ruling societies.

Christianity

A key element of Judaism was the belief that God had promised to send the Jews a **Messiah**, or a savior from their sins. Some of the early Jews felt that that promise was fulfilled when Jesus was born in the Roman province of Judea about 4 to 6 BCE. As an adult, Jesus and his 12 **disciples**, or followers, went throughout the land of Judea, preaching the forgiveness of sins. Jesus was also called Christ, meaning "anointed." When Jesus' teachings were feared as a threat to Roman and Jewish authority, he was tried and put to death by crucifixion.

The network of Roman roads facilitated the spread of Christianity throughout the empire. Missionaries, traders, and other travelers carried the Christian message of forgiveness of sins and an afterlife in heaven for those who believed in Jesus as their savior from sin. The greatest missionary of the early Christian church was Paul of Tarsus. A Roman citizen, he undertook three missionary journeys throughout the Roman Empire in the first century CE. Accounts of Jesus' life in addition to the missionary efforts of Paul and other followers of Jesus are found in the **New Testament** of the Christian Bible.

Several Roman emperors considered Christianity a threat to their rule. Although some, such as Diocletian, persecuted the Christian church, it continued to grow. In 313, the Roman Emperor Constantine changed the position of earlier Roman emperors regarding Christianity. In the **Edict of Milan** he legalized the practice of Christianity in the Roman Empire. Christianity became the official religion of the Roman Empire in 381 under Emperor Theodosius.

After its adoption as the state church of Rome, Christianity in the West began developing an organization under the leadership of the bishop of Rome, or **pope**. In addition to priests who served local churches, monks and nuns withdrew from society to devote their time to prayer and meditation. As it spread throughout the Roman world, Christianity gained popularity because of its appeal to all social classes, especially the poor. Women received new status as Christianity taught that men and women were equal in matters of faith. After the fall of the Western Roman Empire, Christianity spread to northern Europe, the Balkans, and Russia.

› Rapid Review

Although polytheism was the most common religious belief among early agricultural and nomadic peoples, a number of major belief systems arose before 600 CE. Monotheism was the gift of Judaism, which, in turn, became the source of Christianity and Islam. In India, two faiths—Hinduism and Buddhism—emerged from the diverse social structure of South Asia. In China, Confucianism and Daoism blended family and political order with the balance of nature to define Chinese philosophical thought.

› Review Questions

1. Answer Parts A and B.
   (A) Identify TWO similarities between Hinduism and Buddhism.
   (B) Identify ONE major belief most major religions hold in common.

Questions 2 to 5 refer to the following passage.

For thousands of years people have searched for the meaning and truth of their own nature and of the universe, and religions, which deal with the whole of human life and death, are the result. . . . Religions bind people together in common practices and beliefs; they draw them together in a common goal of life. . . . Religions are organized systems for protecting information and for passing it on from one generation to another.

—John Bowker
World Religions: The Great Faiths Explored and Explained, 1997

2. Why did religion assume great importance during the settlement characteristic of the early historical periods?
   (A) It employed the many people no longer required in agricultural or hunting endeavors.
   (B) It provided a sense of belonging.
   (C) It provided gender and social class equality.
   (D) It encouraged the establishment of public educational systems.

3. How did trade networks contribute to the growth of some organized religious systems?
   (A) They provided opportunities for cultural syncretism.
   (B) They allowed exposure to and exchange of ideas.
   (C) They provided markets for religious books and artwork.
   (D) They encouraged the merchant class to act as missionaries.

4. Which of the major religions discussed in this chapter bound people together by considering all social classes equal?
   (A) Christianity
   (B) Confucianism
   (C) Hinduism
   (D) Judaism

5. How do religions pass information from one generation to the next?
   (A) Through missionary work
   (B) Through decrees
   (C) Through texts and ritual
   (D) Through military actions

› Answers and Explanations

1A. Hinduism and Buddhism share beliefs in reincarnation, release from the cycles of reincarnation with achievement of enlightenment (nirvana, moksha), and the power of meditation.

1B. Most major religions share a belief in the "golden rule": do to others what you would have them do to you.

2. B Religions gave a sense of unity to people often drawn together by nothing more than circumstance. It did not employ vast numbers of people who had suddenly been freed from farming or hunting (A). It was decidedly not a means of promoting gender and social class equality (C), but often a means of preserving differences. Public educational systems (D) did not exist until much later.

3. B Merchants carried more than trade goods; they carried ideas, beliefs, and values that often differed from those of their counterparts from different societies. Not all ideas exchanged were accepted, but they exposed merchants to new possibilities. Cultural syncretism (A) usually resulted from prolonged exposure between conquered peoples and their overlords. Religious books and artworks were uncommon (C) and usually the property of the wealthy. While missionaries (D) accompanied merchants, they were members of a distinct class.

4. A Of the major religions, only Christianity made a point of considering all people equal in the eyes of God. Confucianism (B) used familial piety and civil service exams to maintain a patriarchal and class divide. Hinduism (C) separated classes into specific levels. Judaism (D) maintained patriarchal systems.

5. C While general information about a religion may be spread by missionary work (A), decree (B), or military actions (D), texts and especially rituals sustain and share information within a community and within families, thus allowing religion to be passed down through generations.

Major World Belief Systems

	ORIGIN	CENTRAL TENETS	MAJOR TEXTS
Hinduism	1750–1500 BCE Aryan invasions, Indus Valley civilization.	One god in many forms. Reincarnation and progress toward moksha (release) based on karma and dharma (rules of behavior, duties). Caste system.	Vedic literature. *Upanishads; Mahabharata; Bhagavad Gita; Ramayana*
Buddhism	Siddhartha Gautama (sixth c. BCE). Nepal. Carried across Asia by monks and merchants	No personal deity. Life is suffering, caused by desire. Nirvana, the end of reincarnation, is cessation of suffering. Karma.	The Four Noble Truths; Eightfold Path; *Tdripitaka*
Confucianism	Confucius (300 BCE). China.	Jen, the quality that unites all people. Filial piety, five relationships; ancestor worship. Mandate of Heaven, model for Chinese government.	*The Analects*
Daoism	Lao-Tzu (604 BCE). China.	"The way": naturalness, or the way of human life, in accord with the way of the universe. Compassion, moderation, humility.	*Tao Te Ching*
Judaism	Hebrews. Abraham (c. 2000 BCE). Moses (c. 1000 BCE). Canaan, Israel; North Africa, Middle East. Europe.	One God (Yahweh). Chosen people per covenant with God. Laws of Torah—focus on life more than afterlife. Awaiting Messiah. Orthodox, Reform, Conservative branches.	*Torah; Talmud* (oral laws); *Mosaic Law*
Christianity	Jesus of Nazareth (30s CE). Legalized by Emperor Constantine in fourth century CE. Middle East, Europe, worldwide.	One God. Jesus as the Messiah. Eternal life via faith, good works, and atonement. Catholic and Protestant groups whose means of salvation differed.	*Bible, Old and New Testaments*
Islam	Muhammed (570 CE). Arabian Peninsula, Middle East, India, Asia, North Africa, Spain.	One God (Allah). Five Pillars. Sharia Law. Sunni and Shi'a factions.	*Quran*

Change/Continuity Chart

KEY IDEA

REGION	POLITICAL	ECONOMIC	SOCIAL	CHANGES	CONTINUITIES
East Asia	Dynastic rule "Mandate of Heaven" Centralized government Great Wall Civil service exam	Rice, millet Bronze crafts Ironworking Silk production Silk Road trade Paper	Urbanization Patriarchal societies Stratified society Confucianism Daoism	Development of philosophy	Chinese traditions of Confucianism, family Dynastic rule Ancestor veneration "Mandate of Heaven"
Southeast Asia	Chinese influence	Root crops Fruit Trade with South Asia	Urbanization Hinduism Buddhism	Adaptations of Chinese culture Hinduism and Buddhism Urbanization	Agriculture
Oceania	Regional kingdoms	Foraging	Polytheism Animism Tribal organization	Development of kingdoms	Foraging Austronesian migrations
Central Asia	Tribal governments Chinese influence Migrations toward classical empires	Nomadism Trade facilitators	Indo-European migrations	Trade facilitators Invasion of classical empires	Pastoral nomadism Shamanism
South Asia	Community planning Mauryan and Gupta dynasties	Grains Indian Ocean trade	Urbanization Patriarchal societies Hinduism Varna Buddhism Inoculation *Sati*	Hinduism Buddhism Caste system Dynasties	Agriculture Interest in technological advancement Active trade *Vedas* Sanskrit
Southwest Asia	Persian Empire Hellenistic Empire	Grains Wheel Cuneiform Trade with Indus valley and Egypt Camel saddle	Urbanization Polytheism Stratified society Judaism Zoroastrianism Christianity	Development of major religions	Agriculture Irrigation Trade Judaism Zoroastrianism

Change/Continuity Chart (continued)

REGION	POLITICAL	ECONOMIC	SOCIAL	CHANGES	CONTINUITIES
North Africa	Pharaohs Kingdoms of Kush, Axum, Ethiopia	Barley Trade with Sumer and Persia Ironworking Salt/palm oil Use of camel saddle Trade with Rome	Urbanization Village life along the Nile Pyramids Hieroglyphics Polytheism Stratified society Christianity	Long-distance trade Decline of Egyptian civilization Christianity	Regional kingdoms Village life along the Nile
Sub-Saharan Africa	Regional kingdoms	Root crops Trans-Saharan trade Ivory trade/Indian Ocean	Polytheism Animism	Indian Ocean trade Sub-Saharan trade	Regional kingdoms Polytheism Ancestor veneration Bantu migrations
Western Europe	Athenian democracy *Poleis* Hellenistic Empire Roman Empire	Greek trade/colonization Silk Roads trade Roman roads Decline of trade and learning	Phoenician alphabet Olympic games Greek drama Greek philosophy Hellenistic thought *Pax Romana* Latin Roman law Christianity	Fall of Roman Empire	Greco-Roman culture
Eastern Europe	Byzantine Empire Justinian's attempts to recover Roman territory Code of Justinian	Agriculture Center of trade	Greek learning Christianity	Urbanization and trade in Byzantium	Greco-Roman culture
North America	Tribal government Regional empires	Maize Nomadism Some trade with Mesoamerica	Village organization Polytheism	Trade expansion	Village life Nomadism Polytheism Shamanism
Latin America	City-states Mayan civilization Andean societies and civilizations	Maize, potato Llama, alpaca Obsidian, jade Limited trade	Urbanization Quetzalcóatl Stratified society Zero Astronomy Calendar	Pyramids Ceremonial buildings Mayan astronomy	Mesoamerican traditions Shamanism Ancestor veneration

KEY IDEA

Rise and Spread of Islam

IN THIS CHAPTER

Summary: As the empires that lent their grandeur to the classical period of early civilization fell into decline, the barren desert of the Arabian Peninsula witnessed the development of a belief system that evolved into a religious, political, and economic world system. **Dar al-Islam,** or the house of Islam, united sacred and secular institutions.

Key Terms

Allah	*minaret*
arabesque	mosque
astrolabe	Muslim
Battle of Tours	People of the Book
caliph	*Quran*
Dar al-Islam	Ramadan
Five Pillars	*shariah*
Hadith	Shi'ite
hajj	Shia
harem	Sufis
hijrah	sultan
jihad	Sunni
Ka'aba	*umma*
Mamluks	*zakat*

The World of Muhammad

The Arabian Peninsula into which Muhammad was born in 570 was a hub of ancient caravan routes. Although the coastal regions of the peninsula were inhabited by settled peoples, the interior region provided a homeland for nomadic tribes called Bedouins. Located in the interior of the peninsula was the city of Mecca, which served both as a commercial center and as the location of a religious shrine for the polytheistic worship common to the nomadic peoples of the peninsula. Pilgrims were in the habit of visiting Mecca and its revered shrine, the **Ka'aba**, a cubic structure that housed a meteorite. The merchants of Mecca enjoyed a substantial profit from these pilgrims.

Muhammad, an orphan from the merchant class of Mecca, was raised by his grandfather and uncle. He married a wealthy local widow and businesswoman named Khadija. About 610 CE, Muhammad experienced the first of a number of revelations that he believed came from the archangel Gabriel. In these revelations he was told that there is only one God, called *Allah* in Arabic. (*Allah* was one of the gods in the Arabic pantheon.) Although the peoples of the Arabian Peninsula had already been exposed to monotheism through Jewish traders and Arabic converts to Christianity, Muhammad's fervent proclamation of the existence of only one god angered the merchants of Mecca, who anticipated decreased profits from pilgrimages if the revelations of Muhammad were widely accepted. In 622 CE, realizing that his life was in danger, Muhammad and his followers fled to the city of Yathrib (later called Medina), about 200 miles northwest of Mecca. Here Muhammad was allowed to freely exercise his role as prophet of the new faith, and the numbers of believers in the new religion grew. The flight of Muhammad from Mecca to Medina, called the *hijrah*, became the first year in the Muslim calendar.

In Medina, Muhammad oversaw the daily lives of his followers, organizing them into a community of believers known as the *umma*. The well-being of the *umma* included programs concerning all aspects of life, from relief for widows and orphans to campaigns of military defense.

In 629 CE, Muhammad and his followers journeyed to Mecca to make a pilgrimage to the Ka'aba, now incorporated as a shrine in the Islamic faith. The following year they returned as successful conquerors of the city, and in 632 CE, they again participated in the *hajj*. In 632 CE, Muhammad died without appointing a successor, an omission that would have a profound effect on the future of Islam.

The Teachings of Islam

The term Islam means "submission," while the name **Muslim**, applied to the followers of Islam, means "one who submits." Muhammad viewed his revelations as a completion of those of Judaism and Christianity and perceived himself not as a deity, but as the last in a series of prophets of the one god, *Allah*. He considered Abraham, Moses, and Jesus also among the prophets of *Allah*. According to the teachings of Islam, the faithful must follow a set of regulations known as the **Five Pillars**. They include:

- *Faith.* In order to be considered a follower of Islam, a person must proclaim in the presence of a Muslim the following statement: "There is no god but *Allah*, and Muhammad is his prophet."
- *Prayer.* The Muslim must pray at five prescribed times daily, each time facing the holy city of Mecca.

- *Fasting.* The faithful must fast from dawn to dusk during the days of the holy month of **Ramadan**, a commemoration of the first revelation to Muhammad.
- *Alms-giving.* The Muslim is to pay the *zakat*, or tithe for the needy.
- *The* hajj. At least once, the follower of Islam is required to make a pilgrimage to the *Ka'aba* in the holy city of Mecca. The faithful are released from this requirement if they are too ill or too poor to make the journey.

The revelations and teachings of Muhammad were not compiled into a single written document until after his death. The resulting **Quran**, or holy book of the Muslims, was completed in 650 CE. In addition, the sayings of Muhammad were compiled into the books of the **Hadith**. After the death of Muhammad the *shariah*, or moral law, was compiled. In addition to addressing issues of everyday life, the *shariah* established political order and provided for criminal justice.

Split Between the Sunni and the Shia

After the death of Muhammad in 632 CE, the *umma* chose Abu-Bakr, one of the original followers of Muhammad, as the first **caliph**, or successor to the prophet. The office of caliph united both secular and religious authority in the person of one leader. When the third caliph, Uthman of the Umayyad family, was assassinated, Ali, the cousin and son-in-law of Muhammad, was appointed caliph. Soon controversy arose over his appointment. As time progressed, the disagreement became more pronounced, resulting in a split in the Muslim world that exists to the present. After the assassination of Ali in 661 CE, the **Shia** sect, believing that only a member of the family of Muhammad should serve as caliph, arose to support the descendants of Ali. The **Sunni**, who eventually became the largest segment of Islam, believed that the successor to the caliphate should be chosen from among the *umma*, or Muslim community, and accepted the earliest caliphs as the legitimate rulers of Islam.

The Early Expansion of Islam

Shortly after the death of Muhammad, the new religion of Islam embarked upon a rapid drive for expansion. Unlike the Buddhist and Christian religions, which expanded by means of missionary endeavor and commercial activity, Islam at first extended its influence by military conquest. Islam spread swiftly throughout portions of Eurasia and Africa:

- Within a year after the death of Muhammad, most of the Arabian Peninsula was united under the banner of Islam.
- Persia was conquered in 651 CE with the overthrow of the Sassanid dynasty.
- By the latter years of the seventh century, the new faith had reached Syria, Mesopotamia, Palestine, and Egypt.
- At the same time, Islam extended into Central Asia east of the Caspian Sea, where it competed with Buddhism.
- During the eighth century, Muslim armies reached present-day Tunisia, Algeria, and Morocco; Hindu-dominated northwest India; and the Iberian Peninsula (present-day Spain and Portugal).

The earliest Muslim conquerors were not as concerned with the spread of religious belief as they were with the extension of power for the Muslim leaders and people.

The Umayyad Caliphate

After the assassination of Ali in 661 CE, the Umayyad family came to power in the Islamic world. Establishing their capital at Damascus in Syria, the Umayyad were noted for the following:

- An empire that emphasized Arabic ethnicity over adherence to Islam.
- Inferior status assigned to converts to Islam.
- Respect for Jews and Christians as "**People of the Book**." Although required to pay taxes for charity and on property, Jews and Christians were allowed freedom of worship and self-rule within their communities.
- Luxurious living for the ruling families, which prompted riots among the general population.

These riots among the general population led to the overthrow of the Umayyad by the Abbasid dynasty in 750 CE. Although most of the Umayyad were killed in the take-over, one member of the family escaped to Spain, where he established the Caliphate of Córdoba.

Al-Andalus

The flowering of Islamic culture became particularly pronounced in *al-Andalus,* or Islamic Spain. In 711 CE, Berbers from North Africa conquered the Iberian Peninsula, penetrating the European continent until their advance was stopped about 200 miles south of Paris at the **Battle of Tours** in 732 CE. Allies of the Umayyad dynasty, the caliphs of *al-Andalus* helped to preserve Greco-Roman culture, establishing schools of translation, and even enhancing it with the scientific and mathematical developments of the Muslim world. The Caliphate of Córdoba boasted a magnificent library and free education in Muslim schools. It established hospitals and offered health care for all. Interregional commerce thrived, while Arabic words such as *alcohol, álgebra,* and *sofá* were added to the Spanish vocabulary, and Muslim styles such as minarets, rounded arches, and arabesques were used in Spanish art and architecture.

The Abbasid Caliphate

The Abbasids, originally supported by the **Shi'ites (Shia)**, became increasingly receptive to the Sunni also. Establishing their capital at Baghdad in present-day Iraq, the Abbasids differed from the Umayyad in granting equal status to converts to Islam. Under the Abbasids:

- Converts experienced new opportunities for advanced education and career advancement.
- Trade was heightened from the western Mediterranean world to China.
- The learning of the ancient Greeks, Romans, and Persians was preserved. Greek logic, particularly that of Aristotle, penetrated Muslim thought.
- The Indian system of numbers, which included the use of zero as a placeholder, was carried by caravan from India to the Middle East and subsequently to Western Europe, where the numbers were labeled "Arabic" numerals.
- In mathematics, the fields of algebra, geometry, and trigonometry were further refined.
- The **astrolabe**, which measured the position of the stars, was improved.
- The study of astronomy produced maps of the stars.
- Optic surgery became a specialty, and human anatomy was studied in detail.

- Muslim cartographers produced some of the most detailed maps in the world.
- The number and size of urban centers such as Baghdad, Cairo, and Córdoba increased.
- Institutions of higher learning in Cairo, Baghdad, and Córdoba arose by the twelfth century.
- In the arts, calligraphy and designs called **arabesques** adorned writing and pottery.
- New architectural styles arose. Buildings were commonly centered around a patio area. **Minarets**, towers from which the faithful received the call to prayer, topped **mosques**, or Muslim places of worship.
- Great literature, such as poetic works and *The Arabian Nights,* enriched Muslim culture. Persian language and literary style was blended with that of Arabic.
- Mystics called **Sufis**, focusing on an emotional union with *Allah*, began missionary work to spread Islam.

Although responsible for much of the advancement of Islamic culture, the Abbasids found their vast empire increasingly difficult to govern. The dynasty failed to address the problem of succession within the Islamic world, and high taxes made the leaders less and less popular. Independent kingdoms began to arise within the Abbasid Empire, one of them in Persia, where local leaders, calling themselves "**sultan**," took Central of Baghdad in 945 CE. The Persians were challenged by the Seljuk Turks from central Asia, who also chipped away at the Byzantine Empire. The weakening Persian sultanate allied with the Seljuks, whose contacts with the Abbasids had led them to begin converting to Sunni Islam in the middle of the tenth century. By the middle of the eleventh century, the Seljuks controlled Baghdad. In the thirteenth century, the Abbasid dynasty ended when Mongol invaders executed the Abbasid caliph.

It was the Seljuk takeover of Jerusalem that prompted the beginnings of the Crusades in 1095 CE (see Chapter 13). Divisions within the Muslim world allowed Christians from Western Europe to capture Jerusalem during the First Crusade. Under Saladin, however, Muslim armies reconquered most of the lost territory during the twelfth century.

Islam in India and Southeast Asia

Between the seventh and twelfth centuries, Muslims expanded their influence from northwest India to the Indus valley and a large portion of northern India. Centering their government at Delhi, the rulers of the Delhi Sultanate extended their power by military conquest, controlling northern India from 1206 to 1526. Unsuccessful at achieving popularity among the Indians as a whole because of their monotheistic beliefs, the Muslim conquerors found acceptance among some Buddhists. Members of lower Hindu castes and untouchables also found Islam appealing because of its accepting and egalitarian nature. Although militarily powerful, the Delhi Sultanate failed to establish a strong administration. It did, however, introduce Islam to the culture of India.

In Southeast Asia, Islam spread more from commercial contacts and conversion than from military victories. By the eighth century, Muslim traders reached Southeast Asia, with migrants from Persia and southern Arabia arriving during the tenth century. Although the new faith did not gain widespread popularity among Buddhist areas of mainland Southeast Asia, the inhabitants of some of the islands of the Indian Ocean, familiar with Islam from trading contacts, were receptive to the new faith. Hinduism and Buddhism remained popular with many of the island peoples of the Indian Ocean. At the same time, however, Islam also found a stronghold on the islands of Malaysia, Indonesia, and the southern Philippines.

Islam in Africa

The spirit of *jihad*, or Islamic holy war, brought Islam into Africa in the eighth century. Wave after wave of traders and travelers carried the message of Muhammad across the sands of the Sahara along caravan routes. In the tenth century, Egypt was added to the Muslim territories. The authoritarian rulers of African states in the savannas south of the Sahara Desert adapted well to the Muslim concept of the unification of secular and spiritual powers in the person of the caliph. By the tenth century, the rulers of the kingdom of Ghana in West Africa converted to Islam, followed in the thirteenth century by the conversion of the rulers of the empire of Mali to the east of Ghana. Although widely accepted by the rulers of these regions, the common people preferred to remain loyal to their traditional polytheistic beliefs. When they did convert to Islam, they tended to blend some of their traditional beliefs and practices with those of Islam. Some Sudanic societies were resistant to Islam because their matrilineal structure offered women more freedom than did the practice of Islam.

Along the east coast of Africa, Indian Ocean trade was the focal point that brought Islam to the inhabitants of the coastal areas and islands. East African cities such as Mogadishu, Mombasa, and Kilwa became vibrant centers of Islam that caught the attention of Ibn Battuta, an Arab traveler who journeyed throughout the world of Islam in the fourteenth century. Islam did not experience much success in finding converts in the interior of Africa. In East Africa, as in the western portion of the continent, rulers were the first to convert to Islam, followed much later, if at all, by the masses. Women in eastern Africa already experienced more freedoms than did their Muslim counterparts, a fact that made them resistant to the new faith.

Mamluk Dynasties

With the destruction of Islamic power in Baghdad at the hands of the Mongols (see Chapter 14), the **Mamluk** dynasties provided the force that made Egypt a center for Muslim culture and learning. The Mamluks were converts to Islam who maintained their position among the caliphs by adhering to a strict observance of Islam. By encouraging the safety of trade routes within their domain, the Mamluks contributed to the prosperity of Egypt during the fourteenth and fifteenth centuries until internal disorder led to their takeover in the sixteenth century by the Ottoman Turks (see Chapter 16).

Role of Women in Islamic Society

The role of women in Islam underwent considerable change from the time of Muhammad to the fifteenth century. In the early days of Islam, women were not required to veil and were not secluded from the public; these customs were adopted by Islam after later contact with Middle Eastern women. The seclusion of the **harem** originated with the Abbasid court. From the time of Muhammad onward, Muslim men, following the example of Muhammad, could have up to four wives, provided that they could afford to treat them equally. Women, by contrast, were allowed only one husband.

In many respects, however, Islamic women enjoyed greater privileges than women in other societies at the same time. Both men and women were equal before *Allah*, and female infanticide was forbidden. Women could own property both before and after marriage. In some circumstances, Islamic women could initiate divorce proceedings and were allowed to remarry if divorced by their husbands. As time progressed, however, the legal privileges enjoyed by Islamic women were counterbalanced by their seclusion from the public, a situation designed to keep women, especially those from the urban elite classes, away from the gaze of men. This isolation often created barriers against the acceptance of Islam, especially among African women. Furthermore, both the *Quran* and the *shariah* established a patriarchal society.

Slavery in *Dar al-Islam*

Islamic law forbade its followers from enslaving other Muslims, except in the case of prisoners of war. Neither was the position of a slave hereditary; Muslims were frequently known to free their slaves, especially if they converted to Islam during their period of servitude. Children born to a slave woman and a Muslim man were considered free.

› Rapid Review

From the seventh to the fifteenth centuries, Islam served as a unifying force throughout many parts of Asia, Europe, and Africa, contributing to the cultural landscape of all three continents. Islam preserved the learning of the Greeks, Romans, and Persians, blending it with the artistic, scientific, and mathematical knowledge of its own culture. Educational opportunities were extended and urban centers established as *Dar al-Islam* extended its influence into the everyday lives of the inhabitants of the Eastern Hemisphere.

› Review Questions

1. Which of the following sequences of events in the development of Islam is accurate?
   (A) The hijrah → Sunni and Shia factions → death of Mohammed → Abbasid dynasty
   (B) The Abbasid dynasty → the hijrah → death of Mohammed → Sunni and Shia factions
   (C) Death of Mohammed → Sunni and Shia factions begin → hijrah → the Abbasid dynasty
   (D) The hijrah → death of Mohammed → Sunni and Shia factions begin → the Abbasid dynasty

2. Answer Parts A, B, and C.

   The impact of Islam on women is often controversial and sometimes misunderstood.

   (A) Identify and describe one example of a legal protection or right of women under Islam during this period.
   (B) Identify one way in which the rights of women declined under this period.
   (C) Explain how the treatment of women might have limited Islam's spread.

Questions 3 to 5 refer to the following map.

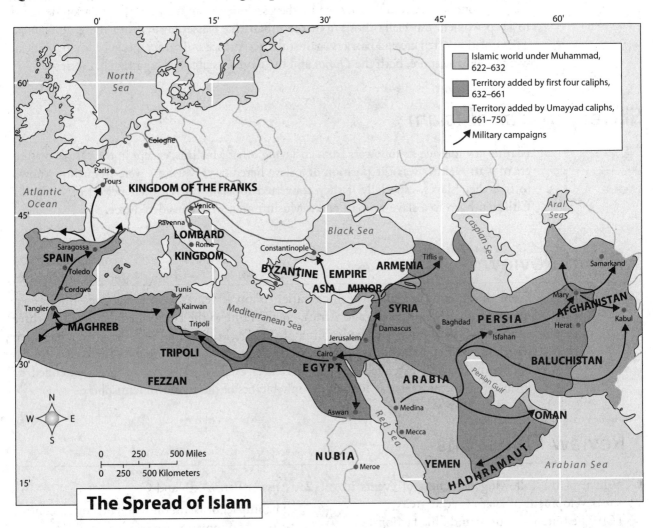

The Spread of Islam

3. According to the map, what was the primary mechanism for the spread of Islam in North Africa?
   (A) Military campaigns and conquest
   (B) Trade and commercial expeditions
   (C) Migration due to population pressure
   (D) Religious missionaries and imams

4. Which of the following best explains why Islam did not penetrate into Europe?
   (A) The values of Islam were rejected by Catholics.
   (B) At Tours, the Muslims suffered a military defeat by the Franks.
   (C) The Muslim army was unprepared for the harsh European winter.
   (D) Most European governments were isolationist at the time.

5. Which of the following is a modern legacy of the interactions shown in the map?
   (A) The use of concrete in modern construction
   (B) The development of cavalry in modern militaries
   (C) The integration of algebra and trigonometry in education
   (D) The legal concept of adhering to precedent

› Answers and Explanations

1. **D** The hijrah refers to Mohammed's flight from Mecca to Medina, which then obviously predates the death of Mohammed (C). The Sunni and Shia factions emerge out of the dispute over whether only direct descendants of Mohammed should lead Islam and the caliphate (A). The Abbasid dynasty was not created until much later, after the fall of the Umayyad dynasty (D).

2A. A thorough answer might include the following:

In contrast with other regions during this era, women under Islam enjoyed certain legal protections. Women were allowed to own property in their own name, both before and after they married. Women could also file for divorce under certain circumstances and were allowed to remarry.

2B. Although the practice of veiling women and secluding them in a harem was not originally part of the Islamic faith, it became increasingly prevalent as Islam mixed with the cultural practices of the Mesopotamian region. This limited women's rights as their freedom of movement and social interactions became increasingly constrained.

2C. These restrictions on women's freedom of movement made Islam less appealing in parts of Africa where women traditionally enjoyed more social and economic autonomy. Where Islam was adopted in Africa, it frequently was in a form adapted to and integrating local customs to make it more acceptable.

3. **A** By reading the map key and studying the map, we see the arrows, together with their direction extending outward from Medina, indicate that this territory was gained through military conquest. Though trade played a key role in the Muslim economy and later conversion to Islam throughout Africa, it was not the mechanism for territorial acquisition, nor is it reflected on the map (B). Religious leaders like Imam and Ulama (Muslim legal scholars) traveled throughout *dar-al-Islam* (the Islamic world) to maintain a degree of conformity in the practice of Islam, but did not acquire territory (D).

4. **B** The Muslims attempted to extend their territory into Northern Europe, but were defeated at Tours by the Franks, led by Charles Martel. For this reason, this battle is considered by some to be one of the turning points in world history. Though Catholics rejected Islam, Muslims still were able to conquer parts of Catholic Spain (A). The Battle of Tours occurred in 732 CE, during which point Europe still had contacts with the wider world through traditional trade networks along the Mediterranean, and with Asia via the Byzantine Empire (D). Although winter has played a role in the defeat of armies, this is most notable for armies invading Russia and is not the case here (C).

5. **C** The flourishing of *dar-al-Islam*, particularly under the Abbasid dynasty, led to a myriad of developments in the arts, sciences, and mathematics, including the development of algebra and trigonometry, which then spread to Europe via trade networks. Concrete had been in use since Roman times and thus was not a result of Muslim expansion (A). The use of horses in combat predates this period and can be seen as early as the Assyrian Empire (B). The use of precedent in deciding legal cases derives from common law that originated in Europe. The Muslim world adhered to *sharia*, or Islamic law, based on the *Quran* and the *Hadith* (collections of Mohammed's sayings).

CHAPTER 12

Changes in European Institutions

IN THIS CHAPTER

Summary: In the centuries after the fall of the Roman Empire, Western Europe underwent a period of political, economic, and social upheaval that continued until about 900 CE. The one stabilizing force throughout most of Western Europe was the Roman Catholic Church. Only in Spain, dominated by Muslim influences between 711 and 1492, did the learning of the Greeks and Romans thrive in Western Europe.

Key Terms

benefice	*Magna Carta*
Black Death	manorialism
chivalry	medieval
excommunication	Middle Ages
feudalism	moldboard plow
fief	parliament
Gothic architecture	Romanesque architecture
investiture	vassal

Manorialism and Feudalism in Western Europe

Even before the fall of the Roman Empire, declining prosperity in the final years of the empire had caused small landowners to sell off their land holdings to the owners of large estates. Although some peasants relocated to urban areas, others remained to work the land, receiving protection from their landlords in exchange for their agricultural labor. As trade continued to decline and political order disintegrated, **manorialism** became more widespread. When a wave of Vikings from Scandinavia invaded Europe in the ninth century, Western Europeans turned to **feudalism** to provide a means of protection.

Feudalism was a political, economic, and social system. Throughout most areas of Western Europe, nobles or landlords offered **benefices**, or privileges, to **vassals** in exchange for military service in the lord's army or agricultural labor on the lord's estate. Often the benefice was a grant of land, called a **fief**. Feudalism was structured so that a person could enjoy the position of a noble with vassals under him and, at the same time, serve as vassal to a noble of higher status. Knights, similar in their roles to the *samurai* of Japan, were vassals who served in the lord's military forces. Like the *samurai*, the knights of Western Europe followed an honor code called **chivalry**. In contrast to the *samurai* code of *bushido*, however, chivalry was a reciprocal, or two-sided, contract between vassal and lord. Whereas the code of *bushido* applied to both men and women of the *samurai* class, chivalry was followed only by the knights.

Occupying the lowest rank on the **medieval** European manor were serfs, whose labor provided the agricultural produce needed to maintain the self-sufficiency of the manor. The life of serfs was difficult. In addition to giving the lord part of their crops, they had to spend a number of days each month working the lord's lands or performing other types of labor service for the lord. The agricultural tools available to them were crude. Only after the invention of the heavy **moldboard plow** in the ninth century did they possess a tool adequate to turn the heavy sod of Western Europe. Serfdom was different from slavery; serfs could not be bought or sold and could pass on their property to their heirs.

Beginnings of Regional Governments

At the same time that feudalism provided protection to the inhabitants of Western Europe, people known as the Franks rose in prominence in the region of present-day northern France, western Germany, and Belgium. The Franks were the descendants of the Germanic tribe that overran Gaul (present-day France) after the fall of Rome. By the fifth century CE, the Franks had converted to Christianity. From the time of the ninth century onward, some areas of Western Europe saw the strengthening of regional kingdoms such as that of the Franks.

Rulers of northern Italy and Germany also gained prominence by the tenth century. Eventually, in an effort to connect with the classical empire of Rome, they began to call their territory the Holy Roman Empire. As the French philosopher Voltaire later commented, however, it was "neither holy, nor Roman, nor an empire." The new empire was but a fraction of the size of the original empire of the Romans. In spite of its grand claims, northern Italy continued to be organized into independent city-states, and Germany into numerous local states also overseen by feudal lords. While providing a measure of unity for a portion of Europe during the **Middle Ages**, the long-term political effect of the Holy Roman Empire was to delay the unification of both Germany and Italy into nation-states until the end of the nineteenth century.

In England, an alternative form of feudalism took hold as a result of the Norman invasion of 1066. In that year, the Duke of Normandy, later called William the Conqueror, arrived in England from his province of Normandy in northern France. Of Viking descent, William transplanted his form of feudalism to England. Rather than following a complex structure of lords and vassals, William imposed a feudal structure that required all vassals to owe their allegiance directly to the monarch.

Growth of Parliamentary Government in England

The political structure of medieval England further distinguished itself by imposing limitations on the power of the monarchy and establishing one of the earliest parliamentary governments. Even under the English style of feudalism, nobles continued to hold considerable influence. In 1215, in an effort to control the tax policies of King John, English nobles forced John to sign the *Magna Carta*. This document endowed the English nobility with basic rights that were later interpreted to extend to the other English social classes as well. The first English **parliament**, convened in 1265, also was an extension of feudal rights of collaboration between king and vassals. The first meeting of this representative body saw its division into a House of Lords representing the clergy and nobility and a House of Commons elected by urban elite classes. Parliaments also arose in Spain, France, Scandinavia, and parts of Germany.

Renewed Economic Growth

Although Western Europe experienced political disorder during the medieval period, by the ninth century the former Roman Empire began to witness signs of renewed economic growth and technological innovation. Contacts with the eastern portion of the former Roman Empire and with people of Central Asia had brought the moldboard plow into use in Western Europe. Also, the military effectiveness of the medieval knight was improved through the introduction of the stirrup.

Improved agricultural techniques resulted in population growth, a trend that also increased the size of urban areas. Warmer temperatures between 800 and 1300 also contributed to urban revival. Landlords often extended their landholdings, sometimes paying serfs a salary to work these new lands. A degree of security returned to Western Europe as many of the Vikings, now Christian, ceased their raids and became settled peoples. In present-day France, palace schools were established to educate local children.

The Crusades

The Crusades between the Western and Eastern worlds and between Christianity and Islam opened up new contacts. As a result of their campaigns to retake the Holy Land from the Seljuk Turks, Western Europeans were exposed to the larger and more prosperous urban areas of the Byzantine Empire with their magnificent examples of Eastern architecture. There was also a flowering of Romanesque architecture, forerunner to the Gothic, particularly visible in pilgrimage churches. The Crusades also introduced the West to sugarcane, spices, and luxury goods such as porcelain, glassware, and carpets from the Eastern world. Trade between East and West increased, although it proved an unbalanced trade; while the West was attracted to the fine goods of the East, the Eastern world displayed little interest in the inferior trade items offered by the West. Western appreciation for the treasures of the East was not universal, however. During the Fourth Crusade, merchants from Venice expressed their intense rivalry with Eastern merchants by looting the city of Constantinople.

As Western Europe widened its knowledge of other peoples through trade, its growing population also extended into neighboring areas. After settling down in Europe during the tenth century, the Vikings explored the northern Atlantic, inhabiting Iceland and establishing temporary settlements in Greenland and the northeastern portion of North America.

Seeking new agricultural lands, the people of Western Europe also pushed into areas of Eastern Europe.

Conflicts Between Church and State

While Western Europeans engaged in commercial rivalries with other societies, a second rivalry had developed in Western Europe: one between church leaders and monarchs. Throughout the Middle Ages, the church had sometimes taken the role of a feudal lord, owning large landholdings. In some cases, the growing wealth of the Roman Catholic Church served as a temptation for priests and monks to set aside their spiritual responsibilities to concentrate on the acquisition of material possessions.

Conflicts between church leaders and secular leaders arose over the issue of **investiture**. Lay investiture was a process by which monarchs appointed church bishops. Especially intense was the controversy between Pope Gregory VII (1073 to 1085) and Holy Roman Emperor Henry IV, which culminated with the **excommunication** of Henry IV. Henry's subsequent confession demonstrated that, in this instance, the pope had gained the upper hand.

Role of Women in Medieval European Society

Throughout the Middle Ages, Western European women carried out traditional roles of homemaker and childcare provider. It is possible that among the elite classes, the position of women declined over that of earlier ages as the code of chivalry reinforced ideas of women as weak and subordinate to men. Women who resided in medieval towns were allowed a few privileges such as participation in trade and in some craft guilds. Convents also offered some women opportunities for service in their communities. For the most part, however, medieval European women were expected to serve as reflections of their husbands or fathers.

High Middle Ages in Western Europe

By the eleventh century, significant changes occurred in Western Europe to indicate the region's gradual emergence from the relative cultural decline of the medieval period. Termed the High Middle Ages, the eleventh to the fifteenth centuries saw the following changes in Western European society:

- Gothic architecture—Cathedrals with tall spires and arched windows with stained glass reflected Muslim designs and Western architectural technology. They reflected the neo-Platonic ideal that urged reconciliation of pagan and Christian values and the belief that contemplation of beauty led to contemplation of the Divine.
- Increased urbanization—The size of Western European cities still could not compare with the much larger urban areas of China.
- Rise of universities (Bologna, Paris, Salamanca), primarily for the study of canon, or church, law.
- Decline in the number of serfs on the manor. Some serfs received wages to work in new agricultural lands, while others fled to towns. A serf who remained in a town for a year and a day and escaped capture by his lord was considered a free person.

- Black Death—or bubonic plague, brought by land and sea from Asia to Europe in the late 1340s; reduced the population by between 25 and 50 percent. Demand for labor put surviving serfs and peasants in a position to earn recompense at increasingly higher levels.
- Emergence of centralized monarchies.
- Strengthening of nation-states. The Hundred Years' War (1337 to 1453) increased the power of both France and England and is considered by many historians as the end of Europe's medieval period.
- Increased Eurasian trade.
- Growth of banking.
- New warfare technology such as gunpowder and cannon that made castles increasingly obsolete.

The renewal of economic and intellectual vigor and the tendency toward centralized regional political authority marked the beginning of a new era on the European continent.

› Rapid Review

The decline of Roman authority in Western Europe resulted in the rise of feudalism as a system of protection. Feudalism in Western Europe bore some similarities to Japanese feudalism. Although Western European feudalism created local governments, in some areas of Europe, such as France, regional kingdoms arose. Characteristic of feudal Europe was a persistent conflict between popes and kings concerning secular authority. Many European women continued in traditional roles. By the eleventh century, Western Europe demonstrated signs of revival as universities were established, trade increased, and some serfs began to leave the manor.

The focus of medieval Europe can be characterized by the "5 Cs":

- Church, and the Holy Roman Empire, which dominated society in Western Europe
- Chivalry, or the idea of a code of honor, followed by knights and characteristic of the first "standing armies"
- Crusades, which along with the goal of spreading Christianity and reclaiming the Holy Lands from the Seljuk Turks, resulted in an exchange of ideas, goods, the arts, and even diseases between East and West
- Commerce, which grew out of both the Crusades and the demographic shifts caused by the black plague and which led to a monetary economy
- Codes of law, including the Magna Carta (1215), which increased popular representation in government

Change might be considered a "sixth C," as encompassing the original "five Cs" and characterizing the era in general.

› Review Questions

1. Answer Parts A and B.
   (A) Identify TWO major changes in patterns of trade and their causes during the period between 600 and 1450 CE.
   (B) Explain how the Black Death contributed to the growth of a monetary economy.

Question 2 refers to the following passage.

The Song of Roland (anon., mid-eleventh century) lists the following elements that make up the knight's code of chivalry.

1. To fear God and maintain His Church
2. To serve the liege lord in valour and faith
3. To protect the weak and defenceless
4. To give succour to widows and orphans
5. To refrain from the wanton giving of offence
6. To live by honour and for glory
7. To despise pecuniary reward
8. To fight for the welfare of all
9. To obey those placed in authority
10. To guard the honour of fellow knights
11. To eschew unfairness, meanness and deceit
12. To keep faith
13. At all times to speak the truth
14. To persevere to the end in any enterprise begun
15. To respect the honour of women
16. Never to refuse a challenge from an equal
17. Never to turn the back upon a foe

2. Answer Parts A and B.
   (A) Identify and explain TWO elements of the code of chivalry that speak to the status of women.
   (B) Identify and explain ONE element that illustrates the power of the Church.

Questions 3 to 5 refer to the following passage.

During the fourteenth and fifteenth centuries, Europe pulled itself together. Nature helped as plagues pruned man's excessive numbers. Man helped, too, and his inventions show where he was going. Four wheeled wagons and square-rigged ships both moved and supplied ever larger concentrations of mankind. The cost of cannon and of the fortifications to withstand them outran the finances and defenses of the independent town and seigniory. Printing gave teaching . . . a uniformity essential for summoning unheard-of numbers for peace or war . . . As the luster of the medieval church dimmed, Europe's secular institutions began to shine ever more brightly . . . It is perhaps the unification of the practical and spiritual in the soul of each man, itself the very essence of later secularism, that is the greatest legacy of the later Middle Ages.

—John A. Garraty and Peter Gay, eds.
The Columbia History of the World, 1972

3. The phrase "ever larger concentrations of mankind" refers to which of the following processes?
   (A) Globalization
   (B) Specialization
   (C) Urbanization
   (D) Industrialization

4. Which of the following best follows medieval chronology?
   (A) Feudalism → parliamentarianism → manorialism → the Crusades
   (B) Manorialism → feudalism → the Crusades → parliamentarianism
   (C) Parliamentarianism → feudalism → manorialism → the Crusades
   (D) The Crusades → feudalism → manorialism → parliamentarianism

5. Secular institutions reflected which of the following medieval innovations?
   (A) Romanesque and Gothic architecture
   (B) Banking
   (C) Advanced wagons and ships
   (D) Universities

❯ Answers and Explanations

1A. Patterns of trade changed as technology (improved ship design, the magnetic compass, the moldboard plow) made passage of goods and exchanges of ideas between Asia and Europe more possible. The Crusades led to increased exchanges of goods as well among the Middle East, Asia Minor, and Europe. Increased urbanization, thanks to settlements along trade routes that served traveling merchants and under Mongol protection, also took place.

1B. The Black Death killed indiscriminately. When workers were required at harvest time, for example, a feudal lord who had lost a large number of serfs was forced to recruit labor for perhaps the first time, and to do that, he often had to pay wages.

2A. Since women were considered the "weaker sex," numbers 3 and 4 refer to their protection. Number 15 makes it clear that women were to be honored.

2B. The first element makes clear that the Church and its protection took top priority in the chivalric code. Numbers 2 and 12 refer to maintaining (religious) faith, while number 9 makes

clear the importance of obeying the powers-that-were.

3. **C** Urbanization was the result of concentrating people in one place. The key word in the question is "concentrations." Globalization (A), specialization (B), and nascent industrialization (D), while all ongoing or beginning during this era, did not involve the same kind of concentration.

4. **B** Manorialism gave rise to feudalism, and they were followed by the Crusades (the first one starting in 1095) and rudimentary parliamentarianism (post-1215). Answers A, C, and D are incorrect in that they are not chronologically ordered.

5. **D** Universities gave rise to urbanization (and the accompanying need for banking, for example) and a more secular power structure (within monarchies and parliaments). Romanesque and Gothic architecture (A) were not institutions and were religious; banking (B) followed the establishment of things like universities; and advanced wagons and ships (C) were also not institutions.

CHAPTER 13

Interregional Trade and Exchange

IN THIS CHAPTER

Summary: Between 600 CE and 1450, pre-existing patterns of contacts gradually increased and intensified through military conquest, migration, and especially trade. In Asia, the Tang and Song dynasties created the stability necessary to revitalize the Silk Road trade routes across Central Asia. Later, the Mongols in the region would facilitate not only trade but also the spread of technology and pathogens like bubonic plague. In sub-Saharan Africa, the migration of the Bantu people continued. Great Zimbabwe stands out as a trade network that remained localized. On the east coast of Africa, trade between the Bantu and Arab mariners from across the Indian Ocean resulted in a new language, Swahili, blending Bantu and Arab elements. A growing Islamic empire, dar-al-Islam, stretched from the Iberian Peninsula to northern India, integrating trade networks, including the trans-Saharan caravan routes, and encouraging the spread of Islam throughout Africa and South Asia. Coastal cities in India became commercial hubs, where merchants exchanged goods from Southeast Asia and China, India, Africa, and the Byzantine Empire. The eastern portion of the Roman Empire gradually lost territory to the Turks as Western Europe built upon Islamic and Greco-Roman traditions to forge a new society on the European continent.

KEY IDEA

Key Terms

age grade

astrolabe

Austronesian

Bantu-speaking peoples

Black Death

caravel

Catholic (Counter) Reformation

Hanseatic League

Humanism

kamikaze

Khan

lateen sail

Malay sailors

Maori

griots	metropolitan
Middle Kingdom	Reformation
Ming dynasty	stateless society
Mongol Peace	steppe diplomacy
perspective	syncretism
Renaissance	Yuan dynasty

Encounter and Exchange: Trans-Saharan Trade

Trans-Saharan trade expanded and intensified, partly due to Islamic control of North Africa. Dar-al-Islam, with its uniform currency, created an integrated commercial zone, whose merchants eventually sought to trade with kingdoms across the Sahara. These kingdoms, like Ghana and later Mali and Songhay, acted as middlemen, trading gold obtained from the south for textiles, pack animals, and salt. Trade cities emerged, like Timbuktu, Gao, and Jenne. To facilitate trade, kings and merchants often converted to Islam, though they continued indigenous religious practices as well, forming the basis of a syncretic religion. Typically, subjects were not encouraged to convert, limiting the extent to which Islam penetrated West African society. Later, Mansa Musa built mosques and established universities, making Timbuktu a center of trade and scholarship.

Encounter and Exchange: Silk Roads

Although this network of trade roads connecting Europe and Asia was established earlier, instability had resulted in a decline in its use. Roads and relay hostels or inns were built by Tang emperors for military and political purposes, but also benefited merchants. Tang economic innovations, like letters of credit (sometimes called "flying money") and paper currency, also promoted trade. (See Chapter 12.) Despite this, costs of overland travel were quite high, limiting trade to high-value items like silk, porcelain, gold, glass, and horses. Cities on the Silk Roads, like Chang'an, Samarkand, and Luoyang, expanded and flourished. Buddhist pilgrims and missionaries both continued to use the Silk Roads, though their presence in China varied depending on who was in power. While Buddhists were tolerated in the early Tang dynasty, later Tang rulers closed monasteries and expelled some Buddhists. The Mongols, discussed later, welcomed Buddhism, Islam, and other faiths.

Encounter and Exchange: Indian Ocean

Like the Silk Roads, Indian Ocean trade networks did not develop during this period, but the volume and frequency of trading voyages intensified. Sailors had long known about the seasonal patterns of monsoonal winds that enabled ships to travel back and forth across the ocean. Advances in maritime technology slowly spread throughout the region, including the magnetic compass from China, and, from India, the triangular lateen sail, which aided maneuverability in the open ocean. Larger ships, like the Arab dhows or the Chinese junks, could handle several hundred tons of cargo, making it more cost-effective to ship bulk goods for mass markets. The expansion of an Islamic empire (dar-al-Islam) created an integrated trading zone from India to the Iberian Peninsula. Islamic banks expanded, with branch offices issuing checks, or *sakk*, reducing the need for cash. Innovations in commerce allowed investors to pool their resources or rent cargo space, further encouraging trade.

East Africa

On the east coast of Africa, the Swahili people benefited from the intensification of trade. The Swahili language fuses Arabic and Bantu, a result of frequent contact with Arab merchants. Powerful city-states like Kilwa and Mogadishu emerged from coastal trading posts. They traded gold, ivory, and slaves from West Africa for porcelain, silk, and glassware from Asia. Trade led to social change, including development of a wealthy merchant class. Elites adopted Islam to facilitate trade with Muslim merchants but often kept their own religious traditions as well.

India

Trade in India centered in large, cosmopolitan port cities like Calicut, home to Persians, Jews, Arabs, Malaysians, and others. Centrally located, they served as clearing houses for goods from China (silk, porcelain, sugarcane), Southeast Asia (rice, spices), and Africa (gold, ivory, slaves). India also exported cotton textiles, leather, steel, pepper, and gems. Merchants exchanged goods in large warehouses known as emporia. The Indian caste system adapted to incorporate migrants and merchants, which helped them integrate into Indian society.

Southeast Asia

This region actively participated in Indian Ocean trade, either as agricultural producers (Angkor) or through control of the shipping lanes (Srivijaya). Hinduism and Buddhism were introduced to the region via Indian merchants, as was Islam around the twelfth century. These religions gained a foothold in the port cities catering to foreign merchants. Southeast Asian rulers and elites used trade to reinforce their positions and found certain Indian practices, like monarchy, to be advantageous. Certain aspects of Hinduism and Buddhism upheld monarchical systems and so were embraced by elites, though the people continued to practice their traditional religions. This is exemplified by a complex of temples at Angkor Wat, incorporating both Hindu and later Buddhist elements, using Southeast Asian architecture. Islam was slower to penetrate the region, at first adopted by some to facilitate trade or by a few inspired by Sufi mystics. By the 1400s, Melaka controlled the sea lanes. Its rulers, who had converted to Islam, used their influence to encourage the spread of Islam throughout the region.

China and Europe in the Indian Ocean

The disruption of overland trade routes fostered by the decline of Mongol power in Eurasia produced increased commercial vigor in the Indian Ocean. China's Ming dynasty (1368 to 1644) responded to the fall of the Yuan dynasty by a renewed focus on Indian Ocean trade. In the early fifteenth century, the Ming sent out massive expeditions into the Indian Ocean to display the glories of the **Middle Kingdom**. In addition to exploring the Indian Ocean, the Chinese expedition entered the Persian Gulf and the Red Sea, carrying with them Chinese porcelain and other luxuries to trade for local merchandise. The expeditions were led by Zheng He, a Chinese general of the Muslim faith.

In 1433, the voyages of Zheng He were abruptly called to an end by the Ming emperors. Confucian scholars had long resented the notoriety that Zheng He enjoyed by virtue of his voyages. To this resentment the Ming emperors now added fear of the cost of the expeditions, taking the opinion that the money would be better spent on resisting the continuing Mongol threat against China's borders and on constructing a new capital at Beijing.

Although China now returned to its more traditional policy of isolation, Ming emperors continued to engage in regional trade in Southeast Asia.

The Mongols

The Song dynasty was overcome in the thirteenth century by the Mongols, a society of pastoral nomads from the steppes of Central Asia. By the end of their period of dominance in the fifteenth century, the Mongols had conquered China, Persia, and Russia, controlling the largest land empire in history. In establishing their empire, the Mongols facilitated the flow of trade between Europe and Asia and brought bubonic plague to three continents.

Accomplished horsemen, the Mongols typified the numerous nomadic bands that migrated throughout Central Asia in search of grazing lands for their livestock. To supplement the meat and dairy products provided by their herds, the Mongols traded with settled agricultural peoples for grain and vegetables. The basic unit of Mongol society was the tribe; when warfare threatened, tribes joined together to form confederations. Although men held tribal leadership roles, Mongol women had the right to speak in tribal councils. Throughout their history, the Mongols were masters of the intrigues of **steppe diplomacy**, which involved alliances with other pastoral groups and the elimination of rivals, sometimes rivals within one's own family.

Early Mongol influence on China had begun as early as the twelfth century, when the Mongols defeated an army from Qin China sent to repel their advances. The leader credited with organizing the Mongols into an effective confederation was Temujin, who was renamed Chinggis Khan when he was elected the ultimate ruler, or **Khan**, of the Mongol tribes in 1206. A master at motivating the Mongol tribes, Chinggis Khan managed to break individual clan loyalties and construct new military units with allegiance to himself as their leader.

In addition to their unparalleled horsemanship, the Mongols became masters of the shortbow. Mongol contact with the Chinese also introduced them to other weapons of war such as the catapult, gunpowder, cannons, flaming arrows, and battering rams. By the time that Chinggis Khan died in 1227, the Mongols controlled an empire that extended from northern China to eastern Persia.

As they consolidated their empire, the Mongols were more preoccupied with collecting tribute than with administering their newly acquired territories. They were generally tolerant toward the religious beliefs and practices of the people they conquered and sometimes eventually adopted the dominant religion of their subject peoples.

Expansion of the Mongol Empire into Russia

The Mongol conquests continued after the death of Chinggis Khan, reaching Russia by 1237. From that year until 1240 the Mongols, or Tartars, as the Russians called them, executed the only successful winter invasions of Russia in history. Cities that resisted Mongol advances saw their inhabitants massacred or sold into slavery. The once-prosperous city of Kiev was burned to the ground. The effects of the Mongol occupation of Russia were numerous:

- Mongols set up a tribute empire called The Golden Horde.
- Serfdom arose as peasants gave up their lands to the aristocracy in exchange for protection from the Mongols.
- Moscow benefited financially by acting as a tribute collector for the Mongols. When neighboring towns failed to make their tribute payments, the princes of Moscow added their territory to the principality of Moscow.
- They strengthened the position of the Orthodox Church by making the **metropolitan**, or head of the Orthodox Church, the head of the Russian church.

- Mongol rule kept Russia culturally isolated from Western European trends such as the Renaissance. This isolation denied Russia opportunities to establish both commercial and cultural contacts with the West in a situation that fostered misunderstanding through the modern period.

After establishing their presence in Russia, the Mongols went on to their next goal: the conquest of Europe. After an attempted conquest of Hungary in 1240 and raids in Eastern Europe, the Mongols withdrew to handle succession issues in their capital of Karakorum in Mongolia. The proposed conquest of Europe never materialized.

Mongols in Persia

After abandoning their plans to add Europe to their empire, the Mongols turned to conquest within the world of Islam. In 1258, the city of Baghdad was destroyed and Persia added to the portion of the Mongol Empire known as the Ilkhanate. Among the approximately 800,000 people slaughtered in the capture of Baghdad was the Abbasid caliph. With his murder, the Islamic dynasty that had ruled Persia for about 500 years ended. Another group of Islamic peoples, the Seljuk Turks, had been defeated by the Mongols in 1243, weakening their dominance in Anatolia.

The Seljuqs (alternative spellings include Seljuk and Saljuq) were a Turkish people originating in the Central Asian steppes near the Aral Sea. The empire was founded by Tughril Beg, who, with his brother Chagri Beg, began migrating westward, using their strong cavalry to take control of parts of modern-day Afghanistan before moving into Persia. Tughril Beg claimed to be a Sultan (protector) of the Sunni Caliphate, a title that was confirmed by the Abbasid Caliph himself after Tughril Beg entered Baghdad and liberated the caliph in 1055. After that, the caliph remained a ceremonial figure, but real power was wielded by the Seljuq sultan and his viziers. From there, the Seljuqs under Tughril Beg's successor, Arp Arslan, invaded Anatolia, defeating the Byzantines at the Battle of Manzikert in 1071. Overburdened by taxes, many Byzantine peasants welcomed the Turks, who brought in Persian traditions and the Muslim faith. At its height, the Seljuq empire also extended into the Levant, prompting the Pope to heed the Byzantine emperor's request for protection and call for the First Crusade. Though the viziers tried to implement Persian administrative practices, the Seljuq empire was divided into mostly autonomous regions run by family members loyal to the sultan. Additionally, they imposed the *iqta* system of tax-farming, in which subjects were awarded responsibility for collecting taxes and maintaining a military in a parcel of land, keeping a portion of the taxes for themselves. This incentivized over-collection of taxes and underfinancing of the military, which limited the cohesiveness of the empire. Though Arabic remained the primary language of law, science, and theology, Persian became the primary language of government and culture, spreading into Anatolia. Seljuq sultans also constructed mosques and universities.

After the death of Malik Shah in 1092, rival claims resulted in the division of the empire. This contributed to its decline during the twelfth century as it contended with Crusaders in the west, Arabs in the south, and Mongols in the east. In addition, there were challenges from the Shi'a Fatimids in Egypt. Though some territory was regained, these victories were short-lived. The defeat of the Seljuqs resulted in a power vacuum and facilitated the conquest of Anatolia (present-day Turkey) by the Ottoman Turks in the fifteenth century. The Mongol threat to the Islamic world ended in 1260 at the hands of the Mamluks, or slaves, of Egypt.

Mongols in China

In China, the Mongols under the leadership of Kubilai Khan, a grandson of Chinggis Khan, turned their attention to the remnants of the Song Empire in the southern part of the country. By 1271, Kubilai Khan controlled most of China and began to refer to his administration of China as the **Yuan dynasty**. The Yuan dynasty would administer China until its overthrow by the **Ming dynasty** in 1368. Under Mongol rule:

- The Chinese were forbidden to learn the Mongol written language, which was the language of official records under the Yuan dynasty.
- Intermarriage between Mongols and Chinese was outlawed.
- The Chinese civil service examination was not reinstated.
- Religious toleration was practiced.
- Chinese were allowed to hold positions in local and regional governments.
- Mongol women enjoyed more freedoms than Chinese women, refusing to adopt the Chinese practice of footbinding. Mongol women also were allowed to move about more freely in public than were Chinese women. Toward the end of the Yuan dynasty, however, the increasing influence of Neo-Confucianism saw greater limits placed on Mongol women.
- The Yuan used the expertise of scholars and artisans from various societies.
- Foreigners were welcome at the Yuan court. Among visitors to the Mongol court were the Venetian Marco Polo and his family. Marco Polo's subsequent account of his travels, perhaps partially derived from other sources, increased European interest in exploring other lands.
- Merchants were accorded higher status in the Mongol administration than they had under the Chinese.
- The suppression of piracy furthered maritime trade.
- Attempts at expansion culminated in the unsuccessful invasions of Japan in 1274 and 1280 and a brief occupation of Vietnam. The attempted invasions of Japan were turned back by treacherous winds known to the Japanese as divine winds, or *kamikaze.*

By the mid-fourteenth century, the court of Kubilai Khan weakened as it became more concerned with the accumulation and enjoyment of wealth than with efficient administration. Banditry, famine, and peasant rebellion characterized the last years of the Yuan dynasty until their overthrow by a Chinese peasant who founded the Ming dynasty.

Impact of Mongol Rule on Eurasia

The most significant positive role of the Mongols was the facilitation of trade between Europe and Asia. The peace and stability fostered by the Mongol Empire, especially during the **Mongol Peace** of the mid-thirteenth to the mid-fourteenth centuries, promoted the exchange of products that brought increased wealth to merchants and enriched the exchange of ideas between East and West. Along the major trade routes, merchants founded diaspora communities that fostered cultural exchange. Among them were Jewish communities along the Silk Roads and the Mediterranean in addition to settlements of Chinese merchants in Southeast Asia. New trading posts and empires encouraged European peoples to later invest in voyages of exploration.

Long-distance travel increased. Ibn Battuta, a Moroccan Muslim scholar, traveled throughout the Muslim world, including Central Asia, China, Southeast Asia, Spain, and East Africa. His journal, as well as the writings of Marco Polo, became valuable resources in the study of cultural exchange in the thirteenth and fourteenth centuries.

Another exchange brought about unintentionally by the Mongols proved devastating to Europe, Asia, and Africa: the spread of the bubonic plague. It is possible that the plague entered Mongol-controlled territories through plague-infested fleas carried by rats that helped themselves to the grain in Mongol feedsacks. The bubonic plague, known also in Europe as the **Black Death**, spread across the steppes of Central Asia to China, where it contributed to the weakening and eventual fall of the Yuan dynasty. In the mid-fourteenth century, the plague also spread throughout the Middle East, North Africa, and Europe. The disease followed Eurasian and African trade routes as merchants carried it from city to city and port to port. As many as 25,000,000 people may have died from plague in China, and Europe lost about one-third of its population; the Middle East also suffered a large death toll. Significant loss of life among Western European serfs helped deal a final blow to manorialism in that region. Some plague-devastated areas required 100 years or more to recover population losses and economic and urban vigor.

Further Nomadic Influences

With the decrease of Mongol dominance in Eurasia came a final nomadic thrust by Timur the Lame, or Tamerlane, a Turk from Central Asia. Although his capital city at Samarkand was noted for architectural beauty, his conquests were known only for their incredible brutality. From the mid-1300s until his death in 1405, Tamerlane spread destruction across Persia, Mesopotamia, India, and a part of southern Russia. His death marked the final major thrust of nomadic peoples from Central Asia into Eurasia.

Encounter and Exchange in Africa: The Bantu Migrations

Sub-Saharan Africa witnessed an exchange of ideas, technology, and language through the migrations of the Bantu-speaking peoples. About 2000 BCE, small numbers of agrarian peoples from the edge of the rainforest in present-day Nigeria began migrating from their homeland, perhaps as a result of population pressures. The migrations escalated throughout the period from 500 BCE to 1000 CE and continued until about 1500 CE.

As the Bantu peoples migrated southward and eastward throughout sub-Saharan Africa, they spread the knowledge of the agricultural techniques that they brought from their homeland. Following the course of the Congo River, they farmed the fertile land along riverbanks at the edges of the rainforest. Their contacts with foraging peoples of Central Africa taught them the techniques of cattle raising. As they migrated, the Bantu also spread the knowledge of ironworking. Historians are unsure whether their skills in ironworking were learned from previous contact with the ironworkers of Kush or were acquired by independent innovation. Whatever the reason, the spread of iron agricultural implements facilitated crop cultivation throughout sub-Saharan Africa.

The Bantu acquired an additional source of nutrition with the arrival of the banana on the African continent. Carried from Southeast Asia through the Indian Ocean to Madagascar by the **Malay sailors** about 400 CE, the banana reached the African continent through interactions between the descendants of the Malay sailors and African peoples. After its arrival on the African continent, the banana spread throughout sub-Saharan Africa in a reverse pattern to that of the migratory Bantu. Today, the inhabitants of Madagascar speak a language belonging to the same **Austronesian** linguistic group as Malaysian tongues.

Interactions in East Africa

The Bantu migrations also resulted in the spread of the Bantu languages. By the thirteenth century, the Bantu had reached the eastern coast of Africa, where they came into contact with Arab traders. The interactions between the two groups of people forged the **syncretism** of the Bantu and Arabic languages into the Swahili tongue. Swahili remains a major African language to the present.

Bantu Society and Government

The Bantu also contributed their social and political organization to the heritage of sub-Saharan Africa. With the village as the basis of Bantu society, **stateless societies** emerged as the political organization of the Bantu. Stateless societies were organized around family and kinship groups led by a respected family member. Religion was animistic, with a belief in spirits inhabiting the natural world. Early Bantu societies did not have a written language; oral traditions were preserved by storytellers called *griots*.

Bantu society centered around the **age grade**, a cohort group that included tribal members of the same age who shared life experiences and responsibilities appropriate to their age group. Woman's role as a childbearer was highly respected, and women shared in agricultural work, trade, and sometimes military duties. All property was held communally; individual wealth was determined not by the acquisition of property but by the acquisition of slaves.

Rise of Western Europe

As the Chinese withdrew from world commercial dominance, the nations of Western Europe stepped in to fill the void. By the 1400s, European regional monarchies possessed the political power and financial resources to allow them to investigate the world beyond their borders. European technology had become more sophisticated, and commercial activity in urban areas contributed to its financial stability. European visitors to the Mongol court learned of advances in Asian technology such as the printing press, gunpowder, and the magnetic compass.

In spite of the increased economic vitality enjoyed by Europeans in the early modern era, there remained a serious imbalance of trade between Europe and the East. Although many Europeans craved the luxury goods of the East, Europe offered very few products attractive to the peoples of the East. Europe's trade goods consisted mainly of items such as wool, honey, salt, copper, tin, and animals for Eastern zoos. The unfavorable balance of trade between Europe and the East meant that Europeans frequently had to pay for their luxury items in gold, a situation that drained Europe of its gold supply.

Although Europe experienced an unfavorable balance of trade with the East, several trading cities in northern Europe capitalized on regional commerce and formed the **Hanseatic League**. By the thirteenth century, this trade association was active in the Baltic and North Sea regions. Eventually both the Hanseatic League and Italian ships from Mediterranean waters extended their commercial activity to the manufacturing centers of Flanders.

The Renaissance

By the beginning of the fifteenth century, the city-states of northern Italy were experiencing a renewed interest in the learning and artistic styles of the Greco-Roman world. This rebirth of learning, or **Renaissance**, owed its origins partly to interactions with the Muslim world. European contacts with the Middle East during the Crusades, the preservation of Greco-Roman learning and scientific advancements by the Muslims during their occupation of Spain, and Islamic and European interactions in the weakening Byzantine Empire invigorated the revival of learning and trade characteristic of the Renaissance. Furthermore, the northern Italian city-states had become wealthy from their role in supplying goods for the Crusaders and in transporting them across the waters of the Mediterranean.

The Renaissance spirit differed from that of the European Middle Ages by focusing on life in this world rather than in the afterlife (humanism). Many Renaissance paintings continued to feature religious subjects; but, at the same time, there was an additional emphasis on paintings of people and nature. Renaissance painting also was characterized by the use of **perspective**, a greater variety of colors, and the use of oil paint on canvas.

In the Late Renaissance, the Reformation would give rise to Protestantism, and the Catholic, or Counter, Reformation would solidify the Roman Catholic Church's theological stances (see Chapter 19).

Early European Explorations

By the early 1400s, European explorations outside the Mediterranean had been primarily confined to the Atlantic islands of the Azores, Madeiras, and the Canaries. Europeans also had carried out some explorations along the western coast of Africa. Lack of European technological expertise prevented further explorations into the waters of the Atlantic. Contacts with Chinese and Arab merchants introduced Europeans to the magnetic compass, the **astrolabe**, and the **caravel**, a lighter vessel with a **lateen sail** and a steerable rudder.

Voyages of exploration soon changed focus to colonization as Spain and Portugal settled the Canary and Madeira Islands and the Azores. The crop initially grown on these islands was sugar, which had been introduced to Europeans by Middle Eastern peoples during the Crusades. Slaves were brought from northwestern Africa to work the plantations.

Oceania

Two regions that by 1450 remained outside the global network were the Americas and Oceania. (The Americas will be discussed in Chapter 15.) After 600 CE, the peoples of Polynesia were involved in migration and expansion from island to island in the Pacific. From their base in the islands of Fiji, Samoa, and Tahiti, Polynesians in canoes sailed northward to the uninhabited islands of Hawaii. For several centuries, Polynesians continued to spread throughout the Hawaiian Islands, establishing agricultural and fishing villages. Inhabitants set up regional kingdoms with a highly stratified class system.

About 1200, another group of Polynesians migrated to the islands of present-day New Zealand. The **Maori**, as these migrants came to be called, learned to adapt to the colder environment of their new home. The Maori set up a stratified society that included slaves.

› Rapid Review

Hemispheric trade accelerated and intensified along previously established trade routes. Empires facilitated trade, either intentionally (e.g., China's "flying money," the Mongols, uniform currency in dar-al-Islam) or incidentally (e.g., roads and inns built by Tang emperors). Though new trade-based kingdoms emerged, like Ghana and Mali, this era is generally associated with the emergence of trade cities like Kilwa, Timbuktu, Calicut, Samarkand, and Chang'an. Housing diasporic merchant communities of Jews, Christians, Muslims, and others, the cities served as centers of cultural, religious, and intellectual exchange. Trade led to, and in turn was enhanced by, technological diffusion (paper, gunpowder), especially maritime advances (e.g., compass, astrolabe, lateen sail) from China, which spread to the Indian Ocean and later to Europe. Trade precipitated cultural changes, too. Caste systems in India adapted to incorporate foreigners and merchants. Access to rare luxury goods reinforced elite classes. Contact with Muslim merchants led to syncretic languages (e.g., Swahili) and religions (e.g., Islam with traditional religions in Africa). New styles of architecture evolved that blended traditions (e.g., African mosques, Angkor Wat).

One of the most significant forces in history throughout the mid-fifteenth century was the movement of the Mongols into Russia, the Middle East, and China. While they were responsible for the massacre of hundreds of thousands of peoples who resisted them, especially in the Middle East, the Mongols deserve credit for forging strong trade connections between Europe and Asia. While the Mongols were establishing their presence in Eurasia, the Bantu-speaking peoples were continuing their migrations throughout sub-Saharan Africa, spreading the knowledge of agriculture and ironworking. Their contacts with Arabs in eastern Africa gave birth to a new language: Swahili. In the Indian Ocean, China engaged in massive expeditions, which were abruptly halted about the time that Europe entered the global trade network. Still outside the global network were Polynesia and the Americas. The inhabitants of Polynesia and the Americas interacted with other peoples in their own regions.

❯ Review Questions

1. Answer Parts A and B.
   (A) Identify TWO differences between Mongol rule in China and Mongol rule in Russia.
   (B) Identify ONE change, and its cause, in the status of women under Mongol rule in China.

2. Answer Parts A and B.
   (A) Give TWO examples of Bantu influence on Central and East Africa.
   (B) Identify the Bantu role in linguistic syncretism.

3. How did the Crusades, religious in nature, contribute to Renaissance secular humanistic ideals?
   (A) They spread Mongol technological advances.
   (B) They preserved Greco-Roman learning.
   (C) They focused on this life rather than the afterlife.
   (D) They indirectly financed economic and secular growth and influence.

4. For what reason might the Islamic reign in Spain, or the Iberian Peninsula (711–1492), be called the "first Western Renaissance"?
   (A) Because of the secularization of Iberian society
   (B) Because of the preservation of ancient texts and traditions
   (C) Because of the institution of Islamic legal systems
   (D) Because of the investigation of monarchical structures

5. Which of the following changes most characterized the voyages of exploration during the early modern era?
   (A) Trade gave way to missionary work.
   (B) Trade gave way to colonization.
   (C) Trade gave way to exploration.
   (D) Trade gave way to technological advances.

› Answers and Explanations

1A. In Russia, the Mongols were more involved in profiting from tribute and trade than in administering the people; in China, the Mongols established the Yuan dynasty to rule. Also in China, the Mongols encouraged the use of foreign advisors. The Mongols protected Chinese and Eurasian trade routes, but kept Russia isolated from Western European trade routes.

1B. The status of women in China, for Chinese women, changed little or not at all during Mongol rule. Mongol women in China, while not subjected to footbinding and being allowed to move about more freely in society, lost many of their freedoms with the rise of Neo-Confucianism.

2A. Bantu influences on Central and East Africa included exchanges of ideas and language; introduction of agricultural techniques and cattle raising; introduction of ironworking; social and political stateless societies, organized around family and kinship groups; property held in common; and without a written language, the oral tradition of storytelling (via *griots*) to preserve their history.

2B. The Bantu language mixed with Arabic and resulted in the creation of Swahili, one of the major languages in present-day Africa.

3. **D** By opening up exchanges of ideas and goods and encouraging urbanization in places that supplied and maintained armies, the Crusades financed nonreligious enterprises. They did not spread Mongol technological advances (A) or preserve Greco-Roman learning (B), and their goals were ostensibly religious and thus concerned with the afterlife (C).

4. **B** Islamic Spain contributed to the collection, preservation, and translation of classical texts and traditions by establishing public libraries and schools of translation, among other centers of learning. It encouraged the Renaissance, or rebirth, of ancient mores, ideals, and intellectual systems. Islamic Spain was religious (A) but tolerant of other faiths. It was not known for instituting legal systems (C) or researching monarchical structures (D).

5. **B** Initially voyages of exploration focused on trade and the discovery of goods that would enrich both voyagers and their sponsors. To control economic rewards and exploit resources, voyagers began to colonize around the globe. While missionaries (A), explorers (C), and scientists and engineers (D) accompanied many expeditions, their work was not often the primary focus.

Hemispheric Exchange

IN THIS CHAPTER

Summary: The period from 1450 to 1750 was one of increased global exchange. While some regions such as China gradually withdrew from long-distance trade, the volume of trade in the Indian Ocean increased with the entry of Europeans into waters that already saw bustling commercial activity among Indian, Muslim, and African peoples. To the trade of the Eastern Hemisphere were added vast interchanges between the Eastern and Western Hemispheres across the Atlantic Ocean.

Key Terms

capitalism   factor
caravel   Northwest Passage
Columbian Exchange

Trading Companies

As European nation-states grew more powerful and involved in colonial expansion, their governments formed trading companies. The governments of Spain, the Netherlands, England, and France gave regional monopolies to these companies. Among the two most prominent companies were the British East India Company, which concentrated on trade in India and North America, and the Dutch East India Company, which focused on trade with Indonesia. With the origin of the great trading companies came increased consumption of Eastern products such as coffee, tea, and sugar. The growth of trade and commerce fostered the growth of **capitalism**, an economic system that is based on the private ownership of property and on investments with the hope of profit.

European Explorations

Technological inventions such as the **caravel**, magnetic compass, and astrolabe, adopted from the Eastern world by the Europeans in the early fifteenth century, facilitated the entrance of Europe into expeditions of exploration. Portugal had already sailed along the western coast of Africa in the early fifteenth century, trading gold and crude iron pots for spices and slaves. The voyage of Vasco da Gama around the Cape of Good Hope to India in 1498 broke the Muslim and Italian monopolies on trade with the Middle East, East Asia, and Southeast Asia. One Portuguese expedition was blown off course and landed in Brazil, giving Portugal a claim to territory in the Western Hemisphere. The Portuguese continued their commercial interests by setting up forts and trading posts on the eastern African coast and also in India at the port of Goa. Portugal also traded in the port of Malacca in Indonesia. From the Chinese port of Macao it entered into trade between Japan and China.

Columbus's rediscovery of the Americas for Spain in 1492 was followed by the Magellan expedition's circumnavigation of the globe, which gave Spain claim to the Philippine Islands. In the sixteenth century, the states of northern Europe joined in voyages of exploration. The defeat of the Spanish Armada by the English navy in 1588 made England the foremost naval power among the European nations.

Both the French and the British turned their attentions to North America, creating rivalries that erupted in warfare in the latter part of the eighteenth century. In 1534, France claimed present-day Canada. In the seventeenth century, the French established settlements and fur-trading outposts in the Ohio and Mississippi River valleys. During the sixteenth century, the British had explored the Hudson Bay area of North America in search of a **Northwest Passage** to the Indies. In the seventeenth century, England established colonies along the east coast of North America to provide the raw materials and markets that were a part of its mercantilist policy.

The Netherlands, which had recently won its independence from Spain, set up colonies in North America and, for a brief time, in Brazil. The Dutch demonstrated their power in the Indian Ocean by removing the Portuguese competition in Indonesia in the early seventeenth century. In 1652, they established Cape Colony, a settlement at the southern tip of Africa, using it primarily as a supply station for ships sailing to Indonesia.

The Columbian Exchange

The voyages of Columbus to the Americas initiated a system of exchange between the Eastern and Western Hemispheres that had a major impact on the Atlantic world. The **Columbian Exchange** was a trade network that exchanged crops, livestock, and diseases between the two hemispheres. Tobacco was introduced to the Eastern Hemisphere. American food crops such as maize and sweet potatoes spread to China and parts of Africa. White potatoes spread to Europe, and manioc to Africa. The introduction of new food crops tended to boost population growth in the Eastern Hemisphere. Coffee, sugarcane, wheat, rice, and bananas made their way across the Atlantic from the Eastern to the Western Hemisphere. The indigenous people of the Americas, however, were largely uninterested in the food crops introduced by Europeans. Sugarcane cultivation was eventually transferred to Brazil and the Caribbean islands, and raw sugar was sold to the Eastern Hemisphere.

The Columbian Exchange brought livestock such as cattle, horses, sheep, and pigs to the Americas. The horse revolutionized the lifestyle of the nomadic Plains Indians of North America by facilitating the hunting of buffalo.

Epidemic disease also found its way to the Americas through the Columbian Exchange. Prior to the voyages of Columbus, the peoples of the Americas had lived in virtual isolation from the rest of the world, a situation that prevented their exposure to the diseases of the populations of the Eastern Hemisphere. When Europeans arrived in the Americas, they brought with them common diseases to which the Native Americans had developed no immunity: diseases such as smallpox, measles, tuberculosis, and influenza. Within 50 years after the voyages of Columbus, approximately 90 percent of American native peoples had died, most of them from epidemic disease.

Patterns of World Trade

By the seventeenth century, Europeans had established ports in East Asia, Southeast Asia, India, and the west coast of Africa. In general, involvement in international trade positively affected local and regional economies. In areas where direct trade was not possible, Europeans negotiated special economic rights. In Russia, Western European shippers known as **factors** established agencies in Moscow and St. Petersburg. In the Ottoman Empire, Western European traders formed colonies within the city of Constantinople where they were granted commercial privileges.

Regions Outside the World Trade System

Until the eighteenth century, large regions of the world lay outside the international trade system. China relied primarily on regional trade, channeling most of its commercial activity through the port of Macao. One reason for China's limits on trade with Europe was disinterest in European products. As a result, Europeans paid for the few items they purchased from China with silver, which was the basis of the Chinese economy. England and the Netherlands compensated for the expense of acquiring fine Chinese porcelain by developing their own porcelain modeled after Chinese patterns. Tokugawa Japan also prohibited foreign trade except for limited commercial activity with the Dutch and Chinese through the port of Nagasaki.

Other world regions carried on only limited long-distance trade. Russia traded primarily with the nomads of Central Asia until the eighteenth century, when it began trading grain to the West. The Ottomans, who dismissed the impact of European technology, showed little enthusiasm for trade with the West. Mughal India encouraged trade with the West but was more preoccupied with imperial expansion. Whereas some trading ports were established by Europeans along Africa's west coast, Europeans were deterred from entering the continent by the risk of contracting malaria and by the lack of navigable rivers.

› Rapid Review

The increased level of exchange between the Eastern and Western Hemispheres began with the voyages of Columbus. Crops, livestock, and diseases changed the demographics on both sides of the Atlantic. Colonies furthered the interchange between the two hemispheres. Some areas such as Japan and China remained largely outside global trade networks, whereas regions such as Russia and the Ottoman Empire concentrated on regional trade.

› Review Questions

Questions 1 to 3 refer to the following image, which shows an early interaction between Europeans and Native Americans. The Native Americans are handing the Europeans a variety of items, including food.

1. Which would be the most appropriate caption for this image?
   (A) The Middle Passage
   (B) The Triangular Trade
   (C) The Mita System
   (D) The Columbian Exchange

2. How did Native Americans eventually benefit from interactions like this?
   (A) Adopting European weapons allowed them regional dominance.
   (B) Adopting metalwork and horses resulted in increased crop yields.
   (C) The introduction of smallpox decimated their population.
   (D) The introduction of maize to the Americas increased reliability of crops.

3. What was the impact of interactions like these on Europe?
   (A) The introduction of diseases from the Americas greatly reduced the population.
   (B) New crops from the Americas led to sharp population growth.
   (C) Insects from the Americas eradicated many staple foods, causing famine.
   (D) New drugs from the Americas led to social and economic unrest.

4. What is the term for a system in which land, labor, and capital are owned and controlled by private individuals?
   (A) Capitalism
   (B) Socialism
   (C) Mercantilism
   (D) Communism

5. Which statement is most accurate about trade during the era 1450 to 1750?
   (A) Trade networks were primarily regional in nature.
   (B) Europeans excluded Muslim regions from trade.
   (C) Trade was global, incorporating all major continents.
   (D) Trade was hemispheric, mostly excluding the South Pacific.

› Answers and Explanations

1. **D** The image reflects the exchange of goods between the Americas and Europeans that characterized the Colombian Exchange system. The Triangular Trade refers more specifically to the trade networks that developed among Europe, Africa, and the Americas, rather than to the exchange of goods themselves (B). The Middle Passage refers to the middle leg of the trade network, characterized by trade in slaves, not reflected in the image (A). The *mita* system was a system of coercive labor that developed in the Spanish colonies, not an exchange of goods (D).

2. **B** One could argue that Native Americans benefited from these interactions in that they were introduced to more efficient agricultural techniques, like using horses and metal tools to increase crop yields. These gains were offset by their eventual domination by European colonial powers (A) and the huge mortality rate due to exposure to European diseases like smallpox (C). Finally, maize was native to the Americas and not introduced by Europeans (D).

3. **B** The Colombian Exchange meant new crops that could be grown under different conditions and that provided a broader range of nutrients, leading to better nutrition and population growth. Though there has been controversy over whether syphilis may have originated in the Americas, the most recent research suggests that it did not. Diseases from the Americas were not

a factor (A). Likewise, there is no evidence that insects from the Americas had any impact on Europe's crops (C). Though there were drugs native to the Americas, like tobacco, that were exported to Europe, these were not associated with any social unrest (D).

4. **A** The system in which the means of production (land, labor and capital) are owned by private individuals is capitalism. In socialism, the means of production (at least for key industries) are owned by the governing body and operated for the benefit of all citizens (B). Communism is considered a higher stage of socialism, in which class distinctions disappear and workers own and operate the means of production for the benefit of all. Instead of wages, citizens are provided with benefits (income, goods) based on their need (D). Mercantilism is an economic policy in which nations try to maximize their wealth by maintaining a favorable balance of trade, often using colonies to do so (C).

5. **D** Though most trade networks started as regional phenomena, this had not been true since at least 600 CE, well before this era (A). Muslims had been integrated into European trade through sea (Indian Ocean) and overland routes (Silk Road) well before this period also (B). However, trade was not truly global in this period, as Oceania and the continent of Australia were still not integrated into the trade networks (C).

CHAPTER 15

Systems of Slavery

IN THIS CHAPTER

Summary: As the Columbian Exchange united the Eastern and Western Hemispheres across the Atlantic Ocean, the exchange of human beings created a new interaction between Africa and the Western Hemisphere. Slave systems, already a part of life in African kingdoms, became a part of life in the Western world. The result was the unification of three cultures—African, European, and American—in the Americas.

KEY IDEA

Key Terms

impressment
indentured servitude

Middle Passage
triangular trade

Beginnings of the Atlantic Slave Trade

Portugal's quest for gold and pepper from African kingdoms brought it into contact with systems of slave trade already in existence in Africa. The subsequent development of the trans-Atlantic slave trade was an extension of trade in human beings already carried out by Africans enslaving fellow Africans. The slave trade within Africa especially valued women slaves for use as household servants or as members of the harem.

The long-existent trans-Saharan trade had already brought some African slaves to the Mediterranean world. In the mid-fifteenth century, Portugal opened up direct trade with sub-Saharan Africa. Portuguese and Spanish interests in the slave trade increased when they set up sugar plantations on the Madeira and Canary Islands and on São Tomé. The first slaves from Africa arrived in Portugal in the mid-1400s. Europeans tended to use Africans as household servants.

Trade in gold, spices, and slaves brought the Portuguese into contact with prosperous and powerful African kingdoms, among them Kongo, Benin, Mali, and Songhay. Mali and Songhay had already become wealthy Muslim kingdoms enriched by the trans-Saharan gold-salt trade that had been in existence for centuries. In Kongo and Benin, Portugal was interested in Christianizing the inhabitants in addition to establishing trade relations. In the late fifteenth century, the rulers of Kongo had converted to Christianity; a few years later the nonruling classes were also converted.

Characteristics of African Kingdoms

Many of the African kingdoms encountered by the Portuguese had developed their own political and court traditions. African monarchs often ruled with the assistance of governing councils and had centralized governments with armies that carried out the state's expansionist policies. Artisans produced works in ivory and ebony and, in Benin, also in bronze. Active trade existed not only in slaves but also in spices, ivory, and textiles. Slaves usually were prisoners of war or captives from African slave raids that were carried out against neighboring kingdoms and villages.

Trans-Atlantic Slave Trade

After Native Americans died in phenomenal numbers from European diseases, European colonists in the Americas turned to Africans as forced labor. West Africans, already skilled in agricultural techniques, were especially sought by Europeans for labor on the sugar plantations of Brazil and the Caribbean and in the rice fields of the southern colonies of British North America. The trans-Atlantic slave trade reached its peak during the eighteenth century. The slave trade was part of a **triangular trade** that involved three segments:

- European guns and other manufactured goods were traded to Africans for slaves. (Guns were then used by Africans to capture more slaves.)
- Slaves were transported from Africa to South America or the West Indies. This **Middle Passage** across the Atlantic placed the slaves in shackles in overcrowded and unsanitary slave ships.
- Sugar, molasses, and rum produced by slave labor were traded to Europe for manufactured goods, and the cycle resumed.

Slaves who crossed the Atlantic came from western and central Africa, particularly from Senegambia, Dahomey, Benin, and Kongo. As many as 25 percent of the slaves who came from Central Africa died on the long march to the coast to be loaded onto slave ships. Perhaps 20 percent of slaves died on the Middle Passage from illness or suicide. If supplies ran low aboard ship, some slaves were thrown overboard.

Of the approximately 9 to 11 million slaves who crossed the Atlantic, only about 5 percent reached the colonies of British North America. Most of the slaves who eventually reached North America did not arrive directly from Africa, but first spent some time in the West Indies in the Caribbean Sea. The rigors of sugar production in the Caribbean islands and in Brazil required especially large numbers of slaves.

Once in the Americas, African slaves blended their culture with that of the Western Hemisphere. Particularly noteworthy was their introduction of African religions to the Americas. Slaves from West Africa often continued to practice Islam in addition to native African beliefs, while others created a syncretism of native African practices and beliefs and those of Christianity.

Slavery in Eastern and Southern Africa

Not all slave routes originating in Africa crossed the Atlantic or led to Europe. The cities of eastern Africa traded with the interior of the continent for gold, ivory, and slaves. Many of these slaves were transported to the Middle East, where they became household servants or members of harems. Other slaves in the Indian Ocean system were used on European plantations on islands in the Indian Ocean. Africans from the Swahili coast, Arabs, and Indians also set up plantation colonies along the eastern coast of Africa and on the islands of the Indian Ocean.

In southern Africa, the Cape Colony established by the Dutch in 1652 depended on slave labor. The first slaves arrived from Indonesia and Asia, but later the Dutch enslaved Africans.

Effects of the Slave Trade on Africa

The African slave trade profoundly altered the demographics of Africa. Family life was disrupted as more males than females were transported across the Atlantic for the heavy work required on plantations. In some areas of Africa, populations were reduced by one-half. The slave trade increased African dependency on the importation of European technology, lessening the technological development of African kingdoms.

Other Forms of Servitude

In addition to their involvement in both the Mediterranean and trans-Atlantic slave trades, Europeans used other forms of servitude such as **impressment** and **indentured servitude**. Impressment involved the seizure of sailors from foreign vessels. Indentured servants were required to work for a master for a specific number of years in exchange for passage to a European colony such as the English colonies of northeastern North America.

› Rapid Review

Europeans did not initiate the African slave trade but tapped into slave trade systems already in place. Europeans involved in the slave trade encountered wealthy and powerful African kingdoms. Although the main focus of the African slave trade in the seventeenth and eighteenth centuries occurred across the Atlantic, there also was an active slave trade in the Indian Ocean. The slave trade significantly reduced the populations of some areas of Africa, created a dependence on European goods, and in turn hampered African economic development.

› Review Questions

Questions 1 and 2 refer to the following passage.

The Atlantic slave trade, however, was not the only slave trade within Africa. Nearly as many Africans were exported across the Sahara Desert, the Red Sea and the Indian Ocean from 650 A.D. to 1900 as were shipped across the Atlantic. Islamic traders probably exported 10 million slaves into northern Africa, Arabia, Yemen, Iraq, Iran, and India. In addition, it now seems clear that during the era of the Atlantic slave trade, many and perhaps most of the enslaved were kept in Africa. It is imaginable that as many as 60 million Africans died or were enslaved as a result of these various slave trades.

The level of slave exports to the New World grew from about 36,000 a year in the early eighteenth century to almost 80,000 a year during the 1780s. By 1750, slavers usually contained at least 400 slaves, with some carrying more than 700.

—Steven Mintz, digitalhistory.uh.edu, 2016

1. Using information from the passage and your knowledge of the slave trade, decide which of the following accounted for the growth in the number of slaves being shipped to the New World in the 1700s.
   (A) An increased need for domestic servants
   (B) Ships with larger carrying capacities
   (C) Economic growth in the West Indies and the United States
   (D) Independence of the United States from Great Britain

2. According to the passage, where did the largest number of enslaved Africans eventually end up?
   (A) Arabia
   (B) The New World
   (C) The Middle East
   (D) Africa

3. Syncretism is best seen in which of the following practices?
   (A) Adaptation of clothing to climatic conditions
   (B) Use of new spices in native African cooking
   (C) Conversion of many native Africans to Islam
   (D) Adaptation of Catholic ritual to include African traditions

4. Answer Parts A and B.
   (A) Identify TWO systems of servitude current between 1450 and 1750.
   (B) Explain ONE difference between two systems of servitude identified in Part A.

Question 5 refers to the following map.

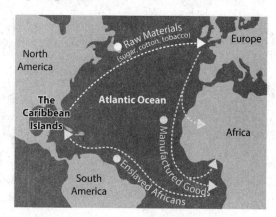

5. What effect did the European importation of raw materials and export of manufactured goods as part of the triangular trade have on African economic development?
   (A) They encouraged production of local goods.
   (B) They increased African trade networks.
   (C) They reduced the number of unmarried females.
   (D) They stopped local industrial development.

› Answers and Explanations

1. **C** As the West Indies and British North America increased production of plantation products (sugar, molasses, rum, cotton), the need for slave labor also increased. The main call for domestic slave labor (A) in the West Indies and British North America was never the primary impetus to the slave trade. While ships increased carrying capacities (B), this was a response to, not a cause of, the need for increased labor. Independence of America from Great Britain (D) was not a determining factor in increased slave labor requirements.

2. **D** The largest numbers of slaves stayed in Africa, not in Arabia (A), the New World (B), or the Middle East (C).

3. **D** Syncretism indicates a blending of elements from two cultures or traditions and was evident in modification of Church rituals to incorporate African music, language, dance, and prayer. Adapting to another situation or tradition (A, B, C) is not evidence of syncretism.

4. **A** Between 1450 and 1750, in addition to slavery, impressment (essentially the kidnapping of able-bodied men who were put to work, frequently as sailors) and indentured servitude were common.

   B Slavery offered little to no hope of eventual freedom. Slaves were purchased and became the permanent property of the buyer. Indentured servitude carried a time limit, and indentured servants could see eventual freedom.

5. **D** By removing raw materials from Africa, Europeans could produce manufactured goods that in turn could be sold back to Africans. Thus, there was no need, and no chance, for Africans to produce manufactured goods. Local industrial development had neither raw materials to work with nor, frequently, the manpower to staff local business. A, B, and C are irrelevant.

CHAPTER 16

Expansion of China

IN THIS CHAPTER

Summary: The political disorder following the collapse of the Han dynasty was reversed by the establishment of centralized government under the Sui dynasty (589 to 618 CE). The brief period of Sui rule was followed by the powerful Tang (618 to 907 CE) and Song (960 to 1279 CE) dynasties. Although the era of the Tang was characterized by trade and agricultural expansion, that of the Song produced significant technological advances. At the same time, the Song emphasized Chinese tradition, including the patriarchal family and Confucian teachings.

Key Terms

abacus	kowtow
bakufu	Neo-Confucianism
bushi	*samurai*
bushido	scholar-gentry
celadon	*seppuku*
daimyo	serf
flying money	Shinto
footbinding	*shogun*
Gempei Wars	shogunate
Grand Canal	tea ceremony
junks	tribute

Tang Dynasty

Internal disorder preceded the rise of the Tang dynasty in 618 CE. The Tang conquered Central Asia to the eastern border of Bactria (present-day Afghanistan), including portions of Tibet, Manchuria, and South Vietnam. In order to solidify control of their vast empire, the Tang used diplomacy and strengthened the Great Wall to ward off the advances of nomadic peoples. The expanding Tang empire centered on a bureaucracy influenced by the **scholar-gentry** and by Confucian perceptions of effective government. During both the Tang and Song eras, the Chinese civil service examination was strengthened.

In spite of the emphasis placed by the Tang government on Confucian principles, Buddhism gained acceptance in China during the Tang period. Buddhism's popularity among both elite and peasant groups resulted in an initial acceptance of the faith by Tang rulers. Thousands of monasteries populated by Buddhist monks and nuns dotted the Chinese landscape under early Tang rule. Especially supportive of Buddhism was Empress Wu (ruled 690 to 705 CE), who supported Buddhist art and sculpture and attempted to promote the faith as a state religion. As imperial tax exemptions and private gifts of property to Buddhist monasteries increased their wealth, the Tang began to fear the increasing power of Buddhism. Consequently, later Tang rulers placed restrictions on gifts of land and money to Buddhist monasteries, a policy that weakened the influence of the Buddhist faith in China. As Buddhism declined in power and wealth, Confucianism gained in popularity as an expression of Chinese tradition.

Decline of the Tang

Following the pattern of earlier Chinese dynasties, the Tang dynasty weakened as internal rebellion spread through the empire. At the same time, the Tang were plagued by invasions of nomadic peoples along their northern borders. By the ninth century, these nomads had placed themselves in control of large portions of northern China. Civil disorder reigned between the fall of the Tang in 907 CE and the accession of the Song in 960 CE.

Achievements of the Tang

Under Tang rule:

- Trade and travel along the Silk Roads was protected.
- Contacts with Islamic peoples increased.
- Ocean-going ships were improved, increasing interest in ocean trade.
- Chinese **junks** were among the world's best ships and Chinese merchants dominated trade in the Indian Ocean.
- Paper money was introduced to China.
- Letters of credit, or **flying money**, facilitated long-distance trade.
- Urban areas grew in size.
- Canals and irrigation systems increased agricultural productivity. The Tang extended the Chinese canal system to supplement the **Grand Canal**, a 1,100-mile waterway constructed under the Sui to ease trade by connecting northern and southern China.
- Large estates were broken up and land redistributed.
- Gunpowder was invented.
- Short stories and poetry were popular.
- Tea and fast-growing rice were imported from Vietnam.
- Population growth in the rice-growing south surpassed that of the millet-growing north.

Song Dynasty

In 960 CE, China was overtaken by the Song dynasty. From its beginnings, the Song dynasty was unable to completely control the Khitan, a nomadic people to the north of the empire that had already assimilated much of Chinese culture. Throughout its 300-year rule of China, the Song had to pay **tribute** to the Khitan to keep them from conquering additional Song territory.

Under the Song dynasty, many Chinese traditions were strengthened. For example:

- Civil service exams were emphasized as a prerequisite for government posts.
- Greater prestige was granted to the scholar-gentry.
- **Neo-Confucianism** arose as a blend of Confucian and Buddhist values. The new philosophy promoted the application of Confucian respect for authority and family to the everyday life of all levels of Chinese society, a feature that made it attractive to Chinese rulers. At the same time, the traditional aspect of Neo-Confucianism heightened the tendency of the Chinese elite classes to withdraw from contact with other peoples. Neo-Confucianism also reinforced gender and class distinctions.

The Song emphasis on the importance of the scholar-gentry over the military weakened its ability to withstand the threat of Khitan conquests of its northern borders. The cost of tribute paid to the Khitan burdened the Song economy as a whole, and especially the peasant class. Efforts at reform ended in the late eleventh century when Neo-Confucians reestablished Chinese tradition.

The faltering Song Empire now faced another threat: invasion by the Jurchens, another nomadic group. The Jurchens had overthrown the Khitan and settled in the region north of the Song Empire. They continued their conquest by dominating most of the basin of the Huang He (Yellow) River and causing the Song to retreat southward. The Song continued to thrive in the basin of the Yangtze River until 1279, during this time achieving noteworthy cultural and technological advances.

Achievements of the Song

During the rule of the Song dynasty:

- Overseas trade begun under the Tang continued.
- Artists expressed themselves through landscape paintings.
- Warfare saw the use of catapults to hurl bombs and grenades. Armies and ships used flamethrowers and rocket launchers.
- Printing with movable type was developed.
- Compasses were used in ocean navigation.
- The **abacus** was developed to aid counting and the recording of taxes.
- The practice of **footbinding** spread among the elite classes. Later, lower classes would often adopt the custom as well.
- The concept of the patriarchal family intensified.

Extension of China's Influence

The reestablishment of tradition among the Chinese during the Tang and Song dynasties did not prevent Chinese culture from expanding to other regions in the East. Throughout the period, Japan built on its previous contacts with Chinese culture, while Vietnam and Korea forged new ones.

Japan

During the seventh century CE, Chinese culture reached Japan. Attempts by the Japanese emperor to mimic the form of Chinese bureaucracy resulted in Japan's adoption of both Confucian thought and Chinese written characters. Buddhism mixed with **Shinto**, the traditional Japanese belief system that revered spirits of nature and of ancestors.

Aristocratic rebellion against the complete adoption of Chinese ways led to the restoration of the elite classes and the establishment of large estates in Japan. Local aristocrats began to acquire their own military. As the power of the Japanese emperor steadily gave way to that of aristocrats in the capital at Kyoto, the power of local lords in the countryside increased. Rather than providing land and labor for the imperial court, local lords ran their own tiny kingdoms. The Japanese countryside saw the construction of fortresses protected by earthen walls and ditches similar to the moats used by European fortresses (Chapter 13).

The small states into which Japan was divided by the eleventh century were led by *bushi*, who not only administered their territories but also maintained their own military. Armed military troops called *samurai* served the *bushi*. Periodically, the *samurai* also were expected to serve in the capital to protect the emperor from bandits. Armed with curved swords, they engaged in battles in which they shouted out the details of their family heritage before engaging in conflicts.

The rise of the *samurai* gradually moved Japan toward a style of feudalism with some similarities to that of Western Europe during the same period. A *samurai* code of honor called **bushido** developed. This code included the practice of **seppuku**, or disembowelment, a form of suicide used by defeated or disgraced warriors to maintain family and personal honor. Japanese peasants gradually became **serfs** bound to the land and considered property of the local lord.

By the twelfth century, powerful families such as the Fujiwara allied themselves with local lords. During the late twelfth century, a series of conflicts called the **Gempei Wars** placed peasants against the *samurai*. The Japanese countryside was destroyed. As a result of the Gempei Wars, in 1185 a powerful family, the Minamoto, established the **bakufu**, or military government. Although the emperor and his court remained, real power now resided in the Minamoto family and their *samurai*. As imperial government broke down, the Japanese increasingly distanced themselves from Chinese Confucian ways.

The Shogunate

During the thirteenth and fourteenth centuries, real Japanese authority lay in the hands of prominent families who, in turn, controlled military leaders called *shoguns*. A period of civil disorder in the fourteenth century lessened the power of both the emperor and the **shogunate**. The resulting power vacuum allowed the *bushi* vassals to acquire lands that they then divided among their *samurai*. The *samurai* were required to pledge loyalty to their lord and provide him with military assistance when needed. Further court rebellions from 1467 to 1477 culminated in the division of Japan into approximately 300 tiny kingdoms, each ruled by a warlord called a **daimyo**.

Japanese warrior culture changed as the code of *bushido* lost its dominance in the fifteenth and sixteenth centuries. Large castles of stone and wood began to dot the Japanese landscape. Poorly trained peasant armies armed with pikes became a major fighting force of *daimyo* armies.

Gradually, some *daimyo* began to impose a degree of centralization upon their vassals and peasants. Taxes were collected to fund public projects such as the improvement of irrigation systems. Trade between villages arose and blossomed into long-distance trade, including trade with China. Merchant and artisan guilds arose; both men and women participated in these organizations. The strengthening of trade in Japan promoted the use of a common currency that assisted the centralization of the Japanese state.

Although trade revived in Japan, Japanese art also was developing its characteristic traditions. Although much Japanese art was an imitation of Chinese models, Japanese artists created their own style in sketches done in ink. Both Shintoism and Buddhism were reflected in two additional examples of Japanese artistry: the **tea ceremony** and decorative gardens.

Korea

Chinese influences in Korea can be traced back as far as the fourth century BCE, when the knowledge of metallurgy and agriculture spread from China to the Korean Peninsula. In the latter part of the Han dynasty, Chinese settlers moved into Korea. Through these contacts Chinese culture, especially Buddhism, found a path into Korea. Chinese writing, which was later modified and made more suitable to the Korean language, was introduced. Confucian classics were read by Korean scholars.

Tang rulers defeated Korean peoples who resisted Chinese rule. The Silla kingdom of Korea, however, routed Tang forces. In 668 CE, the Chinese withdrew from Korea in exchange for an arrangement that made the Silla vassals of the Tang and required them to pay tribute. After the Tang withdrew, the Silla united Korea.

The Silla studied Chinese customs and willingly performed the **kowtow** (a ritual bow) to the Chinese emperor. They introduced the Chinese civil service exam to Korea. The Silla made tribute payments that allowed them to participate in the Chinese trade network and in educational systems with Vietnamese, Japanese, and other Eastern peoples. Korean cultural and commercial opportunities therefore expanded. Buddhism became popular, especially with the Korean elite classes. Techniques of porcelain manufacture made their way from China to Korea; the Koreans modified Chinese porcelain to produce **celadon** bowls with a characteristic pale green color.

The Mongol invasion of Korea in the thirteenth century interfered with cultural contacts between Korea and China. When the Mongols were cast from Korea in 1392, Korea once again established contacts with the Chinese.

Vietnam

Southeast Asians displayed a somewhat different response to the introduction of Chinese culture than the peoples of East Asia had. While the Viets admired the technological advances and political ideals of the Chinese, at the same time they highly valued their own independence. Before the time of the Qin dynasty, the Viets carried on an active trade with the people of southern China. The Viets gradually brought the lands of the Red River valley under their control and began intermarrying with the peoples of present-day Cambodia and others in Southeast Asia. In contrast to the Chinese, the Viets had a different spoken language, lived in villages rather than establishing large urban areas, and based their society on the nuclear family. Vietnamese women enjoyed more privileges than women in China. Additionally, Buddhism gained greater popularity in Vietnam than in China.

When Han rulers attempted to annex South China into their empire, they encountered opposition from the Viets. Initially requiring the payment of tribute from the Viets, the

Han conquered them in 111 BCE. Under Han rule the Viets adopted Chinese agricultural and irrigation techniques, the Confucian concept of veneration of ancestors, and the extended family structure. In spite of their admiration of some aspects of Chinese culture, however, the Viets periodically staged rebellions against Chinese rule. After the fall of the Tang in 907 CE, they staged a major protest, which in 939 CE resulted in Vietnamese independence. After their independence was secured, the Viets continued the Confucian civil service examinations, which had earlier been disbanded. Vietnamese conquests of neighboring peoples succeeded largely because of the military organization and technology they had adopted from the Chinese.

› Rapid Review

The Tang and Song dynasties proved to be an era of active long-distance trade contacts and unprecedented technological innovation in China. During this era, China extended its borders to intensify the diffusion of its culture to regions such as Japan, Korea, and Vietnam. At the same time that China was broadening its influence, it was repeatedly plagued by nomadic invaders from the north such as the Khitan and the Jurchens. The necessity of addressing the problem of nomadic invasions became China's next great challenge.

› Review Questions

Questions 1 to 3 refer to the following passage.

". . . It wears out the strength of the people with constructions of earth and wood, pilfers their wealth for ornaments of gold and precious objects, causes men to abandon their lords and parents for the company of teachers, and severs man and wife with its monastic decrees. In destroying law and injuring mankind, indeed, nothing surpasses this doctrine! Now if even one man fails to work the fields, someone must go hungry; if one woman does not tend her silkworms, someone will be cold. At present there are an inestimable number of monks and nuns in the empire, each of them waiting for the farmers to feed him and the silkworms to clothe him, while the public temples and private chapels have reached boundless numbers, all with soaring towers and elegant ornamentation sufficient to outshine the imperial palace itself."

—Emperor Wuzong's The Edict of the Eighth Month (edict on the suppression of Buddhism)

1. Which line best supports the argument that Buddhism threatened order under Confucianism?
   (A) It wears out the strength of its people.
   (B) It causes men to abandons their lords and parents.
   (C) Monks and nuns [wait] for the farmers to feed [them].
   (D) [It] pilfers their wealth for ornaments.

2. Which has been suggested by historians as another reason for the Tang to suppress Buddhism?
   (A) Tax exemptions and bequests to monasteries made them wealthy enough to rival the Tang dynasty.
   (B) Buddhists opposed the merchant trade on which China relied.
   (C) Buddhists preached that pacifism weakened Chinese military prowess.
   (D) By destroying laws, they created anarchy.

3. Which best describes China's interactions with the neighboring Silla in Korea?
   - (A) China required a strong military presence in these societies to maintain dominion over them.
   - (B) The Silla were willing to pay tribute to China in exchange for access to their trade networks.
   - (C) China adopted Korean traditions of silk manufacture and porcelain production.
   - (D) The Silla conducted regular raids across China's northern border.

4. Which of the following represents a long-term consequence of the feudal period in Japan during the fifteenth century?
   - (A) Women were given political equality.
   - (B) Daimyo centralized taxes and public works.
   - (C) The emperor became the central political figure.
   - (D) The Japanese and Chinese developed an antagonistic relationship.

5. Which is one reason for the fall of the Song dynasty?
   - (A) The cost of an expanded bureaucracy left them vulnerable to nomadic invaders.
   - (B) Famine resulted as peasants protested land reforms.
   - (C) The Silk Roads were blockaded by the Delhi Sultanate.
   - (D) The increased use of opium resulted in social disorder and economic decline.

› Answers and Explanations

1. **B** Only the argument that Buddhism causes people to "abandon their lords and parents" stands in direct conflict with the Confucian traditions of obedience to one's ruler and filial piety. All of the others speak to the availability and efficiency of labor (A) or the diversion of food and wealth to Buddhist monasteries (C, D), but do not directly address the values of Confucianism advocated by the scholar-gentry.

2. **A** The monasteries grew increasingly wealthy through tax exemptions and bequests. These government concerns are reflected in the passage through phrases like "elegant ornamentation sufficient to outshine the imperial palace itself." Buddhism benefited from trade as monks frequently traveled with merchants, and trade caravans often stopped at monasteries located along trade routes. Thus trade facilitated the spread of Buddhism (B). Although Buddhism emphasized nonviolence, it is not commonly associated with weakening of the Chinese military (C). Nor did Buddhism require rejection of laws or lead to anarchy, as precepts of Buddhism included moral aspects like "right action" and "right speech" (D).

3. **B** Although the Silla technically paid tribute to China, they benefitted far more in terms of the access to Chinese trade networks and goods. Part of the tribute system included the withdrawal of Chinese forces from Korea (A). The relationship between China and the Silla, then, was peaceful after the Silla agreed to the tribute system (D). Korea adopted many Chinese practices, including adapting manufacture of Chinese porcelain to include a celadon color (C).

4. **B** During this period, the emperor became more of a figurehead, as power devolved, first to the *bushi*, and later to the regional warlords or *daimyo*, who began to centralize taxes and

public works projects (C). Trade increased with China (D), resulting in new artisan and trades classes. Though women participated in these new guilds, they did not achieve political equality (A).

5. **A** As the Song expanded the size of the scholar-gentry class, which functioned as the bureaucracy, there were fewer resources left to maintain the military, leaving them unable to deal effectively with invasions by groups like the Khitan and Jurchen in the north. Better agricultural techniques helped offset the burden of any additional taxes (B). Though invasions tend to discourage trade, the Silk Road network continued to be used. The Delhi Sultanate never blocked the network's use (C). Opium use did not become widespread in China until much later, in the early 1800s (D).

CHAPTER 17

Empires in the Americas

IN THIS CHAPTER

Summary: Before the voyages of Columbus and the conquests of the Spanish, the civilizations and societies of the Americas developed in isolation from the remainder of the world. Within the Western Hemisphere, many of the peoples of the Americas engaged in long-distance as well as regional trade. When the Europeans arrived in the Americas, they encountered not only societies with their own rich traditions but also mighty empires that dazzled their conquerors.

Key Terms

Anasazi	Mississippians
ayllus	*mita*
calpulli	Moundbuilders
Chimor	parallel descent
chinampas	Quechua
Inca	*quipus*
Mexica	Toltecs

Pre-Columbian Mesoamerica

After the decline of Teotihuacán and of the Mayan civilization, nomadic peoples such as the **Toltecs** moved into central Mexico. Establishing a capital at Tula in the mid-tenth century, the Toltecs created an empire in central Mexico. Their empire included the city of Chichén Itzá in the Yucatán Peninsula. The Toltecs carried on long-distance trade, exchanging obsidian from northern Mexico for turquoise obtained from the **Anasazi** people in the present-day southwestern United States. Another legacy of the Toltecs was the legend of the god Quetzalcóatl, a tradition that would circulate among the various inhabitants of Mesoamerica.

Moundbuilders of North America

A second major concentration of pre-Columbian Native Americans was found among the **Moundbuilders** of North America from about 700 to 1500 CE. Also called the **Mississippians**, these early Americans established their settlements along major rivers such as the Mississippi and the Ohio. Agricultural people, they constructed large earthen mounds that served as burial places or ceremonial centers. Among the most well-known and largest mounds are those found at Cahokia, in present-day southern Illinois. Some historians believe that the pyramid shape of these mounds suggests contact between the Mississippians and the early peoples of Mesoamerica.

The Rise of the Aztecs

When the Toltec empire fell in the mid-twelfth century, perhaps to invaders, another nomadic people called the Aztecs, or **Mexica**, migrated throughout central Mexico. By the mid-thirteenth century, they had settled in the valley of Mexico, establishing their capital city at Tenochtitlán about 1325. Constructed on an island in the center of Lake Texcoco, Tenochtitlán was linked to the mainland by four causeways. To provide additional land for farming, the Aztecs fashioned *chinampas*, or platforms constructed of twisted vines on which they placed layers of soil. These garden plots floated in the canals that ran through the city of Tenochtitlán. Maize and beans became the staple crops of the Aztecs. Like other Mesoamerican peoples, they engaged in agriculture and construction without the use of the wheel or large beasts of burden.

By the mid-fifteenth century, the Aztecs had emerged as the dominant power of central Mexico. After conquering neighboring peoples, the Aztecs established a tribute empire. The Aztec military seized prisoners of war for use as human sacrifices. Although seen in other Mesoamerican and South American societies, human sacrifice was most widely practiced among the Aztecs. Sacrifices were carried out atop truncated, or trapezoid-shaped, pyramids in the Mesoamerican tradition. The Aztecs also worshipped the numerous gods of nature of their Mesoamerican predecessors, among them Quetzalcóatl and the rain god Tlaloc. The chief Aztec god was their own deity, Huitzilopochtli, the god of the sun. Human sacrifices were dedicated to this regional god in the belief that the gods were nourished by the sacrifice of human life. Another aspect of Aztec religious life was its calendar, which was similar to that of the Mayans.

Aztec society was stratified, with classes of nobles, peasants, and slaves, who were often war captives. The social structure was further organized into clans, or *calpulli*, that began as kinship groups but later expanded to include neighboring peoples. Economic life included a marketplace under government regulation that featured items obtained by long-distance trade. Records were kept through a system of picture writing, or hieroglyphics.

Women who died in childbirth were granted the same honored status as soldiers who died in battle. Aztec women who displayed a talent for intricate weaving also were highly regarded. Although Aztec women were politically subordinate to men, they could inherit property and will it to their heirs.

The Incas

Around 1300, about the time that the Aztecs were moving into the central valley of Mexico, the Incas, or **Quechua**, rose to power in the Andes Mountains of western South America. Their empire, or Twantinsuyu, became a model of organization. Building on the contributions of previous Andean societies, the Incas mastered the integration of diverse peoples within their empire.

The immediate predecessors of the Incas were the **Chimor**, who established a kingdom along the western coastal region of South America from 900 CE until the Incas conquered them in 1465 by taking over their irrigation system. At the same time, the southern Andean homelands were inhabited by a number of peoples, among them several *ayllus*, or clans, that spoke the Quechua language. About 1438, under the direction of their ruler, or **Inca**, called Pachacuti, they gained control of the large area around Lake Titicaca. On the eve of its conquest by the Spanish, the Inca Empire extended from present-day Colombia to the northern portion of Argentina and into present-day Chile. As a tribute empire, it required its subjects to supply the *mita*, or labor, on government-controlled lands.

Structure of the Inca Empire

The most noteworthy achievement of Inca rulers was their ability to integrate approximately 11 million people of diverse cultural and linguistic backgrounds under one empire. Unlike the Aztecs, who ruled conquered peoples harshly, the Incas incorporated the conquered into their way of life. The Quechua language was purposely spread throughout the empire to serve as a unifying force. Inca rulers sent groups of Quechua-speaking people to settle throughout the empire to protect it from uprisings among conquered peoples. Another Inca strategy was to settle conquered peoples in an area far from their original homeland. The royal family forged marriage alliances that prevented rivals from obtaining power within their empire.

Although ruins of other urban areas have been discovered, the center of the empire was the capital city of Cuzco. Accurate imperial records were maintained without a system of writing by devices called **quipus**. *Quipus* were groups of knotted cords, with the knots of various sizes and colors representing categories of information, such as finances or religion. The Incas further strengthened the organization of their empire by a dual system of roads, one running across the Andes highlands and the other across the lowlands. Way stations were set up about a day's walking distance apart to serve citizens and armies traveling these roads.

Inca Society and Religion

A polytheistic people, the Incas centered their worship around the sun god, while the creator god, or Viracocha, was also a key element of Inca religion. Local deities were worshipped as well. Society was organized into clans called *ayllus*. Women carried out traditional child-care roles, worked in fields, and achieved special recognition for their skill in weaving cloth for religious and state use. Inheritance was organized along lines of **parallel descent**, with inheritances passed along through both male and female sides of the family.

The Incas based their economy on the cultivation of the potato. They cultivated maize as a supplemental crop. State regulation of trade left little opportunity for long-distance trade, and there was not a separate merchant class among the Incas.

› Rapid Review

Although the Aztecs built on Mesoamerican tradition to establish a powerful empire in the valley of Mexico, the Andean highlands also saw the emergence of a native empire in the centuries before European conquest. The Aztecs ruled other peoples with brutality, whereas the Incas concentrated on integrating subject peoples into their empire. Aztec peoples engaged in long-distance trade, while the Incas were noted for the careful organization of their empire and their system of roads. In addition to the natives of Mesoamerica and Andean America, native peoples of the Mississippian culture of North America constructed large mounds used for ceremonial and burial purposes.

› Review Questions

1. Answer Parts A and B.
   (A) Compare the Aztec and Inca empires by identifying TWO differences in their political or social structures.
   (B) Identify ONE characteristic of a "tribute empire."

2. Answers Parts A and B.
   (A) Identify TWO examples of environmental modifications carried out by pre-Columbian American empires.
   (B) Identify and give ONE example of the use of forced labor in pre-Columbian American empires.

3. Which of the following made long-distance trade more possible for the Aztecs than for the Incas?
   (A) An extensive system of roads
   (B) The use of sea trade routes
   (C) The production of marketable goods
   (D) Environmental and geographical considerations

4. Which of the American peoples was closest to the Persians in their administrative style?
   (A) The Mayas
   (B) The Mississippians
   (C) The Aztecs
   (D) The Incas

5. Answer Parts A and B.
   (A) Identify ONE example of Incan public works.
   (B) Identify TWO forms of writing or communication used by the Incan and Aztec empires.

› Answers and Explanations

1A. To maintain political and social control, the Incas incorporated conquered peoples into the empire and their way of life; the Aztecs treated conquered peoples harshly, frequently using them as sacrifices to the gods. The Incas were sedentary; the Aztecs were nomadic. The Incas established a common language, Quechua, throughout their extensive empire, but the Aztecs did not. The Incas carried out public works (especially roads), and as a tribute empire, required labor from its people. The Aztecs, also a tribute empire, carried on long-distance trade but were not known for their public works.

1B. A tribute empire requires goods, monetary taxes, or labor from subject peoples. The Spanish colonizers would establish a tribute empire based on Native American precedents and traditions.

2A. Environmental modifications carried out by pre-Columbian American empires included the construction of artificial "hills," or mounds, by the Moundbuilders of North America; the Aztec building of *chinampas* (in manmade canals), platforms made of vines that held layers of soil and could be used for farming; and the Aztec building of their capital, Tenochtitlán, in the center of a lake and the building of causeways to connect the city to the mainland.

2B. The *mita* is the most famous use of forced labor. The Incas used it to farm government-controlled lands and in mining endeavors.

3. **D** The Aztecs lived in a more temperate climate than the Incas and did not have the same mountainous obstacles preventing the transport of goods. Both the Incas and the Aztecs had road systems (A); both carried on little sea trade (B); both produced marketable goods (C).

4. **D** Like the Persians, the Incas were adept at integrating subject peoples into their empire as long as their subjects refrained from rebellion. Both the Incas and the Persians also constructed roads to serve as communication links to the various parts of their empires. The Aztecs were noted for their exceptionally harsh treatment of conquered peoples (C). The Mayas (A) did not demonstrate the imperial organizational skills of the Incas, while the Mississippians did not establish an empire (B).

5. **A** The most extensive Incan public works were highway systems, which facilitated travel and trade.

B The Aztecs used the Maya hieroglyphic system of writing; the Incas, while not technically having a writing system, did indeed have a communications system: they used the *quipu*, a means of recordkeeping using strings of various thicknesses and colors and knots. This latter has been tied to theories of binary computer systems.

CHAPTER 18

Empires and Other Political Systems

IN THIS CHAPTER

Summary: About 1450, a major global transition took place with the withdrawal of the Chinese from global interactions and the rise of European dominance. The Byzantine Empire fell to the power of the Ottoman Turks, an empire that by 1750 was in decline. Russia emerged from Mongol control to forge an empire under the rule of the Romanovs. New patterns of world interactions formed as societies of the Eastern and Western Hemispheres exchanged cultural traditions across the Atlantic Ocean.

KEY IDEA

Key Terms

absolute monarchy
boyars
Cossacks
criollos (creoles)
devshirme
divine right
Dutch learning
encomienda
Enlightenment
Estates-General
Glorious Revolution
Hagia Sophia
Janissaries
Jesuits
Manchus
mercantilism

mestizos
Mughal dynasty
mulato (mulatto)
nation-state
parliamentary monarchy
peninsulares
purdah
Qing dynasty
Reconquista (Reconquest)
repartamiento
sovereignty
Taj Mahal
Tokugawa Shogunate
Treaty of Tordesillas
viceroyalty

Spain and Portugal in the Americas

In the mid- and late fifteenth century, events that took place on the Iberian Peninsula culminated in an encounter between Western Europe and the Americas. This encounter profoundly altered the government and society of the peoples of the Americas. In the mid-fifteenth century, Portuguese establishment of a navigation school increased exploration of the western and eastern coasts of Africa. The knowledge and wealth obtained from these ventures created further interest in expeditions of exploration and colonization. In Spain, the marriage of Fernando of Aragón and Isabel of Castile in the mid-fifteenth century united the kingdoms of Aragón and Castile. This union gave its support to three significant events in Spanish history in 1492:

- The *Reconquista* (**Reconquest**) of former Spanish territory from the Muslims with the fall of Granada.
- The expulsion of Jews who refused to convert to Christianity. Spain would suffer serious economic repercussions with the removal of the Jews, who were some of its most well-educated and skilled people.
- The first voyage of Columbus. The unification of central Spain and the end of warfare with the Muslims freed the Spanish monarchs to turn their attention to voyages of exploration.

The Spanish-sponsored voyage of Ferdinand Magellan, beginning in 1519, not only circumnavigated the globe but also gave Spain a basis for its colonization of the Philippines in the late sixteenth century.

Spain's Empire

Control in the Caribbean

Spain's interests in the Americas began in the Caribbean. During his second voyage in 1493, Columbus established a colony on Santo Domingo. In the sixteenth century, the Spaniards took control of Puerto Rico and Cuba and settled Panama and the northern coast of South America. Spanish control of these regions introduced European diseases to the Native Americans, an exchange that significantly decreased the native population. The Spanish crown granted Caribbean natives to the conquerors for use as forced labor.

Conquest in the Americas

In the fifteenth century, the once-mighty empires of the Aztecs and Incas fell to the Spaniards. Tales of riches in the interior of Mexico led the Spaniard Hernán Cortés to attempt the conquest of the Aztec Empire. The Spaniards were aided in their venture by several factors:

- Indian allies from among native peoples who had been conquered by the Aztecs.
- The legend of Quetzalcóatl—Moctezuma II, the Aztec leader at the time of the conquest, believed that Cortés may have been the god who was expected to return to Mesoamerica.
- Superior Spanish weaponry.
- The assistance of Malinche (called Doña Marina by the Spanish), an Aztec woman who served as interpreter between the Spanish and the Aztecs.
- Smallpox—introduced into the Aztec Empire by one infected member of the Cortés expedition, it caused the death of thousands.

On the completion of the Aztec conquest in 1521, the capital city of Tenochtitlán was burned to the ground and a new capital, Mexico City, was constructed on its site. The Spaniards then continued their conquests into northcentral Mexico, Guatemala, and Honduras.

The Spaniards also turned their attention to the region of the Andes Mountains of western South America. By 1535, Francisco Pizarro had conquered the rich Inca Empire, already weakened by years of civil war. The Spaniards then sent expeditions from northern Mexico into what is now the southwestern portion of the United States. From 1540 to 1542, Francisco de Coronado reached as far north as what is now Kansas in an unsuccessful search for seven mythical cities of gold. Further campaigns of exploration led to the conquest of Chile and the establishment of the city of Buenos Aires in present-day Argentina. By the late sixteenth century, the Spaniards had set up about 200 urban centers in the Americas.

Despite constant threats from Caribbean pirates, Spanish galleons carried loads of gold and silver across the Atlantic Ocean to Spain, where the influx of such large quantities of the precious metals caused inflation of the Spanish economy. Eventually, inflation spread throughout Europe. Until the eighteenth century, the Manila galleons sailed the Pacific, transporting silver from the mines of Spain's American colonies to China to trade for luxury goods.

The pursuit of gold and adventure was not the sole motive for the founding of a Spanish colonial empire. Another goal was the desire to spread the Roman Catholic faith to native peoples. Roman Catholic religious orders such as the **Jesuits**, Dominicans, and Franciscans established churches and missions where they educated the Indians and taught them the Christian faith. The Roman Catholic faith became an integral element in the society of the Spanish colonies.

The right of the Spaniards to govern their American colonies was established by papal decree through the **Treaty of Tordesillas** (1494). This agreement divided the newly discovered territories between the Catholic countries of Spain and Portugal by drawing an imaginary line around the globe. Spain received the right to settle the lands to the west of the line drawn through the Western Hemisphere, and Portugal those to the east. Spanish government in the Americas was a massive bureaucracy controlled from Spain by the Council of Indies. The council was further divided into two **viceroyalties**, one centered in Mexico City and the other in Lima, in present-day Peru.

The economic structure of Spain's American colonies was the *encomienda* system. *Encomiendas* were grants from the Spanish crown that allowed the holders to exploit the Indians living on the land they controlled. In Peru, the exploitation of Indians took the form of the *mita,* or forced labor, especially in the silver mines. After Father Bartolomé de las Casas spoke out against the mistreatment of the Indians, the *encomienda* system was restructured as the ***repartamiento***. The new system allowed a small salary to be paid to Indian laborers.

Spanish American Society

Spanish American society took on a hierarchical structure. Four basic classes emerged:

- *Peninsulares*—colonists born in Europe. The *penisulares* initially held the most powerful positions in colonial society.
- *Criollos* (**creoles**)—colonists born in the Americas of European parents. Generally well educated and financially secure, the creoles would eventually become colonial leaders and organizers of colonial independence movements.
- *Mestizos*—people of mixed European and Indian ancestry.
- *Mulatos* (**mulattos**)—people of mixed European and African ancestry. The *mestizos* and *mulatos* occupied the lowest political and social positions in Spanish American society.

Families in the Spanish and Portuguese American colonies were patriarchal. Women were expected to devote themselves to traditional household and childbearing duties. Lower-class women worked in the fields and sometimes managed small businesses. Women could control their dowries, however, and also could inherit property.

Portugal's Empire

The Portuguese colony of Brazil became the first colony based on a plantation economy. Founded by Pedro Cabral in 1500, Brazil was settled in 1532 by Portuguese nobles. Sugar plantations using Indian labor arose; when the Indians died of European diseases, slaves were brought from Africa. Labor in Brazilian gold mines also was supplied by Indians and African slaves. Society in Brazil followed a hierarchy similar to that of the Spanish colonies, and Roman Catholicism was introduced by Jesuit missionaries. In addition to Brazil, the Portuguese Empire included colonies and trade outposts in Africa and Asia.

The Ottoman Empire

The Mongol invasion of eastern Anatolia in 1243 led to the collapse of the Seljuk Turks and the subsequent rise of the Ottoman Turks. The Ottomans migrated into Anatolia to fill the vacuum left by the Seljuks. Named after their leader Osman Bey, the Ottomans established an empire centered around Anatolia. By the late fourteenth century, much of the Balkans were added to the Ottoman Empire.

In 1453, the Ottomans completed their conquest of the city of Constantinople. The Christian church of **Hagia Sophia** was converted into an elaborate mosque, palaces were constructed in the city, and the defense system of Constantinople was repaired. After the conquest of Constantinople, the Ottomans united most of the Arab world by adding Syria, Egypt, and the rest of North Africa to their empire. In the fifteenth century, they became a major naval power until they suffered a decisive defeat by a combined Venetian and Spanish fleet at the Battle of Lepanto in 1571. As late as 1688, the Ottomans threatened the Austrian capital of the Hapsburg dynasty. This siege was not as devastating, however, as a previous siege against Vienna in 1529.

The Ottoman Empire was focused on warfare. Beginning in the middle of the fifteenth century, its armies were largely composed of soldiers called **Janissaries**. Janissaries were Christian boys who were captured and enslaved. Sometimes the boys were turned over to the Ottomans by their own parents in the hope that the education given to them would lead to a prominent position in the Ottoman Empire. The selection process for the Janissaries was called *devshirme;* it placed the boys with Turkish families to learn their language and the teachings of Islam.

Women in Ottoman society maintained a subordinate role to their fathers and husbands. Although some women in the lower classes became involved in trade and small businesses, Ottoman women as a whole were given very little opportunity to acquire an education or participate in politics. Instead, Ottoman women, especially those in elite classes, were restricted by the wearing of the veil and, in some cases, seclusion within the harem.

Ottoman Decline

By the late seventeenth century, the vast Ottoman Empire was so difficult to administer that it fell into a gradual decline. As opportunities to add new territories ran out because of the strengthening military power of other Muslims and of Christians, the Ottomans lost their ability to maintain their large army and bureaucracy. Taxes charged to the lower classes were raised as Ottoman rulers became more and more corrupt. The inflationary trend that affected Europe as a result of the influx of gold and silver in Spain also produced inflation within the Ottoman territories. The Ottomans fell behind in warfare technology because of their reliance on huge weaponry intended for siege tactics. Ignoring the value of Western technological innovations, the Ottomans also disregarded the growing power of Western Europe, a policy that hastened its decline.

Safavid Persia

The Safavid empire originated as a small religious order in Northwest Iran (near Azerbaijan) with Sufi Sheik Safi-al-Din, but as more warlords joined the order, it became more militaristic and Shi'a in its orientation. As the Ottomans expanded across Anatolia, a persecuted Shi'a militia group known as Qizilbash allied with the Safiviyeh, helping them capture Tabriz. The first Shah, Ismail I, came to power in 1501 at age 15. Though he expanded the Safavid territory to the east, repeated Ottoman military incursions by the Ottomans in the West hindered Ismail's territorial ambitions. In 1587, Shah Abbas I came to power. During his reign, he negotiated a settlement with the Ottomans, and reorganized his army around a European model that took advantage of gunpowder-based weaponry. With English assistance, he weakened the Portuguese in Bahrain and the Strait of Hormuz, and established commercial links with both English and Dutch interests who desired access to Iranian carpets, silk, and pearls. When Kurdish tribes rebelled in the early 1600s, Shah Abbas ordered the massacre of many Kurds, as well as the deportation of many more.

The Safavid government was a theocracy, with Shi'ism as the official religion. Though the region was originally Sunni, though a combination of persecution and incentives, the Shi'a religion dominated. The State promoted Shi'ism by sponsoring religious shrines and schools, and by granting land to a new religious elite, who owed their loyalty to the Safavid government. At its peak, the Safavid capital Isfahan was a thriving economic, religious and artistic center. Many Shahs were artists themselves, and the Safavids became known for religious philosophy, calligraphy and painted miniatures.

After Shah Abbas, as so often happens, subsequent rulers were weak, neglecting administrative duties in favor of luxury and indulgence. The focus of trade had shifted, resulting in declining revenue. With the decline of the Ottoman threat, the large military became complacent, rendering them vulnerable to new threats, like the Mughals who expanded into Afghanistan in the 1600s. To prop up the bureaucracy, new taxes were introduced, furthering weakening the empire to raids on its borders.

Mughal India

In 1526, Babur, a descendant of Mongols and of Turks, migrated from the steppes of central Asia to the Indian subcontinent. The founder of the **Mughal dynasty** had lost his kingdom in Central Asia; by 1528, he had used his superior gunpowder technology to conquer a large portion of northern India and had founded a dynasty that would last to the mid-nineteenth century.

The greatest leader of the Mughal dynasty was Akbar (ruled 1560 to 1605). Throughout his reign, he brought more of northern and central India under his control, established a bureaucracy, and patronized the arts. He encouraged cooperation between Hindus and Muslims in India.

Akbar also broke with Hindu and Muslim tradition regarding the treatment of women in society. He encouraged widows to remarry and outlawed *sati,* the practice among Hindu elite classes of burning women on their husband's funeral pyre. Akbar also encouraged merchants to arrange market days for women only so that those following the practice of **purdah**, or confinement in their homes, would have an opportunity to participate in public life. By the declining years of the Mughal Empire, however, the improvements in the position of women had largely been discontinued.

Mughal art and architecture often blended Muslim styles with those of other societies. Mughal artists were known for their miniatures, some of which included Christian religious subjects. Mughal architecture blended the white marble typical of Indian architecture with the arches and domes of the Islamic world. Probably the most well-known architectural structure of the Mughal era was the **Taj Mahal**, constructed by Shah Jahan as a tomb for his wife, Mumtaz Mahal.

The cost of warfare and defensive efforts to protect the northern borders of the Mughal Empire contributed to its decline. Later Mughal rulers failed to bridge the differences between Muslims and Hindus. Centralized government broke down as India returned to numerous local political organizations. The decline of centralized authority opened doors for the entrance of foreign powers, especially the British.

Songhai Empire

The Songhai empire emerged in the mid-fifteenth century in western Africa. Centered around Gao, their traditional home, the Songhai people gained independence from the waning Mali empire in the late 14th century, and then continued to take advantage of the power vacuum, slowly gaining territory to the West. One of their greatest rulers, Sonni Ali, came to power in 1464. A strong military leader, he added key trading cities of Timbuktu and Djenné. Building on Sonni Ali's successes, Askia the Great centralized tax and justice in the bureaucracy, and developed a standing army to protect the gold and salt trade routes. Under his direction, trade flourished with standardization of weights and measures, and trade inspectors in major cities. There were five key provinces in the Songhai empire and the emperor appointed loyal Muslim governors to administer them. Control over peripheral states was maintained through a system of tribute and taxation, but local rulers were left in place, and the Songhai military rarely intervened in local disputes, as long as nothing undermined Songhai policies.

Like many African empires, the Songhai rulers and many elites were Muslim, but the common people maintained traditional African religious practices, often incorporating animism and magic. Social classes in Songhai were determined by one's family clan, which also determined one's trade. Nobles were the highest ranked, followed by artisans and merchants, with slaves and war-captives at the bottom.

Later rulers lacked the strength of character to maintain the empire. The Songhai army quickly became outdated, falling in 1591 to Moroccan forces using firearms.

Monarchies in France and England

In the sixteenth century, European monarchies expanded their power dramatically. Characteristics of these monarchies were:

- Maintenance of strong armies
- Establishment of elaborate bureaucracies
- High taxes to support the frequent wars on the European continent

In France, a system of **absolute monarchy** arose as monarchs stopped convening the **Estates-General**, the medieval parliament. In addition to the characteristics of monarchs listed earlier, absolute monarchs believed in a concept called the **divine right** of kings. Divine right held that monarchs were granted their right to rule by God. Territorial expansion was a goal of the strong military that the absolute monarchies assembled. The most noteworthy of European absolute monarchs was Louis XIV of France (ruled 1643 to 1715), who not only adhered to the doctrine of divine right but also lived extravagantly in his palace at Versailles outside Paris. Keeping with absolutist tradition, Louis XIV also spent huge sums on the military in order to carry out numerous wars to expand French territory.

The prevailing economic theory of the day, called **mercantilism**, encouraged nations to export more than they imported and promoted the founding of colonies. Colonies provided raw materials and ready markets for the manufactured goods produced by the mother country.

The English developed a different model of monarchy in the seventeenth century: **parliamentary monarchy**. Although ruled by a centralized government, England limited the power of its monarchs with a parliament in which they shared power with representatives chosen by voters from the elite classes. The English Civil War (1642 to 1649) and the **Glorious Revolution** of 1689 placed the power of parliament over that of the king. The English parliament met regularly without the consent of the monarch and also retained the authority to tax and appropriate tax revenues.

Development of European Nation-States

Government in Europe was organized around the **nation-state**. Well suited to a continent composed of various cultural groups, a nation-state is defined as a political unit that:

- Governs people who share a common culture, including a common language
- Has definite geographic boundaries
- Enjoys **sovereignty**

European nation-states were governed by either absolute or parliamentary monarchs. The number of nation-states on the small European continent, however, created rivalries and divisions that often led to war.

The Russian Empire

Russia followed the path of absolute monarchy after the final expulsion of the Mongols in 1480. The Mongol occupation of Russia produced a nation with a weakened emphasis on education, as well as depressed trade and manufacturing. Under the tsars Ivan III (the Great) and Ivan IV (the Terrible), Russia expanded from the eastern border of Poland into western Siberia across the Ural Mountains. Russian pioneers called **Cossacks** were sent to the newly conquered territories, taking over land previously held by Asian nomads. In the process of expanding its borders, Russia added a substantial Muslim minority to its population.

The death of Ivan IV without an heir paved the way for the emergence of the Romanov dynasty. In 1613, the Russian nobles, or **boyars**, selected Mikhail Romanov as Russia's new tsar, beginning a dynasty that ruled until 1917. The new tsar continued Russian expansion, adding part of the Ukraine around Kiev and also southern territory that extended to the frontier of the Ottoman Empire. Later Romanovs created state control over the Russian Orthodox Church.

Peter the Great

In 1700, the Russian Empire remained agricultural to a larger extent than East Asian empires or Western European nations. Peter I (the Great), who ruled from 1689 to 1725, launched a new era in Russian history by opening up the country to Western influence. On a trip to Western Europe in a vain attempt to enlist support against the Turks, Peter acquired an appreciation for Western science and technology. When he returned to Russia, he took Western craftsmen with him. In order to bolster trade, Peter fought a war with Sweden in which he not only greatly reduced the military power of Sweden but also gained for Russia a warm-water port on the Baltic Sea. Peter also moved his capital from Moscow to a new city on the Baltic that he named St. Petersburg. He then created a navy for Russia. Continuing his policy of westernization, Peter required boyars to shave their beards and wear Western clothing. He also brought the ballet from France to Russia and allowed women of elite classes to attend public events for the first time.

In spite of his interest in Western technology, Peter the Great did not accept Western democratic trends. Unimpressed with parliamentary government, he continued to favor absolute monarchy. He set up controls over his subjects by creating a secret police and encouraged the continuation of serfdom. Serfdom, which differed from slavery in binding laborers to the land only, kept the Russian economy focused on agriculture, in spite of the westernization policies of Peter the Great.

Catherine II (the Great), who ruled from 1729 to 1796, continued the expansionist and westernization policies of Peter. Laws restricting serfs were harsher than before. Catherine upheld the concept of absolute monarchy but also brought ideas of the **Enlightenment** (see Chapter 19) to Russia. She reduced severe punishments for crimes in order to bring the Russian justice system more in line with that of Western Europe and encouraged Western art and architecture. Catherine added new territory in the Crimea, Alaska, and northern California to the Russian Empire.

Ming China

The Ming dynasty was founded by Zhu Yuanzhang, a warlord who had assisted in the expulsion of the Mongols from China. The Ming dynasty, which reacted against Mongol rule by returning to Chinese tradition, lasted from 1368 to 1644. Under Ming rule:

- The revered position of the scholar-gentry was restored.
- The Confucian-based civil service exam was reinstated and expanded. Women, however, continued to be banned from taking the exam.
- Public officials who were corrupt or incompetent were beaten publicly.
- Thought control, or censorship of documents, was sanctioned by the government.
- Neo-Confucianism, which supported strict obedience to the state, increased its influence.
- Women continued to occupy a subordinate position in the strongly patriarchal society.

Between 1405 and 1423, the Ming dynasty, under the leadership of Zheng He, engaged in several major expeditions of exploration and trade. Designed to impress the remainder of the Eastern Hemisphere with the glories of Ming China, the Zheng He expeditions sailed through the Indian Ocean, the Arabian Sea, and the Persian Gulf. By the 1430s, however, the scholar-gentry had persuaded Ming leaders that the expeditions were too costly in light of the need to spend the empire's funds on restraining continued Mongol threats to China's northern border.

In the late sixteenth century, Jesuits such as the scholar Matteo Ricci were allowed to enter China. More interested in the Jesuits' transmission of scientific and technological knowledge than in Christian theology, the Ming Chinese allowed some Jesuits to remain in China throughout the Ming era.

During the last 200 years of the Ming dynasty, China was ruled by incompetent rulers. The maintenance of dams, dikes, and irrigation systems was neglected, and nomadic peoples continued to exert pressure along the Great Wall. In 1644, the Jurchen, or **Manchus**, a nomadic people on China's northern borders, conquered the Ming dynasty.

Manchu (Qing) China

The Manchu named their new dynasty **Qing**, imposing their rule on the ethnic Han Chinese. Initially, most military and government positions of power were reserved exclusively for Manchu, although as the dynasty matured, non-Manchu were incorporated into most aspects of the government. The Dorgon, a warlord and regent for the young Qing emperor, ordered all Chinese men to adopt the Manchu-style shaved head and ponytail known as a **queue**. Failure to do so signified resistance to Qing rule and was punishable by death.

Many of the early years of the Qing dynasty under Emperor Kangxi were spend consolidating power. First, he eliminated the last strongholds of Ming supporters, including in Taiwan. Second, Emperor Kangxi extended China's western borders, conquering Mongols in Central Asia. Finally, he successfully held off Russia's incursions in the northeast. To gain the support of the Chinese bureaucrats, civil service examinations were reinstated, along with the traditional Confucian-style education and government-sponsored cultural works. The emphasis on religious and philosophical texts without any modern science or mathematics hindered China's technological advancement at a time when Europe was industrializing by leaps and bounds.

Kangxi's grandson Qianlong reigned longer than any other Qing emperor. Though he retired so he would not reign longer than his grandfather, he retained effective control of the government. Under his rule in the 1700s, China enjoyed peace and prosperity, with expansion of trade, skilled crafts, and farming. The Columbian Exchange introduced new crops like corn, and the amount of cultivated land was expanded. Beginning with the reign of Emperor Kangxi and extending through Emperor Qianlong, taxes for peasants remained low. This period is often referred to as a golden age.

The later Qing also faced many challenges. The economic prosperity of the early 1700s led to a population boom, resulting in unemployment and food shortages. Peasant unrest followed. Qianlong neglected his duties in favor of hunting and luxury, allowing for government corruption on a massive scale. International pressure to open to foreign merchants and Christian missionaries also threatened to destabilize the empire. At first Kangxi welcomed Jesuits to his court, respecting their knowledge of languages. Since Jesuits believed Chinese Christians could still practice ancestral rites, conversion to Christianity was permitted. When the Pope disagreed, Emperor Kangxi expelled the Christian missionaries. Foreign merchants had been restricted to certain ports, and the Chinese had limited interest in European goods, preferring to exchange Chinese wares for silver. In the 1800s, European powers like the British, desperate for a more favorable balance of trade, would go to extraordinary lengths to promote the opium trade in China (see chapter 20).

Japan

While the Ming dynasty isolated itself from most foreigners, Japan went through periods of both isolation and acceptance of Western influence. In 1603, the Tokugawa family gained prominence when one of its members acquired the title of *shogun*. Ruling Japan from the city of Edo (present-day Tokyo), the **Tokugawa Shogunate** brought a degree of centralized authority to Japan. Large estates of many of the *daimyo* were broken up and taken over by the Tokugawa family.

Europeans entered Japan in 1543 when Portuguese sailors shipwrecked and were washed up on the shore of the southern island of Kyushu. Additional visits from European traders and missionaries brought Western technology, including clocks and firearms, into Japan. The use of firearms changed Japanese warfare from feudal to modern and assisted the Tokugawa in maintaining their authority. When Christian missionaries arrived to bring Roman Catholicism to the Japanese, the Tokugawa at first protected them from Buddhist resistance. In the late 1580s, however, the Tokugawa stifled Buddhist resistance to their authority. Christianity was perceived as a threat to Tokugawa authority, and Christian missionaries were ordered to leave Japan. Japanese Christians were persecuted and executed. By 1630, foreign trade was allowed only in a few cities and Japanese ships were banned from trading or sailing across long distances. By the 1640s, only the Dutch and Chinese were allowed to trade through the port of Nagasaki. Contacts with the Dutch allowed the Japanese to keep informed about Western developments (**Dutch learning**) and adopt those they considered appropriate to Japanese goals.

› Rapid Review

Western Europe developed models of both absolute and parliamentary monarchy as its advanced technology strengthened its position as a world leader. Russia built a large empire whose rulers continued repressive policies and a system of serfdom that perpetuated Russian backwardness begun under Mongol rule. Spain and Portugal established empires in Mesoamerica and South America, while England and France vied for colonial dominance in North America. The Ottoman Empire conquered the Byzantine Empire, but by the early seventeenth century, could not keep up with Western technological advances and was on a path of decline. Ming China and Tokugawa Japan displayed varying responses to foreign influence. At the conclusion of the period, the Chinese pursued a policy of isolation from foreigners, whereas Japan allowed limited Western influence in order to avail itself of Western technology. Mughal India at first brought centralized government that softened relations between Hindus and Muslims; then later it broke up into regional governments that created openings for foreign intervention.

› Review Questions

Questions 1 to 2 refer to the following map.

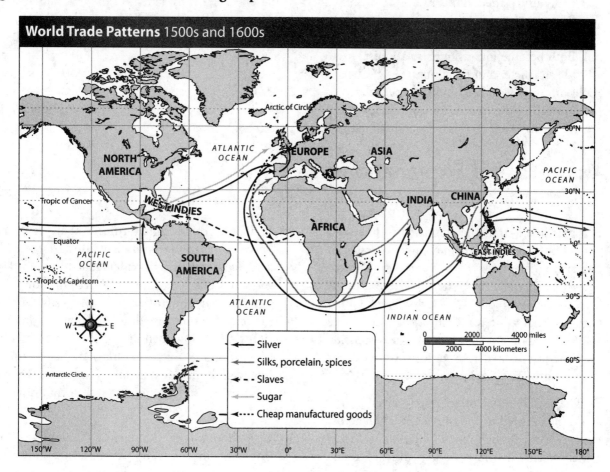

World Trade Patterns 1500s and 1600s

Legend:
- Silver
- Silks, porcelain, spices
- Slaves
- Sugar
- Cheap manufactured goods

1. What is the most likely product to be transported from the Americas to China?
   (A) Native American laborers
   (B) Precious metals like silver
   (C) New food like squash and tomatoes
   (D) Gunpowder and advanced weaponry

2. What was the impact of this commercial exchange?
   (A) High social status of merchants in Neo-Confucian society
   (B) Diseases spread to Asia, destabilizing labor markets.
   (C) China extended its empire into northern India and Russia.
   (D) Inflation destabilized European economies.

3. During the early eighteenth century, in which European nation did citizens enjoy the greatest degree of self-rule?
   (A) Russia
   (B) France
   (C) England
   (D) Spain

4. Which is true of the Mughal Empire?
   (A) It rejected traditional artistic styles in favor of Islamic ones.
   (B) It expanded the empire throughout the Indian subcontinent.
   (C) It reduced tensions between Muslim and Hindu communities.
   (D) It introduced repressive measures for women like *sati*.

5. What would a comparison of the Ming Dynasty and the Tokugawa Shogunate reveal?
   (A) Both feared that Christianity would eventually usurp their authority.
   (B) Both encouraged voyages of discovery to expand their territory.
   (C) Both became increasingly isolationist toward the end of their rule.
   (D) Both were weakened by the expense of protecting their borders from invasion.

〉 Answers and Explanations

1. **B** Hemispheric trade networks led to increased trade, but China was generally only interested in exchanging its products for silver. The Chinese were not especially interested in Western products (D) or new foods (C). Not only was China not particularly interested in labor, but Native American labor was generally not used outside the Americas, as Native Americans were vulnerable to European diseases (A).

2. **D** The rapid influx of so much silver in the world markets led to widespread inflation across Europe. Even though many Chinese merchants gained wealth in the period, it did not translate into substantially higher social status (A). Though disease had been an issue earlier in China, this period was not characterized by widespread epidemics (B). This is partly because China during this era was characterized by isolationism rather than expansionism (C).

3. **C** During this time, England developed a parliamentary system of representative government, characterized by a limited monarchy sharing power with representatives from the upper classes. Most other European nations, including Spain, Russia, and France, were governed by absolute monarchs (A, B, D).

4. **C** Under the Mughal ruler Akbar, tensions between Hindus and Muslims decreased, although later Mughal rulers failed to maintain those cordial relations. Located in northern and central India (B), the Mughals implemented reforms aimed at improving women's rights, including banning the Hindu practice of *sati* (D). Because the Mughal Empire included both Muslim and Hindu traditions, their artistic styles tended to reflect traditions of both cultures.

5. **C** Although the Tokugawa Shogunate was originally intrigued by Western weapons and technology, they later reversed their position, limiting access to outsiders, as did the Ming dynasty. The Ming had ended voyages of discovery by this point, and the Japanese never undertook any during this era (B). In Japan, this isolationism included banning Christianity as a potential threat, but in China Christian missionaries were allowed, though they had limited success (A). Neither the Ming nor the Tokugawa Shogunate spent large sums to defend themselves from outside invaders.

CHAPTER 19

Cultural and Intellectual Changes

IN THIS CHAPTER

Summary: The transformations in the formation of empires, in the slave trade, and in hemispheric connections took place against a backdrop of cultural and intellectual changes. In Europe, a spirit of religious reform created new religious denominations and promoted education. A scientific revolution provided new explanations for the nature of the universe, while Enlightenment philosophers analyzed the nature of political relationships. Enlightenment ideas spread through Europe, Russia, and the Western Hemisphere.

Key Terms

Catholic Reformation
   (Counter-Reformation)
commercial revolution
Deism
empirical research
Enlightenment
excommunication
heliocentric theory
indulgence

laissez-faire economics
natural laws
Ninety-Five Theses
Northern Renaissance
philosophes
predestination
Protestant Reformation
Scientific Revolution
Society of Jesus

Protestant and Catholic Reformations

The Renaissance, which began in the city-states of northern Italy, gradually spread to the states of northern Europe. The **Northern Renaissance** was characterized by a more intense religious focus than the Italian Renaissance. In 1517, to finance the restoration of St. Peter's

Basilica in Rome, the Roman Catholic Church authorized the sale of **indulgences**. Indulgences were documents that granted the purchaser the forgiveness of sins. A German priest and former monk named Martin Luther nailed the **Ninety-Five Theses**, or statements for debate, to the door of the Castle Church in Wittenberg in present-day Germany. Luther's studies of the Bible had led him to believe that salvation was obtained only through faith in Jesus Christ as the savior of the world from sin and was not dependent on following Church practices and traditions. Roman Catholic opposition to Luther's teachings led to his eventual **excommunication** from the Roman Catholic Church. Luther's ideas spread widely throughout Europe as a result of the introduction of movable type, an adaptation of Chinese printing technology, by Johannes Gutenberg in the mid-fifteenth century. Gutenberg also used the new printing technology to produce *The Gutenberg Bible,* written in Latin, about 1455.

The **Protestant Reformation** gained popularity not only for its religious teaching but also because of the political climate in Europe in the sixteenth century. A new wave of nationalism was sweeping through Europe, including the German states, which were part of the Holy Roman Empire. Many Germans resented the authority of the pope and welcomed Protestantism for this reason. Protestantism also looked more favorably on Christian participation in commercial and money-making ventures than did Roman Catholicism, a factor that contributed to the **commercial revolution** of the early modern period.

Spread of Protestantism

A second Protestant Reformation occurred in England when King Henry VIII broke with the Roman Catholic Church over the pope's refusal to annul his first marriage, which had not produced a male heir. Under Henry's daughter Elizabeth I, England officially recognized Protestantism. Another Protestant, John Calvin, preached the concept of **predestination**, which held that God had predetermined those people who would be saved. Calvinism spread not only through much of western and northern Europe but also to North America through the migrations of the Puritans.

Catholic Reformation

The Protestant Reformation produced a movement within the Roman Catholic Church to consider Protestant charges against it. As a result of the **Catholic Reformation (Counter-Reformation)**, a church assembly, the Council of Trent, abandoned the sale of indulgences, but preserved traditional Roman Catholic beliefs and practices. A new religious order, the Jesuits, or **Society of Jesus**, was organized to serve as the missionary and educational arm of the Church. The Jesuits engaged widely in missionary work in the Americas and in Asia, taking both Christianity and the knowledge of European culture and technology to those continents.

Results of the Protestant Reformation

In addition to spreading the belief in salvation by faith alone, the Protestant Reformation:

- Increased European questioning of political authority
- Strengthened the authority of monarchs as papal power decreased
- Encouraged education as Protestants wanted their children to be able to read the Bible
- Improved the status of women within marriage as religious writers encouraged love between husband and wife
- Created new Protestant churches

The Scientific Revolution

The seventeenth and eighteenth centuries saw another kind of revolution: one in scientific thought. Among the key debates of science was a dialogue concerning the nature of the universe. Copernicus, a Polish scientist, abandoned the geocentric theory of Ptolemy to prove that the sun was the center of the solar system (the **heliocentric theory**). The Italian scientist Galileo used a telescope to confirm the discoveries of Copernicus and to study planetary motion and gravity. As a result of his studies, Galileo was taken to court by the Roman Catholic Church and required to publicly recant his theories. A German scientist, Johannes Kepler, discovered the elliptical pattern of planetary motion, whereas Isaac Newton established the basic principles of motion and described the forces of gravity.

New knowledge also was obtained concerning the human body. Vesalius of Belgium studied human anatomy. The Englishman John Harvey explained the circulatory system.

Revolution in Scientific Thought

The **Scientific Revolution** supported additional research. René Descartes encouraged the educated to develop a skeptical approach to learning. Francis Bacon advocated **empirical research** based on observations and carefully obtained and replicable data. Western science took on a nature distinct from scientific thought in East Asia. In contrast to Chinese scientific thought, which generally dealt with specific facts that were practical in nature, Western scientific thought formulated general laws of nature that had roots in Islamic and Greek philosophy. Also characteristic of Western scientific thought were principles that could be used for the improvement of humankind.

The Enlightenment

The revolution in science led to a revolution in thought regarding the nature of politics, economics, and society. The **Enlightenment** involved the application of human reason to improve society. Behind the movement was the belief that human beings were basically good and that education and reason could improve their condition limitlessly. Childhood was recognized as a separate stage of growth, and children's toys and books appeared for the first time. Like the Protestant Reformation, the Enlightenment supported marriages based on love, a concept that raised the status of women in family life.

Beginning and Spread of Enlightenment Thought

The Enlightenment began with the *philosophes*, or French philosophers, many of whom discussed their ideas at Parisian meetinghouses called salons. As the movement spread throughout Europe, Russia, and Europe's colonies in the Americas, the Enlightenment continued to support scientific advances. Some Enlightenment thinkers followed a scientific philosophy called **Deism**, which held that there was a god who created the earth, then left it to operate by **natural law**.

Enlightenment Political Thought

Political philosophers such as the Englishman John Locke and the Frenchman Jean Jacques Rousseau wrote of a social contract in which governments ruled by the consent of the governed to ensure the preservation of the natural rights of humankind. Criminologists advocated rehabilitation for criminals, whereas Mary Wollstonecraft of England spoke out for political rights for women. The Scottish economist Adam Smith wrote *The Wealth of Nations* (1776), in which he set forth the principles of *laissez-faire* economics. Smith's philosophy held that government regulation of the economy should be minimal in order to allow the free operation of the laws of supply and demand. Denis Diderot of France compiled the *Encyclopédie,* which included the scientific and social scientific knowledge of the Enlightenment.

› Rapid Review

The period from 1450 to 1750 witnessed three major cultural and intellectual revolutions. The Protestant Reformation defied established Church traditions and taught salvation by faith alone. The Scientific Revolution explained the nature of the universe and encouraged research. Another movement, the Enlightenment, believed in the basic goodness of humanity and spoke of natural rights that formed the philosophy behind the political revolutions of the eighteenth century.

› Review Questions

1. Answer Parts A and B.
   (A) Identify and explain TWO results of the Protestant Reformation.
   (B) Identify and explain ONE difference in the German and English causes for the Protestant Reformation.

Questions 2 and 3 refer to the following passage.

Sir Francis Bacon (English, 1561–1626) said: "Knowledge is power." He advocated *applying* science and said that the scientific method should include observation of physical realities, collection of data based on such observations, and the drawing of conclusions from these data. As other thinkers refined his ideas, they concluded that a hypothesis, or theory, could prompt initial observation.

—Beth Bartolini-Salimbeni, 2017

2. Which of the following phrases best sums up Bacon's ideas?
   (A) Science over reason
   (B) Reason over religion
   (C) Reality over science
   (D) Theory over practice

3. How does the work of Galileo in support of the idea of a heliocentric universe reflect Bacon's ideas?
   (A) It supplants fact with opinion.
   (B) It confirms the nature of the universe.
   (C) It uses reason to confirm theory.
   (D) It replaces speculation with skepticism.

4. The most likely form of government to come from a "social contract" would be which of the following?
   (A) Conservative
   (B) Theocratic
   (C) Anarchical
   (D) Republican

5. Which of the following concepts of the period 1450 to 1750 did NOT rely on natural laws?
   (A) Predestination
   (B) Deism
   (C) Laissez-faire philosophy
   (D) Social contract

❯ Answers and Explanations

1A. The Protestant Reformation resulted in England's break with the Roman Catholic Church and the establishment of the Church of England; a commercial revolution since Protestantism favored money-making ventures more than did Roman Catholicism; the establishment of diverse Christian, non–Roman Catholic sects—Calvinism, Lutheranism, for example; the belief that faith and good works could lead to salvation.

1B. The English Reformation resulted from a king's desire to divorce and remarry. The German Reformation objected to what it considered corrupt practices in the Roman Catholic Church (i.e., the sale of indulgences), believed that faith and not the following of Church practices and traditions could lead to salvation.

2. **B** "Reason over religion" refers to Bacon's belief that critical thought and the use of rationally applied science were more valid as a means of establishing factual knowledge and truth than was acceptance of "truths" on faith. A, C, and D are incorrect.

3. **C** By advocating observation of physical realities, collection of data, and drawing conclusions, Galileo used reason to confirm his theory of a heliocentric universe. Neither opinion (A) nor skepticism (D) guided Galileo's thought processes or use of the scientific method. Bacon's ideas confirm the scientific method, not the nature of the universe (B).

4. **D** A social contract is an agreement between government and the governed meant to ensure preservation of humankind's natural rights. In a republic, the governed control power by giving their consent to chosen representatives. A, B, and C are incorrect.

5. **A** Predestination is a theological construct that says all that will happen is predestined. Deism (B), the laissez-faire philosophy (C), and the idea of a social contract (D) all rely on the belief that there are natural laws that govern behavior and rights.

Summaries: The Global Tapestry and Networks of Exchange

Timeline
Part I (600–1200)

570 to 632 CE	Life of Muhammad
618 CE to 907	Tang dynasty in China
622	The *hijra*
711 CE to 1492	Muslim occupation of Spain
750 CE to 1258	Abbasid dynasty
960 CE to 1279	Song dynasty in China
1054	Schism between the eastern and western Christian churches
1066	Norman invasion of England
1096	First Crusade

Part II: 1200–1450

Eleventh to thirteenth century	Kingdom of Ghana
Eleventh to fifteenth century	Swahili cities in East Africa
Twelfth to fifteenth century	Kingdom of Great Zimbabwe
Twelfth to sixteenth century	Kingdom of Axum
Thirteenth century	Beginning of chiefdoms in Oceania
Thirteenth to fifteenth century	Empire of Mali
1206 to 1526	Sultanate of Delhi
1211	Beginning of Mongol conquests
1271 to 1295	Marco Polo's travels to China
1279 to 1368	Yuan dynasty
1289	Founding of the Ottoman dynasty
1304 to 1369	Life of Ibn Battuta
1325	Founding of Tenochtitlán by the Mexica (Aztecs)
1330s	Beginnings of bubonic plague in China
1337 to 1453	Hundred Years' War
1347	Beginnings of bubonic plague in the Mediterranean world
1368 to 1644	Ming dynasty
Fourteenth to seventeenth century	Kingdom of Kongo
1405 to 1433	Zheng He's voyages in the Indian Ocean
1441	Beginning of the Portuguese slave trade in Africa

Key Comparisons

1. Feudalism in Japan and Western Europe
2. Mongol rule in Russia and China
3. Muslim Spain and feudal Europe
4. The spread of Islam and the spread of Buddhism
5. Chinese and European presence in the Indian Ocean
6. Urban areas in the Islamic world, non-Islamic Europe, and China
7. Acceptance of Islam in Africa and Europe
8. Mesoamerican and Andean civilizations
9. Polynesian, Viking, and Bantu migrations
10. Gender roles in early Islam and under the caliphate

Change/Continuity Chart

REGION	POLITICAL	ECONOMIC	SOCIAL	CHANGES	CONTINUITIES
East Asia	Japanese feudalism Tang/Song dynasties Mongols Yuan dynasty Ming dynasty	Gunpowder Long-distance trade Technology Flying money Zheng He expedition Grand Canal	Urbanization Neo-Confucianism Buddhism Movable type Celadon pottery Bubonic plague	Japanese shogunate Neo-Confucianism Chinese expansion into Vietnam Mongol domination in China	Nomadic threats Confucianism Footbinding Patriarchal family Shinto
Southeast Asia	Expansion of China into Vietnam	Malay sailors	Islam	Islam	Hinduism Buddhism
Oceania	Regional kingdoms	Agriculture Fishing	Polytheism Polynesian migrations Stratified society	Settlement of Hawaii	Isolation from global trade network
Central Asia	Mongols Steppe diplomacy Tamerlane	Silk Roads trade Moldboard plow	Maori Mongol Peace Women have a voice in tribal councils	Mongol dominance Islam Isolation of Russia from Western Europe	Pastoral nomadism Steppe diplomacy Buddhism
South Asia	Delhi Sultanate Rule of Tamerlane	Arabic numerals Indian Ocean trade	Caste system Islam	Islam	Hinduism Caste system
Southwest Asia	Crusades Mongol destruction of Baghdad	Malay sailors Long-distance trade	Islam Veiling of women *Shariah* *Umma* Bubonic plague	Rise of Islam, Sunni/Shi'ite split Transfer of knowledge of sugarcane to Europeans	Nomadic tribes
North Africa	Regional kingdoms Islam, Mamluk dynasties	Trans-Saharan trade, gold, salt Ironworking	Slavery Travels of Ibn Battuta Bubonic plague	Islam	Trans-Saharan trade

KEY IDEA

Change/Continuity Chart (Continued)

KEY IDEA

REGION	POLITICAL	ECONOMIC	SOCIAL	CHANGES	CONTINUITIES
Sub-Saharan Africa	Stateless societies Islam	Indian Ocean Trade in ivory, ebony, animal skins Trade with Portugal Ironworking	Bantu migrations Swahili *griots* Age grades	Islam Introduction of banana cultivation by Malay sailors	Christianity Slavery Bantu migrations
Western Europe	Feudalism Holy Roman Empire Attempted Mongol incursions Islamic Spain Investiture conflict	Manorialism Moldboard plow Rise of universities Bubonic plague Mediterranean trade routes Hanseatic League	Feudalism Population growth Viking invasions Urbanization Renaissance Palace schools	Islam Increased urbanization and trade Decline of feudalism Renaissance	Christianity Feudalism
Eastern Europe	Byzantine Empire Mongol invasion Seljuk and Ottoman incursion	Expansion of Western Europe Serfdom Trade in fur and timber Hanseatic League	Serfdom Viking invasion	Mongol invasion Viking invasion Serfdom	Eastern Orthodox Christianity Byzantine trade networks
North America	Regional tribal organization	Agriculture Fishing Trade with Mesoamerica	Anasazi and Mississippian cultures Mounds	Trade with Mesoamerica	Isolation from global trade networks
Latin America	Aztec and Inca empires	*Chinampas* Long-distance and regional trade Calendar Incan roads *Quipus*	Human sacrifice Polytheism Quetzalcóatl Parallel descent *Mita* Weaving *Ayllus, calpulli*	Aztec and Inca empires	Isolation from global trade networks

Summaries: Land-Based Empires and Trans-Oceanic Interconnections

Timeline

1453	Fall of the eastern Roman Empire
1464 to 1591	Empire of Songhay
1492	The Reconquest (Spain)
	First voyage of Christopher Columbus
1494	Treaty of Tordesillas
1497 to 1498	Vasco da Gama's voyage to India
1517	Beginning of the Protestant Reformation
1519 to 1521	Spanish conquest of Mexico
1526 to 1858	Mughal dynasty (India)
1532 to 1540	Spanish conquest of Peru
1545 to 1563	Council of Trent
1588	Defeat of the Spanish Armada
1603 to 1867	Tokugawa Shogunate (Japan)
1613	Beginning of the Romanov dynasty of Russia
1643 to 1715	Reign of Louis XIV of France
1644 to 1911	Qing dynasty (China)

Key Comparisons

1. European versus Asian monarchs
2. Empires in Africa, Asia, and Europe
3. European versus Asian economic systems
4. Reactions of Japan versus China to Western influence
5. Slavery versus serfdom
6. Trade in Mughal India versus Ming China
7. Russian versus Ottoman interaction with the West
8. Gender roles in Ming China versus Western Europe
9. Trans-Atlantic versus Indian Ocean trade
10. Western European versus Asian and Ottoman technology

Change/Continuity Chart

KEY IDEA

REGION	POLITICAL	ECONOMIC	SOCIAL	CHANGES	CONTINUITIES
East Asia	Ming/Qing dynasties Tokugawa Shogunate	Japanese trade with the Dutch Chinese trade through Macao	Patriarchal society Population increase	Columbian Exchange (China) Christianity Chinese withdrawal from world trade	Ming dynasty Confucianism Neo-Confucianism
Southeast Asia	Regional kingdoms	Indian Ocean trade European plantations	Slavery Islam	Increased European trade Columbian Exchange	Muslim trade Islam Hinduism
Oceania	Regional kingdoms	Agriculture Fishing	Exposure to epidemic disease	Some European explorations	Relative isolation
Central Asia	Steppe diplomacy Russian Empire	Pastoral nomadism Westernization of Russia	Serfdom Tribal units	Russian expansion	Mongol threats to China
South Asia	Mughal dynasty Entry of the British	European trading empires	Miniatures Temporary improvement in women's status Taj Mahal	Columbian Exchange Return to local governments	Indian Ocean trade Islam Hinduism
Southwest Asia (Middle East)	Ottoman Empire	Decline of trade with the West	Slaves from North Africa Harem	Columbian Exchange Ottoman decline	Slavery Islam
North Africa	Regional kingdoms	Gold-salt trade	Slavery Islam	Columbian Exchange	Trans-Saharan slave trade Islam

REGION	POLITICAL	ECONOMIC	SOCIAL	CHANGES	CONTINUITIES
Sub-Saharan Africa	Regional kingdoms Cape Colony founded	Bronze, ivory, gold, slaves, ebony Indian Ocean trade	Trans-Atlantic slave trade Christianity	Reduced population Columbian Exchange Dependence on European technology	Islam Tribal allegiances Slavery within Africa Native religions
Western Europe	*Reconquista* Defeat of the Spanish Armada Expulsion of the Jews from Spain	Growth of capitalism Slave trade Exploration Inflation Scientific Revolution	Population increase Reformation Enlightenment	Columbian Exchange	Renaissance
Eastern Europe	Fall of Byzantium Ottoman rule	Agriculture	Serfdom	Columbian Exchange Islam	Serfdom Orthodox Christianity
North America	Colonization	Fur trade Plantations	Slavery Triangular trade Indentured servants	Columbian Exchange European presence	Foraging Nomadism Polytheism
Latin America	Colonization	Mining Sugar plantations	Slavery Social classes Triangular trade	Columbian Exchange European conquest	Polytheism

CHAPTER 20

Revolutions and the Consequences of Industrialization

IN THIS CHAPTER

Summary: The period between 1750 and 1900 was one of radical change, especially in the West, Russia, Japan, and China. Political revolutions occurred in the Americas, France, and China. The global population increase caused in part by the Columbian Exchange was followed by a revolution in industry that began in England.

Key Terms

capital
domestic system
economic liberalism
enclosure movement
entrepreneurship
factors of production
gold standard
Industrial Revolution
laissez-faire economics

limited liability corporation
Meiji Restoration
Russo-Japanese War
Second Industrial Revolution
Sino-Japanese War
stock market
transnational company
zaibatsu

Industrial Revolution

The change in the production of manufactured goods from the home to the factory began in the English textile industry in the mid-eighteenth century. The **Industrial Revolution** built on innovations in agriculture that had brought improved farming methods such as crop rotation, scientific breeding of livestock, and the application of fertilizers. A result of increased agricultural output was the **enclosure movement**. Large landholders fenced pastures that previously had been left open for common use, creating a sizable population of landless laborers. England's growing position in global trade contributed to the pursuit of manufacturing interests. The English government supported industrialization by passing laws and instituting policies that promoted its growth. In addition, England possessed the **factors of production**:

- Land (including natural resources such as coal and iron ore)
- Labor (including thousands of dispossessed farmers from southeastern England evicted from their lands as a result of the enclosure movement)
- **Capital** (banking and investment interests capable of funding the costs of factories and machinery)
- **Entrepreneurship** (groups of individuals with the knowledge of combining land, labor, and capital to establish factory production)

The technological advance that initiated the transition of manufacturing from home to factory was the steam engine, invented by James Watt of Scotland in the 1770s. Accompanying factory production were changes in transportation and communication such as the telegraph, canals, steamships, and railroads, all of which served to speed up the movement of goods and information.

Expansion of Financial Institutions

To promote industrial investments, financiers offered a variety of services, including insurance, **stock markets**, and **limited liability corporations**. Many favored the use of the **gold standard** to promote financial stability. The globalization of industrialization gave rise to **transnational companies** such as the United Fruit Company and the Hongkong and Shanghai Banking Corporation. These financial innovations owed their origin to the economists Adam Smith and John Stuart Mill. Both Smith's *laissez-faire* economics and Mill's **economic liberalism** held that government intervention in and regulation of the economy should be minimal.

Social Changes Brought About by Industrialization

The factory system brought a number of changes to family life and society:

- Work was carried out outside the home, a situation that separated family members.
- Factory workers were required to follow schedules and to arrive at work at a specified time.
- Factories required workers to adhere to strict rules.
- Work was done to the noise of machines.
- The pace of work was generally more rapid than at home.
- Women lost manufacturing jobs carried out under the **domestic system**. They were expected to return to the traditional roles of homemaker and childcare provider.
- Social status began to be determined more by wealth than by family position in society.
- Early industrial cities were generally crowded, unsanitary, and poorly lighted, with no police protection.

After 1850, the nature of the industrial setting changed somewhat:

- Workers in Western societies received higher wages and shorter working hours, allowing for more leisure time activities.
- With the increase in leisure time came popular interest in the theater and in sports.
- Additional employment opportunities arose in secretarial work and sales. Some of these jobs were filled by women, especially those who were unmarried.
- The mass production of clothing made it more affordable, allowing the general population to wear similar fashions.
- Popular consumption of manufactured goods led to advertising campaigns.

The Industrial Revolution Begins in Great Britain

In Great Britain, a number of variables fostered the emergence of new industries and modes of production, well before the rest of Continental Europe. First, new agricultural methods in the eighteenth century resulted in a production boom that lowered prices and demand for agricultural labor, while also increasing available money for families to purchase manufactured goods. Britain's mercantilist traditions and extensive colonies resulted in surplus capital for investment, additional markets for manufactured goods, and established credit and banking institutions to finance industrial enterprises, not to mention a culture that embraced wealth, commerce and the associated risks. Britain enjoyed geographic advantages, too, including ample supplies of key natural resources (coal, iron), compact territory that made creation of transportation networks easier, and access to navigable ports and rivers. Political conditions were also favorable, with a stable government that supported private enterprise, few internal trade barriers, and isolation from wars on the European continent. The Crystal Palace, made of glass and steel, constructed for the first industrial fair in 1851, was a symbol of Britain's industrial achievements.

Despite Great Britain's remarkable progress, there were occasional barriers to industrialism. For example, Britain made some limited attempts at protective tariffs, most notably the Corn Laws of 1815, intended to protect British landowners from cheap imported grain (not just corn) that flooded the market after Britain's blockade of Europe during the Napoleonic Wars ended. These laws benefited the nobility, who owned the bulk of fertile land, but hurt both the lower classes now spending the bulk of their income on grain, as well as manufacturers who suffered a drop in demand as disposable income declined. When the Reform Act of 1832 extended suffrage to the merchant class, Parliament became more sympathetic to those opposing the Corn Laws, eventually repealing them in 1846. As industrialism and manufacturing matured in Great Britain, its success spurred other European nations to encourage industrialism within their own borders.

The Factory System and the Division of Labor

The factory system was created in order to better supervise labor. In the old, rural manufacturing system (or cottage industry) that characterized European proto-industrialization, peasants were left on their own to work at the spinning wheel or the loom. Both the quality and the efficiency of their work depended on factors that were beyond the entrepreneur's control. Beginning in the textile industry, new more efficient machines like the spinning jenny and water frame were cost-prohibitive for individuals and required power sources, leading to the development of factories, where workers came to a central location and worked with machines under the supervision of managers.

The factory system employed a technique that has come to be known as the division of labor, whereby formerly complex tasks that required knowledge and skill were broken down into a series of simple tasks, aided by machines. Additionally, larger, centralized factories allowed entrepreneurs to take advantage of power sources required to operate new machines. With the division of labor, skilled craftsman were replaced with unskilled labor, thereby increasing the supply of labor and decreasing the wages that needed to be paid. At the same time, the volume that manufacturers could produce increased, thereby allowing them to sell products for less and still increase profits. As machines did more and more of the work, the number of workers needed decreased, creating unemployment and competition for jobs.

Spread of Industrialization

As described earlier, the Industrial Revolution began in Great Britain, but did not take hold immediately in continental Europe, as those nations did not possess the same favorable conditions. Transportation in Europe was problematic, with few good roads and many customs barriers across its rivers and borders. Guilds were more powerful on the Continent, acting to protect traditional craft systems from industrial change. Particularly with France, wars created political and economic turmoil, limiting access to new technologies from Britain. This was exacerbated by Britain's attempts to maintain its advantage by restricting access to its engineers, technology and industrial equipment.

A key factor in the spread of industrialism was the development of new commercial banking enterprises. As Europe tried to "catch up" with Britain, the scale and cost of industrial equipment had increased beyond individual financing. New commercial banks on the continent held small deposits from numerous customers, allowing them to amass huge amounts of capital which they then invested in new industrial enterprises. Like joint-stock corporations, the liability of shareholders was limited to the original investment. This helped make industry feasible on the European continent. Slowly, industrialization spread from west to east. As it did, the pace and degree of government intervention increased.

France and Belgium

Belgium was one of the first to follow Great Britain, having access to its own reserves of natural resources and the advantage of a compact territory. The Belgian government undertook construction of a railroad to integrate the nation. France's transition to industrialism was more gradual than Great Britain's. Though France's revolution ended medieval guilds, it limited France's population and strengthened the position of the peasantry. During the Napoleon's reign, he sponsored huge infrastructure projects, including roads, canals and ports. The French government also encouraged the construction of railroads through public-private partnerships in which the government paid for much of the construction costs. With the Bourbon restoration came tariffs on inexpensive British goods to protect French industries.

German States

Although the German states had access to large coal and iron deposits, there were a number of barriers to industrialization, including limited access to ports serving Atlantic trade routes. Traditional institutions like serfdom and guilds continued, impeding free movement of labor and establishment of industry. Finally, political fragmentation limited Germany's economic impact. Prussia emerged as an industrial leader, creating *Zollverein*, a protective customs union formed by a coalition of German states. This was influenced by economist Friedrich List, who argued that nations should reduce internal trade barriers but employ protective tariffs to foster the development of fledgling domestic industries. When private capital proved insufficient, the governments of the German states took action, financing railway construction, subsidizing locomotive industry, and even nationalizing railways altogether. The economic and transportation integration of the German states helped facilitate their eventual unification under Prussia. Later government investments in heavy industry and technical education made Germany a world industrial power in the Second Industrial Revolution.

Eastern Europe and Russia

In Eastern Europe, traditional economic systems persisted, including a conservative and powerful landed aristocracy supported by an agricultural peasantry, including serfs. These powerful elites lacked the incentive to invest in modern industries which might threaten the status quo. In Russia, a military defeat in the Crimea highlighted the weakness of its economy. Reforms implemented by Alexander II included creating a mobile labor force by ending serfdom, and agricultural reforms to improve output. The government, under the direction of Sergei Witte, built railroads to connect resources, factories and markets, including the Trans-Siberian railroad. Witte also provided incentives for foreign investment, stabilized the currency, and funded development of telegraph lines and electrical plants. By 1900, Russia was the fourth largest producer of steel in the world.

Social Effects of Industrialization

Rural Areas

The Industrial Revolution transformed European life across all demographic groups, but not always in the same ways or evenly. A general change was population growth, more due to reductions in wars, famines and epidemics than increased birth rates. Ending serfdom created large classes of landless peasants who had to pay rents regardless of harvest. In some rural areas, this overcrowding meant smaller plots of land for families. In Ireland, the potato required a relatively small space to sustain a family, making millions of rural Irish dependent on them. Crop failures led to widespread starvation among the Irish, some of whom emigrated to the United States. In other rural areas, migration of labor to the cities created different problems.

Urbanization

Cities transformed from centers of government and trade to manufacturing. Factories located in cities for access to transportation, energy and labor, while millions migrated to cities in search of work. Not designed to accommodate such a huge influx of people, cities struggled with overcrowding. Housing was scarce and overcrowding was common. Human waste and refuse were thrown in the streets. The waste ran into local water supplies, and outbreaks of diseases like cholera were common. Crime and fraud were widespread. City governments were unwilling or unable to step in to improve conditions, never having had to in the past.

Working Class

For many working-class the nature of their work, and therefore their lives, fundamentally changed. In agriculture, there are busy periods, but also long stretches of inactivity, and the workers could often set the pace. Factory owners couldn't afford to let machines sit idle, so the workers were expected to work constantly for the duration of the shift. Discipline was harsh and unforgiving. No social insurance laws existed to protect workers in case of injury or unemployment, or to guarantee wages. Initially, in coal mines and factories, entire families worked side by side as they had done when farming. Child labor was common, and often preferable, as children's small size afforded them some advantages in mines and around machines, but they typically earned less than a third of a man's wages. Pauper children, orphaned or abandoned by parents, were "apprenticed" by parish authorities to factories or mines, where they received miserable housing and board for hours of unrelenting labor. Eventually, in Great Britain, government inquiries into working conditions led to a minimum age of nine years for child labor (Factory Act of 1833) and limited hours for child and female labor (Ten Hours Act of 1847), though these applied mainly to textile and coal industries.

Industrial workers were particularly vulnerable to the volatility of business cycles and market forces. If an economic downturn was severe enough, an entrepreneur could lose his entire business, but before that, he would fire workers or reduce wages as necessary. In England, guarding against a potentially radicalized poor like that which contributed to the revolution in France, anti-combination laws were passed to limit their organization. Despite this, workers formed trade unions, using collective actions like strikes to improve their position.

Middle Class

The economic benefits of the Industrial revolution were not evenly distributed, but one clear winner was the growing middle class. This included owners and managers of factories and mines, bankers, lawyers, doctors, and skilled artisans, among others. Though investing in industry carried risks, the profits for successful enterprises were sizeable. They were able to move out from cities to suburbs, employ servants, and even purchase large estates alongside traditional aristocrats. These wealthy professionals and businessmen became known as the *bourgeoisie*. Eventually they sought political power to match their economic and social status.

Some artisans and craftspeople who were members of traditional guilds resisted industrialism, fearing competition from cheap, factory-produced goods. One resistance group in the early 1800s, the Luddites, destroyed machines in textile factories in a futile attempt to prevent mechanization of the industry.

Women and Family Life

As previously mentioned, families worked side-by-side in early factories and mines, as they had in the fields. Eventually, responsibilities and hours of parents no longer coincided with children. With restrictions on child labor hours, parents and children no longer had the same schedules. This had implications for female labor. As reform movements examined factory and mining labor practices, the role of women was also examined. Much has been made about new opportunities for women in the workplace, but most women in factories were unmarried. People feared that women and men working together would result in immoral behavior. Restrictions on child labor, too, resulted in changes for women, as they needed to care for children at home, and laws were passed limiting women's factory hours. Family life evolved, with the focus shifting to a nuclear family. As living standards increased, especially in the middle class, marriage was seen less as an economic imperative, and more as a romantic arrangement. Women were perceived as caretakers of the home and family, again, especially in the middle class. Thus female employment, particularly for working-class women, centered on domestic service or work that could be done in the home, like laundry or sewing. For the most economically vulnerable women, prostitution was a means of survival.

Second Industrial Revolution

New Technology

Beginning around 1870, the Second Industrial Revolution was not characterized by innovations in heavy industry, but rather new technologies that improved upon existing methods. Based on the work of Thomas Edison and Nikolai Tesla, electricity was distributed across a public grid, transforming both economic and social life. Combined with the smaller internal combustion engine, electricity extended the use of labor-saving machinery into previously artisanal industries, expanding mass production of goods. These cheaper factory-produced goods and new labor-saving devices began making their way into newly prosperous middle-class homes. Improvements on the Bessemer process made refining iron into the more durable steel more efficient, reducing the price of steel substantially. Railways expanded dramatically as a result. The discovery of petroleum not only changed the fuel needed to run machines, but also led to the development of new materials like vulcanized rubber, plastics, and fertilizers. Refrigerated rail cars, ice boxes, and canning processes dramatically changed food consumption. Steamships provided faster transport of goods across oceans. Communications were also revolutionized, first with the telegraph and later with the telephone. All of these combined to create a truly global marketplace, with the communications systems to handle international orders for raw materials and manufactured goods, and the distribution networks to fulfill them.

Medical Advances

Louis Pasteur demonstrated the importance of microorganisms in natural processes. His work improved food safety through the pasteurization of food, in which it is heated to kill bacteria. It also resulted in the development of vaccines for diseases like cholera, diphtheria and typhoid. Joseph Lister pioneered the use of antiseptics, reducing post-surgical mortality, and anesthesia later broadened the scope of surgical interventions. These gave rise to medical schools with rigorous, scientifically-based curricula, including some for women, notably the London School of Medicine for Women founded by Elizabeth Garrett Anderson (although Dorothea Erxleben of Germany had been granted an M.D. over a hundred years earlier).

Urban Reforms

As cities became more crowded and the problems associated with urbanization grew more acute, reformers attempted to ameliorate the problems. As the British were at the forefront of industrialism, so too, were they pioneers of many reforms. Often driven by a self-interested middle class concerned about the spread of crime, filth and disease, these reform movements were responsible for public works projects like sewers, water purification and plumbing, as well as the gradual assumption of responsibility for public health by government entities. Sir Edwin Chadwick was one such reformer, partly responsible for the modern administrative state. Whether in his 1842 report *The Sanitary Conditions of the Labouring Population,* which demonstrated a causal link between poor sanitation and disease, or in the Poor Law Commission report, which argued for consistent but draconian conditions in poorhouses, he advocated for centralized, efficient public administration of social programs. Internal combustion engines and petroleum made automobiles, street cars, street trolleys and other forms of mass transit possible, which in turn changed residential patterns as middle classes moved from cities to suburbs. Early forms of urban planning began with the garden city movement, pioneered by Sir Ebenezer Howard of Great Britain, which sought to balance greenspaces and countryside with urban areas. Model villages were created like New Lanark (by Robert Owen) and Port Sunlight, based on the idea that providing quality housing and pastoral environments would result in increased productivity. Though these towns charged comparatively low rents, wages were also low and residents were often subject to paternalistic rules set by the industrialist or landowner. Government authorities eventually addressed the lack of affordable housing, through local taxes used to build cheap public housing in Great Britain, and through generous credit terms in France. In Europe, Napoleon III and Georges Haussmann led the way, removing medieval walls, widening streets, and filling city centers with museums, parks, theaters and government buildings, and lining streets with new glowing gas-lamps. Haussmann's vision included apartment buildings with a homogenous, coherent exterior that became part of the urban landscape. Former residents relocated to the suburbs, using new mass transit systems to commute to work.

Business Changes

Although there wasn't a worldwide depression during this time, volatility in the business cycles led to periods of economic hardship in different places and at different times. Protective tariffs were imposed to protect emerging domestic industries from competition by cheap foreign goods. Economic zones emerged, with distinctions between industrial producers of manufactured goods (Western Europe) and agricultural exporters of raw materials (Southern and Eastern Europe). In Germany, cartels, or groups of businesses, coordinated with each other to impose production quotas and to fix market prices. Germany, as a later industrializing nation, also took advantage of economies of scale and new machinery to create mega-sized factory plants, allowing goods to be produced more cheaply and with less labor. Wage-based workers were especially vulnerable to market pressures, as they could be easily fired and hired in response to market fluctuations. Efforts to unionize had mixed success, particularly in England where attempts to create a national federation of unions failed, but local trade unions persisted. Economic historians Karl Marx and Friedrich Engels saw these struggles as a continuation of historic clashes of socio-economic classes, in this case with the capitalist bourgeoisie exploiting the labor of the workers, or proletariat. Articulated in the *Communist Manifesto* in 1848, this theory helped explain the development of class consciousness, especially among the working class.

Social Changes

That each social class now lived and worked together facilitated this class consciousness. An elite class developed, merging aristocratic landholders with newly wealthy industrialists, partly due to changing views on marriage and partly due to elite schools which both attended. This upper class often pursued government or military jobs, reinforcing their influence. Middle classes often worked to create a semblance of an upper class lifestyle. Men provided income and women were seen as the guardians of the perfect family. The cult of domesticity envisioned beautiful, gentle mothers who kept a perfect home, sang and played piano, excelled at domestic arts, and raised perfectly-behaved children. Often the reality was much different, and many middle-class wives who couldn't afford enough domestic servants toiled behind the scenes to create the illusion of perfection. In addition, being excluded from most workplaces served to keep women dependent on fathers and husbands for their economic security, relegating them to marginalized forms of work like piecework sewing in sweatshops. Later opportunities opened up for middle-class women as teachers, nurses or shop clerks, but these were low-wage positions. For some, who lacked family or marital protection, prostitution was the only viable option.

It is important to note that Eastern European nations followed a different pattern. Though some implemented land reforms intended to liberate the serfs and create a mobile workforce, they met with resistance. Landowners, often members of the new local assemblies, retained the best land. Peasants were obliged to repay the landowners, which was difficult given the infertility of their new land, making it difficult for them to leave while they still owed money.

Mass Culture

As standards of living increased and prices declined, a consumer culture developed. Department stores, which aggregated a variety of goods, were created to make shopping easier and more enticing. Mass marketing was used to attract new customers. Advertising found a home in newspapers with mass circulation, as well as on radio shows that captured the public's imagination. With the advent of public education systems, beginning as voluntary elementary education in France in 1833 and later spreading to most Western European nations in the form of compulsory education for boys and girls, literacy rates soared. Public education served to reinforce patriotism, reflected liberal beliefs in science and progress, and created a literate, disciplined workforce. With the standardization of working hours came the standardization of leisure hours. Leisure became commercialized, as mass transit allowed people to travel to entertainment venues. Spectator sports, beaches, recreation centers, dance halls, theaters, and amusement parks all flourished, creating a mass culture through a commonality of shared experiences.

Industrialization in Russia

As the Western nations began to industrialize, Russia remained backward in terms of technology. The emancipation of the serfs in 1861 aided Russia in the transition from a predominantly agricultural to a more industrialized society. Government support for industry led to the construction of a trans-Siberian railroad that linked the European portion of Russia with the Pacific world. By the latter years of the nineteenth century, factories had arisen in Moscow and St. Petersburg. Government-sponsored programs at the turn of the century improved the Russian banking system and applied high tariffs to protect industry. By the beginning of the twentieth century, Russia ranked fourth in the world in terms of steel production.

Industrialization in Japan

During the first half of the nineteenth century, Japan continued to be governed by the Tokugawa Shogunate. Technologically backward to the industrialized West, Japan emerged from its relative isolation after the 1854 arrival of an expedition from the United States under the command of Commodore Matthew Perry. In 1856, Japan opened two ports to trade with the United States. Shortly thereafter, Great Britain, the Netherlands, and Russia were granted similar concessions.

Some of the Japanese *samurai* favored an end to Japan's isolation. In 1868, the Japanese chose a new emperor named Mutsuhito, or "Meiji," meaning "Enlightened One." The **Meiji Restoration** ended feudalism in Japan and centralized its government. The Meiji government sent key *samurai* to Western Europe and the United States to study Western technology, government, and economics. In the 1870s, the Meiji government abolished the position of *samurai*, and in the 1880s, created a bicameral parliament based along Western models.

Japanese social and political changes were accompanied by rapid industrialization. Banks were set up, and the Japanese army and navy were modernized. Key to the success of Japanese industry was strong government support. State-sponsored railroads, steamships, and factories were built. Heavy taxes imposed on Japanese citizens supported industry. By the 1890s, many of the textile mills and other factories were sold off to private investors who formed conglomerates called **zaibatsu**.

In spite of Japan's rapid industrialization, the islands were not fully equipped for industrialization. Japan lacked significant coal and iron ore deposits essential to carry on an industrial economy. By the beginnings of the twentieth century, Japan remained dependent on the West for raw materials and technology.

In the 1890s, Japan's need for raw materials for its industries prompted a quest for empire. In 1895, Japan defeated China in the **Sino-Japanese War**, which was fought over control of Korea. Japan's influence in Korea also led to the **Russo-Japanese War** of 1904 to 1905, in which Japan defeated Russia. In 1910, Japan annexed Korea.

Social Changes in Industrial Japan

The influence of industrialization introduced a number of Western practices to Japan. Public primary education was offered to all children. The Japanese adopted the metric system, clocks, and the Western calendar. Western haircuts became the fashion for Japanese men. In spite of these adaptations to Western ways, however, few Japanese adopted Christianity, and Shinto and Confucianism became even more popular. Family life also maintained its traditions; Japanese women retained their traditional roles of wives and mothers in a patriarchal family.

Industrialization in Egypt

Under the leadership of its ruler Muhammad Ali, Egypt began to industrialize in the early nineteenth century. In order to lessen Egypt's dependence on the Ottomans, Muhammad Ali built up the Egyptian military. He also brought in European advisers to build up industries. To fund the new industries, Egyptian peasants were required to grow cotton and wheat to export to industrialized nations. When Muhammad Ali levied high tariffs on imported goods, the British objected and forced him to discontinue the duties. Egypt's new industries were unable to compete with British manufacturers, and Egypt became dependent on lower-priced manufactured goods from Great Britain.

› Rapid Review

Beginning in Great Britain, the Industrial Revolution spread throughout Western Europe and the United States, altering society and family life. After abolishing serfdom in 1861, Russia began to industrialize, constructing a trans-Siberian railroad to link European Russia to the Pacific coast. The Perry expedition to Japan in 1854 prompted Japan to open its doors to industrialization. Japan ended feudalism and established a centralized empire that built up an industrial sector by the end of the nineteenth century. Japan, however, remained poor in natural resources, a situation that furthered its quest for an empire to acquire resources to run its industries. In Egypt, attempts at industrialization met with limited success because of the intervention of Great Britain.

› Review Questions

Questions 1 to 2 refer to the following passage.

According to Marius Jansen, a Japanese historian: "After decades of weakness, it was good to be a Japanese and to humble the mighty neighbor that had dominated the horizon for so long." In less than four decades Japan went from being a feudal society to a modern state, with sophisticated weaponry, a developed military bureaucracy, advancements in governing structures, and educational institutions.

—Marius B. Jansen, 2002

1. To which event is the quote by Marius Jansen mostly likely referring?
    (A) The Sino-Russo War
    (B) The Sino-Japanese War
    (C) The Taiping Rebellion
    (D) The *zaibatsu* movement

2. What motivated the Meiji government to take the actions referred to in the quote by Marius Jansen?
    (A) A lack of natural resources for further industrialization
    (B) A desire for additional labor sources
    (C) The fear of an increasingly industrialized China
    (D) Obligations imposed by treaties with Western nations

3. Which development was critical to the industrialization of most nations?
    (A) Organization of labor into unions
    (B) The entry of women into the workforce
    (C) State-sponsored railroads
    (D) Direct military involvement

Question 4 refers to the following quotation.

In general, if any branch of trade, or any division of labour, be advantageous to the public, the freer and more general the competition, it will always be the more so.

—Adam Smith

4. Which economic theory is best supported by this quotation?
    (A) Utilitarianism
    (B) Communism
    (C) Corporatism
    (D) *Laissez-faire*

5. Which best reflects a social change resulting from industrialization?
    (A) Working hours could be adapted to the needs of one's family.
    (B) Women eventually returned to more traditional roles of homemaker and mother.
    (C) Populations dispersed and social status was based on estate holdings.
    (D) Children were given more financial responsibilities and independence.

› Answers and Explanations

1. **B** The Qing dynasty and Japan fought in 1894, primarily over control of Korea. The term "Sino" refers to China, and thus the Sino-Russo War would not refer to Japan (A). The Taiping Rebellion was a civil war within China between the Qing dynasty and the Heavenly Kingdom of Eternal Peace, a Chinese movement opposed to the Qing (C). *Zaibatsu* is a Japanese term, referring to large business organizations wielding considerable influence in the Japanese government after the Meiji period. This term is not associated, then, with any foreign war (D).

2. **A** China had been forced to open to trade by the Americans in the mid-1800s and subsequently sought to industrialize. Unhappy with China's traditional dominance, Japan also recognized the value of Korea's natural resources for Japan's industrialization. Japan's population was growing, so labor was not a concern (B). Also China had rejected Western influences and thus had not experienced industrial or technological growth at the time (C). Finally, although required to open to foreign trade, Japan did not have military treaties with or obligations to other nations during this period (D).

3. **C** Industrialization of most nations during this period involved the growth of railroads, through some degree of government sponsorship or intervention. There were necessary to link natural resources, refining and manufacturing, and markets. Labor unions developed after industrialization in response to the problems created by unregulated capitalism (A). Though industrialization offered different opportunities for some women, female labor was not necessary for its initial development (B). While the military may have benefited from industrialization in some places, they were not directly responsible for its development (D).

4. **D** *Laissez-faire* is the economic philosophy based on Adam Smith's ideas that markets function best without government regulations interfering with the "invisible hand." Utilitarianism is not a primarily economic theory, but is based on the belief that the best policies are those that create the most good for the most people. Utilitarians might support regulation if the number of people benefitting were greater than those harmed (A). Communism is an economic theory, but is based on the idea that if capitalism were to disappear, all industries would then be owned by and run for the benefit of all, thus eliminating the competition inventive (B). Corporatism is a political system in which industrial sectors work with the government to manage the economy, and is therefore not based on free competition (C).

5. **B** Although industrialization, in its earliest forms, allowed women to work in textile industries, overall it shifted work to factories and mines, with an emphasis on male labor. The expectation became that women were better suited to childrearing and homemaking. This was partly because the factory system meant work took place outside the home and on a set schedule (A). Industrialization led to concentration of populations in urban areas, with a corresponding decline in importance of agricultural estates (C). Finally, though some poorer families relied on children to supplement the family income, the social expectations (later supported with regulations) were that children should be protected from harsh working conditions (D).

Demographic and Environmental Developments

IN THIS CHAPTER

Summary: The Industrial Revolution brought a number of changes in the environments of industrialized nations. A population increase in the West, China, and Japan during the eighteenth century provided the labor force needed by the factory system but also added new challenges. Industrial pollution plagued urban areas. Migration between the Eastern and Western Hemispheres enriched the cultural makeup of the Americas.

Key Terms

Maori	romanticism
pogrom	theory of natural selection
quantum physics	theory of relativity

Population Revolution in the West

In the middle of the eighteenth century, the population of Western Europe increased dramatically. Among the causes of this increase were the end of episodes of epidemic disease and the improved diets resulting from increased consumption of potatoes. Infant mortality rates decreased, whereas larger numbers of healthy adults resulted in a higher birth rate. Larger populations provided a ready labor supply for the new factories.

Industrialization also contributed to patterns of migration. Substantial numbers of people, especially young adults, migrated from the country to the city in search of employment in factories, upsetting the makeup of the traditional Western family. Another pattern of migration involved the movement of the middle class away from the central city to emerging suburbs.

After 1850, urbanization continued in the West; in Great Britain and other Western countries, the majority of the population resided in cities. Accompanying a drop in death rates was a lowering of birth rates. Families no longer felt as great a need to produce large families to serve as laborers on family farms. Contributing to falling death rates were more hygienic practices used during childbirth following Louis Pasteur's discovery of the germ theory of disease in the 1880s.

Population Growth in the Non-Western World

Population growth was not restricted to the Western world. In the nineteenth century, the population of Latin America doubled. The cultivation of the sweet potato in China increased the population to levels that stressed the country's economy and resources, demonstrating a need for improvement in agricultural methods and technology in China. Also in the nineteenth century, Japan experienced a population explosion because of improvements in nutrition and medical care. Like China, Japan felt the strain in natural resources caused by its growing population. The increased consumption of the potato in the nineteenth century also produced significant population increases in Russia.

Urban Populations and Environments

Sudden population growth was only one of the problems encountered by industrialized urban areas in the West and in Japan. Water supplies were contaminated by human sewage and industrial waste. The dark skies resulting from coal-produced smoke hovering over industrial cities contributed to frequent cases of rickets, a disease of the bones caused by underexposure to sunlight.

Patterns of Migration and Immigration

Migration in the period between 1750 and 1914 took on various forms. Western Europeans continued to colonize and settle regions of the Americas, India, Africa, the Pacific, and Southeast Asia well into the eighteenth century. Settler colonies not only brought about rivalries between Europeans and native peoples but also, as in the Columbian Exchange of the sixteenth and seventeenth centuries, exposed indigenous peoples to European diseases. Among the victims of European diseases were the **Maoris** of New Zealand, whose population was reduced by about one-third, and native Hawaiians, over half of whom fell to diseases such as tuberculosis and syphilis. The decimation of the Hawaiian population created a need for imported workers; in the late 1800s, workers from China and Japan arrived in the Hawaiian Islands and transmitted their culture to the islands.

The need for labor in various regions of Latin America in the late nineteenth century produced a flood of immigration from Europe to Brazil and Argentina. Many of the newcomers to Brazil were immigrants from Portugal and Italy who came to work on Brazil's coffee plantations. Because of the physical strength required to carry out plantation labor, most of these migrants were male, leaving women to remain in their home countries and assume new roles in their society. Some of these Italian immigrants returned to Italy part of the year to work the crops there, but others remained in Latin America permanently, adding a European flair and a new diversity to Brazil and Argentina. In the early years of the twentieth century, Russians, Germans, and Jews also contributed to the immigrant population of Latin America. Many of the Jewish immigrants were refugees from **pogroms**, or mass persecutions, of Jews in Russia.

Many immigrants became victims of racial and ethnic prejudice in their new environment. For example, after anti-Chinese riots broke out in some communities in the western United States, the U.S. Congress passed the Chinese Exclusion Act of 1882, which prevented most Chinese immigration.

Changes in the Educational and Artistic Environment

As the inhabitants of Western industrial cities gradually acquired more leisure time, there was a growing interest in scientific knowledge and theories, as well as in new methods of literary and artistic expression. In early-nineteenth-century literature and the arts, a new manner of expression called **romanticism** explained human experiences and nature through the use of emotion rather than reason. In 1859, Charles Darwin proposed his **theory of natural selection**, which stated that living species had evolved into their current forms by the survival of the fittest species. Darwin's ideas remained controversial because they conflicted with the biblical account of creation. In 1900, the German physicist Max Planck discovered that light and energy flow in small units that he named "quanta," establishing the discipline of **quantum physics**. In 1916, Albert Einstein, also a German physicist, formulated his **theory of relativity**, which argued that time and space are relative to one another. Social scientists used experimental data to explain human behavior; Sigmund Freud of Vienna explained new theories of the workings of the human mind and developed the technique of psychoanalysis.

› Rapid Review

Improvements in medical practices and sanitation, as well as widespread consumption of the potato, increased populations in various world regions. The crowded populations of industrial cities presented new problems in housing developments. Although medical knowledge improved throughout the years from 1750 to 1914, pollution in industrial urban areas presented new health issues. Colonization brought new contacts between East and West, including the spread of epidemic disease. At the same time, European immigrants to the Western Hemisphere contributed customs that enriched the cultural landscape of the Americas. Increased leisure time created popular interest in science and the arts.

› Review Questions

Questions 1 to 2 refer to the following images.

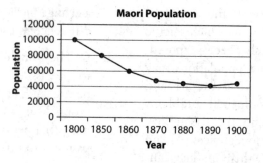

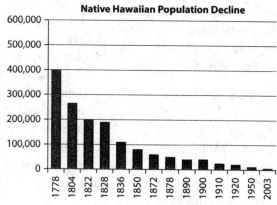

1. What factor was primarily responsible for the decline in both Maori and Hawaiian populations in the early 1800s?
   (A) Intertribal warfare over scarce resources
   (B) Harsh coercive labor systems used by European settlers
   (C) Exposure to European diseases like smallpox
   (D) Famine and war due to environmental degradation

2. Which of the following is a consequence of the trends shown in the graph?
   (A) Labor shortages resulted in Asian migration to Hawaii.
   (B) Maori shamans developed new medicines to combat Western diseases.
   (C) Western Europeans never fully integrated into their Pacific colonies.
   (D) Maoris fled to neighboring islands, spreading their culture and language.

3. Which of the following best explains the population increases experienced by most of the world in the eighteenth century?
   (A) Increased fertility of women
   (B) Better nutrition and decreased mortality
   (C) Higher birth rates among upper classes
   (D) Massive migration from rural to urban areas

4. What were the dominant themes of the Romantic artistic movement?
   (A) Strong lines and angles representing rationalism
   (B) Soft pastel palettes and hazy or blurred focus
   (C) Natural landscapes and appeals to emotion
   (D) Simple childlike forms and primary colors

5. Which characterizes the major scientific developments of this era?
   (A) They reinforced traditional patterns of thinking.
   (B) They relied on physical observations of natural phenomena.
   (C) They challenged long-held understandings of how the world works.
   (D) They were dictated by their practical or commercial uses.

› Answers and Explanations

1. **C** The population decline of native peoples in both regions coincides with the arrival of Europeans and their diseases, to which Pacific peoples had not previously been exposed. Although some Pacific island populations may have died out due to intertribal warfare and scarce resources or environmental problems (i.e., Easter Island), this was not the case in New Zealand or Hawaii. In addition, choices (A) and (D) are so similar as to make them unlikely candidates for the "right" answer. Although Hawaii had some export crops, like sandalwood and, later, sugar, its labor systems were not coercive in the manner of the colonial Americas (B).

2. **A** The resulting labor shortages in Hawaii resulted in an influx of Asian workers to fill the need for workers. Europeans coming to New Zealand especially arrived with family members and the intention to settle permanently, leading them to integrate fully into the colony (C). Maoris never developed medicine to combat these new diseases, but eventually developed some degree of immunity to them (B). Additionally, Maoris did not respond to colonialization by fleeing, but rather stayed, fighting with Europeans over land (D).

3. **B** Although the population increased worldwide during this era, the change was not due to increased fertility (A) or higher birth rates (C), but rather lower infant mortality and higher life expectancy resulting from better nutrition and advances in public health. Rural to urban migration did occur, but would have resulted in a change in the distribution of population, not a difference in the overall numbers (D).

4. **C** The Romantic movement, in part a reaction to the issues of industrialization, emphasized nature and emotion, rather than the extreme rationalism and scientific approaches of the industrial period (A). Although some Romantic painters did use soft colors and focus, these represented technique rather than theme; (B) is not the best response because these are more reflective of later movements like Impressionism. Additionally, the Romantic movement encompassed music, art, and literature; therefore, a response reflecting art only is too restrictive when compared with a response addressing themes relevant across various media. Art with child-like forms and primary colors would be more in keeping with later artistic movements like the primitivism or favusim (D).

5. **C** Scientific discoveries and theories at this time, like Darwin's theory of natural selection, challenged long-held beliefs (A). Rather than rely on observations of the natural world, they used experimentation and data to prove the existence of things that could not be observed, leading to new sciences like quantum physics (B). Many of the new discoveries and theories did not have immediate commercial applications in and of themselves (D).

CHAPTER 22

Political Revolutions

IN THIS CHAPTER

Summary: In the period between 1750 and 1900, the Industrial Revolution was joined by political revolutions. Enlightenment philosophies that society could improve through education and reason led to revolution in the British North American colonies, France, and Haiti in the latter part of the eighteenth century and early nineteenth century. Additional Latin American independence movements flourished in the early nineteenth century. In China, the Qing dynasty faced local revolts as it gradually declined.

KEY IDEA

Key Terms

Bill of Rights
bourgeoisie
Boxer Rebellion
Code Napoleon
communism
Congress of Vienna
conscription
conservatism
Declaration of Independence
Declaration of the Rights of Man and the Citizen
Declaration of the Rights of Woman and the Female Citizen
estates
Estates-General
feminism
Gran Colombia
Jacobins

Jamaica Letter
liberalism
maroon societies
natural rights
proletariat
queue
radicalism
Reign of Terror
Revolutions of 1848
self-strengthening movement
separation of powers
Seven Years' War
social contract
socialism
system of checks and balances
Taiping Rebellion
universal male suffrage

American Revolution

The revolt for independence in the British North American colonies was the child of Enlightenment philosophers, most notably the Englishman John Locke. Locke spoke of a **social contract** in which the people relinquished some of their rights to the government in order to establish order. Governments had the responsibility of safeguarding the "unalienable" rights of "life, liberty, and property." If a government did not preserve these rights, the people had the right to overthrow it and establish a new government.

Britain's North American colonies had gradually developed their own identities since their founding in the early seventeenth century. The colonists particularly resented British policies that levied taxes on them without allowing them their own representative in Parliament. Higher taxes were imposed in 1763 after the end of the French and Indian War (the American phase of the **Seven Years' War**) as a result of British efforts to receive colonial reimbursement for part of the expense of the war that the British had fought on the colonists' behalf. The aftermath of war also brought British restrictions against colonial migration into territories west of the Appalachians once held by the French, territories the British considered unsafe for settlement because of potential conflicts with Native Americans in the area.

The American Revolution began in 1775 as a result of efforts from colonial leaders well versed in Enlightenment thought. In 1776, the colonists set up a government that issued the **Declaration of Independence**, a document modeled after the political philosophies of John Locke. Its author, Thomas Jefferson, altered the **natural rights** identified by John Locke to include "life, liberty, and the pursuit of happiness." With the aid of the French, the British colonists were victorious in 1781. In 1787, the new United States of America wrote a constitution ensuring the **separation of powers** and the **system of checks and balances**, both ideas of the Enlightenment philosopher Montesquieu. A **Bill of Rights** added a statement of individual liberties in keeping with Enlightenment principles. Voting rights were increased to embrace more white male voters; by the 1820s, property rights for voting had been abolished in the new states. Neither the Declaration of Independence nor the United States Constitution addressed the issue of slavery.

French Revolution

Enlightenment thinking also contributed to a revolution in France. In the late eighteenth century, French society was divided into three classes, or **estates**:

- First Estate—the clergy, comprising a little more than 1 percent of the population and paying no taxes.
- Second Estate—the nobility, comprising slightly more than 2 percent of the population and paying only a few taxes.
- Third Estate—the remainder of the population, made up of merchants, artisans, and peasants. The peasants were burdened with heavy taxes and labor requirements that were carryovers from feudal days. The middle class, or **bourgeoisie**, were the merchants, artisans, and professionals who became the driving force of the revolution.

Representatives of the three estates met in the **Estates-General**, the French legislative assembly. In 1789, however, the French monarchs had not called the Estates-General into session for 175 years. Revolution broke out because of:

- Bourgeoisie desire for a wider political role
- Bourgeoisie wish for restraints on the power of the clergy, monarchy, and aristocracy
- Population growth
- Poor harvests in 1787 and 1788

When King Louis XVI was forced to call a meeting of the Estates-General in 1789 in order to raise taxes, the bourgeoisie insisted on changing the voting rules in the Estates-General from one vote per estate to one vote per representative. The king was forced to agree to the new voting arrangement as rioting broke out in Paris. On June 14, 1789, the Bastille, a Parisian political prison, was stormed by a Paris mob. The incident liberated only a handful of prisoners but became the rallying point of the French Revolution.

The new bourgeoisie-dominated National Assembly issued the **Declaration of the Rights of Man and the Citizen**, a document whose content bore a resemblance to clauses in the Declaration of Independence and the United States Constitution. The French declaration identified natural rights as "liberty, property, security, and resistance to oppression." A new constitution guaranteed freedoms of the press and of religion and increased voting rights. Olympe de Gouges countered the French declaration of rights with her **Declaration of the Rights of Woman and the Female Citizen**.

Reign of Terror

In 1792, the revolution entered a more radical phase known as the **Reign of Terror** as the monarchy was abolished, with Louis XVI executed on the guillotine. Under the leadership of a radical club known as the **Jacobins**, thousands were executed during the Reign of Terror. A new constitution provided **universal male suffrage** and universal military **conscription**.

The revolutionaries had to repel foreign armies of Prussia, Russia, Austria, and Great Britain that attempted to preserve the French monarchy. Eventually, the European armies were driven from France, and revolutionaries added new territory in the Netherlands, Germany, and Italy. A wave of nationalism spread throughout France.

Final Stage

The republican gains of the French Revolution came to an end in 1799 with the rise to power of army general Napoleon Bonaparte. Napoleon limited the power of the legislative assembly and returned authoritarian rule to France. Napoleon also:

- Censored speech and the press
- Codified laws in **Code Napoleon**
- Granted religious freedom
- Established universities
- Denied women basic rights

Napoleon declared himself the emperor of a new French empire in 1804. The major powers of Europe fought a number of wars against Napoleon's armies. An 1812 French invasion of Russia led to a decisive defeat for Napoleon, largely as a result of the harsh Russian winter. The European alliance defeated Napoleon in 1814 and again, decisively, in 1815. Although it was a setback for the revolutionary principles in France, Napoleon's empire spread the ideals of the revolution outside France and created a spirit of nationalism throughout Europe.

Aftermath of the Napoleonic Wars

After the final defeat of Napoleon in 1815, European leaders met at the **Congress of Vienna** to restore legitimate monarchs to the thrones of Europe and to create a balance of power. The purpose of the balance of power was to prevent France or any other European nation from dominating the continent again. This spirit of **conservatism** kept Europe largely at peace until the end of the nineteenth century. Other political movements gained strength: **liberalism** sought protection for the rights of propertied classes, whereas **radicalism** wanted broader suffrage and social reforms on behalf of the lower classes. In 1848, a series of revolutions again swept through Europe, bringing the end of monarchy in France. The liberal **Revolutions of 1848** largely failed, however, to bring permanent reform to Europe. Nationalist stirrings in Italy and Germany united the various political units in both regions. The unification of Italy was completed in 1870, while German unification occurred a year later in 1871.

Haitian Revolution

The revolutions in the British North American colonies and in France inspired a revolt in the French Caribbean island colony of Saint-Dominique, or Haiti. The Haitian Revolution was the first incident in world history in which black slaves successfully rebelled against their enslavers. Haiti's colonial economy was based on the production of sugar. Haitian society was divided among slave workers on the sugar plantations, free people of color, and French colonists. During the French Revolution, tensions increased between white inhabitants and free people of color. In 1791, Haitian slaves took advantage of this division to rebel. Under the leadership of a free black named Toussaint L'Overture, the rebellion succeeded, and in 1804 the island declared its independence as the republic of Haiti.

Other Latin American Revolts and Independence Movements

Enlightenment ideas and a succession crisis in Spain created an opportune moment for the realization of independence in Spain's colonies. The placement of Napoleon's brother on the throne of Spain instead of the Spanish king caused the American colonists to question the legitimacy of Spain's ruler. Consequently, independence revolutions broke out in the Americas.

Mexican Independence

In Mexico, the creole Father Miguel de Hidalgo called on *mestizos* and Indians to assist him in a rebellion against Spain in 1810. The creoles, fearing the social reforms that might materialize from *mestizo* and Indian involvement, initially abandoned the independence movement. After Hidalgo was executed, the creoles rejoined the cause under Augustín de Iturbide, a creole officer. In 1821, Mexico declared its independence from Spain. In 1824, Mexico became a republic. The Central American states, which had been a part of Mexico, divided into separate independent nations in 1838.

South American Phase

In the northern part of South America, the creole Simón Bolívar centered his movement for independence against Spain in Caracas. His **Jamaica Letter** (1815) expressed his hope that freedom from Spanish rule would ultimately ensure prosperity for Latin America. By 1822, he had liberated Colombia, Ecuador, and Venezuela, uniting these regions into the nation he called **Gran Colombia**. Regional differences led to the eventual breakup of the new nation.

In the southern portion of South America, José de San Martín emerged as the independence leader from Río de la Plata (present-day Argentina). Río de la Plata declared its independence in 1816. San Martín then crossed into Chile to assist in its liberation. By 1823, all of Spanish America had declared its independence and established republics in all the new nations except Mexico. Independence, however, did not bring prosperity to Latin America, as Bolívar had hoped.

Independence in Brazil

The Portuguese colony of Brazil followed a pattern for independence different from that of the other Latin American countries. In 1807, when the French invaded Portugal, the Portuguese royal family fled to Brazil. The colony of Brazil acquired a status equal to that of Portugal. When Napoleon was defeated, the Portuguese king was recalled and left his son, Dom Pedro, regent in Brazil.

In 1822, Dom Pedro declared Brazil independent after realizing that Brazil was about to lose its representative in the Portuguese parliament. Unlike the other Latin American nations, Brazil did not have to endure a prolonged independence movement. Brazil became a monarchy, and the institution of slavery was left untouched in the newly independent country.

Maroon Societies

Some slaves in Latin America also resisted their colonial government, especially in Brazil and the Caribbean. Runaway slaves who had fled the plantations established their own communities. In the Caribbean, these **maroon societies** were often located in remote areas in the mountains of Jamaica and Hispaniola and in the islands of the Guianas. Initially intended to provide havens for future escaped slaves, some of the maroon societies eventually were granted independence from colonial rulers.

Decline of Qing China

The Manchus who entered China as the Qing dynasty in 1644 had been exposed to Chinese culture as a result of years spent living along the northern Chinese border. The Qing continued Chinese traditions such as the civil service examination and patriarchal family structure. Female infanticide increased. Women were confined to traditional household duties, while women from peasant families also worked in the fields or in village marketplaces. The Manchus required Chinese men to distinguish themselves from them by wearing a **queue**, or braided ponytail.

Although the Qing attempted to control the consolidation of large tracts of land, they had little success. The gap between rural peasants and rural gentry increased. Some men of the gentry began to let their fingernails grow extremely long to indicate that they did not have to do any physical labor.

By the end of the eighteenth century, the Qing dynasty was in decline. The civil service examination had often given way to bribery as a means to obtaining governmental posts.

Dams, dikes, and irrigation systems were in disrepair. Highway bandits were a problem in some areas of China. The importation of opium (see Chapter 22) caused conflicts with Great Britain.

The increased influence of foreign powers on Chinese society and China's defeat in the Opium War produced widespread rebellion in south China in the 1850s and early 1860s. This rebellion resulted from the inability of the Qing to repel foreign influence in China. The **Taiping Rebellion** advocated programs of social reform, more privileges for women, and land redistribution. When the scholar-gentry realized that the rebellion was reaching to the heart of Chinese tradition, it rallied and ended the rebellion.

Later Qing officials attempted to spare the Chinese economy by carrying out a **self-strengthening movement** that encouraged Western investments in factories and railroads and modernized the Chinese army. Reform movements were crushed, however, under the rule of the dowager empress Cixi. The **Boxer Rebellion** (1898 to 1901) was a revolt against foreigners that was backed by Qing rulers. The rebellion, which culminated in the execution of foreigners in China, was put down by a coalition force from Europe, the United States, and Japan.

Sociopolitical Movements: Feminism, Marxism, and Socialism

Feminism

In the eighteenth century, **feminist** movements began to seek political, social, and economic gains for women. Among the goals of these movements were access to higher education and the professions and the right to vote. By 1914, Scandinavian countries and some states in the United States had granted women the right to vote. Within a few years, women's suffrage had extended to all states in the United States and to Great Britain and Germany.

Marxism and Socialism

The sociopolitical theories of the German Karl Marx became significant in Russian history. Marx taught that all history was the result of a class struggle between the bourgeoisie, or middle class, and the **proletariat**, or working class. According to Marx, the proletariat would eventually revolt and establish a "dictatorship of the proletariat" that would ensure social and political freedom. When this occurred, there would no longer be a need for the state, which would wither away. The result would be pure **communism**, or a classless society.

Less extreme forms of **socialism** emerged in European nations as socialist parties arose in Germany, France, and Austria. Many Europeans were fearful of the revolutionary nature of some socialist movements. Socialism in Germany, France, and Austria brought changes such as the recognition of labor unions and disability and old-age insurance.

› Rapid Review

The spirit of the Enlightenment produced revolutions in the British North American colonies, France, and Latin America. Reaction against foreign intervention and the weakness of the Qing dynasty culminated in local revolts in China that weakened centuries-old dynastic rule in that country. Accompanying political revolution was an increasingly vocal movement to grant political rights to women in the Western world. Socialism attempted to create working conditions and societies that would improve the condition of humanity, whereas the Marxist brand of socialism defined a class struggle whose ultimate purpose was the abolition of government.

› Review Questions

1. Answer Parts A and B.
   (A) Identify and explain TWO similarities in the American and the French revolutions.
   (B) Identify ONE unique aspect of the Haitian Revolution and explain its importance.

2. Answer Parts A and B.
   (A) Identify TWO noteworthy political, economic, or social changes that occurred between 1750 and 1900 in Spanish America.
   (B) Identify ONE difference between the Spanish American and Portuguese American revolutions for independence.

Questions 3 to 4 refer to the following passage.

"Caste" originally referred to family; but in colonial Latin America it referred to familial and racial lineage. Created by Spanish elites, the post-Conquest caste system consisted of peninsulares, criollos, mestizos, and mulatos. Both the Spanish colonial state and the Church required more tax and tribute payments from those of lower socio-racial categories. Related to Spanish ideas about purity of blood, which historically also related to its reconquest of Spain from the Moors… [the caste system] was used in the 17th and 18th centuries in Spanish America and the Spanish Philippines.

—Elizabeth Gard Bartolini-Salimbeni, 2017

3. The Mexican independence movement began as a rebellion against foreign control of the Spanish throne and involved which of the following castes?
   (A) Peninsulares, criollos, mestizos
   (B) Criollos, mestizos, Amerindians
   (C) Mestizos, peninsulares, Amerindians
   (D) Mestizos, mulatos, peninsulares

4. The Spanish American caste system left political and social control in whose hands?
   (A) Amerindians
   (B) Criollos
   (C) Mestizos
   (D) Peninsulares

5. Answer Parts A and B.
   (A) Give TWO examples of foreign invasions leading to internal rebellion between 1750 and 1900.
   (B) Identify ONE change that revolution made in the status of women in the Western world between 1750 and 1900.

❯ Answers and Explanations

1A. Both the American and French revolutions were prompted by issues of taxation—the former as a protest against taxation without representation and the latter against taxation of the Third Estate. The American Declaration of Independence and the French Declaration of the Rights of Man and the Citizen both spoke to natural rights. Both revolutions followed Enlightenment ideas that said society could be improved through education and reason.

1B. The Haitian Revolution was the first successful revolution led by black slaves against their enslavers.

2A. The era between 1750 and 1900 witnessed independence from both Spain and Portugal in South America; the growth of feminism; and the birth of new political parties and ideologies, including those representing nationalism, Marxism, and socialism.

2B. The Portuguese American Revolution had as its goal the retention of its monarchy and parliamentary privileges, unlike the Spanish American revolutions.

3. **B** The Mexican independence movement did not involve the peninsulares (A, C, D).

4. **D** The peninsulares, or Spaniards born in Spain of Spanish parents, controlled the highest political and economic positions in the colonies and were at the top of the social scale. While criollos (B) held some political and economic power and a certain social standing, they were secondary to the peninsulares. Amerindians (A) and mestizos (C) were isolated from both power and social standing.

5. **A** Foreign invasions (Great Britain into China, France into Spain, for example) led to the Taiping Rebellion, the Boxer Rebellion, and eventually the North and South American revolutions for independence.

5. **B** Between 1750 and 1900 the major change that revolution made to the status of women was to give them access to education. Revolutions and the rise of feminism also led to a change in economic standing, as women were allowed to retain their dowries in case of divorce or death of a spouse and to receive inheritances in various countries.

Western Imperialism

IN THIS CHAPTER

Summary: The strengthening of European nation-states and the technological changes brought about by the Industrial Revolution gradually began to erode the European balance of power achieved by the Congress of Vienna. As European nation-states competed for power, they turned to colonies to supply them with raw materials and with markets for their manufactured goods. The rivalries among European nations were carried out in the territories of non-Western nations. The United States also realized its imperialist ambitions in Latin America and the Pacific.

Key Terms

Berlin Conference
Boer War
Boers
economic imperialism
Great Trek
imperialism
Indian National Congress

Manifest Destiny
Raj
Sepoy Rebellion
sepoys
Social Darwinism
Spanish-American War

Background of Imperialism

Imperialism, or the quest for empire, was in part a result of the Industrial Revolution. The mechanization of industry and resulting improvements in transportation brought new demands for raw materials, such as palm oil as a machine lubricant and rubber for tires. The industrial age also:

- Produced military weaponry such as the machine gun and the repeating rifle, which gave Western nations a military advantage over developing nations.
- Saw the application of steam to ships. Steamships could travel previously unnavigable rivers, allowing Europeans to reach the interior regions of continents.
- Brought the application of science to the study of health, resulting in preventative measures against the threat of malaria, a common tropical disease to which most Europeans were not immune.

In addition to the impact of industrialization, the concept of **Social Darwinism** contributed to the race for colonies. Social Darwinism was the application of Charles Darwin's theory of natural selection to society to justify the imperial policies of Western powers.

Role of Nationalism

Nationalism, which became less associated with simple "national identity" and came to mean intense pride in one's national culture, also contributed to the new imperialism of the nineteenth and early twentieth centuries. A "new nationalism" has experienced growth in the early twenty-first century. Nationalism served as both a positive and negative force. In 1870, a common language and culture resulted in the unification of the Italian city-states into one nation. The following year, the German principalities also joined to form a single nation-state. The creation and expansion of nation-states were in part the result of a belief in the beneficial nature, not to say superiority, of one's own culture. Nationalism has contributed to justifications of both political and economic imperialism. Nationalism in the United States during the mid-nineteenth century followed a policy of **Manifest Destiny** and led to its expansion from the Atlantic to the Pacific.

Within the Austrian Empire, by contrast, were a number of nations with different languages, religions, and institutions. Among them were Poles, Croatians, Czechs, Slovaks, and Hungarians. The Russian Empire also was ethnically diverse, including not only Slavs but also Turks, Poles, Finns, Estonians, and Jews, as well as other ethnic groups. Its diversity led Russia to try to impose the Russian language on all its subject peoples.

Scramble for Colonies

The main regions of European colonization were India and Africa. British influence in India began as commercial activity during the declining years of the Mughal Empire. The breakup of Mughal rule resulted in minor disputes among local princes. The British took advantage of this situation to help settle disputes, thereby gradually gaining greater influence in India. The Seven Years' War (1756 to 1763), which also was fought in Europe and North America, was the first global war. It brought the British and French into conflict in India. British victories over the French in India gave them control of the country. Many of the Indian soldiers, or **sepoys**, were attracted to the higher-paying British army. India gradually emerged as Britain's key source of raw materials and the main colonial market for Britain's manufactured goods.

British Colonial Society in India

The British who went to India created a stratified society with Europeans occupying the highest positions. English became the language of instruction in Indian schools. The British

Raj (the Sanskrit name for the British government in India) set up telegraph lines to facilitate communications with Great Britain, and railways to carry troops and raw materials. For the most part, the British did not train the Indians in the use of the new technology that they brought to India. With the cooperation of the Western-educated Indian leader Ram Mohun Roy, the British outlawed *sati*.

British rule over India tightened after the 1857 **Sepoy Rebellion**. The cause of this revolt of Indian soldiers in the British army was the issue of new rifles that required the soldiers to use their teeth to tear open the cartridges. These ammunition cartridges were lubricated with animal fat. Muslims, who did not eat pork, were offended by grease that came from animal fat, while Hindus objected to grease from the fat of cattle. Even though the procedure for opening the cartridges was changed, the sepoys rebelled against British authority. The revolt was put down in 1858, but not before several hundred British men, women, and children were massacred.

Schools and universities established by British and American missionaries created an educated class of Indians with a strong nationalist sentiment. In 1885, they founded the **Indian National Congress**, which promoted a greater role for Indians in their country's government. The new organization also sought harmony among Indians of diverse religious and social groups.

Imperialism in South Africa

The first European colonial presence in present-day South Africa was the Dutch way station established at Cape Colony in 1652. Eventually, the Dutch, or **Boers**, moved into the interior of the continent. There they enslaved the inhabitants, the Khoikhoi. Interracial mixing produced the South Africans known as "colored" today.

During the wars of the French Revolution, the British captured Cape Town and annexed it in 1815. A conflict between the Boers, who were slaveholders, and the British over the end of slavery caused many Boers to leave Cape Colony. Their migration, called the **Great Trek** (1834), took the Boers into the interior of South Africa. There they clashed with the Bantu peoples, especially the powerful Zulu. Under the leadership of their leader, Shaka, the Zulu nation fought back against Dutch, then British, rule, only to be defeated by the more advanced British technology.

In the 1850s, the Boers established two republics in the interior of South Africa: the Transvaal and the Orange Free State. When diamonds were discovered in the Orange Free State in 1867, the imperialist businessman Cecil Rhodes and other British moved into the Boer republics. In spite of war between the Boers and the British from 1880 to 1881 that ended in Boer victory, the British continued to pour into South Africa. Migration was especially intense after gold was discovered in the Transvaal in 1885. Continued tension between the British and the Boers culminated in the **Boer War** of 1899 to 1902. After this conflict, the Boers began a period of dominance over native South Africans. In 1902, the individual Boer republics maintained their self-governing status as they were united into the Union of South Africa, controlled by Great Britain.

Partition of Africa

Intense rivalries among European nations played out on the African continent. As the need for raw materials and colonial markets arose, Africa was divided among European colonial powers. The **Berlin Conference** of 1884 to 1885 partitioned Africa into colonies dominated by Great Britain, France, Portugal, Spain, Germany, Belgium, and Italy. Only

Liberia and Ethiopia were not colonized by Europeans. Absent from the Berlin Conference were representatives from any African nation.

The divisions of the Berlin Conference were carried out without regard for ethnic and cultural groups. Boundaries dividing the territorial possessions of one European power from another often cut through ethnic and cultural groups, placing members of a single group in different colonies dominated by different European powers. Traditional African life was disrupted as Europeans imposed on the continent their concept of the nation-state as the unit of government. These colonial divisions would affect African life to the present.

As in India, European imperialist powers in Africa contributed railways, roads, and other public works to the African landscape. Hospitals were set up and sanitation improved. Most of the improvements were intended initially for the welfare of the European colonists. As in India, Europeans in Africa failed to train natives to use the new technology they brought to the continent.

European businesses set up plantations and required local African natives to work long hours at extremely low wages to produce export crops for European benefit. Work on European plantations prevented Africans from tilling their home and village plots, a situation that led to decreased food supplies and malnutrition for their families.

Imperialism in Southeast Asia

Prior to the new imperialism of the nineteenth century, most of Southeast Asia consisted of independent kingdoms. The Malay States (present-day Malaysia) and Burma (presently Myanmar) came under British rule. Indochina was colonized by the French and the East Indies (now Indonesia) by the Netherlands. Siam (present-day Thailand) was the only Southeast Asian country that did not fall to imperialist ambitions. When native populations provided an insufficient labor supply, Europeans brought in immigrants from India and China.

Economic Imperialism

Another pattern of imperialist control was seen primarily in Hawaii and Latin America: **economic imperialism**. Economic imperialism involved the exertion of economic influence rather than political control over the region. In Hawaii, American companies exported Hawaiian-produced goods such as sugar and pineapple. Beginning in the early nineteenth century, missionaries from New England brought Christianity and education to the Hawaiians. Europeans and Americans also brought Western diseases to the islands, killing over half the population. Chinese and Japanese workers were brought in to work on Hawaiian plantations. American planters in Hawaii urged the United States to annex the islands. In 1898, the Hawaiian ruler was overthrown, and Hawaii was annexed to the United States.

The increase in Latin American trade (see Chapter 22) attracted North American and European investors. Businesses based in the United States, Great Britain, France, and Germany invested in Latin American banks, utilities, mines, and railroads. After World War I, U.S. business interests dominated in the region. The nations and islands of Latin America exported food products and raw materials and imported manufactured goods. Western perpetuation of this Latin American trade pattern kept Latin America dependent on the industrialized West. In a swing back toward rightest, nationalist governments, in 2018 Brazil elected Jair Bolsonaro president, who ran on a platform of economic and ethnic nationalism.

In Cuba, U.S. economic imperialism turned to territorial acquisition. U.S. businesses had long invested in Cuban sugar and tobacco plantations. When the Cubans rebelled against Spanish rule in 1895, U.S. businessmen became concerned about their Cuban investments. When the U.S. battleship *Maine* exploded in Havana harbor, the United States went to war against Spain. U.S. victory in the **Spanish-American War** (1898) resulted in Spanish cession of Puerto Rico and Guam to the United States and the U.S. purchase of the Philippines. Cuba became an independent republic subject to control by the United States. The United States was now a world power.

U.S. Interests in Central America and the Caribbean

The nations of Central America and the Caribbean, both dependent on foreign loans, often were threatened by foreign intervention when they could not repay their loans. The United States intervened in Cuba three times during the early twentieth century. During the same period, U.S. troops occupied the Dominican Republic, Nicaragua, Honduras, and Haiti. U.S. support for Panamanian independence led to the decade-long (1904–1914) construction and then opening of the Panama Canal in 1914.

› Rapid Review

European nations colonized India and Africa, providing benefits such as improved medical care and more advanced infrastructures, including better roads and railways. Most improvements were intended more for the benefit of imperialist nations than for native peoples. African village organization was disrupted as European nations divided the continent without regard to ethnic patterns, a practice that proved devastating to Africa's future. Southeast Asia, except for Siam, came under the control of a number of European powers. Economic imperialism supported the interests of U.S. and European businesses and created continued dependence of nonindustrialized nations on the industrialized world.

› Review Questions

Questions 1 to 3 refer to the following passage

VI. All the powers exercising sovereign rights or influence in the...territories bind themselves to watch over the preservation of the native tribes, and to care for the improvement of the conditions of their moral and material well-being and to help in suppressing slavery... They shall, without distinction of creed or nation, protect and favour all religious, scientific, or charitable institutions and undertakings created and organized for the above ends, or which aim at instructing the natives and bringing home to them *the blessings of civilization* [italics added].

—The Berlin Conference
The General Act of February 26, 1885, Chapter 1, Article VI

1. Which of the following best accounts for the phrase "the blessings of civilization" used by the European powers at the Berlin Conference of 1884–1885?
   (A) Economic imperialism
   (B) Social Darwinism
   (C) Manifest Destiny
   (D) Territorial imperative

2. One of the goals of the imperial powers, as stated in the passage, was to preserve "native tribes" and improve their "moral and material well-being." Using your knowledge of this era, decide which of the following people were most likely to fulfill that goal.
   (A) Missionaires
   (B) Scientists
   (C) Health workers
   (D) Engineers

Question 3 refers to the following passage.

Well, they're saved from *the blessings of civilization* [italics added].

—Last line of the John Ford movie *Stagecoach* filmed in 1939 but set in 1885.
It is said sarcastically by one of the main characters as the hero
and heroine flee the reach of the corrupt law.

3. In this case, what does the phrase *the blessings of civilization* mean?
   (A) Access to scientific and material progress
   (B) The right to equal treatment under the law
   (C) Freedom from societal constraints
   (D) The right to take advantage of U.S. alliances

4. Answer Parts A and B.
   (A) Direct imperialism involved political control, and indirect imperialism was more economically focused. Identify TWO examples of direct imperialism.
   (B) Identify ONE example of indirect imperialism.

Question 5 refers to the following cartoon.

5. A caption for this cartoon might be which of the following?
   (A) The Growth of the British empire
   (B) The Death of Freedom
   (C) The Growth of Native Rebellion
   (D) The Death of Western Imperialism

› Answers and Explanations

1. **B** Social Darwinism suggested that some societies were more evolved, more moral, and more economically capable than others and was used to justify the conquering of less advanced countries in the interests of progress and civilization. A, C, and D are incorrect.

2. **A** Missionaries espoused the ideal of improving moral and material well-being among native peoples. Often, as in India, they established (and controlled) schools and universities with an eye to achieving such improvements. B, C, and D are incorrect.

3. **C** *The blessings of civilization* here refers to the constraints society and its corrupt institutions impose on anyone who may differ from the norm. The hero and heroine are being released from these constraints. A, B, and D, while all referring to more positive aspects of *the blessings of civilization,* are not the interpretation appropriate to the situation.

4A. The many examples of direct imperialism might include the British in India; the French, Spanish, and Belgians in Africa; the Dutch (Boers) in South Africa; and the Spaniards in the New World. In these cases, government was under the control of a foreign imperial power.

4B. Indirect imperialism, which generally kept traditional leaders in positions of authority, refers to U.S. economic control of Hawaii; to U.S., British, French, and German control in Latin America; and to French control of Indo-China (Vietnam, Cambodia, Laos).

5. **B** Leopold II of Belgium instituted a policy of absolute control of the Congo colony, based on governmental and religious authority and on foreign economic investment. This meant the end of freedom for those peoples living in what would be known as the Belgian Congo. The area was not under British control (A); native rebellion (C) would not result in independence until the late 1950s; and Western imperialism never died out (D).

CHAPTER 24

World Trade

IN THIS CHAPTER

Summary: The manufactured goods of the industrialized West and the raw materials used to produce them became a primary focus of world trade in the period between 1750 and 1900. In the Atlantic world, trade largely revolved around the plantation system and the economic exploitation of the newly independent nations of Latin America (see Chapter 23). Methods of extracting natural resources from subject nations changed as railroads and roads were constructed to transport raw materials from the interior of colonies to port areas for eventual transport to Europe. Instead of small, independent farm plots owned and cultivated by native peoples, large plantations arose to replace them. On these new agricultural units, native peoples of Africa, India, and Southeast Asia produced crops necessary to the industrialized nations of Europe.

KEY IDEA

Key Terms

extraterritoriality
guano
Monroe Doctrine
Opium War
Qing dynasty
spheres of influence

Suez Canal
Tanzimet reforms
Treaty of Nanking
Wahhabi rebellion
Young Turks

Latin American Trade

The profitable sugar plantations of the Caribbean and Brazil were at the heart of Latin American trade with Europe. Brazil also produced cotton and cacao for European use, and during the late eighteenth century, its seaports were opened to world trade. Trade increased the importation of slaves to the Portuguese colony.

As Latin American independence movements drew to a close in the 1820s, the United States stepped forward to monitor future trade with its southern neighbors. The **Monroe Doctrine** (1823) announced the intention of the United States to maintain a "hands-off" policy with regard to European colonization in the Americas. Great Britain already had trade agreements with the Spanish colonies since the eighteenth century. It now foresaw the newly independent Latin American republics as future trade partners and supported the Monroe Doctrine. A more active trade began with Britain trading manufactured goods to Latin America, especially Brazil, in exchange for raw materials. In the late nineteenth century, the United States, France, and other nations also traded with Latin America.

By the end of the nineteenth century, active trade was carried on in Cuban tobacco and sugar; Brazilian sugar and coffee; Mexican copper, silver, and henequen; Peruvian **guano**; Chilean grain and copper; and Argentinian beef, grain, hides, and wool. Beef exports increased dramatically after the invention of the refrigerated railroad car in the late nineteenth century. Also in the late nineteenth century, as European nations established colonies and increased industrial production, demand for Latin American rubber, especially from Brazil, increased.

Large landholders who exported sugar and hides especially benefited from foreign trade, whereas local independent traders often had to compete with cheaper and better-quality foreign goods. As a result, Latin America became increasingly dependent on the importation of foreign goods, whereas power and wealth concentrated in the hands of large landholders. Foreign investments provided Latin America with necessary capital but also with industry and transportation largely under foreign control. Global trade with the Americas increased after the Panama Canal opened in 1914.

Trade with the Islamic World

Although trade with Latin America increased markedly in the middle and later years of the nineteenth century, foreign trade with the Ottoman Empire continued on a path of gradual decline. The empire was increasingly weakened by successful independence revolts of its subject peoples, including the Greeks in 1820 and the Serbs in 1867. In the early nineteenth century, the **Wahhabi rebellion** attempted to restore Ottoman strength by insisting upon a return to more traditional Islam and strict adherence to *shariah* law. Contributing to Ottoman weakness was the empire's disinterest in industrialization, which led minority groups such as Christians and Jews within the Ottoman Empire to carry on their own trade with Western European nations for manufactured goods. The artisans who produced goods using the domestic system had difficulty competing with European imports.

The threat of European competition produced a wave of political and economic reform from 1839 to 1876 that opened the Ottoman Empire more to Western influence. The **Tanzimet reforms** facilitated trade, but they came too late to make sweeping changes in the Ottoman economy. Further reform efforts by the **Young Turks** failed to achieve permanent change. The corruption of later Ottoman rulers and decreased agricultural revenue took their toll. In return for foreign loans to bolster its faltering economy, the Ottoman Empire was made economically dependent on European imports and influence. Europeans were granted the privilege of **extraterritoriality**, which allowed Europeans in Ottoman commercial centers to live according to their own laws rather than those of the Ottomans.

Egyptian commerce also suffered from European competition. Muhammad Ali's insistence on increasing cotton production diverted farmers from grain production and made Egypt dependent on the export of a single crop. A decline in the price of cotton worldwide could have devastated the Egyptian economy. By 1869, however, Egyptian trade strengthened because a canal opened across the Isthmus of Suez. Connecting the Mediterranean and Red seas, the **Suez Canal** made Egypt a significant commercial and political power between Europe and its colonies in Africa and Asia.

Qing China and the Opium Trade

In 1644, the weakened Ming dynasty was overtaken by the Manchus, a largely nomadic people who lived north of the Great Wall. The new dynasty, calling itself **Qing**, lifted Ming restrictions against foreign travel. Chinese merchants took an increasingly active part in overseas trade, and foreign merchants traded with China through the port of Canton. Trade in Chinese tea, silk, and porcelain brought in large quantities of silver, which was the basis of the Chinese economy. By the nineteenth century, international trade based in southern China was especially profitable.

One of China's chief trading partners, Great Britain, became increasingly concerned over having to pay large amounts of silver for Chinese luxury goods. British merchants solved the trade imbalance by trading Indian opium to China. Indian opium, which was of a higher quality than Chinese-grown opium, took such a hold on Chinese society that soon the Chinese were forced to pay for the product with large quantities of their silver. In addition to this trade reversal, millions of Chinese became addicted to opium, a situation that affected work and family responsibilities. When the Qing emperor took measures to block the opium trade, war broke out in 1839 between China and Great Britain. British victory in the **Opium War** and another conflict in the 1850s resulted in the opening of China to European trade. The **Treaty of Nanking** (1842) that ended the Opium War made Hong Kong a British colony and opened up five ports to foreign commerce instead of only the port of Canton. Opium continued to flow into China. By 1900, more than 90 ports were open to foreign trade. Foreign **spheres of influence** were drawn up in China; within these territories, the controlling nation enjoyed special trade privileges as well as the right of extraterritoriality.

Russia and World Trade

Russia continued to occupy a backward position in trade and technology. The Russians exported some grain to Western Europe in exchange for Western machinery. By 1861, the desire to compete with Western nations in world trade prompted Russia to emancipate its serfs. Still, Russia lagged behind in export crops as the emancipation of the serfs left a labor force that used outdated agricultural methods.

Japanese Entrance into World Trade

The second Perry expedition to Japan in 1854 opened two ports to trade with the United States. Later, the Netherlands, Great Britain, and Russia initiated trade relations with Japan. As Japan industrialized, it depended on imports of Western equipment and raw materials, especially coal.

End of the Trans-Atlantic Slave Trade

The combination of Enlightenment thought, religious conviction, and a slave revolt in Haiti led to the end of the trans-Atlantic slave trade. The British ended their participation in the slave trade in 1807, then worked to get the cooperation of other slave importers to the Americas to end their part in the slave trade. While Britain seized hundreds of slave ships, Cuba and Brazil, with the cooperation of African rulers, continued to import huge numbers of slaves. The trans-Atlantic slave trade did not end until 1867.

› Rapid Review

Although the trade in human beings across the Atlantic was coming to an end, other avenues of trade appeared worldwide. Latin America, Russia, the Islamic world, and Japan developed an increased dependency on Western technology. China saw its favorable balance of trade reversed as its silver supply was diminished to purchase Indian opium from Great Britain. By the beginning of the twentieth century, European products dominated global trade routes.

› Review Questions

1. Which is true of Latin America's economy during the nineteenth century?
   (A) Latin American government investment spurred industrialization.
   (B) It depended on manufactured goods and investment from Western nations.
   (C) Strong regional trade networks made them economically independent.
   (D) Unequal treaties gave European nations unprecedented economic control.

2. Which was a factor contributing to the Ottoman Empire's declining influence?
   (A) Egyptian cotton limited their textile profits.
   (B) The Ottoman Empire shifted from traditional Islamic values and laws.
   (C) The Ottoman Empire never attempted to modernize its industries.
   (D) Several conquered territories successfully rebelled.

Questions 3 to 4 refer to the following image.

3. What prompted the actions taken by the British, reflected in the cartoon?
   (A) Pandemic disease
   (B) Rejection of Christianity
   (C) Military threats
   (D) Trade imbalances

4. What was the impact of the Opium War that resulted from the actions depicted in the image?
   (A) China's territory was reduced substantially.
   (B) China's emperor was replaced with a democratic parliament.
   (C) China lost authority over foreigners in its territory.
   (D) China became politically and economically isolated.

5. Which statement best characterizes trade during this period?
   (A) It shifted power from the Northern to Southern Hemispheres.
   (B) It caused international wars around the globe.
   (C) It benefited Western industrialized nations at the expense of others.
   (D) It facilitated the spread of religious extremism.

› Answers and Explanations

1. **B** In the nineteenth century, Latin America had little industrialization of its own (A). Rather, Western capitalists looked to Latin America as an opportunity for investment in raw materials and as markets for their manufactured goods. Thus, Latin American nations became somewhat dependent on Western nations (C). The unequal treaties were not agreements with Latin American nations, but rather with China (D).

2. **D** The Ottoman Empire was weakened when the Greeks and the Serbs each successfully declared independence. Although the Ottomans initially showed little interest in industrializing, Tanzimat reforms and the Young Turk movement did open trade and tried to modernize industries, making choice (C) less correct. The Wahhabi Rebellion emphasized traditional Islamic laws and values (B). The Ottomans did not have a significant cotton textile trade and therefore were not impacted by the growth of Egyptian cotton (A).

3. **D** The cartoon shows a British officer (representing Britain) forcing opium on a Chinese person, alluding to the Opium Wars. China's disinterest in most Western manufactured goods created an unfavorable balance of trade for Britain, whose people desired Chinese goods. When the British discovered a Chinese market for opium, they encouraged Chinese consumption as a means of redressing the trade imbalance. Though China seized opium stores and attempted to force opium dealers out of business, it was the loss of trade and not fear of a military threat that spurred the British to take military action (C). Opium is not a cure for, or a cause of, any type of pandemic disease (A). Although China was not particularly interested in Christianity, it did not prohibit or persecute its followers at this time, nor was Christianity related to the opium trade (B).

4. **C** Although European powers did not annex Chinese territory (A) and allowed the Chinese emperor to remain in power (B), they were pressured to open to trade with foreign powers (D) through a series of unequal treaties.

5. **C** During this period, Western industrialized powers used their economic and military superiority to their advantage in trade relationships around the world. Economic power remained concentrated in the Northern Hemisphere (A). Though there were conflicts over trade, this era predates international wars (B). This era isn't associated with the spread of religious extremism (D).

Summary: Industrialization and Global Integration: Revolutions and Consequences of Industrialization

Timeline

1750s	Beginnings of the Industrial Revolution in England
1756 to 1763	Seven Years' War
1768 to 1780	Voyages of Captain James Cook in the Pacific Ocean
1775 to 1781	American Revolution
1788	Founding of the first European colony in Australia
1789 to 1799	French Revolution
1793 to 1804	Haitian Revolution
1799 to 1814	Rule of Napoleon Bonaparte
1805 to 1848	Rule of Muhammad Ali in Egypt
1807	End of the British slave trade
1810 to 1825	Independence wars in Latin America
1814 to 1815	Congress of Vienna
1839 to 1842	Opium War in China
1839 to 1876	Tanzimet era
1848	Publication of the *Communist Manifesto*
1850 to 1864	Taiping Rebellion
1854	Matthew Perry's expedition to Tokyo
1857	Sepoy Rebellion
1861	Abolition of serfdom in Russia
1861 to 1865	U.S. Civil War
1865	Abolition of slavery in the United States
1867	Establishment of the Dominion of Canada
1868	Meiji Restoration (Japan)
1869	Opening of the Suez Canal
1870	Unification of Italy
1871	Unification of Germany
1884 to 1885	Berlin Conference
1888	Abolition of slavery in Brazil
1898 to 1899	Spanish-American War
1899 to 1902	Boer War

Key Comparisons

1. Industrial Revolution in Europe, Russia, and Japan
2. Revolutions: American, French, and Haitian
3. Responses to Western influence in China, Japan, India, and the Ottoman Empire
4. Nationalism in Italy and Germany
5. Nationalism in the Austrian Empire and Russia
6. Imperialism in Africa and India
7. Forms of imperialism in Africa and Latin America
8. Roles of European women in upper and middle classes versus women in lower classes
9. Trade in the Atlantic and Indian Ocean basins
10. Trade in Western Europe and the Ottoman Empire

Change/Continuity Chart

REGION	POLITICAL	ECONOMIC	SOCIAL	CHANGES	CONTINUITIES
East Asia	Meiji Restoration Opium War Taiping Rebellion	Spheres of influence Self-strengthening movement Industrialization *Zaibatsu*	Crowded industrial cities Population growth	Dependence on Western technology Bicameral parliament (Japan)	Patriarchal society Shinto Confucianism Buddhism Lack of resources (Japan)
Southeast Asia	Western imperialism	Plantation economy	Influx of Chinese and Japanese	European and East Asian influence	Agriculture Indian Ocean trade
Oceania	Regional kingdoms	Agriculture in Australia	European settlement of Australia and New Zealand	European colonization European diseases	Agriculture Fishing Foraging
Central Asia	Russian expansion Pogroms	Nomads Industrialization Trans-Siberian railway	Emancipation of serfs Russian assimilation of ethnic groups	Abolition of serfdom Industrialization	Tsarist rule Agriculture
South Asia	British Empire Sepoy Rebellion Indian National Congress	Plantation economy Opium trade Hospitals Railroads	End of *sati* English instruction	End of Mughal rule Western political influence	Muslim/Hindu tensions Indian Ocean trade Caste system
Southwest Asia (Middle East)	Ottoman rule Tanzimet reforms Young Turks	Export of raw materials Disinterest in trade	Harem Patriarchal society Islam Wahhabi rebellion	Western influence Extraterritoriality	Ottoman decline
North Africa	Rule of Muhammad Ali European influence Berlin Conference	Suez Canal Industrialization Cotton as a single crop	Islam	Industrialization Foreign influence	Agriculture

KEY IDEA

Change/Continuity Chart (Continued)

REGION	POLITICAL	ECONOMIC	SOCIAL	CHANGES	CONTINUITIES
Sub-Saharan Africa	Imperialism Boer War Berlin Conference	Plantation economy Western technology Gold Diamonds	Ethnic tension Great Trek Strain on village life Sanitation Railroads	Western influence Disruption of village life	Agriculture Slave trade
Western Europe	French Revolution Code Napoleon Unification of Italy and Germany Socialism	Industrial Revolution Jobs for lower-class women	Social Darwinism Abolition of the slave trade Crowded cities Feminism	Industrialization Emancipation of slaves Increased suffrage	Traditional gender roles Agriculture
Eastern Europe	Pogroms Austrian Empire Partition of Poland	Agriculture	End of serfdom	Emancipation of serfs	Agriculture Nationalist sentiment
North America	American Revolution Annexation of Hawaii Spanish-American War Monroe Doctrine	Industrial Revolution End of plantation economies	Abolition of slavery Feminism	Industrialization U.S. Civil War	Agriculture Immigration
Latin America	Independence movements Mexican and Haitian revolutions	Economic imperialism Panama Canal	Immigration from Europe Abolition of slavery	Republican government Monroe Doctrine	Sugar plantations Catholicism Agriculture Poverty Social stratification

CHAPTER 25

Revolutions, World Wars, and Depression

IN THIS CHAPTER

Summary: Because of European competition for colonies in Africa, India, and Southeast Asia, the delicate balance of power that had existed in Europe after the Congress of Vienna gradually eroded. European rivalries negotiated new alliances that led to warfare, while conditions in Russia culminated in a new form of government. Mexico underwent a liberal revolution, and Chinese dynastic rule ended with the fall of the Qing. The economic devastation of World War I led to global depression and extremism in the form of fascist ideology. The conclusion of World War II brought the end of the period of European dominance and the rise of two superpowers: the United States and the Soviet Union.

KEY IDEA

Key Terms

Allied Powers
Anschluss
appeasement
British Commonwealth
Central Powers
Duma
fascism
Great Depression
Holocaust
League of Nations
mandate
Mexican Revolution

Pan-Slavic movement
Potsdam Conference
reparations
Revolution of 1905
Russo-Japanese War
Russification
Spanish civil war
Tehran Conference
Treaty of Brest-Litovsk
Treaty of Versailles
United Nations
Yalta Conference

Revolutions in Mexico and China

Revolution in Mexico

In 1876, Porfirio Díaz was elected president of Mexico. For the next 35 years, he continued the economic growth of the rule of his predecessor, Benito Juárez. Díaz encouraged foreign investment, industries, and exports. In contrast to other Latin American countries such as Argentina and Brazil, Mexico was not the destination of many immigrants; its population, therefore, was largely native. Often economic growth did not benefit the peasants and working classes. Opponents of Díaz were arrested or exiled, and election fraud was common.

In 1910, the middle class began a movement for election reform. Soon joined by workers and peasants, the reform movement escalated into a ten-year-long rebellion known as the Mexican Revolution. The revolution ended in a new constitution that guaranteed land reform, limited foreign investments, restricted church ownership of property, and reformed education.

Revolution in China

The leaders of the movement that brought down the Qing dynasty were Western-educated reformers who wanted to model China's government along Western lines. Sun Yat-sen, one of the movement's chief leaders, also intended to carry out reforms to benefit peasants and workers. Although they admired some aspects of Western society, the revolutionaries envisioned a China free of foreign imperialists. In 1911, opposition to Qing reliance on Western loans for railway improvements led to a final rebellion that toppled the Qing in 1912. Centuries of Chinese dynastic rule had come to an end.

Background of World War I

The forces that interacted to set the scene for World War I may be summed up in the word MANIA:

- Militarism—the creation and maintenance of standing armies
- Alliance system—entangling alliances that pitted groups of nations against other groups of nations
- Nationalism—an intense pride in one's nation and its people
- Imperialism—the acquisition of colonies to supply raw materials to industrializing nations
- Assassination—of the Archduke Franz Ferdinand and his wife

One of the most important of these forces was a system of entangling alliances that complicated international relations in the event of war. Though it was not the immediate cause of the war, it made the war inevitable.

The immediate cause of World War I was the assassination of Archduke Francis Ferdinand and his wife in Sarajevo, Bosnia, by a Serbian nationalist protesting against the Austrian annexation of Bosnia. In the aftermath of the assassinations, Germany supported Austria in a declaration of war against Serbia. Serbia, a Slavic nation, was in turn linked to Russia's ethnic policies. By the early twentieth century, Russia's policy of **Russification**, or insistence on the acceptance of Russian culture by its various ethnic groups, had broadened into a **Pan-Slavic movement** that was designed to bring all Slavic nations into a commonwealth with Russia as its head. Russia therefore began to mobilize its troops in defense of Serbia.

Within a few weeks after the assassination at Sarajevo, the system of European alliances had brought the world into war. Two alliances faced off against each other: the **Central Powers** of Germany, Austria-Hungary, the Ottoman Empire, and Bulgaria; and the **Allied Powers** of Great Britain, France, Russia, Italy (originally part of the Central Powers), Japan, and later, the United States. **British Commonwealth** members Canada, Australia, and New Zealand took an active part fighting on the Allied side. In 1917, China also declared war on Germany. Subject peoples of Europe's colonies in Asia and Africa participated in the war as combatants and support personnel. Many colonial peoples hoped to be granted independence as a result of their war efforts.

Throughout the early war years the U.S. government sold arms to the Allies, while U.S. bankers lent money to the Allied nations. In 1917, the United States was drawn into World War I by two events: Germany's declaration of unrestricted submarine warfare and Great Britain's interception of the Zimmermann Telegram. The telegram proposed that, if Mexico would enter the war as an ally of Germany, the German government would assist Mexico to recover the territory it had lost to the United States as a result of the Mexican War. U.S. entry into World War I provided the Allies with additional supplies and freshly trained troops, two factors that helped turn the tide of war in favor of the Allies.

Revolution in Russia

Nationalism and a mutual desire to control Korea led to war between Russia and Japan in 1904. When the **Russo-Japanese War** ended in Russian defeat in 1905, an uprising known as the **Revolution of 1905** forced Tsar Nicholas II to allow the **Duma**, or Russian Parliament, to convene. When Nicholas abolished the Duma a few weeks later, small groups of radicals began planning the overthrow of tsarist rule.

In March 1917, Russia's decline as a world power, peasant dissatisfaction, political repression, and the human and financial costs of World War I brought about the end of tsarist rule. After a weak provisional government failed to maintain social order, a second revolution in October 1917 brought the Bolsheviks, or communists, into power. The new government, led by V. I. Lenin, decided that Russia was too devastated by revolution to continue the war. In March 1918, Russia and Germany signed the **Treaty of Brest-Litovsk**, which ceded vast amounts of Russian territory to Germany.

Between 1918 and 1921, Russia was engaged in a civil war in which the Bolsheviks, or Red Army, solidified their power over supporters of tsarist rule and wealthy landowners. The opposing forces, or White Army, were supported by troops from the United States, France, Great Britain, and Japan.

Peace Settlements

Several peace treaties were signed following the war's end in November 1918; the most well known was the **Treaty of Versailles** between most of the Allied nations and Germany. As a result of the Treaty of Versailles:

- A war guilt clause placed total blame for the war on Germany.
- Germany was assigned **reparations** payments of $33 billion.
- Germany lost its colonies.
- Alsace and Lorraine were returned to France.

- Germany's military power was severely limited.
- The coal-rich Rhineland was demilitarized.
- A **League of Nations** was established to work for international peace. The dream of U.S. President Woodrow Wilson, the League's future impact was weakened when the United States refused to join. (The United States later signed a separate peace treaty with Germany.) Also, Germany and Russia were forbidden to join the League.

Other Outcomes of World War I

Because of World War I:

- An entire generation of young European men was almost wiped out.
- Italy and Japan were angered at not receiving additional territory.
- The Ottoman Empire was reduced to the area of present-day Turkey.
- China lost territory to Japan and became a virtual Japanese protectorate.
- The Austro-Hungarian Empire was dissolved.
- The new nations of Yugoslavia, Hungary, and Czechoslovakia were formed from Austria-Hungary. All three nations contained within their borders a variety of ethnic groups with their own nationalist aspirations.
- Russia lost territory to Romania and Poland. Finland, Latvia, Estonia, and Lithuania gained their independence.
- Poland was restored to the European map. A Polish Corridor was created to give Poland an outlet to the Baltic Sea.
- The Ottoman Empire was divided into **mandates** with Great Britain controlling Iraq and Pakistan, and France acquiring Syria and Lebanon.

In the newly created or reconstituted nations of east-central Europe—Hungary, Poland, and Yugoslavia—liberal democracy failed to take root, for a variety of reasons. With primarily agrarian societies, these nations lacked the stable, industrial economy, democratic traditions, and experienced politicians necessary. Additionally, arbitrary post-WWI borders were imposed and incorporated minority ethnic groups, resulting in internal conflicts that further eroded the political stability of these states, and ultimately led to right-wing authoritarian regimes coming to power. The social democratic governments of the Scandinavian region fared much better during this period. Generous social services were funded through relatively high taxes, though this didn't seem to hinder economic growth. Several key industries were organized into privately-owned cooperatives, which weathered global economic swings better than in other countries.

The cultural developments of the interwar years also reflected the deep uncertainty of the period. The 1920s have often been referred to as "the Roaring Twenties." The cabaret culture, where men and women mixed easily, seemed to reflect a loosening of social conventions and a pursuit of pleasure after the sacrifices of the war years. But cultural historians have increasingly pointed out that the culture of the interwar years seemed to reflect a deep anxiety for the future.

This was partly fueled by new scientific theories which exacerbated this uncertainty. During the Industrial Revolution, science seemed to march inexorably forward, improving the human condition, and gradually revealing the mysteries of the universe; however, the horrors of WWI highlighted the destructive aspects of technological progress. Even before WWI, Albert Einstein developed his theory of relativity (1905), demonstrating that space and time do not exist as absolutes, but are relative to the observer. Danish physicist Neils

Bohr together with Ernest Rutherford, proposed an atomic model with electrons orbiting a nucleus. Later Bohr posited that electrons can be both particles and waves, though not at the same time. Building on Bohr's work, Werner Heisenberg argued that one cannot know a single particle's exact position and velocity at the same time. The more precisely one measures the first variable, the less precisely one knows the second, and vice-versa. Psychology, too, contributed to this sense of uncertainty with Sigmund Freud's theory that personality was formed through childhood conflicts which were stored in the unconscious mind. His psychoanalysis was an attempt to uncover these previously hidden drivers of conscious behavior and thought. Jung extended this idea to include a "collective unconscious," with ancestral memories from our evolutionary past, which expresses itself in dreams through symbolic forms and archetypes. All of these theories seemed to run counter to the previously dominant Newtonian view, that the world was fixed, orderly and ultimately knowable with careful application of logic and reason.

Social anxiety and uncertainty found expression in interwar artistic movements. Based on the idea that artistic and cultural norms were meaningless in the wake of the atrocities of WWI, Dadaists used elements of chance, absurdity and incongruity in their work. Examples include Marcel Duchamp's *Fountain* (1917), consisting of an upside-down urinal with a fake signature, and Hans Arp's *Squares Arranged according to the Laws of Chance* (1917). Dadaism paved the way for other movements like surrealism, in which images are changes and juxtaposed in a dream-like way, epitomized by Salvador Dali's work *The Persistence of Memory* (1931), with its "melting" watches. Musicians, too, attempted to break with convention during this time. Arnold Schoenberg created atonal music, with a new compositional form based on a twelve-note scale, independent of any traditional key. In architecture, the Bauhaus school in Germany attempted to unite applied arts like furniture and textiles with fine arts of painting and sculpture. Led by architect Walter Gropius, the Bauhaus school helped spread functionalism, in which the purpose of the building takes precedence over its ornamentation. Sometimes simply concrete and steel boxes with glass windows, these buildings were intended to represent the future. Though most movies were aimed at pleasing a mass audience, some filmmakers captured the uncertainty of the time. An excellent example is Fritz Lang's film *Metropolis* (1925). Filmmaking became a popular art form in the interwar years, and film stars became celebrities whose lifestyle seemed to epitomize the Roaring Twenties. However, Lang's *Metropolis* depicted a world in which humans are dwarfed by an impersonal world of their own creation. Similarly, T. S. Eliot's epic poem, *The Waste Land* (1922), depicts a world devoid of purpose or meaning.

Great Depression

The cost of war in Europe devastated the economies of European nations on both sides of the conflict. When Germany announced it was unable to make its reparations payments to the former Allies, Great Britain and France were unable to fully honor repayment of their war debts to the United States. The agricultural sector in Europe and the United States suffered from overproduction that resulted in a decline in farm prices. Farmers in Western Europe and the United States borrowed to purchase expensive farm equipment. Overproduction also resulted in lower prices on plantation-grown crops in Africa and Latin America.

As the economic situation in Europe worsened, banks began to fail. In 1929, when the economy and banking systems in the United States also crashed, the United States was unable to continue its loans to European nations. Global trade diminished, creating massive unemployment not only in Europe and the United States but also in Japan and Latin America.

The economic distress of the **Great Depression** created various reactions in the political arena. In the West, new social welfare programs broadened the role of government. In Italy and Germany, fascist governments developed. Japan's search for new markets was accompanied by increased imperial expansion.

World War II

Prelude to War

The fragmented political order that was the legacy of World War I combined with the economic distress of the Great Depression created the second global conflict of the twentieth century. Fascist governments (nationalist, one-party authoritarian regimes) arose in Germany and Italy. The nationalist Socialist (Nazi) Party of Adolf Hitler sought to redress the humiliation Germany had suffered in the Treaty of Versailles and to expand German territory. **Fascism** in Italy under Benito Mussolini hoped to restore the lost glories of the state. In Japan, competition among extreme nationalists led to the rise of military rule in the 1930s.

Military expansionist policies during the Depression created the stage for war:

- In 1931, the Japanese invaded Manchuria. The goal was to create a buffer zone between the Soviet Union and the Japanese and to make Manchuria's coal and iron deposits available to resource-poor Japan.
- In 1935, Hitler began to rearm Germany.
- In 1935, Mussolini invaded Ethiopia.
- In 1936 to 1939, the **Spanish Civil War** brought into power the fascist regime of Francisco Franco. It served as a dress rehearsal for World War II, as Germany and Italy aided Franco, while the Soviet Union sent supplies and advisers to his republican opponents. Pablo Picasso expressed his view of the horrors of the Spanish Civil War in his painting *Guernica*.
- In 1937, the Japanese invaded China, whose opposition was a threat to their presence in Manchuria. The event signaled the beginning of World War II in Asia.
- In 1938, Hitler proclaimed **Anschluss**, or the unification of Austria with Germany.
- In 1938, Hitler annexed the Sudetenland, the German-speaking western portion of Czechoslovakia.
- In 1938, the Munich Conference followed a policy of **appeasement**, in which Great Britain and France accepted Hitler's pledge not to take any further territory.
- In 1939, Hitler annexed all of Czechoslovakia.
- In 1939, Hitler signed a nonaggression pact with the Soviet Union.
- On September 1, 1939, Hitler attacked Poland, marking the beginning of World War II in Europe.

Opposing Sides

Two opposing sides arose, with the major powers including:

- The **Axis Powers**—Germany, Italy, and Japan
- The **Allied Powers**—Great Britain, France, and the Soviet Union

Course of the War

World War II was fought in two theaters: the Pacific and the European, which included the Middle East and Africa. In an effort to control the oil reserves of Southeast Asia, Japan seized Indochina from France and attacked Malaysia and Burma. When the United States imposed an embargo against Japan as a result of these actions, Japan retaliated by attacking the U.S. fleet anchored at Pearl Harbor, Hawaii, on December 7, 1941. The Japanese attack brought the United States and its greater industrial power into the war on the side of the Allied powers.

The early years of the war showcased Axis strength. In 1941, the tide began to turn in favor of the Allies when Hitler undertook an unsuccessful winter invasion of Russia and the United States entered the war. When Hitler was forced to withdraw his forces from Russia in 1942, Soviet armies began their advance through Eastern Europe and into Germany. After deposing Mussolini, Allied forces pushed into France and met in Germany in April 1945. Hitler's subsequent suicide was followed by Allied victory in Europe in May 1945.

After victory in Europe, the Soviet Union assisted in the Allied effort against Japan. After the U.S. use of atomic bombs against the Japanese cities of Hiroshima and Nagasaki, the Japanese surrendered in August 1945, ending World War II.

Cost of the War

World War II took a devastating toll in human life, killing about 35 million people, including about 20 million in the Soviet Union. The **Holocaust**, Hitler's elimination of European Jews in gas chambers, took the lives of 6 million. Other groups such as Gypsies, Slavs, political prisoners, and Jehovah's Witnesses were also sent to extermination camps during the Holocaust. More than 300,000 were killed by the Japanese offensive in China, most of them in the city of Nanking. The fire bombings of Japanese cities and of the German city of Dresden added tens of thousands to the death toll. Nearly 80,000 were killed in Hiroshima, and tens of thousands were killed in Nagasaki.

Designing the Peace

World War II peace settlements began before the war had ended:

- In 1943, at the **Tehran Conference**, the Allied powers decided to focus on the liberation of France, allowing the Soviet Union to move through the nations of Eastern Europe as it advanced toward France. The Soviet Union therefore gained ground and influence in Eastern Europe.
- In 1945, at the **Yalta Conference**, the Soviet Union agreed to join the war against Japan in exchange for territory in Manchuria and the northern island of Japan. The Yalta Conference also provided for the division of Germany into four zones of occupation after the war.
- In 1945, the **Potsdam Conference** gave the Soviets control of eastern Poland, with Poland receiving part of eastern Germany. It made the final arrangements for the division of Germany and also divided Austria.

After the war had ended:

- The United States occupied Japan.
- Korea was divided into U.S. and Soviet occupation zones.
- China regained most of its territory, but fighting between nationalist and communist forces resumed.
- Latvia, Lithuania, and Estonia became Soviet provinces.

- Czechoslovakia, Hungary, Bulgaria, and Romania were occupied by the Soviet Union.
- Colonies renewed their independence efforts.
- European world dominance ended.
- A new international peace organization, the **United Nations**, was created in 1945, with the United States among its key members.
- International dominance remained in the hands of two superpowers—the United States and the Soviet Union.

Roosevelt and Stalin both preferred to end the war with U.S. and British forces advancing through France and Soviet forces pushing into Germany from the east, leaving the USSR to liberate and occupy Eastern Europe. Stalin harbored some resentment against the allies, particularly the United States, for failing to extend the lend-lease program to the Soviets, for delaying the opening of a second front to relieve pressure on Soviet troops, and (later) for failing to commit funds for Soviet reconstruction after the war. In addition, the United States did not inform the USSR of the atom bomb's development, though they did tell Great Britain. These conditions, together with the USSR's desire for buffer zones to protect them from invasion and the need for strategic resources, set the stage for post-war conflict.

In the eventual settlement, Germany was disarmed and divided into sectors with Western powers controlling the western sector and the Soviet Union controlling the eastern sector. Though Berlin was in the eastern sector, it was also divided into Western-controlled West Berlin and Soviet-controlled East Berlin. Poland lost territory to the Soviet Union in the east, somewhat offset by Polish gains in the west, at Germany's expense.

Although the agreement called for self-determination and democratic elections in Eastern Europe, the Soviets had already begun installing pro-communist governments in the occupied countries, beginning with Poland (despite Poland's government-in-exile in London). Eastern European nations dominated by the Soviet Union eventually included East Germany, Poland, Romania, Czechoslovakia, Hungary, and Bulgaria. Yugoslavia, under Marshall Tito, was communist yet "nonaligned" with the Soviets.

Despite the creation of the United Nations (UN) to promote international peace and cooperation, by 1946 an "Iron Curtain" (a term used by Winston Churchill in a speech given in the United States) had descended over Eastern Europe, stretching from the Baltic Sea in the north to the Adriatic Sea in the south and dividing Europe between a communist East and a capitalist West.

❯ Rapid Review

The forces of nationalism, imperialism, and militarism combined with entangling defense alliances produced the first global war of the twentieth century. Post-war peace settlements created new nations without consideration of ethnic differences within those nations. The Treaty of Versailles left Germany economically and militarily devastated and humiliated by the war guilt clause. The costs of war ruined regional economies and world trade, creating a depression that reached most regions of the world. Out of the despair of the Great Depression arose new political institutions, including fascism in Germany and Italy and military rule in Japan. The world found itself at war for the second time in the twentieth century. Millions died in the Holocaust, while the atomic age was launched with the bombings of Hiroshima and Nagasaki. The lessons of war created an attempt at a new world order that included a stronger international organization, the United Nations.

› Review Questions

Questions 1 to 3 refer to the following image.

1. Which best describes where the event portrayed in the photo would fall in a sequence of events relating to World War II?
   (A) Immediately after the Germans and Soviets signed a nonaggression pact
   (B) Immediately after the announcement of Anschluss
   (C) Immediately after the assassination of Austria's Archduke Franz Ferdinand
   (D) Immediately after the Treaty of Brest-Litovsk

2. Which foreign policy pursued by Great Britain and France is believed by historians to be at least partially responsible for the event shown in the image?
   (A) Containment
   (B) Isolationism
   (C) Appeasement
   (D) Fascism

3. What was the long-term impact of WWII on the majority of Eastern European nations?
   (A) They were granted the right to self-determination.
   (B) They were economically and politically tied to Western Europe.
   (C) They practiced isolationism to avoid future entanglements.
   (D) They were increasingly dominated by the Soviet Union.

4. Answer Parts A, B, and C.

Though World War I was often referred to as "the war to end all wars," students of history know that was not the case.
(A) Identify one underlying (long-term) cause of World War I and explain how it led to war.
(B) Identify one immediate effect of World War I on Europe.
(C) Explain one way in which the Treaty of Versailles created the conditions for future conflicts.

5. Answer Parts A, B, and C.

Both ideologies of fascism and communism gained supporters during this time period.
(A) Explain one similarity between communism and fascism.
(B) Explain one difference between communism and fascism.
(C) Identify one reason why communism became more influential than fascism in the second half of the twentieth century.

› Answers and Explanations

1. **B** Anschluss was the German policy of merging Austria and Germany. This occurred before the Nazi invasion of Poland, pictured in the photograph. The failure of Europe to aid Poland prompted the Soviet Union to sign the non-aggression pact with Germany (A). The assassination of Archduke Ferdinand (C) and the Treaty of Brest-Litovsk (D) are both events of World War I.

2. **C** With the memory of World War I still fresh, European powers followed a policy of appeasement, or giving in to an aggressor, initially allowing Germany to expand unchecked. Isolationism was the policy pursued by the United States (B). Fascism was the political ideology of Nazi Germany, not a foreign policy (D). Containment was a foreign policy, but one pursued by the United States several years later to curb the spread of communism (A).

3. **D** After World War II, the USSR kept a military presence in the Eastern European nations where the Soviet military had pushed back the Nazis. This eventually led to Eastern Europe falling under Soviet control. Although many of its borders remained intact, some countries, like Poland and Czechoslovakia, were forced to cede part of their territory to the USSR, sometimes in exchange for other land (A). Once the Soviets gained dominance, Eastern Europe became isolated from Western Europe (B). Given their subordinate positions to the Soviet Union, total isolationism was not really an option (C).

4A. Nationalism is considered an underlying cause of World War I. The Serbs had long since resented Austria's dominance over them, leading to the rise of nationalistic groups like the Black Hand favoring independence. This is the group that plotted the assassination of Archduke Franz Ferdinand of Austria and of which Gavrilo Princip was a member. When Gavrilo Princip assassinated the archduke in the cause of nationalism, he set into motion the chain of events like Austria's ultimatum, Germany's blank check of support, and Russia's troop mobilization that ultimately led to Germany declaring war on France and Russia in 1914. Other underlying causes would be militarism, imperialism, and alliances.

4B. One immediate effect of WWI on Europe was the changing of borders, often based on the principle of self-determination. The Ottoman Empire was broken up into the mandate system in the Middle East, controlled by Great Britain or France. Austria-Hungary was broken up, and new nations like Yugoslavia, Hungary, and Czechoslovakia were created. Baltic states gained independence, and Russia lost some territory. Other changes that could be discussed include the decline in the population of working-age men and the role that the war's economic devastation played in the Great Depression.

4C. One way in which World War I set the stage for future conflicts was through the conditions imposed by the Treaty of Versailles. Germany, already reeling from the economic devastation of the war, was required to pay a staggering $33 billion in reparations. Together with the Great Depression, this contributed to the hyperinflation Germany experienced in the 1930s. Additionally Germany lost colonies and other territories and was required to demilitarize, both blows to the self-esteem of the German people. Finally, the war guilt clause, in which Germany had to assume total responsibility for all of World War I, engendered tremendous anger and resentment in Germany. This anger and resentment would create the conditions that made Hitler's nationalistic message so attractive to some Germans and led to World War II. Other possible answers could include the mandate system, which set the stage for later conflicts in the Middle East, or Italy's resentment at the terms of the Versailles Treaty resulting in its desire to re-create the Roman Empire through imperialism.

5A. Both communism and fascism are totalitarian, centralized, authoritarian forms of government that rely on propaganda, secret police, and government control of media and schools to foster support.

5B. The primary difference between fascism and communism is in their economic views. Fascism does not address economic disparities within a society and is based on capitalism. Communism, on the other hand, emphasizes that all economic activity is owned in common by all the workers and works toward the elimination of economic disparity. Whereas fascism is a nationalistic ideology, in which the most important ties among the members of society are their national identity, communism is class-based. Since economic classes transcend political borders, communism envisions a worldwide movement, rather than a national one.

5C. Communism became more influential in the second half of the twentieth century because the defeat of Germany and Italy, both fascist states, weakened fascism's influence and appeal. Also, the Soviet Union's influence extended throughout Eastern Europe during the last months of WWII as Soviet troops drove the Nazis out of Eastern Europe. As they progressed, the Soviets left a presence in Eastern Europe that formed the basis for their later influence in the region. Finally, the international perspective of this ideology (see earlier) meant that they encouraged the spread of communism to other nations through propaganda and military intervention.

CHAPTER 26

Cold War and the Post-War Balance of Power

IN THIS CHAPTER

Summary: The decades following World War II were dominated by the relationship between the two superpowers—the United States and the Soviet Union. During the post-war period, the superpowers were almost always on the verge of warfare. As former colonial possessions gained independence, many of them sought aid from the United States or the Soviet Union. As the Soviets extended their dominion throughout Eastern Europe, Asia, and Cuba, the United States attempted to contain communist expansion.

KEY IDEA

Key Terms

Afrikaners
Alliance for Progress
apartheid
ayatollah
Berlin Wall
brinkmanship
coalition
Cold War
collectivization
containment
Cuban Missile Crisis
Cultural Revolution
Five-Year Plans
Geneva Conference

genocide
glasnost
Government of India
   Act
Great Leap Forward
Guomindang
Iron Curtain
Korean Conflict
kulaks
Marshall Plan
May Fourth
   Movement
New Economic Policy
   (NEP)
nonalignment

North Atlantic Treaty
  Organization (NATO)
perestroika
Prague Spring
purges
Red Guard

Sandinistas
Six-Day War
Solidarity
Tiananmen Square
Truman Doctrine
Warsaw Pact

Beginnings of the Cold War

British Prime Minister Winston Churchill described the new post-war world order by stating that an "**Iron Curtain**" dividing free and communist governments had fallen across Europe. In order to prevent communist-dominated nations east of the Iron Curtain from spreading totalitarianism, the United States sponsored a program of European recovery known as the **Marshall Plan** (1947). The program provided loans to European nations to assist them in wartime recovery. The U.S. policy of **containment** of communism was set forth in 1947 in the **Truman Doctrine**. When Greece and Turkey were threatened by communism, U.S. President Truman issued his policy, which pledged U.S. support for countries battling against communism.

In 1946, Great Britain, France, and the United States merged their occupation zones into a unified West Germany with free elections. In 1947, Western attempts to promote economic recovery by stabilizing the German currency resulted in a Soviet blockade of Berlin—the divided city located within the Russian zone of occupation. For nearly 11 months, British and U.S. planes airlifted supplies to Berlin until the Soviets lifted the blockade.

Two opposing alliances faced off during the **Cold War** era. The **North Atlantic Treaty Organization (NATO)**, led by the United States, was founded in 1949. NATO allied Canada, the United States, and most of Western Europe against Soviet aggression. The Soviet Union responded with an alliance of its Eastern European satellites: the **Warsaw Pact**. U.S.-Soviet rivalry intensified in 1949, when the Soviet Union developed an atomic bomb.

The Cold War escalated to military confrontation in 1950 when North Korean forces invaded South Korea. North Korea eventually received the backing of the Soviet Union and communist China, while a United Nations **coalition** led by the United States supported South Korea. The **Korean Conflict** ended with the establishment of the boundary between the two Koreas near the original line.

Beginnings of Decolonization

After the end of World War II, most European nations and the United States decided that their colonies were too expensive to maintain. Within the colonies, renewed nationalist sentiments led native peoples to hope that their long-expected independence would become a reality. In 1946, the United States granted the Philippines their independence. France was alone in wanting to hold on to its colonies in Algeria and Indochina.

Africa

In 1957, Ghana became the first African colony to gain its independence. By 1960, French possessions in West Africa were freed, and the Belgian Congo was granted independence. Independence movements in the settler colonies of Algeria, Kenya, and Southern Rhodesia took on a violent nature. By 1963, Kenya was independent; in 1962 a revolt in Algeria also had ended colonial rule in that country. Southern Rhodesia became the independent state of Zimbabwe in 1980, and in 1990, Namibia (German Southwest Africa, which had been made a mandate of South Africa in 1920) became the last African colony to achieve independence.

In South Africa, the white settler population was divided almost equally between **Afrikaners** and English settlers. Although the white settlers were a minority, by 1948 the Afrikaners had imposed on South Africa a highly restrictive form of racial segregation known as **apartheid**. Apartheid prohibited people of color from voting and from having many contacts with whites. The best jobs were reserved for whites only. Apartheid continued after South Africa gained its independence from Great Britain in 1961.

Egypt won its independence in the 1930s; meanwhile, the British continued to maintain a presence in the Suez Canal zone. After Egypt's defeat in the Arab-Israeli War of 1948, the Egyptian military revolted. In 1952, King Farouk was overthrown; in 1954, Gamal Abdul Nasser was installed as ruler of an independent Egypt. In 1956, Nasser, backed by the United States and the Soviet Union, ended the influence of the British and their French allies in the Suez Canal zone.

In 1967, Nasser faced a decisive defeat once again in the **Six-Day War** with Israel. His successor, Anwar Sadat, strove to end hostilities with Israel after a nondecisive war with Israel in 1973. Sadat's policy of accepting aid from the United States and Western Europe was continued by his successor, Hosni Mubarak, who came to power after the assassination of Sadat by a Muslim fundamentalist.

Effects of Decolonization

Independence did not bring peace or prosperity to most of the new African nations. New states tended to maintain colonial boundaries, meaning that they often cut through ethnic and cultural groups. Sometimes ethnic conflicts turned violent, as in the tribal conflicts in the territories of the former Belgian Congo and the Biafra secessionist movement in southeastern Nigeria.

Soviet Communism

After the Russian civil war, which lasted from 1918 to 1921, Lenin moved quickly to announce a program of land redistribution and a nationalization of basic industries. When his initial programs culminated in industrial and agricultural decline, Lenin instituted his **New Economic Policy (NEP)**. The NEP permitted some private ownership of peasant land and small businesses; it resulted in an increase in agricultural production.

In 1923, Russia was organized into a system of socialist republics under a central government and was renamed Union of Soviet Socialist Republics. The republics were under the control of the Communist Party. When Lenin died in 1924, Joseph Stalin eventually became the leader of the Soviet Union. Stalin's regime was characterized by **purges**, or the expulsion or execution of rivals. Especially targeted were the **kulaks**, wealthy peasants who refused to submit to Stalin's policy of **collectivization**. Collectivization consolidated private farms into huge collective farms worked in common by farmers. Farmers were to share the proceeds of the collective farms and to submit a portion of the agricultural products to the government. Millions of kulaks were executed or deported to Siberia. Even after farmers accepted collectivization, however, lack of worker initiative prevented it from being successful.

Stalin had greater success in improving Soviet industry. He set up a series of **Five-Year Plans** that concentrated on heavy industry. By the end of the 1930s, the Soviet Union was behind only Germany and the United States in terms of industrial capacity.

Expansion of Soviet Rule

During the final weeks of World War II, the Soviet Union liberated Eastern Europe (except Yugoslavia and Greece) from Nazi rule. By 1948, these areas, except for Greece, had communist governments. Yugoslavia's communist rule under Marshall Tito did not become a part of the Soviet bloc, attempting instead to forge a style of communism more responsive to its citizens.

In 1956, a Hungarian revolt against repressive Soviet rule was put down by Soviet tanks. When large numbers of East Germans began migrating to West Berlin, the **Berlin Wall** was constructed in 1961 to stem the tide of refugees. In the **Prague Spring** (1968), Czech leader Alexander Dubcek stood up against Soviet oppression, abolishing censorship; the result of his efforts was Soviet invasion. Only in Poland was Soviet rule somewhat relaxed; religious worship was tolerated and some land ownership was allowed. In the late 1970s, **Solidarity**, Poland's labor movement, challenged the Soviet system.

Soviet Rule after Stalin

In 1956, Nikita Khrushchev rose to power in the Soviet Union. Criticizing Stalin's ruthless dictatorship, Khrushchev eased up on political repression. In 1962, Soviet construction of nuclear missiles in Cuba brought days of tense confrontation between Khrushchev and U.S. President Kennedy. Khrushchev ultimately backed down, and the missiles were removed. The **Cuban Missile Crisis** was a classic example of **brinkmanship**, or the Cold War tendency of the United States and the Soviet Union to be on the brink of war without actually engaging in battle. For example, the Cuban Missile Crisis of October 1963, in which Soviet attempts to install nuclear missiles in Cuba were met with a U.S. blockade of the island, brought the world to the brink of nuclear war until the Soviets backed down and removed the missiles. But, in general, the nuclear capabilities of the United States and the Soviet Union precluded a direct confrontation. Instead, the tensions played out in a series of limited, or "proxy," wars in which the two countries supported opposite sides of existing conflicts in other parts of the world. Many major world events during the second half of the twentieth century were directly related to the Cold War.

In Asia, the civil war in China pitted Soviet-backed communist forces led by Mao Zedong against the nationalist forces of Jiang Jieshi (often known as Chiang Kai-Shek) backed by the United States. The Korean War (1950–1953) involved Soviet- and Chinese-supported North Korean communists and UN- and U.S.-backed South Koreans, producing a stalemate near the 38th parallel (the original post–World War II dividing line between North and South Korea) at the cost of some 1.5 million lives. Later, during the Vietnam War, communist forces led by Ho Chi Minh battled an authoritarian, anticommunist government, increasingly reliant on U.S. military aid for its existence (throughout the 1960s until U.S. withdrawal in 1973). And in Afghanistan, Soviet troops invaded to support a faltering pro-Soviet regime, engineering a coup and installing a new pro-Soviet leader. Rebel "mujahedeen" groups pursued a guerilla war, with funding and training provided by the United States, Pakistan, and Saudi Arabia.

The Middle East was also the scene of U.S.-Soviet conflict. When the United States backed out of an agreement to help build the Aswan Dam, Egypt retaliated by nationalizing the British-controlled Suez Canal. Egypt subsequently benefited from Soviet support in the ensuing battles against Britain, France, and Israel. Pressured by the United States to withdraw, Britain relinquished the Suez Canal; this event marks the decline of British influence in international relations. Moreover, the Soviets then helped build the Aswan Dam when the United States would not, improving the Soviet Union's standing in the Middle East. In 1973, the United States and the Soviet Union again clashed during the Yom Kippur War, in which Soviet-supplied Arab forces attempted to retake the Sinai Peninsula and Golan Heights from U.S.-backed Israel.

Despite these conflicts, the West allowed the Soviet Union a great deal of latitude within its "sphere of influence" in Eastern Europe. For example, in 1956 a popular uprising broke out in Hungary, encouraged by Khrushchev's speech denouncing Stalinist policies. Though Hungary asked for Western support, none was forthcoming for fear of a nuclear confrontation, allowing the Soviets to violently crush the rebellion. Though Khrushchev's speeches had seemed to indicate a softer position, his actions in Hungary proved otherwise.

Later Decades of the Twentieth Century

In December 1979, the Soviet Union invaded Afghanistan to support communist combatants in Afghanistan's civil war. The Soviets withdrew their forces in 1989 after failing to establish a communist government for Afghanistan.

In the 1980s, economic setbacks and the military power of the United States produced a reform movement within the Soviet Union. The new Soviet leader, Mikhail Gorbachev, reduced Soviet nuclear armaments. His reform program revolved around the concepts of **glasnost** and **perestroika**. *Glasnost,* meaning "openness," allowed Soviet citizens to discuss government policies and even criticize them. *Perestroika* was an economic reform program that permitted some private ownership and control of agriculture and industry. Foreign investments were allowed, and industry was permitted to produce more consumer goods.

Latin America

Mexico emerged from its revolution with a one-party system. The Partido Revolucionario Institucional (PRI) dominated Mexican politics for 70 years.

In Argentina, government was under the control of military leaders who wanted to industrialize the country. Some of them were fascist sympathizers, among them Juan Perón and his wife, Evita. Although Perón raised the salaries of the working classes, his government controlled the press and denied civil liberties to its citizens. When he died in 1975, Argentina continued to be ruled by military dictators. In 1982, a short war with Great Britain over the Falkland Islands resulted in Argentine defeat.

From 1934 to 1944 and from 1952 to 1959, Cuba was ruled by dictator Fulgencio Batista. U.S. trade relations with Cuba gave it an influence over the island nation. In 1959, the Cubans revolted against the corruption of the Batista regime, replacing it with the rule of a young revolutionary lawyer named Fidel Castro. During the revolution, Batista lost the support of the United States because of his corrupt government.

Shortly after assuming power in Cuba, Castro proclaimed himself a Marxist Socialist. He seized foreign property and collectivized farms. In 1961, Castro terminated relations with the United States and gradually aligned Cuba with the Soviet Union. Also in 1961, the United States sponsored an unsuccessful invasion of Cuba by Cuban exiles. Cuba's dependence on the Soviet Union led to the Missile Crisis of 1962.

Throughout Central America, U.S. businesses such as United Fruit invested in national economies, resulting in a U.S. presence often resented by Central Americans. In Nicaragua, the **Sandinistas** carried out a protest against U.S. intervention that resulted in a socialist revolution in the 1980s.

The United States attempted to contain communism in Latin America by supporting governments that professed adherence to democratic principles. It also sponsored programs such as the **Alliance for Progress**, begun in 1961 and intended to develop the economies of Latin American nations. By the final decades of the twentieth century, the United States changed its position to one of less intervention in Latin America. Under the Carter administration, the United States signed a treaty with Panama that eventually returned control of the Panama Canal to Panama. By the 1980s, the United States was again assuming a more direct role in Central America. In 1990, the United States helped end the Noriega government, which was known for its authoritarianism and control of the drug trade.

Decolonization of India

Indian independence from Great Britain was accomplished largely through the efforts of Mohandas Gandhi, who believed in passive resistance to accomplish his goals. In 1935, the British Parliament passed the **Government of India Act**, which increased suffrage and turned provincial governments over to Indian leaders. Indian independence was delayed by the insistence of some Muslims on a separate Muslim state. In 1947, the British granted India its independence; India followed a path of **nonalignment** with either superpower.

At the same time that India received its independence, the new nation of Pakistan was created. Pakistan was then divided into eastern and western regions separated by over 1,000 miles of Indian territory. A few years later, Burma (Myanmar) and Ceylon (Sri Lanka) also gained independence. Unequal distribution of wealth between the two Pakistans ended in civil war in the early 1970s; in 1972, East Pakistan became the independent nation of Bangladesh.

Conflict in Palestine

The Holocaust strengthened international support for a homeland for the Jews. As the Nazis continued their policy of **genocide** against the Jews, immigration to Palestine increased. When Arab resistance turned to violence against Jewish communities in Palestine, the British placed restrictions on Jewish immigration. In 1948, the United Nations partitioned Palestine into Jewish and Arab countries; the independent state of Israel was proclaimed. Almost immediately, war broke out as Arabs protested the partition. A Jewish victory resulted in the eventual expansion of the Jewish state at the expense of hundreds of thousands of Palestinian Arabs who were exiled from their homes.

Iran

In 1979, the U.S.-backed Iranian government of Reza Shah Pahlavi was overthrown by Islamic fundamentalists. The middle classes were opposed to the shah's authoritarian and repressive rule; Iran's *ayatollahs*, or religious leaders, opposed the shah's lack of concern for strict Islamic observance. Iran also was suffering from a fall in oil prices prior to the 1979 revolution.

The new Iranian ruler, the Ayatollah Khomeini, rejected Western culture as satanic and imposed strict Islamic law, including the veiling of women, on Iran. Saddam Hussein, leader of Iraq, took advantage of Iranian weakness by annexing its oil-rich western provinces. When peace came in 1988, Iran was devastated economically.

Postrevolutionary China

One of the key leaders of the 1911 to 1912 revolt against the Qing dynasty was Western-educated Sun Yat-sen. He briefly ruled China's new parliamentary government until he relinquished his place to warlord rule. After World War I, the **May Fourth Movement** (1919) attempted to create a liberal democracy for China. In the same year, Sun Yat-sen and his followers reorganized the revolutionary movement under the **Guomindang**, or Nationalist Party. Marxist socialism also took hold in China, however; and in 1921, the Communist Party of China was organized. Among its members was a student named Mao Zedong.

After the death of Sun Yat-sen in 1925, Jiang Jieshi (Chiang Kai-shek) seized control of the Guomindang. A 1927 incident in which the Guomindang executed a number of communists in Shanghai so enraged the communists that civil war broke out. Except for the years during World War II, the Chinese civil war lasted until 1949, when Mao Zedong's communists, whose land reforms gained peasant support, were victorious. After their defeat, Jiang Jieshi's forces fled to the island of Taiwan (Formosa) off the coast of China, while Mao proclaimed the birth of the People's Republic of China on the Chinese mainland.

After gaining control of China, the communists contained secessionist attempts in Inner Mongolia and Tibet; some Tibetan opposition exists to the present. China also supported North Korea in its conflict with South Korea in the 1950s.

Once in power, Mao began organizing China along Soviet models. Farms were collectivized, leading to a lack of peasant initiative and a decrease in agricultural production. Eager to increase the participation of rural peoples, Mao instituted the **Great Leap Forward**, which attempted to accomplish industrialization through small-scale projects in peasant communities. The Great Leap Forward proved a resounding failure.

In 1960, Mao was replaced as head of state, although he retained his position as head of the Communist Party. The new leaders, Zhou Enlai and Deng Xiaoping, instituted some market incentives to improve the Chinese economy. In 1965, Mao launched his **Cultural Revolution**, a program that used student **Red Guard** organizations to abuse Mao's political rivals. Especially targeted were the educated and elite classes; universities were closed. Opposition from Mao's rivals led to the end of the Cultural Revolution, whereupon relations were opened between China and the United States.

In 1976, both Zhou Enlai and Mao Zedong died, paving the way for the leadership of Deng Xiaoping. Deng discontinued collective farming and allowed some Western influence to enter China. His government did not, however, permit democratic reform, as shown in the government's suppression of students demonstrating for democracy in **Tiananmen Square** in 1989.

Vietnam

After World War II and the end of Japanese occupation of Vietnam, France was eager to regain its former colony. During Japanese occupation, however, Vietnamese nationalism had materialized under the leadership of Marxist-educated Ho Chi Minh. In 1945, in a document whose preamble echoed that of the U.S. Declaration of Independence, Ho Chi Minh proclaimed the independence of the nation of Vietnam.

Ho Chi Minh's party, the Viet Minh, had control over only the northern part of the country. The French, aided by Great Britain, occupied most of the south and central portions. In 1954, the Vietnamese defeated the French. The **Geneva Conference** (1954) gave the Viet Minh control of the northern portion of the country while providing for elections throughout Vietnam in two years. With U.S. support, Ngo Dinh Diem was installed as the president of South Vietnam. The required free elections were not held, and pockets of communist resistance, the Viet Cong, continued to exist in the south.

When Diem's government proved corrupt and ineffective, the United States arranged for his overthrow. By 1968, hundreds of thousands of U.S. troops were fighting in Vietnam. In 1973, the United States negotiated an end to its involvement in Vietnam; in 1975 the government in the south fell, and all of Vietnam was under communist control. The neighboring countries of Laos and Cambodia also fell to communism.

› Rapid Review

The post-war world saw the emergence of two superpowers: the United States and the Soviet Union. The Cold War period was one of constant threats of aggression between the superpowers as the Soviet Union sought to expand communism and the United States sought to contain it. Communism spread outside the Soviet Union to Eastern Europe, China, Southeast Asia, North Korea, and Cuba.

After World War II, most colonial possessions gradually achieved their long-awaited independence. Newly independent nations often aligned themselves with either the United States or the Soviet Union. Other nations such as India, however, chose the independence of nonalignment. New nations often experienced conflicts that continue to the present; the first Arab-Israeli war occurred immediately after the establishment of the nation of Israel, and sub-Saharan Africa has experienced a continuing history of ethnic strife.

› Review Questions

Questions 1 to 3 refer to the following image.

1. Which adjective best describes the artist's attitude toward the likelihood of an independent, united India?
   (A) Hopeful
   (B) Skeptical
   (C) Despairing
   (D) Angry

2. What is the artist's purpose in creating this cartoon?
   (A) To highlight the abuses of the British Empire in their relations with India
   (B) To indicate support for India's fight for independence
   (C) To warn that Indian Muslims may not support a single Indian state
   (D) To show that India was not capable of self-rule

3. What was the ultimate outcome of the conflict shown in the cartoon?
   (A) Burma and Ceylon became Buddhist nations.
   (B) India maintained its traditional borders as a Hindu nation.
   (C) Great Britain delayed granting Indian independence for 30 years.
   (D) India was divided and the Muslim state of Pakistan created.

4. Answer Parts A, B, and C.
   The post-war era of the twentieth century was characterized by a movement toward decolonization, especially in Africa.
   (A) Explain how France's reaction to decolonization differed from that of other colonial powers.
   (B) Describe one example of decolonization that illustrates France's reaction that you identified in Part A, and explain how it illustrates this reaction.
   (C) Identify and explain one long-term effect of decolonization on Africa.

5. Answer Parts A, B, and C.
   Although both the Soviet Union and China established communist regimes in the twentieth century, the nature of these regimes differed.
   (A) Identify and explain one similarity between the early economic policies of the Soviet Union and communist China.
   (B) Identify and explain one similarity in the Soviet Union's and communist China's economic reforms in the later decades of the twentieth century.
   (C) Identify and explain one way in which the policies of the Soviet Union and communist China differed.

› Answers and Explanations

1. **B** The cartoonist's tone is best described as skeptical, given the possibility of disaster posed by the explosives. The cartoon doesn't quite rise to the level of angry (D) or despairing (C), as nothing terrible has yet happened, although the potential is there. The presence of the explosives indicates that the cartoonist is not especially hopeful regarding the success of an independent India (A).

2. **C** The cartoonist is warning, through the actions of Muhammad Ali Jinnah, that Muslim Indians might be working against the success of a united India. There is no indication that Nehru is not capable of controlling the elephant that is India, with the exception of the sabotage of Muhammad Ali Jinnah (D), and the cordial exchange between Nehru and the British official would imply that the cartoonist isn't focused on past British abuses (A). Though the cartoonist might support Indian independence, the cartoon doesn't take a position with regard to its righteousness, only its chances of success (B).

3. **D** Because of the tensions between Hindus and Muslims in India, the state was divided and the independent Muslim nation of Pakistan was created (B). The conflict in the cartoon is set in the 1940s, and India gained independence in 1947, so (C) cannot be true. Burma and Ceylon have both been Buddhist nations for over 1,000 years, so this cannot have been a consequence of the events in the cartoon (A).

4A. Unlike other countries, France resisted decolonization. While Great Britain negotiated with its colonies like India, using legal means for their eventual independence, France's resistance to the self-determination of its colonies in Algeria and Indochina meant that those regions gained independence only through conflict.

4B. France had promised Algeria a greater degree of autonomy but then failed to follow through on its promises after WWI, prompting Algerians to form a liberation movement that engaged in guerilla-style tactics against the French in Algeria. The most intense fighting occurred in the Battle of Algiers, which had so many casualties and employed such brutal tactics that the French desire for the colony weakened, and Algeria eventually became independent in the 1960s.

4C. Decolonization of Africa has not led to strong, peaceful, democratic republics as many originally hoped. When the borders of African nations were drawn up by Europeans at the Berlin Conference, there was no consideration for tribal, ethnic, religious, or linguistic territories. Thus, a single nation might contain traditionally rival groups. As African nations decolonized, they typically maintained the colonial borders. In the absence of order imposed by a colonial power, traditional tribal, ethnic, and religious divisions resurfaced in many African nations after decolonization. An example of this would be the hostilities between the Hutu and the Tutsi people of Rwanda, resulting in genocide against the Tutsi people in the 1990s.

5A. One similarity between the economic policies of the Soviet Union and communist China would be the practice of collectivizing agriculture. Both Mao and Stalin wanted to increase agricultural production to feed their large populations. In both places, peasants and poor farmers had their land taken by the state and combined into huge collective farms, where they were expected to work. Part of both systems included ambitious quotas, with corresponding rewards and penalties. Both hoped to take advantage of economies of scale and both failed. In the Soviet Union, workers earned less under collectivized farming than they did on private lots, so they resisted by slowing work or refusing to work altogether. Both countries used unsound agricultural techniques that resulted in lower yields. Both management systems resulted in lowered agricultural output.

5B. The later decades of the twentieth century both saw a change or moderation in China's and the Soviet Union's economic positions. In the Soviet Union, Mikhail Gorbachev introduced *perestroika*, a restructuring of the government and economy. As part of that he allowed, for the first time since Lenin, some capitalism and private ownership of business. He also relaxed the centralized planning of the economy in favor of market forces. In China, Deng Xiaoping similarly allowed the gradual adoption of private business and some capitalism.

5C. The eventual outcomes of these two similar approaches was very different because in the Soviet Union, Mikhail Gorbachev combined *perestroika* (political and economic restructuring) with *glasnost*, or a new political and social openness. *Glasnost* opened the doors to a torrent of previously repressed dissent and dissatisfaction by the different ethnic groups that had been subjugated by the Russian-dominated Soviet Union. Deng Xiaoping, though, maintained strict governmental control over other aspects of its citizens' lives and the media, quelling any dissent. This could be seen in the Chinese government's reaction to the protest for democracy in Tiananmen Square. When support for the protestors spread, the Chinese military used force to end the protest. China's economic liberalization was not accompanied by political or democratic liberalization.

CHAPTER 27

End of the Cold War and Nationalist Movements

IN THIS CHAPTER

Summary: By the late 1980s, economic setbacks in the Soviet Union were producing social unrest. Worldwide nationalist movements were weakening the hold of communist regimes upon their people. The fall of the Berlin Wall in 1989 precipitated the end of other communist governments, culminating in the overthrow of communist governments in the Soviet Union. As former Soviet republics declared their independence, democratic movements continued throughout the world, especially in Latin America and Africa. The end of communism in the Soviet Union saw the emergence of a single superpower—the United States.

KEY IDEA

Key Terms

al-Qaeda
cartels
International Monetary Fund

Persian Gulf War
World Bank

Breakup of the Soviet Union

While Gorbachev was instituting reforms to save the Soviet Empire, the small nations of Eastern Europe were steadily moving toward independence. In 1988, Poland inaugurated a noncommunist government. In 1989, the people of Berlin dismantled the Berlin Wall; by the end of 1990, the two Germanys were reunited. In Czechoslovakia, resurgent nationalism split the country in half, as the Slovak region split off to form the republic of Slovakia, leaving the Czechs to form the Czech Republic. Meanwhile, in the former Soviet republic of Azerbaijan, traditional tensions with Armenians reemerged, with alleged violence against Armenians, resulting in Armenians declaring an autonomous sate in the Nagorno-Karabakh region of Azerbaijan. In the Russian Republic, Chechens began a guerrilla war against Russian troops when their demands for independence were refused.

Yugoslavia: Fragmentation

During the Cold War, Yugoslavia was composed of six ethnically self-conscious member "republics" held together by the Communist Party. As the communist regime began to collapse, the ethnic rivalries of Yugoslavia quickly reasserted themselves. The fragile multi-ethnic system fell apart as Slovenia and then Croatia declared independence in 1991. Serbia, as the largest "republic" of Yugoslavia, tried to hold the union together, but war erupted between Serbia and Croatia, and about the same time, the Serbian province of Kosovo revolted against Serbian rule. In Bosnia-Herzegovina the situation degenerated into a vicious, multisided war with acts of genocide committed on all sides. In the end, Yugoslavia split into seven independent nations—the six former republics of Yugoslavia plus Kosovo (although the independence of Kosovo is not recognized by Serbia and some other countries, including Russia).

Social, Economic, and Political Changes in Post–Cold War Europe

Globalization

While politics in the post–Cold War era often seemed to regress, the unity of the world's economies, societies, and cultures continued to move forward. Near the end of the twentieth century, the term globalization became prominent to describe the increasing integration and interdependence of the economic, social, cultural, and even ecological aspects of life. The term refers not only to the way in which the economies of the world affect one another but also to the way that the experience of everyday life is becoming increasingly standardized by the spread of technologies that carry with them social and cultural norms.

During this time, improvements in transportation, communication, and automation intensified, reducing the cost of producing and distributing goods internationally and creating a truly global economy, with both multinational and transnational corporations. As Europe transitioned from an industrial, factory-based economy to a post-industrial, service economy, social class structures changed, most notably with an expansion of the middle class. In addition to typical middle-class occupations, an educated class of professional managers and administrators emerged. The expansion of a prosperous middle class further encouraged a culture of mass consumerism begun earlier in the twentieth century.

Student Revolts

During the 1960s, philosophers like Herbert Marcuse contended that capitalist societies encouraged materialism and consumerism because they eroded the dissatisfaction of the proletariat necessary to advance communism; however, small groups of committed students could overthrow the ruling classes. Partly driven by theories like these, partly reacting to international events like the Vietnam War, and partly driven by frustrations over outdated and overburdened university systems, a series of student revolts erupted around Western Europe. In France in 1968, student and worker movements combined, resulting in student takeovers of university buildings and widespread strikes. Germany, too, experienced student protests. In both countries, police quashed the student violence, though the issues prompting them remained unresolved.

Green Party Movements

The increase in scope and pace of global post-industrial economies, in conjunction with technological advances, has given rise to environmental movements in Europe. Beginning in the 1970s, the ecological consequences of industrial and post-industrial economies became all too apparent. Air quality suffered due to vehicle and factory emissions, causing health concerns and even damaging buildings. Waterways became polluted with runoff from pesticides and fertilizers, as well as chemicals dumped by industrial concerns. As populations expanded, wildlife habitats like forests contracted.

Challenges to the Welfare State

The end of communism did not come without discord. A key example was Yugoslavia, where bitter conflict broke out in Bosnia among Muslims, Serbs, and Croats in the early 1990s. Fighting continued in 1998 to 1999 between Serbs and Albanians in the province of Kosovo. In 2004, Kosovo again became the scene of ethnic conflict in the newly founded republics of Serbia and Montenegro. The province declared its independence in 2008.

Final Days of the Soviet Union and Thereafter

In the summer of 1991, the Baltic republics declared their independence. Independence movements spread throughout the European border republics of Belarus, Ukraine, and Moldova and also in the Muslim regions of central Asia. In December 1991, the Soviet Union was dissolved and replaced by the Commonwealth of Independent States. The Communist Party was terminated, and the elected president of the Russian Republic, Boris Yeltsin, became the leader of the Commonwealth of Independent States.

The new commonwealth was faced with conflicts between ethnic groups and economic difficulties resulting from its new status outside the Soviet economy. Yeltsin, who initiated policies that allowed for a move toward private enterprise, was faced with continuing opposition during his rule and resigned in 1999. In 2000, a new president, Vladimir Putin, was elected; he was reelected in 2004, and in 2008 was appointed prime minister by the newly elected Russian president. Russia continued to struggle with economic weakness and organized crime. Ethnic clashes, especially within the Muslim-dominated province of Chechnya, plagued the commonwealth.

In 2008, violence broke out as Russian forces entered the democratic republic of Georgia in retaliation for Georgia's attempt to put down a separatist revolt in the province of South Ossetia. Because Georgia had a security relationship with the United States, the Georgia-Russia conflict renewed concerns of increasing tensions between the Putin government and the United States.

Latin America

At the end of the Cold War, more Latin American nations were moving toward democracy. Still, resistance to democratic rule was seen in groups such as the leftist Sendero Luminoso in Peru, which attempted to disrupt free elections in 1990. El Salvador remained under the control of its military, and the government of Nicaragua, no longer under the control of the Sandinistas, had to chart a new course under the direction of its elected president, Violeta Chamorro. The end of the twentieth and the beginning of the twenty-first centuries also saw new challenges to democracy in Colombia, Brazil, and Venezuela. In Colombia, violence caused by drug traffickers and armed rebels resulted in the flight of some Colombian citizens to neighboring countries. In Brazil, right-wing nationalist Jair Bolsonaro won the presidency in 2018. In Venezuela, the left-leaning Hugo Chávez was elected president in 1999. Concerned over fluctuating oil prices, Chávez nationalized a number of Venezuelan industries, including petroleum. In 2007, Venezuelans voted down proposed constitutional changes that would have given Chávez additional powers. With Chavez's death in 2015, Nicolas Maduro, also left-leaning, became the new president. In 2019, Maduro's presidency was being contested.

Additional issues plagued Latin American nations. Some of them owed large foreign debts; and in some, huge international drug **cartels** threatened government stability. The end of the twentieth century, however, saw renewed hope for enduring democracies and popular participation in Latin America. In Mexico in 2000, for example, the PRI lost its dominant status with the election of Vicente Fox of the PAN party as president. The Fox administration and the succeeding one led by Enrique Peña Nieto, of the PRI, continued to struggle with poverty and illegal immigration to the United States. With the election of left-leaning Andrés Manuel López Obrador, or AMLO, to the presidency in 2018, Mexico's national policy was projected to continue the fight against poverty, crime, and illegal immigration to the United States.

New Challenges

As communism dissolved in the Soviet Union, new challenges arose in the noncommunist nations. In 1990, Iraqi leader Saddam Hussein annexed oil-rich Kuwait, precipitating the **Persian Gulf War** between Iraq and a U.S.-led coalition of United Nations forces. Saddam Hussein's defeat and the liberation of Kuwait led to only a short truce. In 2003, the Iraqis were again at war with a U.S.-led coalition over Saddam Hussein's repressive regime and his potential for unleashing weapons of mass destruction. A new democratically elected Iraqi government executed Saddam Hussein in December 2006.

In 1998, India and Pakistan, long in conflict with each other over the territory of Kashmir, announced their development of nuclear weapons. A 2008 terrorist attack in the city of Mumbai, India, attributed by some to Pakistani terrorist organizations, increased global concern over the unstable relationship between the two countries. The nuclear capacity of North Korea also remained a troublesome issue.

In Africa and Asia, new nations often did not have the resources to further their development and had to look to developed nations or international organizations such as the **World Bank** and the **International Monetary Fund** for assistance. Violent ethnic conflicts plagued both regions. Repeated negotiations failed to bring lasting peace in the Middle East or to settle the problem of Palestinian refugees. U.S. President Obama ended

U.S. involvement in Iraq in 2011, although ethnic and religious divisions remain. Also in 2011, U.S. military forces located and killed Osama bin Laden. President Obama originally planned for withdrawal of U.S. forces in Afghanistan in 2014. In 2016, however, he announced that he would allow his successor to decide on the withdrawal date.

The end of the twentieth century saw a series of economic problems throughout parts of Asia and Southeast Asia, especially Japan. By 1999, some recovery was apparent. Hong Kong was returned to the People's Republic of China in 1997.

In spite of challenges in Africa and Asia, the future appeared hopeful. India remained the world's largest democracy. In the 1990s, South Africa ended apartheid and held elections in which all adult South Africans had the right to vote. New governments based on increased civil rights were emerging in both Afghanistan and Iraq. By 2014 Syria broke out in a civil war and the Islamic State in Iraq and Syria (ISIS) increased violence in the region. ISIS targeted fellow Muslims, especially Shiites, causing massive death and destruction. Jews and Christians were also targets of ISIS.

› Rapid Review

The breakup of the Soviet empire in 1991 resulted in the formation of a loose organization of former Soviet republics. Ethnic rivalries continued in the former Soviet republics and in Yugoslavia. Newly founded republics battled with economic problems. In Latin America, repressive governments gradually gave way to more widespread democracy. South Africa saw the end of apartheid and the beginnings of universal suffrage. Challenges remained, especially in the Middle East and South Asia, where Arab-Israeli conflicts continued and U.S.-backed coalitions had been engaged in Afghanistan and Iraq.

❯ Review Questions

Questions 1 to 3 refer to the following images.

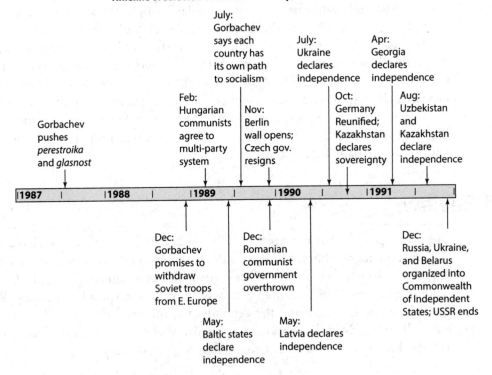

Timeline of selected events in the collapse of the USSR

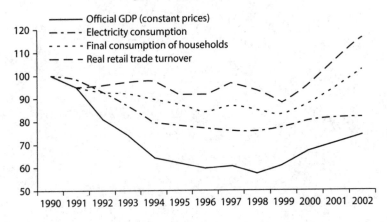

Measuring Economic Change in Russia, 1990–2002

1. Based on the information and your knowledge of world history, what was a likely contributing factor to the fall of the Soviet Union?
   (A) The large number of subordinate regions declaring independence
   (B) Military pressure by Western Europe and the United States
   (C) Growing religious fundamentalism and traditionalism
   (D) An increase in official GDP measured in constant prices

2. Based on the information and your knowledge of world history, which of the following could one infer was an immediate consequence of the fall of the Soviet Union?
   (A) Widespread homelessness
   (B) Decline in trade with the West
   (C) Declining household income
   (D) Growing importance of the energy sector

3. If a historian believed the Soviet Union primarily fell as a result of domestic factors, which information would he or she be most likely to add to the timeline?
   (A) Soviet troop withdrawal from Afghanistan
   (B) The nuclear disaster at Chernobyl
   (C) The declaration of sovereignty by Slovenia
   (D) Development of the U.S. Strategic Defense Initiative (Star Wars) program

4. Answer Parts A, B, and C of the following question.

   The later decades of the twentieth century have seen mixed results with respect to reduction of conflict and hostilities around the world.

   (A) Identify and describe one example of a new conflict in Asia or in Latin America that developed in the later decades of the twentieth century.
   (B) Identify and describe one example of an ongoing conflict in Asia or Latin America that has yet to be resolved.
   (C) Identify and describe one example of a previous conflict in any region that was resolved in the later decades of the twentieth century.

5. Which of the following has been a common problem of both Japan and Russia in the later years of the twentieth century to the present?
   (A) Ethnic conflicts
   (B) Political instability
   (C) Economic downturns
   (D) Huge foreign debt

› Answers and Explanations

1. **A** The timeline illustrates the number of smaller subordinate units within the USSR and the communist bloc seeking sovereignty and becoming independent. Some of these included nationalist movements that may have had religious or traditional elements, but these are not reflected in the timeline or the graph (C). Nothing on the timeline refers to actions taken by the United States or Western Europe (B). Although the graph does illustrate an increase in GDP, this does not happen until later in the 1990s, after the Soviet Union collapsed, and thus cannot be the reason for its failure (D).

2. **C** To answer this, one must use the graph as it reflects the time period after the fall of the Soviet Union. The decline of GDP in the years right after the fall of the Soviet Union, together with

declining consumption of households in the same period, supports the conclusion that household income declined (although these measures are not exactly the same). To say that this resulted in widespread homelessness, though, would be too strong a statement and not supported by the evidence given (A). The early 1990s show a decline in electricity consumption, which could indicate a lessening of its importance. It also would not represent the entire energy sector (D). There are no trade data in the graph (B).

3. **B** "Domestic," used in the context of history, means "at home" or "within one's own borders." The nuclear disaster at Chernobyl was the only event that took place within the Soviet Union. Although the USSR participated in the Afghanistan war, the fighting took place in

Afghanistan, and so was not a domestic concern. Also, military engagements are typically considered to be foreign policy, rather than domestic, making (A) a weaker response than B. Slovenia was part of Yugoslavia, which, though communist, was not part of the Soviet bloc of nations (C). The Strategic Defense Initiative was a defense system proposed by the United States and therefore does not fit the definition of "domestic" (D).

4A. In South Asia new conflicts arose over oil supplies. Iraq under Saddam Hussein invaded and annexed oil-rich Kuwait, located on its southeastern border. In response, a U.S.-led, United Nations coalition of military forces drove them from Kuwait but stopped short of invading Iraq in the first Persian Gulf War. After the terrorist attack on New York City on September 11, 2001, by members of a radical Islamic group called al-Qaeda, a U.S.-led (but not UN-sanctioned) military coalition drove Saddam Hussein from power. The primary justification was that Iraq was hiding weapons of mass destruction. Fighting continued, as Iraqi insurgent groups used guerilla warfare tactics to oppose the occupying forces.

4B. In Colombia, internal conflicts arose among left-leaning or communistic groups like FARC, right-wing paramilitary groups, criminal organizations, and the government. All of these groups are vying for increased control and power in Colombia. Many of the groups have been accused of drug trafficking as a means of financing their activities. Nearly all of them have been accused of human rights abuses in

pursuit of their goals. The Colombian government and FARC have negotiated a treaty, but other groups continue to battle for control of the drug trade.

4C. South Africa, with its history of institutionalized racism known as apartheid, had known periodic internal conflict and violence between the minority white population and the majority black citizens throughout the second half of the twentieth century. Although the white government gave black South Africans some concessions in the 1970s, including legalization of black labor unions and limited property rights, the African National Congress and its supporters were not placated. In the 1980s, violence escalated with strikes, boycotts, and riots. Black policemen and officials, perceived as tools of the government, were also attacked by black South Africans. The government responded with torture and violence. International condemnation grew, and foreign investment declined. Eventually, in the early 1990s, the government held a whites-only referendum on the repeal of apartheid laws. It passed overwhelmingly, and open elections were held shortly afterward. Though South Africa struggles with inequality and poverty, legacies of apartheid, it has remained peaceful.

5. **C** Japan's economy weakened sharply in the early 1990s, while Russia continued to struggle with the establishment of a market economy. Only Russia experienced ethnic conflicts (A). Neither has seen political instability nor huge foreign debt (B, D).

Global Trade

IN THIS CHAPTER

Summary: The twentieth century witnessed active commercial and trade interactions in virtually every region of the globe. The Great Depression illustrated the impact of a decline in trade in one region over trade throughout the world; an example was the manner in which the imposition of national tariffs in Western Europe and the United States weakened global trade in general. Price and supply manipulations by oil-producing nations in 1973 and 1979 affected the globe. Multinational corporations, often using cheap labor in developing nations, increased their influence. Especially after the decline of communism, more nations implemented free-market economies. Regional trade associations were organized to facilitate trade, and mass consumerism created a truly global marketplace. The following sections summarize key events in global trade between 1914 and the present.

Key Terms

euro
European Economic Community
European Union
import substitution
    industrialization
McDonaldization

North American Free Trade
    Agreement (NAFTA)
Organization of Petroleum
    Exporting Countries (OPEC)
World Trade Organization (WTO)

Early Twentieth Century

While the twentieth century is characterized by globalization of the economy, it is important to note that this was not an entirely new development, but rather the continuation of increasing economic integration. Early empires like Rome had their own regional trade networks, and Asian societies have long been connected with other parts of the world via the Silk Road and Indian Ocean trade. With the addition of Atlantic-based trade routes incorporating the Americas, trade truly became global, if not universal. What distinguishes the twentieth century, then, is the intensification of the pace and scope of economic integration.

The path of this integration, though, has not been consistent or continuous. While the dawn of the twentieth century reflected the economic prosperity created by industrialization, the aftermath of World War I was marked by a period of economic contraction and a worldwide depression. Nations turned to protectionism and tariffs to bolster domestic industry, but with little success. The poor economy is believed by many to have created the conditions favorable for the rise of dictators like Hitler in Germany.

The Changing Role of Government

Governments were more likely to take an active trade role in the early years of the twentieth century than at its close. In communist countries like the Soviet Union and China, this was more pronounced. Stalin's Five-Year Plans, for example, were government-created plans for rapid industrialization, shifting resources into heavy industry and collectivizing agriculture in attempts to spur economic growth. In China, Mao Zedong also collectivized agriculture and directed many workers and resources into increasing steel production as part of his Great Leap Forward program. Fascist corporatism, like Mussolini's Italy, was another form of government management of the economy, in theory with the cooperation of privately owned corporations. And in the United States, the New Deal created government-sponsored programs covering social benefits, job creation, infrastructure projects, and labor regulations. In Latin America, European exports were no longer available during WWI, forcing Latin Americans to adopt import substitution industrialization, a process by which nations developed domestic industries to produce goods previously imported and supported these new industries with protectionist tariffs.

Government intervention was also a tool of developing nations. Gamel Abdel Nasser implemented economic policies, including an increase in state ownership of businesses, as well as land and agricultural reforms in Egypt, though he is best known for nationalizing the Suez Canal. In East Asia, the "Four Tigers" (Hong Kong, South Korea, Taiwan, Singapore) emphasized export-led growth, in which governments focused on exporting goods for which they had a comparative advantage. These industries, including textiles (Taiwan, Hong Kong), automobiles (Japan, South Korea), and electronics (Japan, South Korea), often benefited from government subsidies or protectionist tariffs on foreign competition.

Gradually, support for government intervention in the economy gave way to a support for neoliberalism, an economic philosophy characterized by support for free markets and a reduction in trade barriers, a global market for goods and capital, privatization of state industries, and cuts in both spending and taxes. The nature of labor also changed, with a global, mobile, temporary workforce. The economic and political turmoil of communist nations with tightly controlled economies only reinforced this trend.

Free Trade

Increasingly, communism and socialism gave way to neoliberal policies in countries around the world, though with different results. With the rise of Putin, many reforms have gone by the wayside. *Glasnost* led to an explosion of dissent, resulting in many ethnic nations declaring independence. Market reforms were continued under Boris Yeltsin. China, by contrast, also began some free market reforms under Deng Xiaoping in the early 1980s, including transitioning to privately owned businesses. Nevertheless, China still has some state-owned monopolies, regulations restricting access of foreign-owned businesses to Chinese markets, and protective tariffs. Moreover, the economic liberalization was not accompanied by democratic reforms. After Chile experienced hyperinflation rates of up to 140 percent, the pro-market Pinochet took power in September 1973 in a coup that ousted Salvador Allende. In the new millennium, power has returned to a democratically elected president. He encouraged international investment and reduced trade barriers, though high unemployment resulted.

Post World War II, many regional and international trade agreements and organizations developed that served to increase the free flow of trade goods, which also increased global interdependence. Institutions like the World Bank and the International Monetary Fund (IMF) were created to facilitate international investment and trade and to maintain the stability of the international currency system. Committed to neoliberal values, these organizations frequently made loans to developing nations conditional on adopting free market systems and on deregulation and privatization of state industries. The General Agreement on Tariffs and Trade (GATT) eventually became the World Trade Organization (WTO), which encourages the reduction of trade barriers and adjudicates trade disputes among nations. The influence of these institutions is far-ranging, given that the WTO has 164 members and the IMF and World Bank have 189 members. However, the economic conditions imposed by the IMF and World Bank are sometimes blamed for additional social and economic hardships suffered by the people living in nations receiving these loans. In addition, power within these groups is not always evenly distributed, with wealthy nations having more influence.

The twentieth century is also notable for the growth of regional trading blocs, formed through trade agreements like the European Economic Community (EEC) and the North American Free Trade Agreement (NAFTA). The EEC was originally formed in 1958 to create a customs union (free trade within and external tariffs) and common policies to facilitate economic integration within Europe. This became the forerunner of the European Union (EU) today, with 28 members, 19 of which have adopted the euro as a common currency. Not all members of the European Union have equally robust and stable economies, especially the southern members like Greece and the newest members that are former members of the Soviet bloc. This has caused some tension as their economies and labor markets become intertwined, as we shall see later. In fact, in what is known as the Brexit vote, Great Britain voted to leave the European Union in 2016.

NAFTA is a trade agreement among Canada, the United States, and Mexico, eliminating barriers to trade and investment within the region. Although two related agreements were signed to protect workers and the environment, NAFTA continues to be criticized in the United States and Canada for shifting jobs to Mexico, due to its lower wages and looser regulatory standards. Prompted by fear of communism and the growing power of China, the Association of Southeast Asian Nations (ASEAN), which includes nations like the Philippines, Thailand, Singapore, Burma, Malaysia, and Indonesia, was created to promote economic, political, and cultural integration among its members (though not to the extent of the EU). Most recently the Trans-Pacific Partnership (TPP) would have included Pacific Rim nations, (the United States, Peru, Mexico, Canada, Australia, New Zealand, Thailand, Japan, and Brunei, to name a few). As of this writing, its future is unclear, as President Trump declared the United States will withdraw from the partnership.

One reason these trade agreements are so controversial is that more-developed nations fear that jobs will move to less developed nations, where labor is cheaper and regulations less extensive. This has given rise to a new type of business, the transnational corporation. Multinational corporations (MNCs) operate in many countries, and may open subsidiaries in them, but there remains a centralized management system and a "home country." Transnational corporations (TNCs) are truly global, in that their management system is global, rather than based in any one country; thus, there is no loyalty to the values or people of a "home" nation. They are highly mobile, in that they will open or close operations around the world to take advantage of the lowest labor and regulatory costs. Even the location of the company's official headquarters may quickly be shifted from one country to another to take advantage of tax laws and government regulations.

Labor

Labor markets have also become global, as workers migrate in search of better employment, usually from poorer nations to more developed ones, and sometimes from former colonies to the colonial power. Thus, there are many West Africans and Algerians in France, and Indians and Pakistanis in Great Britain, and Filipinos in the United States Geographic proximity also plays a role, with Mexicans, Cubans, and Haitians migrating to the United States for work. Sometimes these migrants enter illegally, which makes them vulnerable to exploitation, with substandard wages and conditions. Women, particularly, can be vulnerable to exploitation as sex workers. Beginning in the 1960s, other nations, like the Persian Gulf regions and Germany, have had guest worker programs to fill labor needs. In Europe, the freedom of movement among workers in member nations has caused concern that wealthier Western European nations will be flooded with migrants from Eastern Europe and the Baltic states. Foreign workers often send remittances (money) home to their families, contributing to the international circulation of currency. Cheap labor also leads to cheaper products, contributing to the global circulation of goods.

Globalization and the rise of TNCs have led to concern about outsourcing, where companies have functions filled by cheaper labor overseas. Information technology jobs, customer service, and manufacturing jobs have been shifted to places like India, the Philippines, and China. Increasingly, white-collar jobs like computer programming are being shifted overseas as well, to places like India and Eastern Europe. Fears of job loss have increased support for protectionist policies in some Western nations like the United States and Great Britain.

The Role of Technology

Improvements in communications and transportation have intensified the scope and pace of these developments. To handle increasing amount of goods circulating worldwide, transportation evolved, including the development of containerized shipping and supertankers. Passenger air travel facilitates international business, reducing travel time among countries from days to hours in most cases. Information can be shared instantly among corporate offices around the world using computers. Laptops and mobile phones have expanded on this capacity by making information accessible nearly everywhere. Telephones have given way to mobile phones and videoconferencing. These changes have given rise to new work patterns, where telecommuting allows for a widely dispersed workforce.

Consequences of Globalization

One of the primary consequences of globalization is interdependence, whereby the fortunes of each nation's economy are inextricably linked to the fortunes of others around the world. The global depression in the 1920s and 1930s is one example. Another is the oil embargo of the 1970s in which Arab petroleum exporting nations (members of OPEC, including Saudi Arabia, Iraq, and Iran) cut oil production and embargoed (halted) oil exports to nations that had supported Israel in the Yom Kippur War. The ensuing oil shock led to skyrocketing oil prices, erosion of trade surpluses, rationing of oil, increasing unemployment, and declining GDP in the United States and Europe.

This interdependence was particularly pronounced during the recession of 2008, in which the U.S. housing market, whose prices were inflated, suffered a sharp downturn. Mortgage lenders, insurance companies, and banks suffered; some went out of business and others were bailed out by the U.S. government. Credit dried up, businesses contracted, unemployment rose, and foreclosures increased. Globally, exporting nations in Asia suffered as demand for goods decreased. Smaller nations lost foreign investment. Major European banks were on the brink of collapse and were bailed out by their governments. Economic output decreased globally to the lowest level since 1970. Some European nations with high debt levels, like Ireland and Greece, were at risk of defaulting. Since banks in other countries (like Crédit Agricole in France) had financial investments in these nations, people feared that it could cause panic in the Eurozone banking sector and devalue the euro, used by 17 countries. Loans by the European Central Bank and the IMF loans to these countries came with stringent requirements that they take measures to reduce their debt through spending cuts, triggering mass protests in Greece. Given that many African currencies are tied to the euro, it is clear that these events could have even further-reaching effects.

The benefits of globalization have not been evenly distributed, leading to a growing North-South divide (as contrasted to the West-East divide earlier in history). The North includes Western Europe, North America, Australia, and New Zealand (the latter two are not in the North, but share similar economic and cultural characteristics). Usually more developed Asian nations are also included in this category, but not always. The South is generally thought to include Africa, Latin America, and Southeast Asia. Though the North has only about 25 percent of the world's population, it controls nearly all of the world's manufacturing and approximately 80 percent of the world's income. Access to health care, food, clean water, and housing are nearly universal in the North, but much scarcer in the South. One criticism of globalization is that wealthier nations in the North can take advantage of their superior economic power when negotiating trade agreements with the South, leading to exploitation of labor and environment. Inequality is also growing within nations. For example, the wealthiest 1 percent of people in the United States have increased their income twofold since the 1950s, the widest gap since the 1920s. Currently they earn 184 times what the rest of the country earns. The top 10 percent in India have more than 350 times the wealth of the rest of the nation. And in Russia, more than 80 percent of the population has less than $10,000 in personal assets, though there are more than 100 billionaires and over 150,000 millionaires.

Globalization: Criticisms and Concerns

Globalization has had its critics. Environment degradation has resulted; since transnational corporations have no obligation to work within the regulatory framework of any specific country, they will move operations where environmental rules are lax, lowering production costs, but causing deforestation, air pollution, and water pollution in the countries where they operate. TNCs are also accused of exploitive labor policies, especially in developing nations. By shifting operations to nations with low wages and few labor regulations, TNCs maximize profits for investors, while workers may suffer unsafe working conditions and low standards of living. Reducing costs of production can also lead to the use of child labor. Undocumented migrant workers are also vulnerable to exploitation, as employers leverage workers' illegal status to prevent complaints about substandard wages and working conditions. A related phenomena is known as McDonaldization, in which businesses value efficiency, productivity, and standardization over regional variation and quality. For example, even though a McDonald's hamburger might not be high cuisine, the company can make it cheaply and McDonald's customers worldwide know what they are getting.

The creation of a single global market has also led to concerns about the cultural homogenization of the world, as Western language, products, music, film, and fashion penetrate the cultural norms and practices of other nations.

These concerns have created antiglobalization protests (especially at G-20 summits) and a backlash against unrestricted free trade. As manufacturing and skilled jobs move from industrialized nations to developing ones with lower labor and regulatory costs, and automation reduces the number of available jobs, workers in industrialized nations face unemployment, reduced wages or benefits, and economic uncertainty. This has led to growing protectionist and anti-immigration sentiment around the world. Protectionist measures include tariffs on imports, antidumping measures (tariffs to prevent markets being flooded by imports sold below market values), increased bureaucratic regulations intended to discourage imports, and subsidies to lower the costs of exports. For example, Argentina taxed imported luxury items more than 30 percent; China has quotas on imported wheat, rice, and corn; and the United States has imposed a 35 percent tariff on Chinese tires. In 2016, the WTO warned that protectionist measures by member countries were on the rise. In Western industrialized nations, immigrants are frequently blamed for being willing to work for lower wages, and thus "taking" jobs from native-born workers. This has led to growing support for politicians supporting restrictions on immigration, like Marine Le Pen of France's National Front party, and Donald Trump, president of the United States.

› Rapid Review

Twentieth- and twenty-first-century global economies were so interconnected that a crisis in one sector affected nearly all regions of the globe. Former colonial economies often had difficulty recovering from the production of a plantation cash crop to a diversified economy. East Asian nations proved fierce competitors in the export of automobiles, textiles, and electronics. OPEC oil prices became a major focus of world attention. Mass consumerism characterized the latter years of the twentieth century and the beginning of the twenty-first century as U.S. values and products diffused throughout most of the world.

› Review Questions

Questions 1 to 3 refer to the following quotations.

[An] effective strategy for encouraging democracy is the spread of markets.

—Chris Coyne

Globalization and free trade do spur economic growth, and they lead to lower prices on many goods.

—Robert Reich

1. Which economic philosophy best represents the ideas expressed in the quotes?
   (A) Marxism
   (B) Utilitarianism
   (C) Neoliberalism
   (D) Conservatism

2. Which nation would best serve as a counter-example to Chris Coyne's statement?
   (A) China under Mao Zedong
   (B) China under Deng Xiaoping
   (C) Cuba under Castro
   (C) The Soviet Union under Josef Stalin

3. Which organization would both speakers be least likely to support?
   (A) NAFTA
   (B) The Eurozone
   (C) ASEAN
   (D) OPEC

4. Answer Parts A, B, and C.
   Globalization, though an increasing part of the twentieth century, has many critics.
   (A) Explain the concept of globalization.
   (B) Identify ONE technological development that facilitated globalization, and explain how it facilitated globalization.
   (C) Identify and discuss ONE negative consequence of globalization.

5. Answer Parts A, B, and C.
   Although the latter part of the twentieth century was characterized by free markets, many countries began their economic development through government intervention.
   (A) Describe the economic concept of collectivization, and discuss ONE example of how it was used in the twentieth century.
   (B) Describe the concept of nationalization of industries and discuss ONE example of how it was used in the twentieth century.
   (C) Describe the economic concept of protectionism and discuss ONE example of how it was used in the twentieth century.

› Answers and Explanations

1. **C** Neoliberalism is characterized by a support for free-markets as the best means of guaranteeing economic growth. Marxism is the belief that capitalism, the driver of free markets, exploits workers and leads to revolution. Utilitarianism is the belief that the best policies are those that promote happiness for the greatest number of people. Though an argument could be made that free-market policies benefit the most people, this could be disputed if one considers the environmental consequences, for example. Moreover, utilitarianism is not an economic philosophy per se, making neoliberalism the better answer. Likewise conservatism is not an economic philosophy, but rather a political one favoring traditional institutions and resisting change (D).

2. **B** Chris Coyne's statement implies that development of economic freedom is likely to lead to political freedom. Although China implemented market reforms under Deng Xiaoping, these have not led to increased political freedoms. China under Mao Zedong with its Great Leap Forward (A), the Soviet Union under Stalin and his Five-Year Plans (D), and Cuba under Castro (C) were all associated with state control of the economy.

3. **D** OPEC is a group formed to increase profits for oil-exporting nations by limiting production and setting prices, both of which violate free market ideals. NAFTA (A) and ASEAN (C) are both free trade zones instituted through multilateral treaties. The Eurozone is a single-currency zone among European Union members, created to facilitate the free flow of capital and goods within the zone (B).

4A. Globalization is characterized by increasing economic interdependence and the free flow of goods and capital in a global marketplace though the reduction of trade barriers.

4B. Globalization was facilitated by improvements in technology, like those in the transportation industry. Lower energy costs made passenger air travel much cheaper and more widely available, allowing businesses executives to travel easily among international offices. Containerized shipping increased the amount of goods that freighters could carry at a time, reducing costs.

4C. One negative consequence of globalization is that the economic interdependence of nations makes them more vulnerable. Economic downturns in one part of the world can have ripple effects throughout the world. For example, the U.S. recession in 2008 with its resulting unemployment led to a decrease in the demand for goods from exporting nations. There was also a contraction of credit and international banks failed, decreasing investment and leading to business failures and unemployment internationally.

5A. When governments take over and consolidate many small, private enterprises, it is known as collectivization. One example of this is the move by Josef Stalin in the Soviet Union to collectivize agriculture by forcing farmers to work on large-scale, state-owned farms. Though the intent was to take advantage of economies of scale, without the profit motive, farmers were less productive. Stalin also set unrealistic production targets, and managers of the collectives often lied about meeting them, making economic planning more difficult.

5B. Nationalization is the process by which a government takes over an industry or enterprise previously owned by private investors, often in foreign nations. An example of this was Nasser's nationalization of the Suez Canal in Egypt, which had previously been controlled by Great Britain.

5C. Protectionism is the policy of protecting domestic industries through the imposition of protective tariffs on imports and/or subsidies. One example is the use of import substitution industrialization in Latin America when governments encouraged the development of domestic industries to replace imported goods. One way they encouraged those industries was by using protective tariffs on foreign imports. The governments also provided financial assistance to companies developing those industries (subsidies).

CHAPTER 29

Technological Developments

IN THIS CHAPTER

Summary: The period since 1900 was one of rapid technological developments. From new medical discoveries, to more sophisticated military technology, to improvements in transportation, technology dominated the twentieth and twenty-first centuries. Labor-saving devices in the household increased leisure time, and new forms of mass entertainment filled that leisure time. The space race increased Cold War tensions as the development of nuclear weapons raised new uncertainties.

Key Terms

deoxyribonucleic acid (DNA)   International Space Station
Helsinki Accords   service industries
Hubble Space Telescope   Sputnik

World War Firsts

Many technological innovations with commercial and practical applications were first developed with military use in mind. In the first half of the twentieth century, world wars provided the impetus for large-scale, more institutional scientific research and development, often with government, research university, or corporate assistance. Scientific developments in the twentieth century tended not to be the product of a single researcher in a small lab, as they had in the past. World War I was the initial conflict in which several new types of technology were used for the first time. Airplanes were used in combat. Dirigibles, tanks, more sophisticated weaponry, and poison gas also made their debut during the First World War. Radio technology was used during World War I for communication purposes. Leaders of warring nations used radio to promote nationalism, ushering in an age of mass culturalism. After the war, radio was extended to commercial and private use. In 1920, the first commercial radio broadcast was aired in Philadelphia. By 1930, millions of U.S. citizens owned radios, which they used to listen to news, sportscasts, and serials (soap operas). Government control of the airwaves in Europe made radio ownership less common on that continent.

World War II and the dropping of the atomic bomb ushered in a new scientific age. The Second World War also added jet engines, tape recordings, and radar to its list of firsts.

Postwar Period

Technology assisted Europe in its recovery from the world wars. Tractors and combine harvesters, powered by internal combustion engines, synthetic fertilizers, and pesticides like DDT, as well as improved seeds, increased agricultural yields, while modern industrial equipment increased production of textiles and metal goods, including automobiles and appliances.

In the 1950s, scientific technology led British and U.S. scientists to discover the composition of **deoxyribonucleic acid (DNA)**. Scientific farming based on genetics led to further improvements in seeds and pesticides. Genetic research produced the first incident of animal cloning (a cloned sheep) in Scotland in 1997.

Medical treatments and sanitation improved. New antibiotic drugs, such as penicillin (discovered in 1928), as well as immunizations against diphtheria and poliomyelitis lowered the death rate. X-rays, ultrasound, and imaging assisted medical diagnoses. Indoor plumbing improved sanitation.

In 1949, the Soviet Union developed its own atomic bomb. From that time until the 1980s, both the United States (1952) and the Soviet Union (1953) built hydrogen bombs and developed ever more sophisticated weapons of war and defense. In 1972, as a result of the nuclear arms race, European countries convened a conference on security issues in Helsinki, Finland. In 1975, the **Helsinki Accords** called for contacts between nations on both sides of the Iron Curtain and addressed the issue of human rights. The Human Genome Project, an international public-private research effort to sequence the nucleotides in human DNA, was begun in 1990. The first complete sequence of a single individual's genome was published in 2007, though study of genetic variations continues. Advances in genetics show great promise in the treatment of disease, but have raised ethical concerns about the ability to genetically engineer life, as well as concerns over privacy of genetic information.

Power, Energy, and Materials

Although some of the inventions discussed in this section were actually developed before 1900, the twentieth century saw their widespread improvement and expansion. One example is electrification. Today more than 60 percent of the world has access to electricity. Hydroelectric dams brought electricity to regions whose topography might otherwise have made it impractical. Transmission of electricity became more efficient, with lines able to handle more power, and large regions integrated into power grids, which could adapt to local variations in load.

Gas turbine engines, with a high power-to-weight ratio, supported the development of jet airplanes. The speed of transportation also increased, with improved automobiles, high-speed trains, and the Concorde supersonic jet.

Similarly, crude oil had been used in the 1800s, but the twentieth century saw improvements in extraction (like fracking) and refining, as well as increased importance of the reliability of industrialized nations' oil supply. Oil refining techniques led to the development of plastics, which were nonconductive, and thus useful in electrical devices. Scientists quickly realized that the energy released by an atomic bomb could be adapted and harnessed to create steam and drive a turbine, producing electricity. Metal alloys were developed for specific qualities: strength, magnetism (or its absence), corrosion resistance, and light weight. Synthetic materials like nylon, notable for combining flexibility with high tensile strength, were developed as women's stockings, then adapted for military purposes, like parachutes.

Concerns about dependence on energy based on nonrenewable sources like fossil fuels and radioactive material, has led to searches for alternative fuels. Solar panels harness the energy of the sun, and wind "farms" use the wind and giant turbines to generate power, though these technologies have not yet been widely adopted. Other concerns over nuclear power center on disposal of radioactive waste and fears over nuclear accidents like the one in 1986 in Chernobyl, the Soviet Union, or the Fukushima Daiichi nuclear meltdown in Japan in 2011.

Space Age

The twentieth century saw the exploration of new horizons in space. In 1957, the Soviet Union launched **Sputnik**, the first satellite, and in 1961 sent the first manned flight into space. The United States soon followed in the space race, succeeding in landing astronauts on the moon in 1969. In the 1970s, the United States and the Soviet Union cooperated in docking spacecraft and later cooperated in work on the **International Space Station**. Cooperation between the United States and European nations led to the development in 1990 of the **Hubble Space Telescope**, which is capable of observing objects in remote areas of the universe. U.S. orbiter landings on Mars have provided opportunities for investigation of potential landing sites on the Red Planet.

Entertainment Technology

The film industry created new opportunities for entertainment, especially after the addition of sound in the late 1920s. By the early 1950s, television had begun to enter many homes in the West, further promoting mass consumerism. In the 1970s, the entertainment industry born in Hollywood was surpassed by Bollywood, the name given to the film industry based in Mumbai, India. Since the 1970s, India has ranked as the world's largest film producer.

Technology in the Information Age

The first computer, nicknamed ENIAC, took up 1,800 square feet of floor space and used 2,000 vacuum tubes. Vacuum tubes were first developed in 1906 and relied on heating up a filament that generated a flow of electrons to a positively charged plate inside. These formed the basis of many early communication technologies, such as radar, telephone networks, sound recording and reproduction, radio, television, and early computers. While they connected and integrated the world, vacuum tubes were also large, fragile, and generated a lot of heat, necessitating energy-intensive cooling systems.

Personal computing did not develop until the introduction of transistors, using semiconductor technology. This miniaturized the storage and transfer of information, while solving the problems of vacuum tubes. Later the integrated circuit, or chip, further refined the process. Personal computers became available in the 1980s and were in widespread use within ten years. The invention of the modem allowed data to be transferred along phone lines, making data communication cheaper and more accessible.

Around the 1960s, new communications networks were being developed with the help of the Defense Department in the United States. The Internet was intended to integrate multiple computer networks and was used primarily for emails and file transfers. With the invention of the World Wide Web in 1989 and its implementation two years later, hyperlinked documents were accessible from any point on the network, leading to a truly global information age. Browsers and search engines were created to bring content to nontechnical users. Web 2.0 is sometimes used to discuss user-generated content on sites like YouTube, WordPress (blogging), Wikipedia, and Facebook.

Mobile phones provide the intersection of portability, computing, and communication. Developed in 1973, the first one went on sale in 1983 for approximately $4,000. Since then, improvements in battery life, memory, processing power, graphics, and networking have made mobile phones ubiquitous. They allow instantaneous communication through phone, email, text, or video chat anywhere in the world. Access to encyclopedic information, news alerts, and maps with real-time traffic have changed how we research, process, and store information. Although mobile phones have democratized the information age in the sense that mobile phones are available everywhere (there are more mobile phones than there are indoor toilets), they have also raised concerns about virtual interactions supplanting face-to-face ones and the ability of people, especially employees, to "disconnect" from technology. Robots, first used in Japan and adopted in Europe for use in mines and the automobile industry, increased industrial productivity. More people in the post-industrial world worked in **service industries** because of increased mechanization of agriculture and industry.

The power of technology in political conflict was apparent in the Middle East and North Africa during the Arab Spring of December 2010 to May 2011. In this series of events, pro-democracy protesters effectively used social media to organize and communicate throughout the uprisings.

❯ Rapid Review

World Wars I and II saw a number of technological firsts, from improved transportation and communications to more elaborate weaponry. The atomic bomb ushered in a nuclear age that was among the focal points of the Cold War era. Technology created new leisure time activities, improved sanitation, and helped in the discoveries of new breakthroughs in medical science. The use of technology to transmit information characterizes the twenty-first century.

› Review Questions

1. Answer Parts A, B, and C.

   Many new technological innovations were first developed or used for military purposes.

   (A) Identify ONE new technology in energy or power that was initially developed for or used in the military, and explain how it was used by the military.

   (B) Explain how the innovation in Part A was refined or adapted for civilian use.

   (C) Explain ONE modern-day concern regarding energy or power technology.

2. Answer Parts A, B, and C.

   (A) Explain ONE difference in the process of scientific discovery or technological innovation in the nineteenth century and the twentieth century.

   (B) Identify and explain how ONE example of a scientific discovery or technological innovation in the medical field developed in the new manner explained in Part A.

   (C) Discuss ONE valid ethical concern regarding advances in the medical field in the twentieth century.

Questions 3 to 5 refer to the following images.

A.

B.   The photograph shows a boy and an old woman with a laptop in front of a typical house in Myan-mar, Asia.

3. Which statement best represents the theme of image B?
   (A) Young people are inherently better with computers.
   (B) Technology is destroying indigenous cultures.
   (C) Cloud computing allows one to conduct business from anywhere in the world.
   (D) Computers are ubiquitous; they are found virtually everywhere.

4. Which statement would be an appropriate theme for image A?
   (A) Technology is so inexpensive now, even children can afford it.
   (B) Children are better able to understand technology than their parents.
   (C) Technology enhances children's enjoyment of the outdoors.
   (D) Technology is changing how children interact, not necessarily for the better.

5. Which technological discovery in the twentieth century made it practical to transfer information along home telephone lines?
   (A) Vacuum tube
   (B) Transistor
   (C) Modem
   (D) Cathode ray tube

› Answers and Explanations

1A. One innovation in energy or power technology that was initially developed for use by the military was nuclear power. This was first used in the military when the United States dropped atom bombs on Hiroshima and Nagasaki in World War II.

1B. Scientists saw the energy produced by the atom bomb and realized that energy could be harnessed to produce steam, drive a turbine, and produce electricity. This was the birth of the modern nuclear power plant.

1C. Nuclear power has raised concerns about its safety. Nuclear power creates radioactive waste that does not lose its radioactive properties for many, many years, making its safe storage or disposal a problem, both for our generation and those to come. People also fear what might happen if there is an accident or equipment failure at the plant, exposing people, plants, and animals to toxic radiation for years and years. Such fears are not unfounded given the disasters at Chernobyl and Fukushima Daiichi.

2A. While most scientific or technological discovery in the nineteenth century was the result of one or a small group of researchers working in a single laboratory or at home, scientific discovery in the twentieth century was accomplished on a much grander scale, with scientists collaborating across multiple facilities in multiple locations, or in one giant research lab. Such discoveries require investment, and so in the twentieth century, research was funded by corporations, private nonprofit foundations, universities, and governments.

2B. One such discovery in the medical field would be the Human Genome Project, which was funded through public-private partnerships and on which teams of researchers in multiple countries worked (and continue to work).

2C. Although the Human Genome Project has enormous potential for the cure or eradication of genetically based diseases, possibly without medication and its side effects if the genes can be "turned off," there are ethical concerns about how this new information will be used. Some are concerned that it might be used to create "designer babies," with superior genetic characteristics. This creates the ethical dilemma about "playing God" to determine how life develops. It also raises a societal ethical dilemma if this kind of genetic engineering is only available to those who can afford it, leading to two distinct classes of people, based on genetic talents and their parents' ability to buy them.

3. A The artist's purpose in the image is to show all of the different tasks that can be accomplished using technology. There are a variety of people (B), many of whom are likely using technology for work (email, documents, etc.) (C). The clouds in the image represent the innovation of cloud computing, not "heaven" (D).

4. D The children are outside, but there is no personal or face-to-face interaction. Even though all the children have smartphones, there is no indication regarding their price (A) or a comparison with their parents' technological skills (B). Though the setting is outside, there is no indication that the children are especially enjoying being outside or interacting with their environment. Their activities wouldn't be much different if they were indoors (C).

5. C The modem converted data into sound and back again, allowing information to be transferred along telephone lines and making home computing practical. Vacuum tubes were the invention that allowed for the earliest computers, but those were too big to be used at home (A). Transistors allowed for the miniaturization of computers, but were not related to data transfer (B). Cathode ray tubes were used for graphics technology in televisions and computer monitors, though they are now obsolete (D).

CHAPTER 30

Social Changes

IN THIS CHAPTER

Summary: The twentieth-century world wars produced two basic responses—the first, a feeling of skepticism concerning the future, and the second, the desire to possess the many new products on the market after both world wars. In an attempt to secure a comfortable future for their citizens, Western and Japanese governments established social welfare systems, particularly for the aged. Women's rights increased at the same time that traditional female roles persisted. Universal suffrage became law in the United States (1920) and in other nations around the world (for example, Japan in 1945, India in 1947, and Brazil in 1932). A new global culture saw the dominance of Western influence, balanced somewhat by the rise of Asian popular culture's influence; Netflix production of streaming shows from around the world; Bollywood; the worldwide reach of culinary traditions, products, and restaurants; and, of course, the World Wide Web. At no time has it been more clear that *all* history is world history.

Key Terms:

cubism
evangelical
fundamentalism
globalization
Kabuki theater
Liberation Theology

mass consumerism
National Organization for Women (NOW)
New Deal
No theater
welfare state

Society After World War I

During the 1920s, Western society, most noticeably in the United States, saw a rise in **mass consumerism**, especially in household appliances and in automobiles. The automobile decreased isolation and allowed new freedoms for some adolescents in the United States. Some women turned to fashions that called for shorter skirts and hairstyles and behavior that allowed freer self-expression.

The movie industry was not only an outlet for artistic expression but also a new source of family entertainment. Modern painters such as Pablo Picasso, Juan Gris, and Georges Braque introduced to visual art Einstein's idea of relativity (as a means to express the relationship among mass, energy, space, and time), and they combined geometric figures with non-Western art styles, particularly African, to create a new style called **cubism**, which emphasized the idea that the artist's subjective view, not external appearance, constituted reality. Modern architecture featured the use of concrete, steel, and broad expanses of glass.

At the same time, post-war Western society was characterized by a general feeling of skepticism. The devastation brought by the century's first global war was heightened by the despair of the Great Depression. All social classes faced the prospect of unemployment or reduced salaries. In Japan, the depression increased suspicions of the Western way of life. Western states provided old age and medical insurance that eventually led to the institution of the **welfare state**. In the United States, the **New Deal** took government spending to new heights in an attempt to resolve the economic stagnation of the Depression and to provide for social security programs. Western European governments began to provide assistance to families with several children.

Post–World War II Western Society

In 1948, the United Nations General Assembly proclaimed its Universal Declaration of Human Rights. This document would set the stage for post–World War II societies. After World War II, some of the women who had assumed traditionally male roles in the workforce retained those roles, and more women entered the workforce. Divorce was made more accessible, and effective birth control became more conveniently available with the introduction of the birth control pill. For the first time, women could control their own fertility; they could delay pregnancy in favor of developing their careers. Many European countries provided day care centers for working mothers. In the United States, the **National Organization for Women (NOW)**, founded in 1966, campaigned for women's rights. The role of the church in family life declined as church attendance fell, especially in Europe.

In the 1950s and 1960s, the United States experienced a civil rights movement that ended segregation of African Americans and increased voting rights. In South Africa, the Anti-Apartheid Movement; in China, the Tiananmen Square Protest; and globally, the student revolts of 1968–1969 all aimed to provide nonviolent alternatives to the societal status quo. Campuses themselves had changed, as they expanded to accommodate newly enfranchised students from the middle and lower classes. Student protests against U.S. involvement in the Vietnam War swept university campuses in the 1960s and early 1970s. These protests, including those in Western Europe, eventually focused on growing opposition to materialism and **mass consumerism**.

In the 1970s and 1980s, some Westerners began to question the concept of the welfare state. Both Great Britain and the United States elected leaders who adopted more conservative approaches toward government responsibilities and spending. Welfare programs were decreased under the leadership of Britain's Prime Minister Margaret Thatcher and U.S.

President Ronald Reagan. Western European economic growth soared during the 1980s, producing a marked increase in consumer goods. Educational opportunities broadened throughout the world. Social, political, and economic changes following World War II would also prompt a struggle between capitalism and communism and a Cold War among the superpowers.

Society in the Soviet Union

In the post–World War II period, the USSR was in many ways forced to start from scratch. Both Allies and Axis powers followed a "scorched earth" policy to deprive their enemies from gaining or retaining goods. Almost 2,000 towns, 70,000 villages, countless livestock, 32,000 factories, and approximately 40,000 miles of railroad tracks had been destroyed during the war. Population was down by at least 14 percent, including almost 10 million military deaths. While England suffered from rationing until well into the 1950s, the USSR experienced severe famine. Soviet leaders began to build a system of welfare services, including protection for the sick and aged. Soviet schools inculcated communist values and praised the "motherland." Religion was considered a myth; Western styles of art were denounced as decadent.

By the 1950s, the Soviet Union and most Eastern European nations were industrialized. Unlike the Western world, factories in the communist bloc forced the production of heavy goods over consumer goods. Research led to a successful space program, for example. And women enjoyed noteworthy progress in educational and professional opportunities.

With the disbanding of the USSR on December 31, 1991, and the conversion to a market-based economy, Russia was faced with the need to provide social service (child care, housing) previously provided by state-run, but now privatizing, factories. This switch to a more capitalistic society resulted in a widening gap between the rich and everyone else. Living standards dropped, and social services collapsed. Health, education, and welfare systems all suffered. Women lost many of the privileges they had enjoyed previously.

By the turn of the century, the Russian Federation had begun to regain some economic ground, though the rich-poor gap remained notable. Privilege remained tied to tradition and family position.

Japan

In the 1920s, Japan also experienced a rise in **mass consumerism**. The film industry became popular, and secondary education reached greater numbers of students than ever before. After World War II, the new U.S.-influenced government in Japan provided for women's suffrage and abolished Shintoism as the state religion. The Japanese preserved respect for their elders by creating a social security system for the elderly. After the end of the U.S. occupation, the Japanese government began asserting more control over the lives of its citizens, including controlling the content of student textbooks. Traditions such as the tea ceremony, **Kabuki**, and **No theater** continued.

Japanese work schedules allowed for less leisure time than in Western societies. One leisure activity that became (and remains) extremely popular was baseball, introduced to Japan during the U.S. occupation.

The 1950s and 1960s were characterized by a technological revolution in Japan. Research and mass communication developed to a high degree, and continues. The rapid industrialization of the country—as well as expanded educational opportunities and mass communication, urbanization, and population growth—resulted in significant changes in social structure. Still, there is a traditional elite, based not solely on ancestry but also on educational levels achieved and financial success. Housing and land remain costly; food prices are high; and many farming villages have disappeared, leading to an imbalance of trade because of food imports.

China

China's May Fourth Movement (1919) honored the role that women had played in the Chinese revolution by increasing women's rights. Footbinding was outlawed, and women were given wider educational and career opportunities. Although the Guomindang attempted to return Chinese women to their more traditional roles, Chinese communists gave them a number of positions in their revolution. Women were allowed to bear arms in the military. After the institution of Mao's government in 1949, Chinese women were expected to work outside the home while maintaining their traditional responsibilities in the home as well. Following the second revolution, Mao's Cultural Revolution (1966–1976), whose goal was to cultivate a sense of permanent, or ongoing, revolution and to achieve a classless society, China became more globally oriented. The one-child policy, introduced in 1979 to control population growth, was changed to a two-child policy in 2015 and became law on January 1, 2016.

Latin America

After the Mexican Revolution, Mexican artists such as Diego Rivera used murals painted on public buildings to depict both scenes from the revolution and the hopes for social progress in the future. Latin American folk culture includes strong elements of the Native Indian and African cultures. Although the region remains largely Roman Catholic, the later decades of the twentieth century and the beginning of the twenty-first century have seen significant increases in the popularity of **evangelical** Protestant denominations throughout Latin America. Also popular in Latin America as well as in sub-Saharan Africa is **Liberation Theology**, a belief that focuses on social justice for victims of poverty and oppression.

Throughout the twentieth century, Latin American women tended to retain their traditional roles. Women were not allowed to vote until 1929, when Ecuador became the first Latin American nation to allow women's suffrage. By the later part of the twentieth century, however, women controlled small businesses, were found across the professions, and were active at all levels of politics.

Africa

Between 1957, when Ghana achieved independence under the leadership of Kwame Nkrumah, and the early 1970s, as many as 30 nations emerged from the colonies that had governed the continent for approximately 150 years. Women's suffrage was written into the constitutions of many of the new nations, resulting from the participation of women in African independence movements. Many of the new nations also granted women increased opportunities for education and employment. Early and arranged marriages, however, often continued to confine women to traditional roles. Government imposition of *shariah* law in regions of Nigeria and other Muslim-dominated African nations threatened not only the independence but also the security of women.

In South Africa, the Anti-Apartheid Movement would succeed in allowing judicial equality for whites and nonwhites, men and women, only in the final years of the twentieth century.

A Global Culture

In today's world, the global culture has been dominated by Western trends and styles, a situation that has especially produced disapproval in East Asian and Islamic cultures. English is the language of commerce and of the Internet. The Western appreciation for science has been a hallmark of the global age.

Sometimes reactions to globalization created changes in religious beliefs and practices. Beginning in the 1960s, New Age religions, dependent on astrology and frequently on the older Eastern religions, emerged. **Fundamentalism**, or the return to traditional beliefs and practices, became the goal of many practitioners of major religions, especially of Christianity and Islam, worldwide.

The new global culture placed more emphasis on monetary wealth, education, and professional position rather than on land ownership or inherited position. Traditions, however, continued to hold sway. In India, for example, remnants of the caste system caused some Indians to cling to caste restrictions even though they had been outlawed. Laws of almost all nations recognized women's suffrage. The global culture continued to display regional traditions and characteristics, while national pride surfaced in international athletic competitions such as the Olympic Games and World Cup Soccer, or the Federal International Football Association (FIFA).

❯ Rapid Review

In the interim between the world wars and after World War II, labor-saving devices transformed leisure time in Europe and the United States. Movies and television provided family entertainment, and the automobile created a new lifestyle for Western teenagers. Governments instituted welfare programs, and women's political rights were broadened worldwide. Religion declined in popularity, especially in Europe, and the Soviet Union denounced the importance of religion. Although women's rights increased, women were often expected to continue to carry out traditional roles. The new global culture emphasized the importance of professional status and education over family social position. The dominance of Western culture and the English language met with disapproval in cultures around the world.

› Review Questions

Questions 1 to 4 refer to the following passages.

Where Do Universal Rights Begin?

In small places, close to home—so close and so small that they cannot be seen on any maps of the world. Yet they are the world of the individual person; the neighborhood he lives in; the school or college he attends; the factory, farm or office where he works. Such are the places where every man, woman, and child seeks equal justice, equal opportunity, equal dignity without discrimination. Unless these rights have meaning there, they have little meaning anywhere. Without concerted citizen action to uphold them close to home, we shall look in vain for progress in the larger world.

—Eleanor Roosevelt, Chair of the United Nations Commission that wrote the Universal Declaration of Human Rights in 1948.

. . . recognition of the inherent dignity and of the equal and inalienable rights of all members of the human family is the foundation of freedom, justice and peace in the world,

. . . disregard and contempt for human rights have resulted in barbarous acts which have outraged the conscience of mankind, and the advent of a world in which human beings shall enjoy freedom of speech and belief and freedom from fear and want has been proclaimed as the highest aspiration of the common people,

. . . it is essential, if man is not to be compelled to have recourse, as a last resort, to rebellion against tyranny and oppression, that human rights should be protected by the rule of law,

. . . the peoples of the United Nations have in the Charter reaffirmed their faith in fundamental human rights, in the dignity and worth of the human person and in the equal rights of men and women and have determined to promote social progress and better standards of life in larger freedom . . .

. . . effective recognition and observance, both among the peoples of Member States themselves and among the peoples of territories under their jurisdiction . . .

—Preamble to the Universal Declaration of Human Rights

1. The Preamble to the Universal Declaration of Human Rights, written in 1948, may be considered a specific response to which twentieth-century phenomenon?
   (A) Population growth
   (B) World wars
   (C) Feminism
   (D) The welfare state

2. Eleanor Roosevelt indicates that human or universal rights are essentially upheld by which of the following?
   (A) Regional action
   (B) Religious belief
   (C) Individual effort
   (D) Legal documents

3. Which of the following may have been inspired by the Universal Declaration's expressed sentiments?
   (A) The Civil Rights Act of 1964
   (B) The Great Depression
   (C) The welfare state
   (D) A surge in religious faith

4. How is Liberation Theology a natural outgrowth or continuation of ideals expressed in the passages?
   (A) It advocates rebellion.
   (B) It advocates individual action.
   (C) It advocates social justice.
   (D) It advocates freedom.

5. What did the Soviet Union, Japan, the United States, and Western Europe have in common in the twentieth century?
   (A) A program of social security for the aged
   (B) Free elections
   (C) An emphasis on the production of consumer goods
   (D) An appreciation for Western styles of art

› Answers and Explanations

1. **B** Prepared in 1948, the Universal Declaration of Human Rights responded to the idea that war could be avoided and that "peace in the world" was possible. Population growth (A) was not a consideration in the declaration; Feminism (C) and the welfare state (D) predate the proclamation.

2. **C** Roosevelt specifically mentions the "world of the individual person" as being critical to the process. A, B, and D are incorrect.

3. **A** The Civil Rights Act of 1964 targets all human beings, specifically mentioning equal rights. The Great Depression (B) and the welfare state (C) both predate the Universal Declaration. There was no surge in religious faith (D) following the world wars; if anything, there was a decline.

4. **C** Liberation Theology specifically called for social justice, especially for the disenfranchised. While it would have supported rebellion (A), individual action (B), and freedom (D), its focus was on social justice and progress.

5. **A** All have social security programs for the elderly, whereas the Soviet Union did not have free elections (B), an emphasis on consumer goods (C), or an appreciation for Western art styles (D).

CHAPTER 31

Demographic and Environmental Developments

IN THIS CHAPTER

Summary: Although the Industrial Revolution generated overall improvements in living standards, it also caused atmospheric pollution in both industrialized cities and the countryside. Environmental challenges of the twentieth and twenty-first centuries included efforts to resolve poor environmental quality from industrial and automobile emissions. Potential threats to the environment also result from oil spills, the devastation accompanying warfare, and the danger of meltdowns from nuclear power plants. Climate change became a major concern and a political football.

Since 1900, warfare, famine, disease, and migration have affected global population distribution. Most migrants moved from developing to developed nations in search of improved economic opportunities, or from war-torn areas in search of safety or asylum.

Key Terms

Green Revolution
guest workers

ozone depletion
xenophobia

War Years

World War I resulted in more than 38 million casualties (11 million military deaths, around 20 million wounded, and 7 million civilian deaths) and eliminated a generation of young European men. The lack of potential husbands forced many European women to remain unmarried. The drastic decline in marriages lowered the European birth rate and population growth in future generations. Bombs and troop movements destroyed cities, factories, and agricultural lands. World War II claimed another 35 million people. Because of post-war boundary changes, hundreds of thousands of displaced persons were forced to relocate.

Population Changes

Rapid population growth, especially in developing nations, became a persistent concern of the twentieth and twenty-first centuries. Sometimes religious and cultural beliefs prohibited efforts at population control. In the early twentieth century, efforts to eradicate disease and improve sanitation led to marked population increases in developing nations in Asia. In Africa, which began the century with low population levels, high birth rates and lower mortality rates resulted in significant population increases. These population trends continued in spite of the high incidence of AIDS in Africa. In the United States, a "baby boom" lasting from the end of World War II until the 1950s led to population increases. More advanced and available health care, including the use of penicillin and the development of a polio vaccine, also contributed to this growth.

Despite advances in health care, those living in poverty continued to struggle with diseases such as cholera, tuberculosis, and malaria. New epidemics emerged, such as the influenza pandemic of 1918–1919, Ebola, and AIDS. The incidence of diseases such as Alzheimer's disease, heart disease, cancer, and diabetes increased, perhaps because of increases in life expectancy and lifestyle changes.

In Europe, the population decline and labor shortages of the 1950s and 1960s caused Western European governments to seek workers from Southern Europe and the non-Western world. Many of these **guest workers** migrated to Western Europe from the West Indies, North Africa, Turkey, and Pakistan. Guest workers received low wages and were often subjected to discrimination and violence. This discrimination heightened in the 1980s because of a slowdown in European economies and the growing size of the guest worker population. Not all immigrants were welcomed. **Xenophobia**, an intense fear of foreigners, often provoked protests, race riots, and government policies restricting citizenship.

In contrast to European demographic patterns, East Asian countries experienced high population growth. By the 1980s, for example, South Korea had the highest population density in the world. As a result, many South Koreans migrated to other countries. The government of South Korea encouraged its people to limit the size of their families, while the Japanese government addressed its ever-increasing population by promoting birth control and abortion.

The People's Republic of China attempted to control its huge population by instituting policies designed to limit family size. In the 1960s, rural couples were limited to one child and urban couples to two. By the 1980s, only one child per family was allowed. These programs greatly reduced the Chinese birth rate at the expense of forced abortions and sterilizations. Female infanticide increased. Other infants were hidden among family members in rural areas where recordkeeping was not as accurate as in urban areas. By 2007, the one-child policy had relaxed in some regions of China to permit urban couples who themselves were only children to give birth to two children; and in 2015 the law was changed to accommodate everyone, allowing all families two children.

The Soviet Union lost approximately 14 percent of its population in World War II. The Stalin-era purges further reduced population, so emphasis during the second half of the twentieth century was on rebuilding. With the dissolution of the USSR in 1991, however, population increased, in part because of immigration.

Efforts to Improve Agricultural Production

One of the solutions to growing population concerns was to improve agricultural productivity in developing nations. The **Green Revolution** was a program that increased crop yields through the use of high-yield, disease-resistant crops, as well as of fertilizers, pesticides, and efficient irrigation methods. Especially effective in India and other parts of Asia, it also experienced some success in Latin America. The Green Revolution was criticized for its use of pesticides and fertilizers that caused pollution and cancer. Also, chemicals were expensive, making the program mostly accessible to large landowners and agricultural businesses.

In Egypt, President Nasser attempted to improve agricultural productivity through the construction of the Aswan Dam. Although the project provided additional arable land, its interference in the normal flood patterns of the Nile River deprived the land of the fertile silt deposited by the Nile's flooding. It also allowed an increase in parasites that caused blindness and in salt found in the soil.

Migration Patterns

The causes of migration are many and varied. For example, they can include economic, including few jobs, forced labor systems, expropriation of wealth; environmental, such as deforestation, drought, desertification, natural disasters, and pollution, all of which can lead to famine; personal; and political, involving dissent. Early in the twentieth century, immigrants often viewed their status as temporary, working in a host country and sending money home until they could return. This changed as war destroyed (and continues to destroy) homelands and left immigrants with nothing to return to. Furthermore, the distinction between migrants and refugees became noteworthy. Countries that refused or imposed quotas on migrants sometimes considered refugees more welcome. Refugees often were seeking asylum (or sanctuary) from political or religious oppression and persecution, discrimination, blatant death threats, or ethnic cleansing.

After World War I, the population of Latin America swelled as immigrants continued to pour into Argentina and Brazil as well as into other Latin American countries. Urban areas grew rapidly. Latin America experienced sizable migration within the continent as the inhabitants of rural areas migrated to urban regions in search of employment. Newcomers often were forced to live in shantytowns on the outskirts of urban areas. Sometimes these settlements were incorporated into urban areas, resulting in somewhat improved living conditions within the former shantytowns.

In the 1920s, workers from Mexico crossed into the United States at the same time that Central Americans were crossing into Mexico in search of employment. During the 1940s, the United States set up programs with Mexico to provide workers. Hundreds of thousands of migrants, both legal and illegal, continued to cross the border into the United States. Throughout Latin America, migration in search of employment occurred across national borders. Other migrants reached, or attempted to reach, the United States to escape political oppression and warfare. This last group included immigrants from Cuba, Haiti, Nicaragua, and El Salvador.

Population flight from countries undergoing ethnic or religious strife or alterations in political boundaries remained an issue in the period since 1914. The largest displacement of people in history occurred in South Asia in 1947 and 1948, when the partition of India and Pakistan produced a major migration of Muslims to Pakistan and Hindus to India. The first Arab-Israeli War in 1948 created hundreds of thousands of Palestinian

Arab refugees. In 1998, in the Balkan region of Kosovo, thousands of ethnic Albanians of the Muslim faith fled the region in the face of Serbian massacres. From 2000 to 2004, religious conflict in Nigeria caused Christians and Muslims to flee to areas where their religion was the majority faith. In the Sudan, inhabitants of the southern region of the country, most of them Christians or practitioners of native religions, were displaced from their homes when Sunni Arabs from the northern regions of Sudan attempted to impose Islamic law upon the southern regions. By 2004, the Sudanese conflict focused on the region of Darfur and involved a conflict between Arab and non-Arab Muslims. In 2016, conflicts arose in both Europe and the United States as Syrian refugees fleeing ISIS attempted to migrate across the Mediterranean Sea to settle in Europe. The controversy over admitting Syrian refugees to the United States became a major focus in the 2016 U.S. presidential election.

Another pattern of migration involved the movement of South Asians and Arabs toward the oil-producing regions of the Middle East. Also, workers from developed nations, including the United States, sought employment with their own nation's companies in the oil fields of the Middle East.

Environmental Concerns

The world faced a number of environmental issues: damage to marine life from oil spills, the dangers of meltdowns from nuclear plants, and the devastation of warfare. During the Vietnam War, for example, the United States extensively employed chemical defoliants. Post-war disease and genetic mutations have been attributed to this usage. During the Persian Gulf War, Iraq's Saddam Hussein spilled huge amounts of oil into the Persian Gulf and set fire to Kuwaiti oil fields. Industrial pollution and human waste continued to plague many of the world's waterways. In Eastern Europe industrialization severely polluted half the area's rivers and endangered farmlands. Pollution was responsible for respiratory diseases and higher rates of infant mortality. Population growth in rural areas of Africa and Asia often led to overgrazing and deforestation; depletion of the rainforest in part caused global warming.

There has been some progress in protecting the environment. Governments of industrialized nations identified the chemicals that cause **ozone depletion** in the upper atmosphere and limited their use. Antipollution devices were installed on automobiles, planes, and industrial smokestacks. In the early twenty-first century, the Paris Agreement (ratified April 22, 2016) saw almost 200 countries adopt a legally binding global climate pact and provided national climate action plans to keep global average high temperatures to within 2 percent of pre-industrial levels.

› Rapid Review

Population issues in the period since 1914 have revolved around migration and control of population growth. Migration in the period has most frequently been from developing to developed nations and, second, from rural to urban areas. The latter often has resulted in the establishment of shantytowns along the perimeters of major urban areas. Guest workers often became the victims of discrimination, especially in Europe. Although some government programs limited population growth, many rural areas in Africa and Asia suffered from depleted farmland insufficient to handle their populations. Issues of poor air and water quality, global warming, and the devastation wrought by warfare remained.

〉 Review Questions

1. Answer Parts A and B.
   (A) Identify and explain TWO reasons for a decline of death rates after 1950.
   (B) Identify and explain ONE reason, different from those in Part A, for the twentieth-century population explosion.

2. Answer Parts A, B, and C.
   (A) Identify and explain ONE twentieth-century or twenty-first–century environmental concern.
   (B) Identify and give ONE example of a guest worker program.
   (C) Explain how either A or B has contributed to xenophobia.

Questions 3 to 5 refer to the following passage.

Still they come—grape-pickers and bricklayers, nannies and schoolteachers, computer programmers and sex-workers, these and millions more head for foreign lands in search of work, or higher pay, or just the opportunity to make a better life. Around 190 million people are "foreign-born," living outside their country of origin, and every year they are joined by two to three million more emigrants. This number also includes 10 million or so refugees, driven from their homes by war, or famine, or persecution. Bangladeshi laborers fly to construction sites in Malaysia. Desperate Nigerians perch on flimsy craft to cross the treacherous Straits of Gibraltar. Mexican laborers clamber across the walls and fences that mark the long and porous border with the United States. These 190 million people may only represent 3 percent of the world's population. But they generate controversy and debate out of all proportion to their modest numbers, largely because as they travel, migrants expose many of the social and political fault lines—race, gender, social class, culture and religion—that underlie the seemingly settled terrain of modern nation states.

—Peter Stalker, 2008

3. Which of the following best defines the difference between migrants and refugees?
   (A) The number in each group
   (B) The reasons for leaving the home country
   (C) The destinations of each group
   (D) The preponderance of women in the latter group

4. Why does this small percentage of the world population have a disproportionately large social and political effect?
   (A) Because they change the economic status quo in receiving countries
   (B) Because they expose the behavioral status quo in receiving countries
   (C) Because they introduce foreign concepts
   (D) Because they oppose established religions

5. Which of the following is the *least* common migration pattern in the late twentieth and early twenty-first century?
   (A) From Asia to Europe
   (B) From Europe to the United States
   (C) From Mexico to the United States
   (D) From the Middle East to Europe

> Answers and Explanations

1A. The decline in death rates can be attributed to improved health, thanks to medical discoveries (polio vaccine, for example), more efficient food production and availability, and improved sanitation systems.

1B. Any of the reasons from Part A works here, just so long as it isn't one used in Part A. Thus, the connection between lower death rates and the population explosion becomes clear.

2A. Any of the following is of primary environmental concern: oil spills, nuclear plant meltdowns, and global warming. All tie into the chain of resource production and the availability of life-sustaining products.

2B. A guest worker program, designed to offer work to migrants and to alleviate labor shortages, was that instituted in Western Europe using workers from Turkey, the West Indies, Africa, or Pakistan. It often paid lower wages, and workers were the target of discrimination and persecution.

2C. A shortage of resources or goods, as well as one of labor, often prompted a nationalistic and xenophobic response based on fear of outsiders taking nationals' jobs and goods.

3. B Immigrants often make a voluntary move from one country to another, while refugees are forced to leave their homes as a result of war, discrimination, or persecution. Migrants are often in search of work and a better life; refugees are in search of survival. Numbers vary (A); both migrants and refugees have varied destinations (C); there is not a preponderance of women in either group (D).

4. B Migrants bring a different point of view to an established, sometimes static, society and expose behavioral "fault lines." The economic status quo (A), introduction of foreign concepts (C), and opposition to established religions (D) may indeed have an effect on a receiving society, though not necessarily an overweening one.

5. B Since the most common pattern of migration in the twentieth century has been from developing to developed nations, migration from Europe to the United States would be the least common of the patterns listed. A, C, and D describe migrations from developing to developed areas.

Summary: Accelerating Global Change and Realignments (c. 1900 to the present)

Timeline

1904 to 1905	Russo-Japanese War
1905	Revolution of 1905 (Russia)
	Einstein's Theory of Relativity
1908 to 1918	Young Turk era
1910 to 1920	Mexican Revolution
1911 to 1912	Chinese Revolution; end of Chinese dynastic rule
1914	Opening of the Panama Canal
1914 to 1918	World War I
1917	Bolshevik Revolution
1918	Treaty of Brest-Litovsk
1918 to 1919	Influenza pandemic
1918 to 1920	Russian civil war
1919	Treaty of Versailles
	May Fourth Movement in China
1921 to 1928	Lenin's New Economic Policy
1923	End of the Ottoman Empire
	Establishment of the Republic of Turkey
1928 to 1932	First of Stalin's Five-Year Plans
1929	Beginning of the Great Depression
1931	Japanese invasion of Manchuria
1933	Hitler's rise to power in Germany
1935	Government of India Act
1937	Japanese invasion of China
1939	German invasion of Poland
1945	Atomic bombs dropped on Hiroshima and Nagasaki
	End of World War II
1947	Truman Doctrine
	Partition of India
1948	Marshall Plan
	Creation of Israel
	Establishment of apartheid in South Africa
	Universal Declaration of Human Rights
1949	Division of Germany
	Establishment of NATO
	Establishment of the People's Republic of China
1950 to 1953	Korean War
1954	Division of Vietnam
1955	Establishment of the Warsaw Pact
1956	Suez Crisis
	Soviet invasion of Hungary
1957	Independence in Ghana
1958 to 1961	Great Leap Forward in China
1959	Cuban Revolution
1960	Establishment of OPEC

1961	Construction of the Berlin Wall
1962	Cuban Missile Crisis
1964	Sino-Soviet Rift
1967	Establishment of the European Community
1968	Prague Spring
1972	Beginning of détente
1973	Arab-Israeli War
	Beginning of Arab oil embargo
1975	Fall of Vietnam
1979	Iranian Revolution
1980 to 1988	Iran-Iraq War
1989	Fall of the Berlin Wall
1990	Reunification of Germany
1990 to 1991	Gulf War
1991	Fall of the Soviet Union
	End of the Cold War
1993	Establishment of NAFTA
1995	Establishment of the World Trade Organization
1997	Transfer of Hong Kong to China
2001	Terrorist attacks on the United States
2003	U.S. Coalition–Iraq War
2008 to 2010	Global economic crisis
2010-2011	Arab Spring protests
2011	Rise of ISIS
2014	Russian annexation of Crimea
2016	Migrations of Syrian refugees
2016	Brexit

Key Comparisons

1. Post-war governments of Western nations versus the Soviet bloc
2. Decolonization in Africa versus India
3. Effects of World War I versus the effects of World War II
4. Russian Revolution versus the Chinese Revolution
5. Reactions of Western versus non-Western nations to U.S. consumer society
6. Female roles in China and the West
7. Patterns of immigration in the Eastern versus the Western Hemispheres
8. Patterns of economic development in Africa versus Latin America
9. Global trade in the Pacific Rim versus the West
10. Political and economic conditions in Russia before and after communism

Change/Continuity Chart

REGION	POLITICAL	ECONOMIC	SOCIAL	CHANGES	CONTINUITIES
East Asia	End of the Qing dynasty World wars Japanese occupation Chinese communism Korean War	Great Leap Forward Electronics Automobiles Textiles	Chinese one-child policy Women working outside home (China) Baseball	Depression Footbinding outlawed High-tech industries	Shintoism Buddhism Confucianism U.S. recognition of China
Southeast Asia	Vietnam War Communism	Rice	Buddhism	Decolonization Communism Tourism Immigration from Asia	Buddhism
Oceania	Participation in world wars British Commonwealth	Tourism Farming Sheep-raising Industry	Greater rights for aborigines	Introduction of capitalism in Russia	Herding Grazing
Central Asia	Russian Revolution World wars Cold War *Glasnost* End of communism	NEP Five-Year Plans Collective farming *Perestroika*	Allowance of some Western influences	Decolonization Partition Nuclear power	Economic difficulties Ethnic conflict
South Asia	World wars Independence movements	Green Revolution	Laws against caste system	Mandates Creation of Israel Arab-Israeli wars	Hinduism Islam Buddhism
Southwest Asia (Middle East)	Iranian Revolution, Iran–Iraq War Persian Gulf War War in Afghanistan Terrorism U.S. Coalition–Iraq War	OPEC Oil	Guest workers	Decolonization Guest workers	Islam Arab-Israeli conflicts

Change/Continuity Chart

KEY IDEA

REGION	POLITICAL	ECONOMIC	SOCIAL	CHANGES	CONTINUITIES
North Africa	Independence movements Suez Crisis	Oil OPEC Aswan Dam	Shantytowns (Cairo)	Decolonization End of apartheid	Islam
Sub-Saharan Africa	Independence movements Ethnic conflicts	Oil Native art Famine	AIDS Population increase Apartheid	Depression Loss of world dominance Economic prosperity, guest workers	Poverty Unstable governments
Western Europe	World wars Fascism Berlin Wall Terrorism	European Union Euro Auto industry	Population decrease Drop in religious observance	Industrialization Emancipation of slaves Increased suffrage	Racism
Eastern Europe	End of empire World wars Communism	Solidarity Industry	Religious freedom (Poland)	Depression End of communism	Ethnic conflict
North America	World wars Cold War U.S. as superpower Civil rights movement	Depression NAFTA	Transmission of U.S. culture Feminism	Fight against terrorism Transmission of U.S. culture	Dominance of the United States
Latin America	Mexican Revolution Coups PRI Cuban Revolution Sandinistas Democracy	Depression Industry Oil Panama Canal	Immigration from Europe Shantytowns	Industry Increased trade Popularity of Protestantism	Agriculture Roman Catholicism

STEP **5**

Build Your
Test-Taking Confidence

Practice Test One

Practice Test Two

Practice Test One

ANSWER SHEET

1 Ⓐ Ⓑ Ⓒ Ⓓ	16 Ⓐ Ⓑ Ⓒ Ⓓ	31 Ⓐ Ⓑ Ⓒ Ⓓ	46 Ⓐ Ⓑ Ⓒ Ⓓ
2 Ⓐ Ⓑ Ⓒ Ⓓ	17 Ⓐ Ⓑ Ⓒ Ⓓ	32 Ⓐ Ⓑ Ⓒ Ⓓ	47 Ⓐ Ⓑ Ⓒ Ⓓ
3 Ⓐ Ⓑ Ⓒ Ⓓ	18 Ⓐ Ⓑ Ⓒ Ⓓ	33 Ⓐ Ⓑ Ⓒ Ⓓ	48 Ⓐ Ⓑ Ⓒ Ⓓ
4 Ⓐ Ⓑ Ⓒ Ⓓ	19 Ⓐ Ⓑ Ⓒ Ⓓ	34 Ⓐ Ⓑ Ⓒ Ⓓ	49 Ⓐ Ⓑ Ⓒ Ⓓ
5 Ⓐ Ⓑ Ⓒ Ⓓ	20 Ⓐ Ⓑ Ⓒ Ⓓ	35 Ⓐ Ⓑ Ⓒ Ⓓ	50 Ⓐ Ⓑ Ⓒ Ⓓ
6 Ⓐ Ⓑ Ⓒ Ⓓ	21 Ⓐ Ⓑ Ⓒ Ⓓ	36 Ⓐ Ⓑ Ⓒ Ⓓ	51 Ⓐ Ⓑ Ⓒ Ⓓ
7 Ⓐ Ⓑ Ⓒ Ⓓ	22 Ⓐ Ⓑ Ⓒ Ⓓ	37 Ⓐ Ⓑ Ⓒ Ⓓ	52 Ⓐ Ⓑ Ⓒ Ⓓ
8 Ⓐ Ⓑ Ⓒ Ⓓ	23 Ⓐ Ⓑ Ⓒ Ⓓ	38 Ⓐ Ⓑ Ⓒ Ⓓ	53 Ⓐ Ⓑ Ⓒ Ⓓ
9 Ⓐ Ⓑ Ⓒ Ⓓ	24 Ⓐ Ⓑ Ⓒ Ⓓ	39 Ⓐ Ⓑ Ⓒ Ⓓ	54 Ⓐ Ⓑ Ⓒ Ⓓ
10 Ⓐ Ⓑ Ⓒ Ⓓ	25 Ⓐ Ⓑ Ⓒ Ⓓ	40 Ⓐ Ⓑ Ⓒ Ⓓ	55 Ⓐ Ⓑ Ⓒ Ⓓ
11 Ⓐ Ⓑ Ⓒ Ⓓ	26 Ⓐ Ⓑ Ⓒ Ⓓ	41 Ⓐ Ⓑ Ⓒ Ⓓ	
12 Ⓐ Ⓑ Ⓒ Ⓓ	27 Ⓐ Ⓑ Ⓒ Ⓓ	42 Ⓐ Ⓑ Ⓒ Ⓓ	
13 Ⓐ Ⓑ Ⓒ Ⓓ	28 Ⓐ Ⓑ Ⓒ Ⓓ	43 Ⓐ Ⓑ Ⓒ Ⓓ	
14 Ⓐ Ⓑ Ⓒ Ⓓ	29 Ⓐ Ⓑ Ⓒ Ⓓ	44 Ⓐ Ⓑ Ⓒ Ⓓ	
15 Ⓐ Ⓑ Ⓒ Ⓓ	30 Ⓐ Ⓑ Ⓒ Ⓓ	45 Ⓐ Ⓑ Ⓒ Ⓓ	

AP WORLD HISTORY PRACTICE TEST ONE

Section I

Time: 1 hour, 45 minutes

Part A: Multiple-Choice Questions

Recommended Time for Part A: 55 Minutes

Directions: Each of the following incomplete statements or questions is followed by four answer choices. Select the choice that best answers the question and fill in the corresponding oval on the answer sheet provided.

Questions 1 to 3 refer to the following passage.

The condition of foreign states is not what it once was; they have invented the steamship, and introduced radical changes in the art of navigation. They have also built up their armies to a state of great efficiency and are possessed of war implements of great power and precision, in short have license to be formidable powers. If, therefore, we persistently cling to our antiquated systems, heaven only knows what a mighty calamity may befall our Empire.

—Adapted from a letter written by Lord Ii to Lord Tokugawa, 1847

1. Which event or period in Japan's history best reflects Lord Ii's concerns?

    (A) The expulsion of Christian missionaries from Japan
    (B) The adoption of Chinese imperial customs in the Japanese court
    (C) The annexation of Manchuria by the Japanese
    (D) Commodore Perry forcing Japan to open its ports to trade

2. How did Japan respond to the concerns raised by Lord Ii during this era?

    (A) The government dismantled the Chinese-style civil service system.
    (B) The government undertook a program of conquest in the Pacific.
    (C) The country sent emissaries to study western democracies and industry.
    (D) The country turned inward and closed its ports to all foreigners.

3. The era in Japanese history following this passage is known as the

    (A) Meiji Restoration.
    (B) Heian period.
    (C) Tokugawa Shogunate.
    (D) Jomon period.

Questions 4 to 6 refer to the following passage.

He contains all works and desires and all perfumes and all tastes. He enfolds the whole universe and in silence is loving to all. This is the Spirit that is in my heart, this is Brahman. To him I shall come when I go beyond this life, and to him will come he who has faith and doubts not.

—*The Upanishads*, India, c. 1000 BCE

4. Based on the quotation, what is true of Brahman?

(A) He is found everywhere and contained in everything.
(B) He resides in a form of paradise, like Heaven.
(C) He is found only inside the hearts of the faithful.
(D) He is a vengeful God, punishing those who sin.

5. Based on the quotation, which statement is true of the speaker's religion?

(A) Salvation is based on the correct completion of rituals.
(B) There is an expectation of an afterlife.
(C) Right actions and right speech earn favor with the gods.
(D) It is a polytheistic religion.

6. To which religion does the speaker most likely belong?

(A) Hinduism
(B) Buddhism
(C) Shintoism
(D) Zoroastrianism

Questions 7 to 9 refer to the following quotation.

The invaders had brought in wheat and other Eurasian and African grains; peach, pear, orange, and lemon trees; chick-peas, grape vines, melons, onions, radishes, and much more. A Spanish nobleman come to America could require his Indians to furnish his table with the fruits of his ancestors.

—Alfred Crosby, historian, 1972

7. The comment quoted resulted from which of the following processes?

(A) The Green Revolution
(B) The Columbian Exchange
(C) The triangular trade
(D) The Middle Passage

8. What was the impact of this process on Europe?

(A) The population increased due to the increased diversity of crops.
(B) The population declined as a result of imported disease.

(C) The population increased due to New World immigrants.
(D) The population declined because of famine caused by the mass export of crops.

9. What economic practice is referred to by the phrase "his Indians" in the quote?

(A) Slavery
(B) Indentured servitude
(C) The encomienda system
(D) The apprentice system

Questions 10 to 14 refer to the following image, which shows the use of a pre-Columbian wooden foot plow.

—Felipe Guaman Poma de Ayala, 1616

10. What can one infer from the illustration?

(A) Farming practices relied on human labor.
(B) There was extensive use of irrigation.
(C) Farming was the exclusive purview of women.
(D) Animals were valued too highly to be used in the fields.

11. Metal work and animal-drawn plows were essential parts of the development of complex societies in Africa and Eurasia, but not in the Americas. This would indicate which of the following?

(A) The role of religion in economic development
(B) The influence of environmental factors in patterns of development
(C) That the earliest Americans emphasized warfare at the expense of their own economic development
(D) That the earliest Americans depended primarily on trade rather than on agriculture to sustain their economies

12. Which of the following was *the* major difference between the Aztecs and other early empires?

(A) The Aztecs had no writing system.
(B) The Aztecs did not use metallurgy.
(C) The Aztecs had no wheeled transportation.
(D) The Aztecs never developed overland trade networks.

13. A historian arguing that there were limited interregional networks in the Americas might use which of the following as evidence?

(A) The llama was domesticated in Andean culture, but was not found in Mesoamerica.
(B) The Andean civilization had extensive roads and bridges, but Mesoamerica did not.
(C) There was no strong religious tradition in Andean culture, compared with the Maya.
(D) The Andeans had a system of writing, but the Maya did not.

14. Chinampas and terraces, used in Aztec and Incan agriculture, both show which of the following?

(A) Societies adapting to their environments
(B) Cultural diffusion
(C) Efforts to reform land ownership
(D) Coercive labor systems

Questions 15 to 18 refer to the following map.

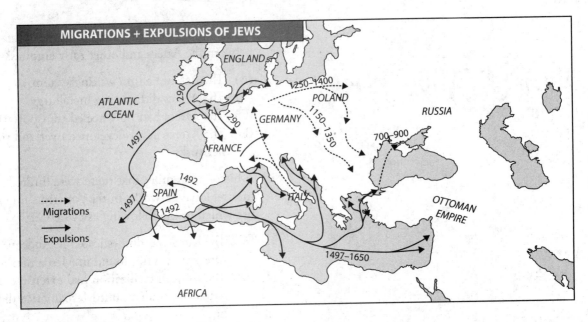

15. Based on the map, most of the relocation of Jews was due to expulsion from which country or region?

   (A) Spain
   (B) Germany
   (C) The Ottoman Empire
   (D) Africa

16. Based on the map, which of the following statements is true?

   (A) The Jewish people were more likely to migrate of their own accord than be expelled.
   (B) Jews were more likely to be expelled than to migrate voluntarily.
   (C) The migration of Jews typically occurred later than the expulsion of Jews.
   (D) The Jews were expelled as punishment for plotting against Christian rulers.

17. Based on the map and your knowledge of history, which statement is true?

   (A) Muslim regions were more likely to expel Jewish people than Catholic ones.
   (B) Most of the Jewish expulsions originated in Protestant regions.
   (C) Catholic regions were more likely to expel Jewish people than other regions.
   (D) Jews migrated voluntarily to the regions with the most economic prosperity.

18. Based on the maps and your knowledge of history, identify one consequence of these migrations.

   (A) Increased tension between Muslims and Jews in the Holy Land
   (B) Increasing interest in exploration and colonization by Spain
   (C) Increased anti-Semitism in Central Europe
   (D) A decline in religious conflicts in Europe

Questions 19 to 21 refer to the following political cartoon.

—Chain of Friendship, American political cartoon, 1914

19. The political cartoon best illustrates which political concept?

    (A) Imperialism
    (B) Nationalism
    (C) Alliances
    (D) Militarism

20. The order of the countries shown in the cartoon—Serbia–Austria–Russia–Germany–France—supports which of the following statements?

    (A) World War I was a politicians' war.
    (B) France attacked all the countries that were in front of it in line.
    (C) Russia supported Serbia; France supported Russia.
    (D) World War I was strictly a European war.

21. Countries that also took part in World War I for varying amounts of time included which of the following?

    (A) Poland, Denmark, and Great Britain
    (B) Switzerland, Greece, and Turkey
    (C) Bulgaria, Italy, and the United States
    (D) Great Britain, Spain, and France

Questions 22 to 24 refer to the following passage.

In 1797 Toussaint L'Ouverture, as general-in-chief of the French forces in Saint Domingue, sent this report to the Directory, which was then in charge of France. In dialogue form he recounts his conversation with Léger Felicité Sonthonax, the head of the French commission to the island.

Commissioner Sonthonax: Do you know what we are going to do first? The blacks are worried for their freedom. We have here colonists of whom they are suspicious. They must all be slaughtered. Everything is ready. You only have to be in agreement with me.

General Toussaint: What? You want to slaughter all the whites? Aren't you white yourself?

Commissioner Sonthonax: Yes, but not all of them. Only those who are enemies of freedom.

General Toussaint: (With an impatience he can no longer hide) Let's talk of other things. . . .

(The next morning)
Commissioner Sonthonax: Let's talk about the affair.

General Toussaint: What affair?

Commissioner Sonthonax: That which we broached yesterday evening. I am very happy to see you head of the armed forces of the colony. We are in a perfect position to do all we want. You have much influence over the inhabitants. We must carry off our project; it is the perfect moment. The circumstances have never been more favorable, and there's no one better than you to act together with me.

General Toussaint: You mean, Commissioner, that you want to ruin me... Kill the whites? Take our independence? Did you not promise me that you'd never again talk of these projects? . . .

Commissioner Sonthonax: No, it's to chase them out. We won't kill them.

General Toussaint: Today you say you want to chase them out, but yesterday and just now you said they had to be killed. But if a white was killed here it is I who would be held responsible. ...

Commissioner Sonthonax: I give you my word of honor. I swear to you never to speak of this again. But promise me that you'll keep this secret. This isn't something your officers should know about. Give me your word of honor that you won't speak of this to anyone.

General Toussaint: (With ill-humor) Alright then. I give you my word. Farewell.

22. The incident depicted most likely occurred as part of which historical conflict?

    (A) The Haitian Revolution
    (B) The Mexican Revolution
    (C) The U.S. Civil War
    (D) The Algerian War

23. Based on the passage, which statement best reflects Toussaint's reasons for refusing Commissioner Sonthonax's suggestion?

    (A) Toussaint was also white.
    (B) Toussaint wished to reinstate slavery in the colony.

    (C) Toussaint feared he will be blamed.
    (D) Toussaint objected to the plan on moral grounds.

24. Which historical disciplinary practice or thinking skill would be most relevant to evaluate properly the accuracy of this source?

    (A) Chronology
    (B) Point of view
    (C) Cause and effect
    (D) Continuity over time

Questions 25 to 27 refer to the following poem.

You are the United States,
you are the future invader
of the native America that has Indian blood,
that still prays to Jesus Christ and still speaks Spanish.
. . .
you are Alexander-Nebuchadnezzar.
You think that life is fire,
that progress is eruption,
that wherever you shoot
you hit the future.

No.
. . .
But our America, that has had poets
since the ancient times of Netzahualcoyotl,
. . .
that consulted the stars, that knew Atlantis
whose resounding name comes to us from Plato,
that since the remote times of its life
has lived on light, on fire, on perfume, on love,

America of the great Montezuma, of the Inca,
the fragrant America of Christopher Columbus,
Catholic America, Spanish America,
the America in which noble Cuauhtémoc said:
"I'm not in a bed of roses"; that America
that trembles in hurricanes and lives on love,
it lives, you men of Saxon eyes and barbarous soul.
And it dreams. And it loves, and it vibrates, and it
is the daughter of the sun.
Be careful. Viva Spanish America!

There are a thousand cubs loosed from the Spanish
lion.
Roosevelt, one would have to be, through God
himself,
the-fearful rifleman and strong hunter,
to manage to grab us in your iron claws.

And, although you count on everything, you lack
one thing: God!

—Adapted from "To Roosevelt" by Ruben Dario, 1904

25. What events might have prompted the poet to compose this piece?

(A) The discovery of the Zimmerman Telegram
(B) The embargo of Cuba after Castro's revolution
(C) U.S. involvement in Panama's independence
(D) U.S. involvement in the Haitian Revolution

26. What was the poet's purpose in discussing "our America, that has had poets since ancient times, . . . that consulted the stars"?

(A) Latin America has excelled in poetry.
(B) Latin America had made significant scientific contributions.
(C) Latin America had a prophecy regarding these events.
(D) Latin America has had a rich culture for centuries.

27. Which statement best reflects the theme of the poem?

(A) Latin Americans are too naive and should fight back.
(B) Latin America has survived many invaders and will endure.
(C) The Spanish have already destroyed Latin American culture.
(D) Change is necessary for progress.

Questions 28 to 31 refer to the following passage.

Bonesteel's prime consideration was to establish a surrender zone as far north as he thought the Soviets would accept. He knew that the Russian troops could reach the southern tip of Korea before American troops could arrive. He also knew that the Russians were on the verge of moving into Korea, or were already there. The nearest American troops to Korea were on Okinawa, 600 miles away. His problem, therefore, was to compose a surrender arrangement which, while acceptable to the Russians, would at the same time prevent them from seizing all of Korea. If they refused to confine their advance to north Korea, the United States would be unable to stop them. . . . He decided to use the 38th parallel as a hypothetical line dividing the zones within which Japanese forces in Korea would surrender to appointed American and Russian authorities.

—Adapted from U.S. Army Lt. Paul C. McGrath's account of Colonel Bonesteel's decision in the 1940s

28. What was the world history event occurring in the stated time frame that caused the Soviet Union to enter Korea?

(A) The Crimean War
(B) World War I
(C) World War II
(D) The Seven Years' War

29. Which best describes the relationship between the United States and the Soviets as depicted in the passage?

(A) Uneasy allies
(B) Comrades-in-arms
(C) Mortal enemies
(D) Distant strangers

30. How did the events depicted here affect Koreans?

(A) They became a part of Japan's territory.
(B) The Americans established freedom for all Koreans.
(C) The Korean economy never recovered.
(D) Korea remains divided into two nations near the 38th parallel.

31. Which U.S. Cold War policy, developed later, is consistent with the U.S. concern over limiting how much Korean territory the Soviet Union would occupy?

(A) Détente
(B) Mutual Assured Destruction
(C) Dollar Diplomacy
(D) Containment

Questions 32 to 34 refer to the following passage.

As for their men there is no sexual jealousy in them. And none of them derives his genealogy from his father but, on the contrary, from his maternal uncle. A man does not pass on inheritance except to the sons of his sister to the exclusion of his own sons. . . . They are Muslims keeping to the prayers, studying fiqh (Islamic jurisprudence) and learning the Qur'an by heart. With regard to their women, they are not modest in the presence of men; they do not veil themselves in spite of their perseverance in the prayers. He who wishes to marry among them can marry, but the women do not travel with the husband, and if one of them wanted to do that, she would be prevented by her family. The women there have friends and companions amongst men outside the prohibited degrees of marriage [i.e., other than brothers, fathers, etc.]. Likewise for the men, there are companions from amongst women outside the prohibited degrees. One of them would enter his house to find his wife with her companion and would not disapprove of that conduct.

—Adapted from an account by Ibn Battuta of his travels in Mali during the 1300s

32. What evidence is there in the passage that the Malians take their Muslim faith seriously?

   (A) The genealogy is derived from the maternal side.
   (B) They study Islamic law faithfully.
   (C) The men do not yield to sexual jealousy.
   (D) They enjoy friendship with all, regardless of gender.

33. What was the likely cause of women not wearing the veil?

   (A) They were probably rebelling against the oppression of women in Islam.
   (B) It was a continuation of a preexisting cultural pattern.
   (C) As sexual objects, they were prevented from veiling themselves.
   (D) The climate of Mali makes veiling women impractical.

34. The most likely source of Islam in Mali came from

   (A) wandering Berber mystics.
   (B) conquering Mughal armies.
   (C) contact with Muslim trade caravans.
   (D) pilgrims to Islamic shrines in Ethiopia.

Questions 35 to 37 refer to the following poem.

The following poem refers to an incident in Sharpeville, South Africa, in 1960. To protest the requirement that they carry papers documenting their identity and residence, black South Africans gathered in front of police stations without their papers. Though other protests ended peacefully, in Sharpeville, police fired into the crowd.

What is important
about Sharpeville
is not that seventy died:
nor even that they were shot in the back
retreating, unarmed, defenceless

and certainty not
the heavy caliber slug
that tore through a mother's back
and ripped through the child in her arms
killing it

Remember Sharpeville
bullet-in-the-back day
Because it epitomized oppression
and the nature of society
More clearly than anything else;
it was the classic event

Nowhere is racial dominance
more clearly defined
nowhere the will to oppress
more clearly demonstrated

What the world whispers
apartheid declares with snarling guns
the blood the rich lust after
South Africa spills dust

Remember Sharpeville
Remember bullet-in-the-back day

And remember the unquenchable will for freedom
Remember the dead
and be glad

—Dennis Brutus, 1973

35. What does the poet mean by "what the world whispers"?

(A) The world is too afraid of South Africa to oppose apartheid.
(B) The world engages in subtler forms of discrimination.
(C) The world condemns South Africa's discrimination.
(D) The world economy promotes South Africa's discrimination.

36. The discriminatory system referred to in the poem was known as

(A) Jim Crow.
(B) spheres of influence.
(C) Boer division.
(D) apartheid.

37. What event symbolized the end of South Africa's institutionalized discrimination?

(A) The election of F. W. de Klerk
(B) The election of Nelson Mandela
(C) The bombing of Lesotho
(D) The Boer War

Questions 38 to 40 refer to the following chart, which provides information regarding the First Fleet, the earliest British colonists in Australia.

26 Jan. 1788	Landed with supplies for 2 years Initial rations for marines and convicts: Beef: 7 lb or Pork: 4 lb Dried peas: 3 pints Bread: 7 lb Butter: 6 oz Flour: 11 lb or Rice: ½ lb Female convicts and marine wives receive 2/3 male ration. Convicts excused from work Saturday afternoons to tend their own gardens.
13 March 1788	Beef rations reduced 12% and pork rations reduced 8%.
April 1788	Chief Surgeon expressed concern about the number of convicts with scurvy. Fish is served wherever possible.
July 1788	36 marines and 66 convicts under medical treatment. 52 convicts unfit for labour due to old age or infirmity. Chief Surgeon wrote to governor regarding shortages of medical equipment and unsatisfactory "salt diet" for the ill.

38. Based on the information provided, what was one of the primary purposes of the Australian colony?

   (A) A place in which to exile criminals
   (B) A place to create Pacific trading posts
   (C) A haven for persecuted religions
   (D) A base to establish military control of the Pacific

39. Which entry date provides evidence that the colony was intended to be self-sustaining?

   (A) April 1788
   (B) January 1788
   (C) July 1788
   (D) March 1788

40. What would a historian be most likely to use this information for?

   (A) Understanding the farming practices of early Australians
   (B) Determining the age and sex ratios of the early Australian colonists
   (C) Researching the hardships facing the early Australian colonists
   (D) Examining the medical practices of the early Australian colonists

Questions 41 to 43 refer to the following map.

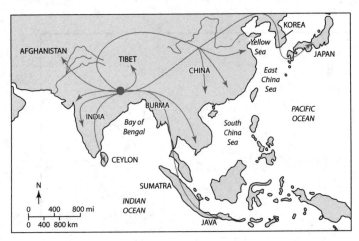

41. A historian would use the above map to illustrate which of the following?

(A) Major trade routes in the classical era
(B) The spread of communism from 1900 to today
(C) One aspect of cultural diffusion
(D) The monsoonal wind patterns of Asia

42. Which religion's spread followed the cultural diffusion pattern shown in the map?

(A) Hinduism
(B) Buddhism
(B) Christianity
(D) Islam

43. How did this religion primarily spread?

(A) With merchants
(B) With monks
(C) With military officers
(D) With diplomats

Questions 44 to 46 refer to the following passage.

Although in Protestant Europe, [Peter the Great] was surrounded by evidence of the new civil and political rights of individual men embodied in constitutions, bills of rights and parliaments, he did not return to Russia determined to share power with his people. On the contrary, he returned not only determined to change his country but also convinced that if Russia was to be transformed, it was he who must provide both the direction and the motive force. He would try to lead; but where education and persuasion were not enough, he could drive—and if necessary flog—the backward nation forward.

—Robert K. Massie, *Peter the Great: His Life and World*

44. Based on the passage, what kinds of reforms did Peter the Great embrace?

(A) Creation of an elected assembly
(B) Declarations of human rights
(C) Development of a constitutional monarchy
(D) Reduction of aristocratic influence

45. What term best describes Peter the Great's ruling style as described in the passage?

(A) Egalitarian
(B) Absolutist
(C) Republican
(D) Theocratic

46. When Peter the Great ruled Russia, he continued the practice of which of the following?

(A) Decentralization of power
(B) Isolationism
(C) Serfdom
(D) Reform

Questions 47 to 50 refer to the following passage, which is taken from testimony before Parliament.

Joshua Drake, called in; and Examined.

You say you would prefer moderate labour and lower wages; are you pretty comfortable upon your present wages?
—I have no wages, but two days a week at present; but when I am working at some jobs we can make a little, and at others we do very poorly.

When a child gets 3s. a week, does that go much towards its subsistence?
—No, it will not keep it as it should do.

Why do you allow your children to go to work at those places where they are ill-treated or over-worked?
—Necessity compels a man that has children to let them work.

Then you would not allow your children to go to those factories under the present system, if it was not from necessity?
—No.

—Testimony given before the Sadler Committee, 1831–32

47. Which period in history is associated with the conditions described in the passage?

(A) The Enlightenment
(B) The Green Revolution
(C) The Scientific Revolution
(D) The Industrial Revolution

48. According to the passage, why does the witness allow his children to work in a place where they will be ill treated?

(A) A factory owner is forcing him to do so.
(B) He doesn't earn enough on his own.
(C) The children need discipline.
(D) Their labor is only moderately difficult.

49. Which style of government is most associated with limited regulations on business and working conditions similar to those described in the passage?

(A) *Laissez-faire*
(B) Totalitarian
(C) Utilitarian
(D) Corporatist

50. Which type of organization was partially responsible for improving the hours, wages, and working conditions of workers in this era?

(A) Guilds
(B) Joint-stock companies
(C) Labor unions
(D) Zaibatsu groups

Questions 51 to 55 refer to the following image, which shows students taking the imperial examination in China c. 960–1279 CE.

51. From which social class were the students depicted in the painting most likely to be drawn?

   (A) Coastal merchants
   (B) Rural peasants
   (C) Conscripted military
   (D) Noble families

52. What would be the most likely content of these exams?

   (A) Legal statutes
   (B) Engineering principles
   (C) Economic theory
   (D) Confucian essays

53. Why were Japan's early attempts at introducing the Chinese-style imperial exam largely unsuccessful?

   (A) The Japanese were unable to adapt to the Chinese style of examination.
   (B) Merchants resisted, fearing that efficient administrators would lead to increased taxes.
   (C) Japanese nobles feared that their power base would be weakened.
   (D) Christian missionaries discouraged the adoption of pagan practices.

54. Which social phenomenon within China during the Song and Tang dynasties resulted from the imperial examination system?

(A) Improved conditions for women
(B) Development of state-run education
(C) Integration of nomadic border tribes
(D) Opportunity for social mobility

55. Which Chinese emperor or ruler would be most likely to disapprove of candidates who were successful on an exam like this?

(A) Mao Tse Tung
(B) Emperor Han Wudi (Han dynasty)
(C) Emperor TaiZong (Tang dynasty)
(D) Deng Xiaoping

GO ON TO PART B

PART B: SHORT-ANSWER QUESTIONS

Recommended Time for Part B—40 minutes

Directions: You need to answer a total of three short-answer questions. You are required to answer questions 1 and 2, but you may choose to answer either question 3 or question 4. The short-answer questions are divided into parts; answer all parts of the questions. Each question is worth a total of three points. Note that short-answer questions are not essay questions—they do not require the development and support of a thesis statement.

Question 1 refers to the following passage.

> The arbitrary and compulsory feudal marriage system, which is based on the superiority of man over woman and which ignores the children's interests, shall be abolished. . . . The new democratic system, which is based on free choice of partners, on monogamy, on equal rights for both sexes, and on protection of the lawful interests of women and children, shall be put into effect. . . . Husband and wife are in duty bound to love, respect, assist, and look after each other, to live in harmony, to engage in production, to care for their children, and to strive jointly for the welfare of the family and for the building up of a new society.

> —1950 Marriage Law, People's Republic of China

1. Answer Parts A and B.

   A. Discuss ONE major change in the status of men or women under the new marriage law.

   B. Identify TWO additional changes brought about by the Marriage Law.

Question 2 refers to the following map, which shows the progress of the Bubonic Plague, or the Black Death, during the 1340s.

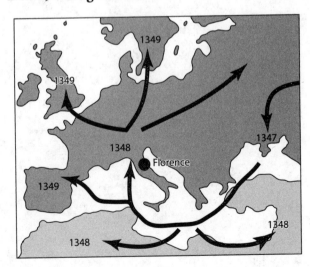

2. Answer Parts A and B.

   A. Discuss ONE way in which the plague spread from one region to another.

   B. Identify and discuss TWO effects of the plague in Europe.

Answer EITHER Question 3 OR Question 4.

3. Answer Parts A and B.

    A. Identify and discuss TWO examples of popular culture whose influence has spread throughout the world during the twentieth and twenty-first centuries.

    B. Discuss ONE reaction that non-Western societies have demonstrated when confronted with Western popular culture.

4. Answer Parts A and B.

    A. Identify two examples of diseases spread between the Old and New Worlds during the Columbian Exchange.

    B. Identify and explain the role of disease in the conquest of the Americas.

STOP. END OF SECTION I.

Section II

Time: 100 minutes

PART A: DOCUMENT-BASED QUESTION (DBQ)

Recommended reading time for Part A—15 minutes
Recommended writing time for Part A—45 minutes

Directions: The question is based on the following documents. The documents have been edited and adapted for this exam.

- Read the question carefully.
- Then read all the documents.
- Begin by grouping the documents into categories that reflect the documents' points of view, theme, or intended audience.
- Create a thesis that addresses the entire question.
- Analyze the documents that support the thesis. You must use all (or all but one of) the documents.
- Give careful attention to the purpose, point of view, source, and historical context of each document.
- Do NOT list the documents or analyze them one at a time in your essay; they should be incorporated into your argument.
- Bring in historical examples that support your argument.
- Create a persuasive essay that upholds your thesis, connects your argument to historical context, and draws conclusions.

1. Using the following documents, and your knowledge of world history, discuss in what ways the modern (twentieth-century) Olympic games have become a platform for international political disputes and how this contradicts their original purpose.

Document 1

Source: Encyclopaedia Britannica, 11th edition, 1910–1911, s.v. "Olympia"

The regular catalogue of Olympic victors begins in 776 B.C. . . . It was at Elis, in the gymnasium, that candidates from all parts of Greece were tested, before they were admitted to the athletic competitions at Olympia. To have passed through the training (usually of ten months) at Elis was regarded as the most valuable preparation. . . . The list of contests was enlarged to invest the celebration with a Panhellenic character. Exercises of a Spartan type—testing endurance and strength with an especial view to war—had almost exclusively formed the earlier programme. . . . As early as the 25th Olympiad the four-horse chariot race was added. Horse races were added later. Besides the foot race . . . there were now "long" foot races. Wrestling and boxing were combined. Leaping, quoit-throwing, javeline-throwing, running and wrestling were also added. Hellenes from all cities were to have peaceable access to the Olympian festival. . . . An expression of the Greek ideas that the body of man has a glory as well as his intellect and spirit, that body and mind should alike be disciplined.

Document 2

Source: Pierre de Coubertin, founder of the International Olympic Committee, 1894

May joy and good fellowship reign, and in this manner, may the Olympic Torch pursue its way through the ages, increasing friendly understanding among nations, for the good of a humanity always more enthusiastic, more courageous and more pure.

Document 3

Source: On This Day, BBC, October 17, 1968

Two black American athletes have made history at the Mexico Olympics by staging a silent protest against racial discrimination.

Tommie Smith and John Carlos, gold and bronze medalists in the 200m, stood with their heads bowed and a black-gloved hand raised as the American National Anthem played during the victory ceremony.

The pair both wore black socks and no shoes and Smith wore a black scarf around his neck. They were demonstrating against continuing racial discrimination of black people in the United States. Within a couple of hours the actions of the two Americans were condemned by the International Olympic Committee.

. . . Two days later, the two athletes were suspended from their national team, expelled from the Olympic village and sent home to America.

Document 4

Source: "Massacre Begins at Munich Games," *This Day in History* (September 5, 1972), *History* (www.history.com)

During the 1972 Summer Olympics at Munich, in the early morning of September 5, a group of Palestinian terrorists stormed the Olympic Village apartment of the Israeli athletes, killing two and taking nine others hostage. The terrorists were part of a group known as Black September. In return for the release of the hostages, they demanded that Israel release over 230 Arab prisoners being held in Israeli jails and two German terrorists. In an ensuing shootout at the Munich airport, the nine Israeli hostages were killed along with five terrorists and one West German policeman. Olympic competition was suspended for 24 hours to hold memorial services for the slain athletes.

Document 5

Source: U.S. Department of State Archive, 1980

In 1980, the United States led a boycott of the Summer Olympic Games in Moscow to protest the late 1979 Soviet invasion of Afghanistan. In total, 65 nations refused to participate in the games, whereas 80 countries sent athletes to compete.

In early 1980, the movement toward either boycotting the games altogether or moving them out of the Soviet Union gained momentum. Calls for boycotts of Olympic events were not uncommon; just four years prior, most of the nations of Sub-Saharan Africa boycotted the Summer Games in Montreal to protest the attendance of New Zealand after the latter sent its rugby team to play against the team from apartheid South Africa. In 1956, several Western European governments boycotted the games in Melbourne over the Soviet invasion of Hungary that year. Although the Olympic ideal was to place sport above politics, in reality there were often political goals and messages promoted through the games.

Document 6

Source: "Track Star Jesse Owens Defiantly Bucks Hitler," by Mike Morrison, posted on Infoplease (www .infoplease.com)

Twenty-two-year-old American Jesse Owens didn't care much for Hitler's politics—or any politics for that matter. He just wanted to show off his immense skills and represent his country to the best of his abilities. Just over a year earlier, on May 25, 1935, Owens recorded one of the more mind-boggling performances in track and field history. He broke three world records and tied another at the Big Ten Track and Field Championships in Michigan—in just 45 minutes! Hitler viewed African-Americans as inferior and chastised the United States for stooping to use these "non-humans." Despite the endless racial epithets and the constant presence of the red and black swastika, Owens made Hitler eat his words with four gold medals.

Document 7

Source: Jaime Fuller, writing in the *Washington Post,* February 5, 2014

The United States was trying to get the Olympics moved to a permanent location to avoid "unwarranted and disruptive international politics." (Then New Jersey Sen. Bill Bradley, who won a gold medal in the Tokyo Olympics as part of the American basketball team, recommended Greece.) But these people weren't paying very close attention to the Olympic games if they thought this was a recent phenomenon. Politics have been an essential part of the Olympics since Thucydides was covering them.

GO ON TO PART B

PART B: LONG-ESSAY QUESTION

Recommended Time for Part B—40 minutes

Directions: Answer ONE of the following questions.

1. Analyze the effects of physical environment (including geography and climate) on the longevity of the Chinese imperial system and culture.
2. Analyze the effects of physical environment (including geography and climate) on the longevity of the Mongol imperial system and culture.
3. Analyze the effects of physical environment (including geography and climate) on the longevity of (or lack of) the Incan Empire.

STOP. END OF SECTION II.

› Answers and Explanations

Section I, Part A: Multiple-Choice

1. **D** When Commodore Perry's ship entered Japan's harbor and forced the Japanese to open their ports to trade, it became clear to the Japanese that other nations had superior technology and that this put Japan at a disadvantage, as Lord Ii described. Christian missionaries were expelled from Japan during the Tokugawa Shogunate, which led up to the time when the letter was written (A). The adoption of Chinese imperial customs occurred during the Japanese Heian period, during the 800s to 1100s, and well before the steamship was invented (B). Manchuria was annexed by Japan in the 1930s, well after the era of the letter (C).

2. **C** In the 1970s, top Japanese leaders traveled to Europe and the United States to study Western-style economic and political practices. Japan briefly implemented a civil service system like the Chinese during the Heian period, but it never fully developed (A). Japan had been inward-looking prior to this time. Although some Japanese argued for expansion, in the hopes that they would gain power, this did not occur until the later 1890s and then did not occur in the Pacific (B). The turning inward happened prior to these events, during the Tokugawa Shogunate, and thus was not a response to them (D).

3. **A** The Meiji Restoration refers to the period starting in 1868 with the restoration of imperial rule. It was characterized by strong centralized government, opening to the West, land reforms, and dismantling of the samurai classes. The Heian period lasted from the 800s to the 1100s and was characterized by strong Chinese influence (B). The Tokugawa Shogunate period lasted from the 1600s to 1868 and was characterized by a feudal system with a strong samurai class (C). The Jomon were a Japanese Neolithic culture.

4. **A** The phrase "he enfolds the whole universe" indicates that Brahman is everywhere. There is no discussion of a specific location or place like Heaven (B). Because he is everywhere,

Brahman is not found *only* in the hearts of the faithful, although he is found in the heart of the speaker (C). He is described as "loving to all" and therefore is not vengeful (D).

5. **B** The speaker states that he will go to Brahman after his death, indicating that he believes that there will be some form of afterlife. The speaker is probably referring to *moksha*, the transcendent state reached after being released from the cycle of reincarnation. There is no discussion of rituals or religious practices (A), not even proper deeds or speech (C). According to Hinduism, Hindus worship one being that has many aspects or forms, and thus, they are not truly polytheistic (D).

6. **A** Brahman is the supreme cosmic entity and also means the underlying reality of all things in the Hindu religion. In Buddhism, there is a cycle of rebirth until Enlightenment is achieved, but there is no concept of a supreme God (B). Shintoism, from Japan, focuses on nature deities (C). Zoroastrianism, an ancient Persian religion, has a supreme God, Ahura Mazda, and focuses on a cosmic struggle between the forces of good and evil (D).

7. **B** The Columbian Exchange refers to the exchange of crops, animals, and disease between the "Old World," meaning Europe, Africa, and Asia, and the "New World," meaning the Americas. The Green Revolution refers to the use of agricultural science to create high-yield crops, fertilizers, and pesticides, starting in the mid-1960s (A). The triangular trade was the system of Atlantic trade networks around the 1500s (C). The Middle Passage was the part of the triangular trade network that shipped slaves from Africa to the Americas (D).

8. **A** Increased diversity of crops meant a greater and more varied food supply, which in turn led to increased population in Europe. There is some speculation regarding whether any diseases entered Europe via the Columbian Exchange, but, in any event, such introductions were not sufficient to cause any significant decline in the European population (B). Immigration from the Americas to Europe was not a widespread phenomenon (C). Though

Europeans brought crops to the Americas, it was not in quantities that would have caused a famine or a population decrease (D).

9. **C** The encomienda system granted land and an allotment of Indians to a Spaniard. The Indians were required to work for free, and in exchange the Spaniard was supposed to protect them and provide for their Christian education. Slavery of Indians (though not of Africans) was officially banned by Spain in 1542 (A). Indentured servitude refers to the system of repaying one's passage to the Americas by working for a specified period of time for free. It was primarily used by Europeans (B). The apprentice system is a system of learning a trade by working for a master craftsman for a specified period for low or no wages (D).

10. **A** Human, not animal, labor was used to prepare the land and to plant and harvest crops. There is no evidence of irrigation in the image (B), and both men and women are at work (C). Animals were not generally used in farm work, not because they were "too valuable" but because they fulfilled other tasks (D).

11. **B** The Americas lacked horses and oxen, the animals that were most commonly used for agricultural work. And while the indigenous cultures were practiced in decorative metal work (using gold and silver especially), they did not use metals for weaponry. Religion and trade did not play substantial roles in economic development (A, D); warfare, however, did contribute to economic development (C), thanks to the resulting extensive system of tribute.

12. **C** While the Aztecs used the wheel for non-essential items (toys, for example), they did not use it for transport vehicles. The Aztecs did have a system of writing (A), used metals for decorative work (B), and had significant overland trade networks (D).

13. **A** There was little to no north–south traffic in the Americas, and certainly not among indigenous peoples between Mesoamerica and South America. The Andean and Mesoamerican cultures both had extensive roads and bridges (B) and strong religious cultures (C). The Maya had a system of writing (D); the Andean cultures did not.

14. **A** Chinampas, or "floating gardens," made use of the lakes and swamplands of Mesoamerica;

terraces made agriculture possible in the mountainous Incan homeland. There was no overlap of agricultural techniques between the two cultures (B). Land ownership did not undergo reform (C), and coercive labor systems were not common to the two cultures (D).

15. **A** Most of the solid arrows (indicating expulsion) originate in Spain. There are no arrows indicting Jewish migration from Africa (D), and both Germany (B) and the Ottoman Empire (C) have only dotted arrows originating in those regions, indicating migrations as opposed to expulsion of Jews.

16. **B** Most of the arrows are solid lines, rather than dotted lines, indicating forced expulsions rather than voluntary migration (A). The dates of the expulsions range from 1290 in England to 1492 and 1497–1650 in Spain. The dates of the voluntary migrations range from 700–900 from the Ottoman Empire to 1150–1450 in Germany. Because there are more expulsions from Spain, with the later date range, (C) is incorrect. There is nothing on the map indicating the reasons for expulsion, which is where the directions state to look for the information. Moreover, historically there is little to no association with Jewish people and political conspiracies during this era (D).

17. **C** Most of the expulsions originated in Spain, which was a Catholic nation at this time. This explains why (B) is incorrect but also, while England eventually becomes Protestant, when it expelled Jews in 1290, the Protestant Reformation hadn't yet begun. Muslim regions at this time generally practiced religious toleration, as evidenced by the very few arrows originating in the Ottoman Empire and North Africa (A). Finally, throughout history Jews have generally migrated en masse when forced to by governments or due to persecution (D).

18. **C** Most of the Jews expelled from other regions ended up in Central Europe, causing increased anti-Semitism in this region, which ultimately found its expression in events like the Dreyfus Affair and World War II. Though there is tension between Muslims and Jews in the Middle East today, this is not the best answer because the conflict is not directly connected to events on the map (A). Choice (B) is incorrect, as there is no connection between migration of Jews and

Europeans' desire for colonies. Finally, during the time periods indicated, and shortly afterward, there was an increase in religious conflict in Europe, as Catholics and Protestants battled for control (D).

19. **C** Alliances, which were characteristic of the nineteenth and early twentieth centuries, constrained the allied countries to support one another and were one of the major causes of World War I. An attack on Serbia, for example, was considered an attack on Russia and its allies, France and Great Britain. Imperialism is an expansive policy of conquest and control (A). Nationalism refers to national identity (B). Militarism (D) refers to the buildup of armies and materiel.

20. **C** The alliances that led to World War I were the Triple Entente (Great Britain, France, and Russia) and the Triple Alliance (Germany, Austria-Hungary, and Italy). Serbia was supported by Russia, which needed access to (winter) warm-water ports. As part of the Triple Entente, France supported Russia (B). World War I may well be known as a "politicians' war," but the cartoon does not show this (A). World War I is aptly named, as it involved non-European countries (D).

21. **C** Bulgaria, Italy, and the United States were all engaged in World War I. Denmark (A), Switzerland (B), and Spain (D) were all neutral, although Switzerland did declare a "state of siege."

22. **A** Toussaint L'Ouverture was one of the key leaders in the Haitian Revolution, the only successful slave revolt in the colonies. Saint Domingue was the original French name for Haiti. The Mexican Revolution occurred slightly later (B), and Toussaint L'Ouverture was not associated with Mexico. Though the wars in both the other choices involved racial conflicts, when looking at the date 1797, neither the U.S. Civil War in 1860 (C) nor the Algerian War in 1954 (D) fits the year specified in the introduction.

23. **C** When General Toussaint stated that he would be held responsible for violence against whites, the implication is that he would likely be blamed because he is black. From one's knowledge of the Haitian Revolution, one should know that Toussaint L'Ouverture was a freed black slave (A) who won emancipation of the slaves and eventual independence for Haiti (B). There is no evidence in the passage that he had moral objections to the killing of white colonists (D).

24. **B** Before assuming that the passage is an accurate depiction of events, one should consider the point of view of the source. Specifically, could he have exaggerated or even lied to the French government about what transpired? He certainly would have benefited by making himself seem noble and a potential rival for power or an enemy seem murderous or treasonous. Chronology, which is placing events in a historical period or sequence, would not help evaluate the accuracy of a source (A). Similarly, neither causation (C) nor continuity over time (D) are relevant to assessing accuracy or credibility of a source.

25. **C** Theodore Roosevelt advocated intervention in Latin America when U.S. interests were at stake. The United States supported Panama's independence from Colombia in 1903 because Colombia did not support the Panama Canal. The Zimmerman Telegram was sent to Mexico by Germany in 1917 (A), the Cuban embargo took place in 1962 (B), and the Haitian Revolution began in 1791 (D). They all occurred either substantially earlier than the writing of the poem, or after. In addition, Haiti was a French colony and would not have been considered part of Latin America.

26. **D** The phrase indicates that Latin America has had both poets and civilizations that used "the stars" in its history. Answers including only poetry (A) or only science (B) are therefore insufficient. There is nothing in the passage to suggest prophecy (C).

27. **B** The theme is that Latin America has survived many invaders and will continue to survive, as indicated by references to Columbus, Catholics, and Spain and the use of phrases like "it lives" and "Viva Spanish America!" The only references to violence are in connection with the United States' warlike actions and are critical of the violence (A). The poem refers to the rich culture of Latin America in the present tense: "it lives" (C). The poet is critical of the U.S. focus on industry and progress ("You think progress is eruption . . . . No.") (D).

28. **C** The introduction states that the events occurred in the 1940s, which was during the World War II era. The Crimean War occurred between 1853 and 1856 and therefore is the wrong era (B). World War I occurred between 1914 and 1918, which is also the wrong era (B). The Seven Years' War occurred in Europe, primarily between 1755 and 1763. It is therefore from the wrong era and also occurred in a different location.

29. **A** The United States was allied with the Soviet Union primarily because the Soviet Union had been invaded by Germany. There was some distrust, though, as the Soviets had earlier signed a non aggression pact with Germany. The Soviets also felt that the United States, by refusing to open an Eastern Front to take the pressure off Soviet troops, had been lukewarm in its support. That distrust meant that the two were not exactly comrades or friends (B). They also were not enemies, because the United States was looking for a solution that was acceptable to the Soviets (C). That the Soviets' views were considered means that they were not strangers (D).

30. **D** Korea is currently separated into a communist dictatorship in the north and a democratic, capitalist regime in the south. The Japanese have no authority over or ownership of Korea (A). The Americans established a democratic regime in the south, but North Korea limits the individual liberties of its citizens (B). Though North Korea has suffered economic hardship in the late twentieth century, South Korea has enjoyed rapid economic growth over the same period (C).

31. **D** Containment refers to the policy of limiting the spread of communism by limiting the amount of territory the communist powers occupied. Détente refers to a thawing of relations, which is incorrect given the distrust of the Soviets implied in the passage (A). Mutual Assured Destruction refers to the idea that both the Soviets and the United States would be deterred from using nuclear weapons by the fact that they would both be destroyed if they did so. The passage predates Soviet nuclear capabilities and is therefore incorrect (B). Dollar Diplomacy emphasized the U.S. use of economic influence to achieve political ends in Latin America (C).

32. **B** The people of Mali study the fiqh, which is part of Muslims' religious law. Ibn Batutta expresses surprise that the genealogy is derived from the maternal side, indicating that this is not a common Muslim practice (A). Although he does not explicitly state that the men do not yield to sexual jealousy, it can be inferred from the fact that women had male friends and companions (C). Likewise, he is surprised at the casual acceptance of such interactions between unrelated members of opposite sexes (D).

33. **B** Women wearing the veil is a cultural practice found in Southwest Asia (the Middle East) that predated the founding of Islam. Women of Africa did not have that custom and so were less likely to adopt it as part of Islamic practice. Muslim women do not always perceive the veil to be a means of oppression, not to mention the fact that the passage did not indicate that the Muslim women of Mali were oppressed (A). That women could have male friends indicates that they were not merely sexual objects (C). The climate of Mali would be similar to that of Southwest Asia, where wearing the veil was a common practice (D).

34. **C** Mali was near the trans-Saharan trade routes dominated by Muslim merchants in the 1300s. Those merchants frequently exposed local African merchants to Islam. Berbers are North African tribes, but they are not associated with any religious or mystical movement (A). The Mughal empire lasted from the mid-1500s to the mid-1800s and so is out of period. The Mughals also were located in India and never entered Africa (B). Ethiopia was one of the earliest Christian nations in Africa, and therefore was unlikely to have many Islamic shrines (D).

35. **B** By "whispering" sentiments similar to those that apartheid "declares," the world also engages in discrimination, just in a less noticeable manner. There is no discussion of the world's fear of South Africa (A) or of the world's condemnation of the policy of apartheid (B). Although "oppression" is the nature of the society, there is no discussion of its being caused by the world economy (D).

36. **D** Apartheid was the policy of legal discrimination against black South Africans from 1948 to 1994. Jim Crow refers to legal segregation in the United States South from Reconstruction after the Civil War until the 1960s (A). Spheres

of influence refers to the system during the late 1800s in which European powers gained trading privileges within their own region, or "sphere," in China (B). Boer is a Dutch and Afrikaans term for farmer and is associated with South Africa, but "Boer division" is not an official term (C).

37. **B** Nelson Mandela was an anti-apartheid activist and head of the African National Congress Party. He was the first black president of South Africa, elected in 1994 after years of imprisonment for his anti-apartheid activities. Even though F. W. de Klerk worked to repeal apartheid laws after his election as South Africa's president in 1989, as he was a white politician, his presidency didn't symbolize the end of apartheid (A). There was no major bombing of Lesotho (C). The Boer War was fought by the British and the Boers (Dutch descendants) for control of South Africa at the end of the 1800s, and is therefore out of the time period.

38. **A** The information states that the settlers included marines, marine wives, and both male and female convicts. The presence of the convicts shows that Australia was intended to be a penal colony, to house convicted criminals. There is no evidence of any intention to trade or to build a trading post (B). There is no discussion of religion (C) or of the weapons or arms that would be needed for military bases (D).

39. **B** Convicts were given the afternoons to tend their own gardens, which implies that they were hoping to grow their own food eventually. April's entry discusses illness (scurvy) (A); July's entry discusses medical shortages and the age of some convicts (C); and March's entry discusses food shortages (D).

40. **C** The passage gives some indication concerning the hardships faced by the early Australian colonists, including famine, disease, and shortages of important supplies. There is no detailed discussion of the gardening methods used (A). Although there are mentions of age and sex, one cannot determine the ratios because no exact numbers are provided (B). Likewise, there is no information regarding any specific medical practices and procedures beyond a "salt diet," which could apply to all colonists (D).

41. **C** The spread of religion is one of the best-known examples of cultural diffusion, and the map shows the spread of Buddhism. Trade routes (e.g., the Silk Roads) in the classical era (A) originated in China and continued to the Mediterranean. Communism (B) is primarily a twentieth-century phenomenon that did not originate in India. The paths shown have nothing to do with weather (D).

42. **B** Buddhism originated in India, although it eventually became a minority religion there and spread to other countries, incorporating or adapting to local customs and needs. Hinduism (A), Christianity (C), and Islam (D) did not begin in India.

43. **B** Monks served as the leaders and missionaries for Buddhism. They gave up earthly goods in order to guide lay believers. Although merchants (A), military officers (C), and diplomats (D) all helped to transport beliefs, they did not dedicate their lives to doing so.

44. **C** Peter the Great brought a great many ideas back from his travels to the West, among them those dealing with individual rights and parliamentary government, but he retained control, instituting a sort of constitutional monarchy. He did not create an elected assembly (A), make declarations of guaranteed human rights (B), or reduce aristocratic influence to any great degree (D).

45. **B** By retaining control and power, Peter the Great was more absolutist than he was egalitarian (A), republican (C), or theocratic (D).

46. **C** Peter the Great did not free the serfs; it took the Industrial Revolution in Russia to make that feasible. He did nothing to decentralize power—in fact, he consolidated it (A). He worked hard to reverse the isolationism (B) that had left Russia on the margins of modernization. He did not *continue* reform, but he initiated it in many instances (D).

47. **D** The Industrial Revolution was characterized by a lack of regulation, leading to poor working conditions, long hours, and low wages, including for children. The Enlightenment was primarily a philosophical movement occurring in the seventeenth and eighteenth centuries (A). The Green Revolution used scientific methods to increase crop yields. It is also a twentieth-century phenomenon and is therefore out of the era (B). The Scientific Revolution predates this, having occurred

around the sixteenth to eighteenth centuries, and refers to the prolific scientific discoveries in fields like physics, astronomy, and anatomy. (C)

48. B The witness states that he has work only about two days each week and that he needs to let his children work (necessity compels him). There is no owner forcing him. The phrase "necessity compels a man" refers to his own need for his children to work (A). There is no indication that the children need discipline (C). The phrase "moderate labour" does appear, but the speaker is saying that he would prefer reasonable hours, even if he earns less (D).

49. A *Laissez-faire* ("leave it alone") is the principle that governments should not interfere in or regulate industries, businesses, or markets. Totalitarian governments typically have total control over their economies, making "A" the better answer (B). Utilitarian philosophers advocate policies that create the greatest amount of happiness for the largest number of people. It is not a style of government per se, nor would it be consistent with systems that used child labor (C). Corporatists include interest groups (like labor and industry) in the government, and therefore provide more government involvement in the economy than *laissez-faire* systems (D).

50. C Labor unions, whose workers are organized and act collectively, fought for better wages, hours, and working conditions in the 1800s and 1900s. Guilds were medieval organizations and therefore are out of the time period (A). Joint-stock companies allowed investors to purchase shares in a business. They did not advocate for workers (B). Zaibatsu groups are Japanese industrial conglomerates that controlled parts of Japan's economy in the late 1800s and early 1900s. This answer is incorrect because they did not support improved conditions for workers and because it relates to a different region (D).

51. D Most of the people taking the exams came from the Chinese nobility. Even though the civil service exam offered the possibility of social mobility for the lower classes, the reality was that, since the exams were so difficult and there was no public education, few peasants could afford to devote that amount of time to studying (B). Conscripted military would also have been unable to take the time to study for the exam

(C). Coastal merchants would not have been a large enough group to make an impact (A).

52. D The civil service exam was created during the Han dynasty to provide a professional bureaucracy. It was based on Confucian essays, literature, and poetry. It did not cover legal statutes (A) or engineering principles (B). It also would not have covered economic theory, especially as the Chinese tended to look down on trade and merchants (C).

53. C Even though the civil service exams did not result in large degrees of social mobility, the Japanese nobles and Buddhist monks balked at the prospect of diluting their power. The Japanese had adopted Chinese writing and other elements of the imperial court system, so there is no reason to think that they would not have been able to adapt to that style of exam (A). Japanese merchants at this time weren't significant enough to affect the decision (B), and Christian missionaries did not have enough influence to affect such decisions (D).

54. D Although most of the candidates were drawn from the upper classes, the civil service exam did offer an opportunity for a few bright candidates from rural villages. Conditions for women were unchanged, as women could not take the exam (A). Candidates had to pay for their studies themselves (B). The imperial exam was unrelated to nomadic border tribes (C).

55. A Mao Tse Tung was opposed to intellectuals, and sought to reeducate them during the Cultural Revolution. Both the Han dynasty and the Tang dynasty used and supported the imperial exam, so they would have approved of successful candidates (B, C). Deng Xiaoping is the twentieth-century Chinese leader who modernized China, improving education and opening markets. Although he might not have supported the Confucian element, the fact that he supported education means that this is not the best response (D).

Section I, Part B: Short-Answer Questions

1A. You should mention ONE of the following in your answer: men are no longer considered superior to women, women will enjoy equal rights in the marriage, men and women can now choose the person they want to marry, or men and women are constrained to be monogamous. (1 point possible)

1B. The TWO additional changes can include any of the answers from 1A, so long as you didn't use them to answer 1A. You can also mention the care of children or the consideration of marriage as a way to contribute to the societal good. (2 points possible)

2A. As the map shows, the plague spread both by land and by sea. Drawing on your knowledge of world history, you might discuss merchants or crusaders as being responsible for this spread of the disease. (1 point possible)

2B. TWO effects of the plague in Europe can include, for example, a death blow to the feudal class system caused by the loss of serf labor and the beginning of a wage labor system; a drastic decline in population; increased persecution of Jews and alleged witches, since they were considered to have been responsible for the plague; or the production of literary works (e.g., Boccaccio's *Decameron*). (2 points possible)

3A. You may mention any two of various styles of popular music—rock 'n' roll, heavy metal, or reggae, for example. Movies have become globally popular, from Italian neorealism to Hollywood to Bollywood, to name just a few forms. Food has gone global, including fast food, like McDonald's. Jeans, jazz, and sports have all become global. (2 points possible)

3B. While many non-Westerners admire and, to some degree, emulate American cultural icons, many others resent the diffusion of American culture. As a result, citizens of non-Western cultures often experience a resurrection of traditional practices in their countries. Some have gone so far as to ban the use of Western language or terminology and replaced it with native terms. (1 point possible)

4A. You should mention at least two of the following in your answer. From the East and Old Worlds: the Black Plague, smallpox, measles, mumps, chickenpox, typhus, typhoid, cholera, whooping cough, scarlet fever, malaria, or influenza. From

the New World to the Old World: hepatitis, encephalitis, or syphilis. (2 points possible)

4B. It is sufficient to note that of the millions of Native Americans who died during the conquest, as many as 90 percent died from diseases previously unknown to them. As a result, African workers (slaves) were brought to the New World to carry on agricultural endeavors. (1 point possible)

Section II, Part A: Document-Based Question

This question has two parts: in reverse order, you must decide the original purpose of the Olympic games, and the purpose of the modern games as well; then you must discuss how the modern games have deviated from that original purpose and become, frequently, political. You must sustain a thesis that takes both parts of the question into consideration. For example, you could say that the original purpose of the games was to use sport to establish or maintain peace among different peoples (Documents 1 and 2) but that with globalization, or with modern interweavings of different nations and different aspects of life, politics have crept into sports. You may decide that this is inevitable. Or you may take to heart the idea of establishing a permanent venue for the games that asks participants to check their politics at the gate (Document 7).

A good response will draw on six or seven (that is, all or all but one of the) documents to explain how the nature of the modern Olympic games has changed—not always but frequently enough to be noteworthy. You should begin by analyzing the documents. A definition of just what the modern Olympic games represented, or their overall goal, would be to promote peace and understanding among nations (Documents 2 and 5). This is based on the Classical era's idea that the games should be all-inclusive (Document 1).

You should incorporate further analysis of the documents, perhaps by dividing them into those that contain evidence in support of the idea of using the games as a political soapbox (Documents 3, 4, and 5) and those that present an opposing point of view (Documents 2, 3, 5, 6, and 7). There will be an obvious overlapping of documents, since many of them present both perspectives. Simply listing the characteristics of individual documents, however, does not answer the question or sustain your thesis.

Having considered the differing points of view, your task is to connect them, within a historical context, in order to show that the Olympics were never intended to be political and that today, in an effort to remove politics from the Olympic arena, the establishment of a permanent venue has been suggested (Document 7).

There are various conclusions that can be drawn here. You may feel that globalization has made the political nature of any international event inevitable. On the other hand, you may conclude that athletes should take the moral high road and simply carry out and show off their athletic talents (Document 6). In other words, you may show that while political gamesmanship contradicts the original intent of the Olympic games, it is an unavoidable by-product of a world in which not only are nations inextricably intertwined (economically, politically, culturally) but so are the things—sports, religion, entertainment, business—that make up any given culture.

Section II, Part B: Long-Essay Question

In a strong response, you may begin by explaining what "longevity" means in the context of the question. The Chinese imperial system lasted from approximately 1500 BCE to 1912 CE, or almost 3,500 years. The Mongol Empire, the largest ever in the history of the world, lasted from approximately 1206 until 1368, though a remnant would survive until the 1600s. (For purposes of comparison, the Western Roman Empire lasted about 500 years, and the Spanish Empire lasted about 300 years.)

In this essay, you can make the case either for or against the causal effects of physical environment on the longevity of either the Chinese or the Mongol imperial system. Both China and the Mongols controlled large landmasses. In a sense, they had only one frontier to defend from invaders. The Chinese fortified their frontier with the Great Wall. In the Chinese case, geography contributed to the longevity of the empire

as well as to a sense of national identity. Geographic barriers kept invaders out and, to a degree, kept inhabitants in.

China's climate is varied simply because the country covers a great deal of territory. Arable land, however, has always been relatively restricted. This geographic feature made China more inclined to cultivate trade, and thus the Silk Roads developed. Under Mongol rule, trade engendered a lasting peace, and conquest followed the trade routes.

Culturally, China believed that its leaders were semidivine and that continued environmental benevolence depended on maintaining harmony between the rulers of the cosmos and the terrestrial rulers. Thus, natural or environmental disasters—floods or droughts, for example—could prompt changes in rulers or even whole dynasties, although the system remained intact. The Mongols incorporated distant parts of their empire by keeping local rulers in place and not physically centering overall power. Physical environment was less a contributing factor in the empire's survival than was the cultivation of political alliances.

The Incan Empire (c. 1425–1532) on the western coast of South America was, by contrast, short-lived. Its geography—the Pacific Ocean on the west, the Andes Mountains on the east—allowed expansion on a north–south axis. This made for varied environmental and climatic conditions. It did not, however, prevent invasion as might have been expected.

As had the Mongols, the Incas cultivated (or enforced) alliances. Unlike the Mongols, they established a center of government, in Cusco, to which regional rulers reported and paid tariffs.

The development of technology would make the role of the physical environment much less important. At this point, you could argue that geography and climate (including natural resources), while important to the way in which a society develops or the directions that it takes, are not THE determining factor in longevity. Technological superiority allowed the Spaniards to destroy the Incan Empire quickly and definitively. In early times, it was a response to the environment that partially determined the success or failure of an empire; after the Industrial Revolution, however, society could control the physical environment. In any case, in modern times, empires are no longer the dominant model of governing.

Practice Test Two

ANSWER SHEET

1 Ⓐ Ⓑ Ⓒ Ⓓ	16 Ⓐ Ⓑ Ⓒ Ⓓ	31 Ⓐ Ⓑ Ⓒ Ⓓ	46 Ⓐ Ⓑ Ⓒ Ⓓ
2 Ⓐ Ⓑ Ⓒ Ⓓ	17 Ⓐ Ⓑ Ⓒ Ⓓ	32 Ⓐ Ⓑ Ⓒ Ⓓ	47 Ⓐ Ⓑ Ⓒ Ⓓ
3 Ⓐ Ⓑ Ⓒ Ⓓ	18 Ⓐ Ⓑ Ⓒ Ⓓ	33 Ⓐ Ⓑ Ⓒ Ⓓ	48 Ⓐ Ⓑ Ⓒ Ⓓ
4 Ⓐ Ⓑ Ⓒ Ⓓ	19 Ⓐ Ⓑ Ⓒ Ⓓ	34 Ⓐ Ⓑ Ⓒ Ⓓ	49 Ⓐ Ⓑ Ⓒ Ⓓ
5 Ⓐ Ⓑ Ⓒ Ⓓ	20 Ⓐ Ⓑ Ⓒ Ⓓ	35 Ⓐ Ⓑ Ⓒ Ⓓ	50 Ⓐ Ⓑ Ⓒ Ⓓ
6 Ⓐ Ⓑ Ⓒ Ⓓ	21 Ⓐ Ⓑ Ⓒ Ⓓ	36 Ⓐ Ⓑ Ⓒ Ⓓ	51 Ⓐ Ⓑ Ⓒ Ⓓ
7 Ⓐ Ⓑ Ⓒ Ⓓ	22 Ⓐ Ⓑ Ⓒ Ⓓ	37 Ⓐ Ⓑ Ⓒ Ⓓ	52 Ⓐ Ⓑ Ⓒ Ⓓ
8 Ⓐ Ⓑ Ⓒ Ⓓ	23 Ⓐ Ⓑ Ⓒ Ⓓ	38 Ⓐ Ⓑ Ⓒ Ⓓ	53 Ⓐ Ⓑ Ⓒ Ⓓ
9 Ⓐ Ⓑ Ⓒ Ⓓ	24 Ⓐ Ⓑ Ⓒ Ⓓ	39 Ⓐ Ⓑ Ⓒ Ⓓ	54 Ⓐ Ⓑ Ⓒ Ⓓ
10 Ⓐ Ⓑ Ⓒ Ⓓ	25 Ⓐ Ⓑ Ⓒ Ⓓ	40 Ⓐ Ⓑ Ⓒ Ⓓ	55 Ⓐ Ⓑ Ⓒ Ⓓ
11 Ⓐ Ⓑ Ⓒ Ⓓ	26 Ⓐ Ⓑ Ⓒ Ⓓ	41 Ⓐ Ⓑ Ⓒ Ⓓ	
12 Ⓐ Ⓑ Ⓒ Ⓓ	27 Ⓐ Ⓑ Ⓒ Ⓓ	42 Ⓐ Ⓑ Ⓒ Ⓓ	
13 Ⓐ Ⓑ Ⓒ Ⓓ	28 Ⓐ Ⓑ Ⓒ Ⓓ	43 Ⓐ Ⓑ Ⓒ Ⓓ	
14 Ⓐ Ⓑ Ⓒ Ⓓ	29 Ⓐ Ⓑ Ⓒ Ⓓ	44 Ⓐ Ⓑ Ⓒ Ⓓ	
15 Ⓐ Ⓑ Ⓒ Ⓓ	30 Ⓐ Ⓑ Ⓒ Ⓓ	45 Ⓐ Ⓑ Ⓒ Ⓓ	

AP WORLD HISTORY PRACTICE TEST TWO

Section I

Time: 1 hour, 45 minutes

Part A: Multiple-Choice Questions

Recommended Time for Part A: 55 Minutes

Directions: Each of the following incomplete statements or questions is followed by four answer choices. Select the choice that best answers the question and fill in the oval on the answer sheet provided.

Questions 1 to 3 refer to the following passage.

Hello, Yankee Brothers. This is your Japanese sister, the Voice of Truth. . . . This morning [your superiors] are making you attempt the impossible. For it is impossible for you to dislodge our forces on Iwo Jima. . . . I'm filled with sadness for you because of the thousands of Japanese soldiers safe in caves and pillboxes [which] your bombs and shells can't touch, reluctantly waiting to slaughter you. They do not want to harm you because they know that what you are attempting to do this morning is not of your own choice. They know as you know and I know that you are making a futile sacrifice for people who sit snug and secure 11,000 miles away. . . . Listen, Yankee brothers, to these headlines. "Strike continues in critical war industry." "Three year buying spree clears shelves as public clamors for more merchandise." "Workers claim nightclub curfew limits amusement spending." Does that sound like a people who want war? Who are supporting you and your sacrificial attempts to carry on this useless war? Think it over, Yankee brothers. They do not want the war. They are doing their best to let you know they are not behind you. This is the Voice of Truth. I will be with you again tomorrow, those of you who are left to listen.

—Tokyo Rose, February 1945, transcribed from Periscope Film LL Archives

1. Which of the following elements identifies the above passage as Japanese propaganda from World War II?

   (A) Reference to the high level of American support for Allied troops
   (B) Reference to the technological superiority of Japanese troops
   (C) Reference to the safety of Japanese soldiers
   (D) Reference to an energetic war effort

2. The terms "Yankee brothers," "Japanese sister," and "Voice of Truth" are intended to do what to the listener?

   (A) Assure the accuracy of the broadcast
   (B) Engender empathy for the Japanese
   (C) Demoralize the war command
   (D) Recruit future soldiers

3. What is the point of the phrase "for people who sit snug and secure 11,000 miles away"?

   (A) To convince Allied soldiers that they stand no chance of winning
   (B) To convert American soldiers to the Japanese cause
   (C) To place the blame for World War II on Allied politicians
   (D) To suggest that the war is a worthless endeavor

Questions 4 to 6 refer to the following passage.

[Mansa Musa] extended the borders of Mali in every direction. To the north, he added the important trading centers of Walata and Timbaktu. To the east, he added Gao. To the west, he expanded into Senegal and Gambia, reaching the Atlantic Ocean. Mali thus became the owner of the north-south as well as east-west trade routes and the repository of important centers of learning. . . . Mansa Musa (1307–1337) consolidated the administration of the state, encouraged trade and protected trade routes. In 1324, he performed his Hajj. . . . He took with him an entourage of 12,000. . . . The Malians were rich and carried with them a plentiful supply of gold. They spent so much of it during their trip that the price of gold fell in North Africa and Egypt. . . . On his return from Hajj, Mansa Musa stopped off in Cairo and Kairouan, brought a large number of books and returned home accompanied by Maliki jurists, administrators and Qur'anic scholars. He richly endowed the African universities, built mosques, patronized scholarship, encouraged mass education and established closer relations with the Muslim powers of North Africa. . . . Mansa Musa is known in history as a pious man, a scholar, a generous patron and a farsighted ruler.

—*An Encyclopedia of Islamic History*
s.v. "Mansa Musa"

4. Mansa Musa expanded and consolidated the Malian empire using which of the following tactics?

   (A) He established a state religion, outlawing others in the process.
   (B) Through universal education and military service, he standardized language in the empire.
   (C) He performed his Hajj and required all citizens to do the same.
   (D) He spread Malian culture through trade, diplomacy, and patronage.

5. Why did Mansa Musa bring legal and religious scholars and bureaucrats to Mali from other regions?

   (A) To expose his court to modern technology
   (B) To strengthen trade in the growing empire
   (C) To reinforce Malian traditions
   (D) To incorporate successful imperial practices

6. During Mansa Musa's reign, trade routes served as conduits for various goods and products (textiles, gems, gold, salt, and ivory). According to the passage above, what else was spread because of the trade routes?

   (A) Diseases
   (B) Weaponry
   (C) Ideas
   (D) Medicines

Questions 7 to 10 refer to the following quotation.

"Gunga Din"
Now in Injia's sunny clime,
Where I used to spend my time
A-servin' of 'Er Majesty the Queen,
Of all them blackfaced crew
The finest man I knew
Was our regimental bhisti, Gunga Din . . .
"You squidgy-nosed old idol, Gunga Din."
The uniform 'e wore
Was nothing' much before,
An' rather less than 'arf o' that behind,
For a piece o' twisty rag
An' a goatskin water-bag
Was all the field equipment 'e could find. . . .
'E would dot an' carry one
Till the longest day was done;
An' 'e didn't seem to know the use o' fear.
If we charged or broke or cut,
You could bet your bloomin' nut,
'E'd be waiting' fifty paces right flank rear. . . .
I shan't forgit the night
When I'd dropped be'ind the fight

With a bullet where my beltplate should 'a' been.
I was chokin' mad with thirst,
An' the man that spied me first
Was our good old grinnin', gruntin' Gunga Din.
'E lifted up my "ad,
An' he plugged me where I bled,
An' 'e guv me 'arf apint o' water green.
It was crawlin' and it stunk,
But of all the drinks I've drunk,'
I'm gratefullest to one from Gunga Din. . . .
'E carried me away To where a dooli lay,
An' a bullet come an' drilled the beggar clean.
'E put me safe inside,
An' just before 'e died,
"I 'ope you liked your drink," sez Gunga Din. . . .
Though I've belted you and flayed you,
By the livin' Gawd that made you,
You're a better man than I am, Gunga Din!

—Edited and adapted from "Gunga Din"
Rudyard Kipling

7. Written about a native nineteenth-century Indian water carrier, "Gunga Din" reveals British stereotypes of locals in what way?

   (A) By using animal imagery to describe Gunga Din
   (B) By explaining specific battle formations and roles
   (C) By referring to physical differences between the narrator and Gunga Din
   (D) By using dialectical language

8. What does the narrator mean when he calls Gunga Din a "better man"?

   (A) Gunga Din is in better physical condition than the narrator.
   (B) Gunga Din is more willing to make sacrifices for the greater good.
   (C) Gunga Din knows more about warfare than the narrator does.
   (D) Gunga Din was more religious than the narrator.

9. In this poem, the author takes what view of the cultural superiority of the "white man's burden"?

   (A) Accepting
   (B) Resigned
   (C) Critical
   (D) Condescending

10. Kipling may well have written this poem as a response to which of the following social theories?

    (A) Socialist Realism
    (B) Social Darwinism
    (C) Marxism
    (D) Positivism

Questions 11 to 13 refer to the following illustration.

11. In the political cartoon, the United States is seen as fulfilling which of the following roles?

(A) Oppressor
(B) Imperialist
(C) Savior
(D) Isolationist

12. The Spanish Empire included lands on five continents. After the Spanish-American War, which treaty included Spain's cession of the Philippines to the United States?

(A) The Treaty of Paris
(B) The Treaty of Tordesillas
(C) The Treaty of Westphalia
(D) The Treaty of Guadalupe-Hidalgo

13. In 1904, President Theodore Roosevelt opened the door to U.S. military intervention in Latin America with the Roosevelt Corollary to the Monroe Doctrine. In part, this was mitigated by which policy?

(A) Gunboat diplomacy
(B) Humanism
(C) Revisionism
(D) Dollar diplomacy

Questions 14 to 16 refer to the following passage.

I wish this Lady to have knowledge of letters, music, painting, and to know how to dance and make merry, accompanying the other precepts that have been taught the Courtier with discreet modesty and with the giving of a good impression of herself. . . . In her talk, her laughter, her play, her jesting, in short, in everything, she will be very graceful, and will entertain appropriately, and with witticisms and pleasantries befitting her and everyone who shall come before her. And although continence, magnanimity, temperance, strength of mind, prudence, and the other virtues seem to have little to do with entertainment, I would have her adorned with all of them . . . in order that she may be full of virtue. . . . Do you not know that Plato, who certainly was no great friend to women, gave them charge over the city and gave all other martial duties to the men? . . . But I have not laid these [martial] duties on them because I am fashioning a Court lady and not a queen. . . . There have even been those who waged wars and won glorious victories, governed kingdoms with the highest prudence and justice, and did everything that men have done. As for the sciences, do you not remember having read of many women who were learned in philosophy? Others who were excellent in poetry? Others who conducted suits and accused and defended eloquently before judges?

—Taken from Castiglione, *Il Cortegiano*, a sixteenth-century Italian book of etiquette

14. How does Castiglione distinguish a court lady from a queen?

   (A) Court ladies should be conversant in the sciences, but queens should not.
   (B) Queens must be adept at military strategy, but court ladies need not be.
   (C) A queen's primary quality must be the ability to entertain, whereas court ladies must be able to have a profession.
   (D) Ladies have no need to be literate, but queens do.

15. According to the passage, how is Castiglione an example of a Renaissance humanist?

   (A) He values the potential of all individuals.
   (B) He values military skill.
   (C) He reconciles Greek philosophy with Christian doctrine.
   (D) He places no value on literacy for women.

16. What other civilizations have had similar visions of the role of women?

   (A) Song Empire
   (B) Abbasid Empire
   (C) Tokugawa Shogunate
   (D) Mongol Empire

Questions 17 to 19 refer to the following illustration.

McDonald's restaurant in Shenzhen, China

17. Which phenomenon in world history is best illustrated by the above image?

   (A) Globalization
   (B) Nationalism
   (C) Syncretism
   (D) Communism

18. What is one consequence of trends such as the one illustrated above?

   (A) The health and safety conditions of workers worldwide have improved.
   (B) Jobs created by multinational corporations have reduced migration.
   (C) The economies of most nation-states are now interdependent.
   (D) American corporations are adopting Chinese economic practices.

19. Some people argue that closer economic ties with the West will lead to improved human rights in authoritarian regimes. Which twentieth-century event contradicts this?

   (A) Britain's decision to leave the European Union
   (B) The implementation of the Marshall Plan
   (C) The formation of the European Union
   (D) China's response to protests in Tiananmen Square

Questions 20 to 23 refer to the following passage.

THE TURKISH LETTERS, 1555 CE–1562 CE, sent by a Flemish diplomat to the Ottoman Empire on behalf of the Austrian Empire.

. . . No single man owed his position to aught save his valor and his merit. . . .

The Sultan . . . examines carefully into the character, ability, and disposition of the man whose promotion is in question. It is by merit that men rise in the service, a system which ensures that posts should only be assigned to the competent. . . . This is the reason that they are successful in their undertakings, that they lord it over others, and are daily extending the bounds of their empire. These are not our ideas; with us [Austrians] the prestige of birth is the sole key to advancement in the public service. . . .

. . . The Turkish monarch going to war takes with him over 40,000 camels and mules, loaded with rice and other kinds of grain. . . . They are well aware that they will have to retreat over districts wasted by the enemy, . . . as if they had been devastated by locusts; accordingly they reserve their stores as much as possible for this emergency. Then . . . a ration just sufficient to sustain life is daily weighed out to the Janissaries and other royal troops. From this you will see that it is the patience, self-denial, and thrift of the Turkish soldier that enable him to face the most trying circumstances. What a contrast to our men! Christian soldiers on a campaign call for . . . dainty dishes! If these are not supplied, they grow mutinous and work their own ruin. . . .

The sons of Turkish Sultans are in a wretched position. As soon as one of them succeeds his father, the rest are doomed to certain death. The Turk can endure no rival to the throne, and, indeed, the conduct of the Janissaries renders it impossible for the new Sultan to spare his brothers; for if one of them survives, the Janissaries are forever asking largesses. If these are refused, forthwith the cry is heard, 'Long live the brother!'—a broad hint that they intend to place him on the throne. Turkish Sultans are compelled to celebrate their succession by imbruing [staining] their hands in the blood of their nearest relatives.

20. According to the passage, what is the author's view of the Ottoman Empire's bureaucrats compared with the Austrians?

   (A) The Ottomans don't have a single man in office because of his valor or merit.
   (B) The Austrian system according prestige to birth is preferable.
   (C) The system of rewarding ability is the source of the Ottoman Empire's success.
   (D) The Ottoman bureaucracy is too large to be sustainable.

21. In which other society was a bureaucracy based on merit central to its success?

   (A) France under Louis XIV
   (B) Athens under Pericles
   (C) The Aztecs under Moctezuma
   (D) China under the Tang and Song

22. Which term best describes the Ottoman military as described in the passage?

   (A) Overindulged
   (B) Self-disciplined
   (C) Egalitarian
   (D) Shortsighted

23. Use your knowledge of world history and the passage to answer: Why might the Janissaries be considered both an asset and a weakness for the Ottoman Empire?

   (A) They demanded both the greatest and the richest resources.
   (B) Their loyalty was contingent upon bribes.
   (C) Though great in numbers, they were unskilled.
   (D) As native Turks, they supported regional lords.

Questions 24 to 27 refer to the following passages.

Their arms are bows, iron maces, and in some instances spears; but the first is the weapon at which they are most expert, being accustomed, from children, to employ it in their sports. They wear defensive armor. . . . They are brave in battle, almost to desperation, setting little value upon their lives, and exposing themselves without hesitation to all manner of danger. . . . They are capable of supporting every kind of privation, and when there is a necessity for it, can live for a month on the milk of their mares, and upon such wild animals as they may chance to catch. Their horses are fed upon grass alone, and do not require barley or other grain. The men are trained to remain on horseback during two days and two nights, without dismounting. . . . No people on earth can surpass them in fortitude . . . nor show greater patience. . . . They are most obedient to their chiefs and are maintained at small expense.

—*Travels*
Marco Polo, 1298

One woman will drive twenty or thirty wagons, since the terrain is level. . . . It is the women's task to drive the wagons, to load the dwellings on them and to unload again, to milk the cows, to make butter and grut [curds and cheese], and to dress the skins and stitch them together, which they do with a thread made from sinew. The men make bows and arrows, manufacture stirrups and bits, fashion saddles, construct the dwellings and the wagons, tend the horses and mares, churn the comas [mare's milk], produce the skins in which it is stored, and tend and load the camels.

—*A Report on Gender Relations*
William of Rubruck, a Franciscan friar who visited the Mongols in the 1250s, on behalf of the King of France

24. The above passages reveal Mongol society to be primarily of which kind?

    (A) Bucolic
    (B) Nomadic
    (C) Urban
    (D) Agricultural

25. According to the above passages, the nature of Mongol society resulted in which of the following?

    (A) Class distinctions that were carefully observed
    (B) Division of labor, which made gender equality possible to a large degree
    (C) Self-sustaining characteristics, which allowed for the creation of political alliances
    (D) Technological advances, which outweighed tradition

26. Overall, the Mongols appear to have been what type of people?

    (A) Carefree
    (B) Hardy
    (C) Resigned
    (D) Innovative

27. Based on the passage, and using your knowledge of world history, what were the long-term effects of the Mongols' military prowess?

    (A) New scientific discoveries
    (B) Frequent interclan wars that weakened the Mongols
    (C) Spread of the Mongol religion through Central Asia
    (D) The conquest of many established empires

Questions 28 to 31 refer to the following passage.

The word quipu means both knot or to knot; it was also used for accounts, because they were kept by means of the knots tied in a number of cords of different thicknesses and colors, each one of which had a special significance. . . . In order to make an inventory of the arms of the imperial army, they first counted the arms that were considered to belong in a superior category, and any other arms that were used. In order to ascertain the number of vassals in the Empire, they started with each village, then with each province: the first cord showed a census of men over sixty, the second, those between fifty and sixty, the third, those from forty to fifty, and so on, by decades, down to the babes at the breast. Every year, an inventory of all possessions was made. . . . And indeed, it may be said that everything that could be counted, was counted in this way, even to battles, diplomatic missions, and royal speeches. But since it was only possible to record numbers in this manner, and not words, the quipucamayus assigned to record ambassadorial missions and speeches, learned them by heart, at the same time that they noted down the numbers, places and dates on their quipus; and thus, from father to son, they transmitted this information to their successors. . . . The quipucamayus never let their quipus out of their hands, and they kept passing their cords and knots through their fingers so as not to forget the tradition behind all these accounts. In fact, their responsibility was so great and so absorbing, that they were exempted from all tribute as well as from all other kinds of service.

—*Royal Commentaries of the Incas*
Inca Garcilaso de la Vega, 1609

28. The quipu primarily served which of the following purposes?

(A) They recorded and transmitted the Incas' historical data.
(B) They were the basis for textile artworks.
(C) They acted as road maps to the corners of the Incan Empire.
(D) They maintained and updated the empire's population census.

29. Based on the passage, quipucamayus were comparable to which of the following?

(A) An African griot
(B) A European priest
(C) A Japanese samurai
(D) A Native American shaman

30. Which of the following demonstrates most clearly the importance of the quipucamayu?

(A) The low tribute he was responsible for paying
(B) His military commission
(C) His creation of diplomatic speeches
(D) The lack of other demands made on the quipucamayu's time

31. Measuring which of the following would be an inappropriate interpretation of the use of the quipu?

(A) Economic activity
(B) Population censuses
(C) Extent of military skill
(D) Life expectancy

Questions 32 to 35 refer to the following passage.

Now the Law of Nature was never more apparent in them. People are equal everywhere. [But] Europeans, thirsting for blood and for this metal that greed calls gold, have made Nature change in these happy lands. . . .

Trading people! Heavens! And Nature does not quake! If they are animals, are we not also like them? How are the Whites different from this race? It is in the color . . . . Why do blonds not claim superiority over brunettes who bear a resemblance to Mulattos? Why is the Mulatto not superior to the Negro? Like all the different types of animals, plants, and minerals that Nature has produced, people's color also varies. Why does not the day argue with the night, the sun with the moon, and the stars with the sky? Everything is different, and herein lies the beauty of Nature. Why then destroy its Work?

. . . When submissiveness once starts to flag, what results from the barbaric despotism of the Islanders and West Indians? Revolts of all kinds, carnage increased with the troops' force, poisonings, and any atrocities people can commit once they revolt. Is it not monstrous of Europeans, who have acquired vast plantations by exploiting others, to have Blacks flogged from morning to night? These miserable souls would cultivate their fields no less if they were allotted more freedom and kindness. Is their fate not among the most cruel, and their labor the hardest, without having Whites inflict the most horrible punishments on them, and for the smallest fault? Some speak about changing their condition, finding ways to ease it, without fearing that this race of men misuse a kind of freedom that remains subordinate.

—*Reflections on Negroes*
Olympe de Gouges, February 1788

32. By which philosophical movement would the author most likely have been influenced?

(A) Existentialism
(B) The Enlightenment
(C) The Reformation
(D) Scholasticism

33. What is the author's purpose in referring to day and night?

(A) To emphasize the benefits of the light over the dark
(B) To illustrate that the Law of Nature is ever changing
(C) To emphasize that differences do not imply inequality
(D) To show that mulattoes are superior to Africans

34. What is the author's main purpose?

(A) To encourage rebellion among the slaves
(B) To legally end the institution of slavery
(C) To argue for better treatment of slaves
(D) To justify the institution of slavery

35. Which nation's revolution would have been most influenced by the arguments in this essay?

(A) Haiti
(B) France
(C) The United States
(D) Mexico

Questions 36 to 38 refer to the following passage.

Sixteen million Americans either defend their rights or suffer repression at the hands of Spain, which, although once the world's greatest empire is now too weak to rule the new hemisphere. . . . We are a young people . . . young in the ways of almost all the arts and sciences, although, in a certain manner, we are old in the ways of civilized society. . . . But we scarcely retain a vestige of what once was; we are, moreover, neither Indian nor European, but a species midway between the legitimate proprietors of this country and the Spanish usurpers. In short, though Americans by birth we derive our rights from Europe. . . . The monarchs of Spain made a solemn agreement with the discoverers, conquerors, and settlers of America [our social contract] prohibiting them from drawing on the royal treasury. In return, they were made lords of the land, entitled to organize the public administration and act as the court of last appeal, together with many other exemptions and privileges that are too numerous to mention. The King committed himself never to alienate the American provinces, inasmuch as he had no jurisdiction but that of sovereign domain. Thus, for themselves and their descendants, the *conquistadores* possessed what were tantamount to feudal holdings. . . . Americans today, who live within the Spanish system occupy a position in society no better than that of serfs. . . . Yet even this status is surrounded with galling restrictions, such as being forbidden to grow European crops, or to store products which are royal monopolies or to establish factories of a type the Peninsula itself does not possess. To this add the exclusive trading privileges and the barriers between American provinces, designed to prevent all exchange of trade, traffic, and understanding. . . . The American provinces are fighting for their freedom, and they will ultimately succeed. Some . . . will form federal and central republics; the larger areas will inevitably establish monarchies, some of which will fare so badly that they will disintegrate in either present or future revolutions.

—"The Jamaica Letter," Simón Bolívar, September 6, 1815

36. How does Bolívar, a nineteenth-century South American leader in the fight for independence from Spain, justify rebellion?

   (A) He suggests that monarchy is inappropriate to the New World.
   (B) He says that Spain's mercantilist policies keep the inhabitants of the New World weak and members of the lower class.
   (C) He contends that Spain's rule should be replaced by one New World nation.
   (D) He claims that the Peninsula (Spain) should emphasize agriculture in South America.

37. What does Bolívar, mean by "the legitimate proprietors" of the country?

   (A) Young people
   (B) Spaniards born in America
   (C) Indigenous peoples
   (D) Spaniards, by right of conquest

38. Which Enlightenment ideals are evident in Bolívar's, letter?

   (A) Believing in the inherently evil nature of man
   (B) Using laissez-faire economics
   (C) Maintaining social hierarchies
   (D) Accepting political authority

Questions 39 to 41 refer to the following passage.

. . . farmers are sedentary and live amid their own sewage, thus providing microbes with a short path from one person's body into another's drinking water. . . . Sedentary farmers become surrounded . . . by disease transmitting rodents, attracted by farmers' stored food. . . . the rise of cities [and] more densely packed human populations festered under even worse sanitation conditions. . . . The development of world trade routes, effectively joined the populations of Europe, Asia, and North Africa . . . but plague didn't begin to hit Europe with full force as the Black Death epidemics until 1346, when a new route for overland trade with China provided rapid transit, along Eurasia's east-west axis, for flea-infected furs from plague-ridden areas of Central Asia to Europe.

Jared Diamond, *Guns, Germs, and Steel*, 1997

39. According to the author, the preconditions for the spread of infectious diseases included which of the following?

(A) Rural to urban migration
(B) Local, concentrated trade
(C) A rise in the rodent population
(D) The decline of farming

40. The overall tone of this passage, taken as only a partial contextual analysis, is on the whole which of the following?

(A) Condemnatory
(B) Optimistic
(C) Informative
(D) Resigned

41. According to the passage and your knowledge of world history, what should be done to limit the spread of infectious diseases?

(A) Isolate farmers from city dwellers
(B) Curtail international trade
(C) Remove raw sewage from the environment
(D) Store crops only in airtight facilities

Questions 42 to 45 refer to the following passage.

Within a few decades [after Columbus's voyages] the European world would be transformed. The dominant Island of the Earth, a connected body of *land* comprising six-sevenths of the surface, was displaced by a dominant Ocean of the Earth, a connected body of *water* comprising two-thirds of the surface. Never before had the arena of human experience been so suddenly or drastically revised.

Daniel Boorstin, *The Discoverers*, 1983

42. Exploration of a newly defined world, made more of water than of land, would rest on technological innovation, dissemination of which was made possible at first by the work of which groups?

   (A) Soldiers
   (B) Missionaries
   (C) Merchants
   (D) Explorers

43. Technological innovations specifically geared to overseas exploration and discovery included which of the following?

   (A) Cartography
   (B) Shipbuilding
   (C) Magnetic compass
   (D) All of the above

44. How did nation-states promote, sustain, and develop both land-based and maritime empires?

   (A) Through the spread of religion
   (B) The establishment of mercantilistic policies
   (C) The development of profitable industries in newly discovered lands
   (D) Control through force, even war, of national rivals

45. The role of global trade, made possible by technological innovation and the exploration it encouraged, also resulted in which of the following?

   (A) Economic hegemony
   (B) Sociocultural syncretism
   (C) Population decline
   (D) Growth of cottage industries

Questions 46 to 49 refer to the following passage.

We will do everything that depends on us to expand cooperation with socialist states to enhance the role and influence of socialism in world affairs. . . . The Soviet Union has always supported the struggle of peoples for liberation from colonial oppression. And today our sympathies go out to the countries of Asia, Africa and Latin America, which are following the road of consolidating independence and social renovation. For us, they are friends and partners in the struggle for a durable peace, for better and just relations between peoples. (March 1985)

The U.S. is carrying out its gigantic space weapons program and constantly designs and manufactures new weapons...It is a reason for special concern that the arms race is a basis on which the U.S.A. and its closest allies build their adventuristic strategic policy concepts. They are planning to win over socialism through war or military blackmail.[. . .] U.S. top echelons started hoping they would be able to use their considerable technological advantage against the socialist economies. (October 1985)

We are convinced that only through democratization is it possible to build a well-functioning, healthy and dynamic economy. Radical economic reform, which blends together planned regulation and the market, will help us devise a new economic mechanism, harmonize the numerous forms of socialist ownership and economic activities, and give ample room to producers' initiative and enterprise.

We have formulated a new agrarian policy, seeking to tear down the administrative-command system in agriculture; various forms of leasing help to restore the status of farmer-peasant, his right to be in control of land, machinery and the product of his work.

Excerpts from Mikhail Gorbachev's speeches to the Soviet Union Communist Party congress during the 1980s

46. Which best describes the economy of the Soviet Union prior to the 1980s?

   (A) Centrally planned
   (B) Laissez-faire
   (C) Mercantilist
   (D) Privatized

47. Which is a likely contributing factor to the cumulative economic weaknesses in the Soviet Union by the 1980s?

   (A) A series of poor wheat harvests in Ukraine
   (B) Lost revenue from newly independent Baltic states
   (C) Diversion of economic resources to arms race with United States
   (D) High wages paid to newly unionized Soviet workers

48. What was the long-term impact of the new policy of economic and political openness under Gorbachev?

   (A) The Communist Party's support was strengthened domestically.
   (B) Demand for greater political and economic freedoms undermined the Soviet Union.
   (C) Loyalty of satellite countries like Bulgaria and Romania intensified.
   (D) The Soviet Union government became a Western-style democracy.

49. Which other communist nation has experimented with limited private enterprise?

   (A) China under Deng Xiaoping
   (B) Cuba under Fidel Castro
   (C) China under Mao Zedong
   (D) North Korea under Kim Il-Sung

Questions 50 to 52 refer to the following passage.

U.N. Resolution 181 (II). Future government of Palestine
A

The General Assembly,

Having met in special session at the request of the mandatory Power to constitute and instruct a special committee to prepare for the consideration of the question of the future government of Palestine at the second regular session; [. . .]

Having received and examined the report of the Special Committee (document A/364) 1/ including a number of unanimous recommendations and a plan of partition with economic union approved by the majority of the Special Committee,

Considers that the present situation in Palestine is one which is likely to impair the general welfare and friendly relations among nations; [. . .]

Recommends to the United Kingdom, as the mandatory Power for Palestine, and to all other Members of the United Nations the adoption and implementation, with regard to the future government of Palestine, of the Plan of Partition with Economic Union set out below; [. . .]

PLAN OF PARTITION WITH ECONOMIC UNION . . . 3. Independent Arab and Jewish States and the Special International Regime for the City of Jerusalem, set forth in part III of this plan, shall come into existence in Palestine two months after the evacuation of the armed forces of the mandatory Power has been completed but in any case not later than 1 October 1948. The boundaries of the Arab State, the Jewish State, and the City of Jerusalem shall be as described in parts II and III below.

50. Which best describes the Mandate System to which the passage makes reference?

   (A) A system imposing a religious government on a subject state
   (B) A system of totalitarian government
   (C) A system of tariffs and trade preferences in East Asia
   (D) A system of political "guardianship" by Western Allies after WWI

51. Based on the passage, what was a key point of conflict between the two parties?

   (A) Reduction in nuclear weapons
   (B) Agreements against use of terrorism
   (C) Control of Jerusalem and other holy sites
   (D) Building of settlements on contested land

52. The formation of which other state is the most similar to the situation in the passage?
   (A) Pakistan
   (B) Liberia
   (C) Taiwan
   (D) Estonia

Questions 53 to 55 refer to the map/chart below.

Life expectancy, 2019

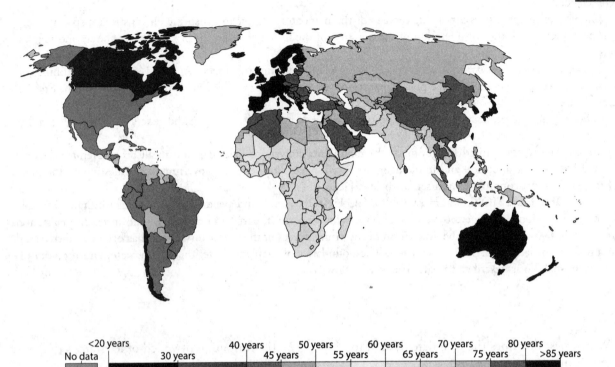

	<20 years		40 years	50 years	60 years	70 years	80 years	
No data		30 years	45 years	55 years	65 years	75 years		>85 years

Source: https://ourworldindata.org/life-expectancy.

53. Which of the following is true based on the data shown?

(A) Life expectancy is increasing worldwide.

(B) Life expectancy is increasing the most in places like Western Europe, Canada, and Australia.

(C) Life expectancy is generally lower in African countries than in other regions.

(D) Life expectancy is generally higher in Asian countries than in other regions.

54. Using the chart and your knowledge of world history, what health patterns might one expect to see in countries like Australia, France, or Canada?

(A) High rates of diseases like heart disease and Alzheimer's.

(B) Lower rates of asthma in countries like India and Russia.

(C) High rates of infant mortality in China.

(D) Greater exposure to pandemics caused by new diseases

55. Which of the following is the most likely cause of lower life expectancy across the continent of Africa?

(A) Increased access to birth control and family planning services for women

(B) Greater incidence of diseases associated with poverty like malaria, tuberculosis, and cholera

(C) Increased desertification has disrupted agricultural patterns

(D) The intervention of international organizations such as the World Health Organization (WHO)

GO ON TO PART B

PART B: SHORT-ANSWER QUESTIONS

Recommended Time for Part B—40 minutes

Directions: You need to answer a total of three short-answer questions. You are required to answer questions 1 and 2, but you may choose to answer either question 3 or question 4. The short-answer questions are divided into parts; answer all parts of the question. Each question is worth a total of three points. Note that short-answer questions are not essay questions—they do not require the development and support of a thesis statement.

Question 1 refers to the following passage.

Water supply almost entirely from shallow wells, often uncovered, mostly in the cottage garden, not far from a pervious privy pit, or a huge collection of house refuse, polluted by the foulness soaking into it. The liquid manure from the pigsty trickles through the ground into the well. Often after heavy rain the cottagers complain that their wellwater becomes thick. . . . In these days of investigation and statistics, where results are described with microscopic exactness and tabulated with mathematical accuracy, we seem to think figures will do instead of facts, and calculation instead of action. We remember the policeman who watched his burglar enter the house, and waited to make quite sure whether he was going to commit robbery with violence or without, before interfering with his operations. So as we reach such an account as this we seem to be watching, not robbery, but murder going on, and to be waiting for the rates of mortality to go up before we interfere; we wait to see how many of the children playing round the houses shall be stricken down. We wait to see whether the filth will really trickle into the well, and whether the foul water really will poison the family, and how many will die of it. And then, when enough have died, we think it time to spend some money and some trouble to stop the murders going further, and we enter the results of our 'masterly inactivity' neatly in tables; but we do not analyse and tabulate the saddened lives of those who remain.

Florence Nightingale, *Rural Hygiene*, 1854

1. Answer Parts A and B.

   A. Discuss TWO sources of the pollution of well water in rural areas during the nineteenth century.

   B. Explain ONE factor involved in the action, or inaction, of the government to remedy the situation.

Question 2 refers to the excerpted poems below.

If I should die, think only this of me:
That there's some corner of a foreign field
That is for ever England. There shall be
In that rich earth a richer dust concealed . . .

"The Soldier," Rupert Brooke, Nov.–Dec. 1914

Does it matter?—losing your legs? . . .
For people will always be kind,
And you need not show that you mind.

. . .
Does it matter?—losing your sight? . . .

There's such splendid work for the blind;
And people will always be kind,
As you sit on the terrace remembering
And turning your face to the light.

. . .
Do they matter?—those dreams from the pit?
You can drink and forget and be glad,
And people won't say that you're mad;
For they'll know you've fought for your country
And no one will worry a bit.

"Does It Matter," Siegfried Sassoon, 1918

2. Answer Parts A and B.

  A. Discuss TWO changes in attitudes evident in
     these poems from the beginning (1914) and
     the end (1918) of World War I.

  B. Identify ONE example of a soldier's disillu-
     sionment with war.

Answer EITHER question 3 OR question 4.

Syncretism refers to the combination of cultural elements, such as the Buddha clothed in Greek fashions from the
Hellenistic Age or the mix of architectural elements (medieval and Renaissance) in a single building.

3. Answer Parts A and B.

  A. Discuss TWO examples of syncretism in
     the Eastern Hemisphere. Consider religion,
     the arts, and governmental institutions and
     practices, for example.
  B. Identify ONE example of syncretism in
     either Latin America or sub-Saharan Africa.

4. Answer Parts A and B.

  A. The collapse of modern empires (Ottoman,
     Ching, British) shows many discrete char-
     acteristics and causes. Discuss ONE cause
     for the fall of empires in the modern period
     (the nineteenth and twentieth centuries).
  B. Explain TWO reasons for the fall of
     empires that most societies have had in
     common.

STOP. END OF SECTION I.

Section II

Time: 100 minutes

PART A: DOCUMENT-BASED QUESTION (DBQ)

Recommended reading time for Part A—15 minutes
Recommended writing time for Part A—45 minutes

Directions: The question is based on the following documents. The documents have been edited and adapted for this exam.

- Read the question carefully.
- Then read all the documents.
- Create a thesis that addresses the entire question.
- Describe a wider historical context that is relevant to your thesis and the prompt.
- Analyze the documents that support your thesis. You must use all of the documents.
- Give careful attention to the purpose, point of view, source, and historical context of each document.
- Do NOT list the documents or analyze them one at a time in your essay; they should be incorporated into your argument.
- Bring in historical examples that support your argument.
- Create a persuasive essay that upholds your thesis, connects your argument to historical context, and draws conclusions.

1. Using the following documents and your knowledge of world history, discuss the evolution of the concept of human rights from 1215 to the present. Analyze universal and national changes.

Document 1

Magna Carta
1215 CE

JOHN, by the grace of God King of England, Lord of Ireland, Duke of Normandy and Aquitaine, and Count of Anjou, . . . TO ALL FREE MEN OF OUR KINGDOM we have also granted, for us and our heirs for ever, all the liberties written out below, to have and to keep for them and their heirs, of us and our heirs: (6) Heirs may be given in marriage, but not to someone of lower social standing. Before a marriage takes place, it shall be made known to the heir's next-of-kin.

(7) At her husband's death, a widow may have her marriage portion and inheritance at once and without trouble. She shall pay nothing for her dower, marriage portion, or any inheritance that she and her husband held jointly on the day of his death. She may remain in her husband's house for forty days after his death, and within this period her dower shall be assigned to her.

(8) No widow shall be compelled to marry, so long as she wishes to remain without a husband. But she must give security that she will not marry without royal consent, if she holds her lands of the Crown, or without the consent of whatever other lord she may hold them of.

(9) Neither we nor our officials will seize any land or rent in payment of a debt, so long as the debtor has movable goods sufficient to discharge the debt.

Document 2

Recopilación de leyes de las Indias
1680

Those [Colonists] who should want to make a commitment to building a new settlement in the form and manner already prescribed, be it of more or less than 30 vecinos (freemen), (know that) it should be of no less than twelve persons and be awarded the authorization and territory in accordance with the prescribed conditions.

Having made the selection of the site where the town is to be built, it must, as already stated, be in an elevated and healthy location; [be] with means of fortification; [have] fertile soil and with plenty of land for farming and pasturage; have fuel, timber, and resources; [have] fresh water, a native population, ease of transport, access and exit; [and be] open to the north wind; and, if on the coast, due consideration should be paid to the quality of the harbor and that the sea does not lie to the south or west; and if possible not near lagoons or marshes in which poisonous animals and polluted air and water breed.

They [Colonists] shall try as far as possible to have the buildings all of one type for the sake of the beauty of the town.

Within the town, a commons shall be delimited, large enough that although the population may experience a rapid expansion, there will always be sufficient space where the people may go to for recreation and take their cattle to pasture without them making any damage.

The site and building lots for slaughter houses, fisheries, tanneries, and other business which produce filth shall be so placed that the filth can easily be disposed of

Document 3

French Declaration of the Rights of Man and of the Citizen
1789

The representatives of the French people, constituted as a National Assembly, and considering that ignorance, neglect, or contempt of the rights of man are the sole causes of public misfortunes and governmental corruption, have resolved to set forth in a solemn declaration the natural, inalienable and sacred rights of man: so that by being constantly present to all the members of the social body this declaration may always remind them of their rights and duties; so that by being liable at every moment to comparison with the aim of any and all political institutions the acts of the legislative and executive powers may be the more fully respected; and so that by being founded henceforward on simple and incontestable principles the demands of the citizens may always tend toward maintaining the constitution and the general welfare.

In consequence, the National Assembly recognizes and declares, in the presence and under the auspices of the Supreme Being, the following rights of man and the citizen:

1. Men are born and remain free and equal in rights. Social distinctions may be based only on common utility.
2. The purpose of all political association is the preservation of the natural and imprescriptible rights of man. These rights are liberty, property, security, and resistance to oppression.
3. The principle of all sovereignty rests essentially in the nation. No body and no individual may exercise authority which does not emanate expressly from the nation.
4. Liberty consists in the ability to do whatever does not harm another; hence the exercise of the natural rights of each man has no other limits than those which assure to other members of society the enjoyment of the same rights. These limits can only be determined by the law.

5. The law only has the right to prohibit those actions which are injurious to society. No hindrance should be put in the way of anything not prohibited by the law, nor may any one be forced to do what the law does not require.
6. The law is the expression of the general will.

Document 4

United States of America Bill of Rights
1791

RESOLVED by the Senate and House of Representatives of the United States of America, in Congress assembled, two thirds of both Houses concurring, that the following Articles be proposed to the Legislatures of the several States, as amendments to the Constitution of the United States, all, or any of which Articles, when ratified by three fourths of the said Legislatures, to be valid to all intents and purposes, as part of the said Constitution . . . **Article the third**. . . Congress shall make no law respecting an establishment of religion, or prohibiting the free exercise thereof; or abridging the freedom of speech, or of the press; or the right of the people peaceably to assemble, and to petition the Government for a redress of grievances. . . . **Article the sixth**. . . .The right of the people to be secure in their persons, houses, papers, and effects, against unreasonable searches and seizures, shall not be violated, and no Warrants shall issue, but upon probable cause, supported by Oath or affirmation, and particularly describing the place to be searched, and the persons or things to be seized.

Document 5

The Universal Declaration of Human Rights
1948

PREAMBLE
Whereas recognition of the inherent dignity and of the equal and inalienable rights of all members of the human family is the foundation of freedom, justice and peace in the world,

Whereas disregard and contempt for human rights have resulted in barbarous acts which have outraged the conscience of mankind, and the advent of a world in which human beings shall enjoy freedom of speech and belief and freedom from fear and want has been proclaimed as the highest aspiration of the common people,

Whereas it is essential, if man is not to be compelled to have recourse, as a last resort, to rebellion against tyranny and oppression, that human rights should be protected by the rule of law,

Whereas it is essential to promote the development of friendly relations between nations,

Whereas the peoples of the United Nations have in the Charter reaffirmed their faith in fundamental human rights, in the dignity and worth of the human person and in the equal rights of men and women and have determined to promote social progress and better standards of life in larger freedom,

Whereas Member States have pledged themselves to achieve, in co-operation with the United Nations, the promotion of universal respect for and observance of human rights and fundamental freedoms,

Whereas a common understanding of these rights and freedoms is of the greatest importance for the full realization of this pledge,

Now, Therefore THE GENERAL ASSEMBLY proclaims THIS UNIVERSAL DECLARATION OF HUMAN RIGHTS as a common standard of achievement for all peoples and all nations, to the end that every individual and every organ of society, keeping this Declaration constantly in mind, shall strive by teaching and education to promote respect for these rights and freedoms and by progressive measures, national and international, to secure their universal and effective recognition and observance, both among the peoples of Member States themselves and among the peoples of territories under their jurisdiction.

Document 6

The Cairo Declaration of Human Rights
1990

The Member States of the Organization of the Islamic Conference,

Reaffirming the civilizing and historical role of the Islamic Ummah which Allah made as the best community and which gave humanity a universal and well-balanced civilization, in which harmony is established between hereunder and the hereafter, knowledge is combined with faith, and to fulfill the expectations from this community to guide all humanity which is confused because of different and conflicting beliefs and ideologies and to provide solutions for all chronic problems of this materialistic civilization.

In contribution to the efforts of mankind to assert human rights, to protect man from exploitation and persecution, and to affirm his freedom and right to a dignified life in accordance with the Islamic Shari'ah.

Convinced that mankind which has reached an advanced stage in materialistic science is still, and shall remain, in dire need of faith to support its civilization as well as a self motivating force to guard its rights;

Believing that fundamental rights and freedoms according to Islam are an integral part of the Islamic religion and that no one shall have the right as a matter of principle to abolish them either in whole or in part or to violate or ignore them in as much as they are binding divine commands, which are contained in the Revealed Books of Allah and which were sent through the last of His Prophets to complete the preceding divine messages and that safeguarding those fundamental rights and freedoms is an act of worship whereas the neglect or violation thereof is an abominable sin, and that the safeguarding of those fundamental rights and freedom is an individual responsibility of every person and a collective responsibility of the entire Ummah;

ARTICLE 6:

(a) Woman is equal to man in human dignity, and has her own rights to enjoy as well as duties to perform, and has her own civil entity and financial independence, and the right to retain her name and lineage.
(b) Human beings are born free, and no one has the right to enslave, humiliate, oppress or exploit them, and there can be no subjugation but to Allah the Almighty.
(c) Colonialism of all types being one of the most evil forms of enslavement is totally prohibited. Peoples suffering from colonialism have the full right to freedom and self-determination. It is the duty of all States peoples to support the struggle of colonized peoples for the liquidation of all forms of and occupation, and all States and peoples have the right to preserve their independent identity and control over their wealth and natural resources.

Document 7

> 1967 ASEAN DECLARATION Bangkok, Thailand on 8 August 1967
>
> [http://www.aseansec.org/1212.htm]
>
> The Presidium Minister for Political Affairs/Minister for Foreign Affairs of Indonesia, the Deputy Prime Minister of Malaysia, the Secretary of Foreign Affairs of the Philippines, the Minister for Foreign Affairs of Singapore and the Minister of Foreign Affairs of Thailand:
>
> **MINDFUL** of the existence of mutual interests and common problems among countries of South-East Asia and convinced of the need to strengthen further the existing bonds of regional solidarity and cooperation;
>
> **DESIRING** to establish a firm foundation for common action to promote regional cooperation in South-East Asia in the spirit of equality and partnership and thereby contribute towards peace, progress and prosperity in the region;
>
> **CONSCIOUS** that in an increasingly interdependent world, the cherished ideals of peace, freedom, social justice and economic well-being are best attained by fostering good understanding, good neighbourliness and meaningful cooperation among the countries of the region already bound together by ties of history and culture;
>
> **CONSIDERING** that the countries of South East Asia share a primary responsibility for strengthening the economic and social stability of the region and ensuring their peaceful and progressive national development, and that they are determined to ensure their stability and security from external interference in any form or manifestation in order to preserve their national identities in accordance with the ideals and aspirations of their peoples;
>
> **AFFIRMING** that all foreign bases are temporary and remain only with the expressed concurrence of the countries concerned and are not intended to be used directly or indirectly to subvert the national independence and freedom of States in the area or prejudice the orderly processes of their national development;
>
> **DO HEREBY DECLARE:**
>
> **FIRST,** the establishment of an Association for Regional Cooperation among the countries of South-East Asia to be known as the Association of South-East Asian Nations (ASEAN).
>
> **SECOND,** that the aims and purposes of the Association shall be:
> 1. To accelerate the economic growth, social progress and cultural development in the region through joint endeavours in the spirit of equality and partnership in order to strengthen the foundation for a prosperous and peaceful community of South-East Asian Nations;
> 2. To promote regional peace and stability through abiding respect for justice and the rule of law in the relationship among countries of the region and adherence to the principles of the United Nations Charter.

GO ON TO PART B

PART B: LONG-ESSAY QUESTION

Recommended Time for Part B—40 minutes

Directions: Answer ONE of the following questions.

1. Using specific examples, discuss short-term and long-term effects, or legacies, of European imperialism.
2. Using specific examples, discuss five legacies that the British Empire left the modern world.
3. Using specific examples, discuss five legacies that the Spanish Empire left the modern world.

STOP. END OF SECTION II.

› Answers and Explanations

Section I, Part A: Multiple-Choice

1. **C** By discussing the safety of the Japanese troops, the radio broadcasters hope to emphasize the futility of any attack by American soldiers. Both A and B are incorrect because they both reference high levels of support and effort back in the United States, which is contradicted by the headlines cited by Tokyo Rose. The passage does not reference technological superiority of Japanese troops but, rather, their superior position in Iwo Jima.

2. **B** These terms are supposed to evoke familial ties (sister, brother) or credibility (Truth) to increase their emotional appeal. A is incorrect, as the terms "sister" and "brothers" are metaphorical, rather than strictly accurate. C is incorrect because the target audience is not the war command (of either side) but, rather, the enlisted soldiers who will actually participate in the raid. D is incorrect because the intent is not to recruit new soldiers but, rather, weaken the resolve of those already in the U.S. military.

3. **C** The phrase makes it clear that the powers directing the war are far from the action. The overall tone of the passage is directed at supporting the sense of futility and worthless efforts of those on the front lines (A, B, D).

4. **D** The passage establishes that Mansa Musa encouraged and protected trades, established closer relations with other rulers (diplomacy), and was a patron to many scholars. Although he did encourage mass education, there is no mention of universal military service (B) or that he required all citizens to perform the Hajj (C). While Mansa Musa was a devout Muslim and provided government support for Islamic scholars and jurists, there is nothing in the passage to indicate that other religions were banned.

5. **A** In order to spread both religion and education, Mansa Musa imported expertise of various kinds. He strengthened trade and imperial relations (B, D), but is not known for singling out existing traditions (C) as needing shoring up.

6. **C** Trade routes are often the routes of cultural diffusion, or the spread of ideas, as indicated by the descriptions of the legal and religious scholars whom Mansa Musa brought to Mali, as well as many books. The passage does not discuss diseases (A) or weaponry (B) or medicines (D), although all of these have certainly been spread via trade routes in other historical eras and regions.

7. **C** The narrator describes Gunga Din as "black-faced" and "[s]quidgy-nosed old idol." He also describes Gunga Din's physical appearance in terms of his clothing, as rags that didn't cover much in front or behind. All of these would have been British stereotypes of native populations. Although the language is a colloquial dialect, it is that of the narrator, not Gunga Din (D). The passage does not focus on battle descriptions, except to say that the water carrier was always "right flank rear," which doesn't connect to stereotypes of indigenous peoples (B). The passage doesn't use animal imagery to refer to Gunga Din (A).

8. **B** In the poem, despite prior harsh treatment at the hands of the narrator ("I've belted you and flayed you"), Gunga Din pulled him to safety during battle and even gave him a drink, despite his own fatal wounds. Although Gunga Din was able to carry the narrator, there is no direct reference to Gunga Din's physical prowess (A). Because the comment about Gunga Din being the better man was in response to his kindness toward his abuser, even as Gunga Din was dying, B is the better choice. Though Gunga Din was in the army, he was only a water carrier, and there is no indication he had battle knowledge (C). Likewise the only reference to religion is "by the livin' Gawd that made you" that is stated by the narrator and thus does not reveal anything about Gunga Din's religious nature (D).

9. C By showcasing the selflessness of the simple water carrier and claiming that he is a better man than the British narrator, Kipling is implicitly criticizing the cultural superiority underlying the "white man's burden." Although the beginning of the poem describes Gunga Din in a somewhat condescending manner (D), leading you to think that he is either accepting (A) or resigned (B) to the white man's burden, none of these is the best choice, since the point of the poem is the transformation of the narrator's attitude at the end.

10. B The theory of Social Darwinism, which is Darwin's theory of natural selection applied to human societies through the lens of class, race, or culture, is often associated with European imperialism and the "white man's burden." Socialist Realism was an artistic style in twentieth-century communist countries, which means it is from the wrong era (A). Marxism is the theory of history as a series of economic stages culminating in communism. Although it was developed in the nineteenth century, it focused on conflict between economic classes in capitalist economies, not imperialism or nationalities (C). Positivism refers to a Western philosophy that the only true knowledge is based on data or experience and not metaphysical ideas or theories. Since this poem is not about data or science and references the "livin' Gawd," (D) is not the correct choice.

11. C The perspective of the cartoonist is that the United States has been a savior to the nations brought under its control, saving them from poverty or oppression and bringing them trade, prosperity, and democratic governments. Although one might be tempted to cast the United States in the role of imperialist (B), the purpose of the cartoon is to highlight the positive transformation of the people due to their "rescue" by the United States, rather than the benefits to the United States. Because the cartoon claims the people are better off for having been "rescued" by the United States, the United States is not seen as an oppressor (A). Since isolationists do not support foreign intervention, (D) cannot be the correct answer.

12. A The Treaty of Paris was signed in 1898, ending the Spanish-American War, guaranteeing Cuban independence and granting the United States rights to Guam, Puerto Rico, and the Philippines. Since there are many treaties signed in Paris, one way to approach this question is by process of elimination. The Treaty of Tordesillas was signed by Portugal and Spain, recognizing the Pope's Line of Demarcation that divided the Americas between Portugal and Spain. The Treaty of Guadalupe-Hidalgo ended the Mexican-American War, resulted in the United States acquiring territory in the southwestern United States, and recognized the Rio Grande River as the border between the United States and Texas (D). The Treaty of Westphalia was signed in 1648, ending the Thirty Years' War fought in the Holy Roman Empire primarily over conflicts between Protestant and Catholic states (C).

13. D Dollar diplomacy was used by President Taft to extend U.S. influence throughout Central and South America through economic means, like guaranteed loans, rather than military might. Gunboat diplomacy uses a nation's superior naval force to blockade, attack, or otherwise force concessions from another country. Thus, it would not mitigate (lessen) the Roosevelt Corollary but, rather, strengthen it (A). Humanism refers to a school of thought that focuses on the individual and his potential for good, rational thought and worldly life rather than the afterlife. It is most often associated with the Renaissance period in Europe and is therefore unrelated to the topic (B). Revisionism may seem like a possible choice, in that it means changing one's interpretation of an idea, but it is most often applied to followers of Marx who reject his ideas of violent conflict in favor of a less violent evolution of economic stages (C).

14. A Castiglione states that he has not laid martial (military) duties on them because he is fashioning or creating a court lady, not a queen. In this statement, he implies that queens must have knowledge of military matters but that this is not necessary for court ladies. At the end of the passage, Castiglione states many women in history have been learned in philosophy, poetry, and law/rhetoric. This comes right after the statement about queens who have governed kingdoms with prudence and justice, implying that queens, too, should know the sciences (A). The beginning of the passage emphasizes a lady's need to master music, dancing, and the art of witty conversation to entertain appropriately (C). They also must "have knowledge of letters," which means they must be literate (D).

15. **A** Renaissance humanist focused on the potential of all individuals, as well as looking to classical Greece and Rome for inspiration. Because Castiglione emphasizes that women should master a variety of skills, including dancing, painting, poetry, and "knowledge of letters," his views are consistent with individuals maximizing their potential, as well as the idea of a classical or well-rounded education. This directly contradicts D. While Castiglione might value military skill, this is not the primary focus of the passage, nor is it part of the humanist philosophy (B). The passage briefly discusses philosophy, but not Greek philosophy specifically, and does not address Christian theology (D).

16. **D** The Mongol Empire allowed women the most freedom of any of the choices. Although the Mongol Empire was patriarchal, there is evidence that some women were warriors, herders, property owners, and advisers to leaders. In Song China, the rise of neo-Confucianism limited women's rights. They were expected to remain indoors, obey husbands or sons, and refrain from discussing the matters of men (A). The Tokugawa Shogunate was also influenced by neo-Confucian ideals. Women, especially from the elite classes (which is what the passage discusses), were also expected to remain in the home and remain subservient to male family members (C). Similarly, in the Abbasid Empire, women (at least in the elite classes) were expected to cloister themselves and refrain from public life (B).

17. **A** The image shows a quintessentially American fast-food restaurant, McDonald's, located in Shenzhen, China. This illustrates the concept of globalization, which is characterized by interaction and integration of corporations and people on an international scale. Nationalism, or extreme pride in one's own nation and

national traditions, would be the opposite of this in many ways, with people preferring traditional foods (B). Syncretism refers to a blending of cultural beliefs but is usually used in the context of religion or art (C). Traditionally, communist societies are opposed to capitalist organizations like McDonald's (D).

18. **C** One consequence of global economies is that the economic situation in one country can affect the economies of other nations. In this situation, if China experiences an economic decline, it will affect McDonald's profits. By seeking out cheaper labor markets with weaker regulations, corporations have weakened the conditions and bargaining power of workers (A). Globalization has also led to migration as labor flows to find available work, especially in urban areas (B). Being located in a different country does not necessarily mean that the corporation will adopt that nation's economic practices, however (D).

19. **D** When Chinese students gathered in Tiananmen Square to demand greater freedoms, the Chinese government responded by sending the military, who fired upon its own citizens. The Marshall Plan was implemented in post-WWII Europe to bolster damaged Western European economies against the spread of communism, resulting in stronger democratic governments. The formation of the European Union is an agreement among Western European nations to form a free-trade zone with a political organization to legislate on matters requiring regional cooperation (C). Although Britain's withdrawal from the European Union stands as a counterpoint to this cooperation, it is not an authoritarian regime, nor does it constitute a violation of human rights (A).

20. **C** The author states that "it is by merit that men rise in the [Sultan's] service" and that "this is the reason they are successful." The phrase "no single man owed his position to aught save his valor or merit" means that he only owes his position to those qualities. "Aught save" means "nothing except" (A). The author does not feel the Austrian system of allocating positions according to birth is not preferable. On the contrary, he is using it as a contrast to the Ottoman's very successful system. (B) Although

the Ottoman bureaucracy may have gotten too large eventually, this is not reflected in the passage (D).

21. **D** The Tang and Song dynasties developed a merit-based civil service in which applicants took a test based on Confucian texts to demonstrate their ability, regardless of social class, in theory. Although Louis XIV did hire some "intendants" from the middle classes, these were not based on objective demonstrations of competence, but more on personal loyalty and Louis XIV's desire to weaken the power of the nobility (A). Neither the Aztecs nor the Athenians were noted for their effective bureaucracies (B, C).

22. **B** The passage describes the Turkish army as being very self-restrained with respect to rations, saving them for emergencies. By taking the bare minimum needed for survival, they are the opposite of overindulged (A), and by planning for possible emergencies, they are the opposite of shortsighted (D). Although the passage does not directly address the equality of the troops, and is therefore not the best choice, it does mention the Janissaries as distinct from other royal troops, implying that they might not all be equal (C).

23. **B** According to the passage, the Janissaries would ask for "largesses" (essentially gifts or bribes) to secure their loyalty, or risk them supporting a rival for the throne. The Janissaries were the Ottoman sultan's household guards, originally Christian youth taken from conquered provinces in Central Europe or the Balkans, and therefore owing no loyalty to the Turkish people (D). They were considered elite soldiers (C). Although they often required bribes to favor one candidate for sultan over another, to say they demanded the greatest and richest resources would be too extreme (A).

24. **B** The passage makes reference to wagons and to loading the dwellings on them, all of which indicates temporary housing, which can be easily transported. While they lived in the steppes of Central Asia and not cities (C), they would not have been considered "bucolic," which refers to a pleasant, romanticized view

of the countryside (A). Given that they did not have fixed settlements and tended to herds rather than fields and crops, they were not agricultural (D).

25. **B** The passage describes the roles of Mongol men and women, giving their tasks equal consideration, both of which are equally critical to their survival. This type of society often leads to more gender equality than agriculturally based ones. There is no discussion of social classes within the passage (A). Nor does the passage discuss political alliances, although the Mongols were largely self-sustaining (C). The passage doesn't indicate any new technology or innovations but, rather, a continuation of traditional patterns (D).

26. **B** Hardy best describes the Mongols who, according to the passage, can endure "every kind of privation," stay on horseback for days, and survive for a month on the milk of a mare. The passage gives no indication of lightheartedness or fun, which would support a conclusion that they are carefree (B), nor is there any indication that they found their lifestyle disagreeable but suffered it anyway (C). As discussed earlier, there is no indication that they broke away from their traditional patterns of living, which means they are not innovative (D).

27. **D** The Mongols' maneuverable and skilled cavalry, together with their ruthless tactics, enabled them to conquer territory from Russia to Persia to China. Eventually this would facilitate the flow of trade and ideas, but that was not directly due to their military prowess, and thus, (A) is not the best choice. Although there were interclan wars early in their history, the question asks for the long-term effects, which occur after they were united under Chinggis Khan (B). Once the Mongol Empire was established, it was known for being tolerant of local religions, which meant that there was little incentive to adopt the Mongol religion (C).

28. **A** The passage indicates that the quipu were used for all kinds of historical data, from recording arms, to the census, to the number of battles or diplomatic speeches. They were not merely artwork (B). Because of the variety

of things the quipu was used for, (D) is insufficient. Since the quipu could only record numerical data, it could not provide the kind of information required for a road map (C).

29. **A** African griots maintained the oral traditions and history of their people in the same way the quipucamayus did. A European priest (B) and a Native American shaman (D) would be the keepers of religious traditions, but there is no indication the quipucamayus held any religious significance. Finally, Japanese samurai are warriors, but the quipucamayus are historians (C).

30. **D** The author states that the quipucamayus' responsibility was so great they were exempted from all other kinds of service, which means they had no other responsibilities save that as keeper of the history. It also states that they were exempted from all tribute, but (A) specifies low tribute, which makes it incorrect. Though the quipucamayu memorized speeches and recorded military data, there is no indication that they wrote speeches (C) or served in the military (B).

31. **B** The passage explicitly states that one of the functions of the quipu was to record the census of the empire. Although the quipu was used to records numbers of weapons, it could only record raw numbers and thus couldn't accurately record the effectiveness of troops (C). Similarly, though it could record the numbers of people in various age cohorts, it couldn't be used to extrapolate life expectancy, as it didn't record age at death (D). The use of the quipu appears to be confined to government records and data; therefore, it could not be used to track amounts or types of goods that were traded, which is a key part of economic activity (A).

32. **B** Olympe de Gouges was most influenced by the Enlightenment. This can be determined by the date (1788) as well as the topics she addresses: equality, nature of man, and a just society. Existentialism is a philosophy dedicated to examining human choice in an essentially purposeless universe. It developed in the nineteenth century and gained prominence in the 1930s, and is therefore out of the time period (A). Both the Reformation (a sixteenth-century movement criticizing practices of the Catholic Church) and Scholasticism (a medieval movement attempting to reconcile reason and the Catholic faith) were both overtly religious and also significantly predate this passage (C and D, respectively).

33. **C** The author discusses day and night as an extension of the previous line, which describes all of the variation in Nature as being natural and, therefore, none is inferior. We know she is not suggesting the benefits of light over dark because elsewhere she says that the "white race" is similar in that there are variations (blonde/brunette), but we do not claim one is superior to the other (A). Although there is a cycle with day and night, the preceding lines about Nature's variation, together with the phrase "everything is different," shows that the author's point is about differences throughout Nature and not its changing nature (B). In the same vein, the author is saying that Europeans do not consider mulattos superior to Negroes, even though the degree of their difference is similar to the difference between blondes and brunettes (D).

34. **B** There are multiple indications that the author is opposed to slavery altogether rather than just arguing for better treatment of slaves. These include the phrase "people are equal everywhere" as well as her exclamation "Trading people! Heavens! And Nature does not quake?" We can then infer that the author prefers ending slavery to mere improvement of conditions (C). The target audience is not slaves themselves, so the purpose is unlikely to be encouraging a slave rebellion (A). Finally it is clear from her tone and description of the slave owners ("monstrous," "barbaric") that she is not defending the institution of slavery.

35. **A** The most likely group influenced by writings like this would be the Haitians in their revolution against France, since that was the only revolution in which black people (slaves and former slaves) successfully ousted the European colonial power. The French Revolution occurred shortly after this writing, but that revolution was primarily class-based and driven by desire for economic and political rights (B).

The revolution in the United States in 1776 occurred before this passage was written. Additionally, as a nation with an economic interest in the slave trade, this issue would have been more divisive than unifying (C). Finally, the Mexican Revolution occurred in 1910, more than 100 years after this passage was written. It was fought primarily over the dictator Porfirio Diaz's policies favoring wealthy landowners at the expense of the poor but not over slavery (D).

36. **B** Bolivar's complaints about the Spanish treatment of Latin America center around typical mercantilist policies like a prohibition on economic activity, which would compete with Spain's, as well as trade barriers (tariffs). We know he does not abhor all monarchies (A) or expect a single Latin World nation (C), since he says some will form monarchies and others republics. He also isn't in favor of agriculture exclusively, since he also criticizes the ban on factories, which might provide competition with Spain. Rather, he is opposed to the restrictions on the types of crops they are allowed to cultivate (D).

37. **C** One can infer that Bolivar considers the indigenous people to be the "legitimate proprietors" of the nation, in that he claims that they are neither Indian nor European but midway between the legitimate proprietors and the Spanish usurpers. If the Europeans are the Spanish usurpers, that would make the Indians the legitimate proprietors (D). The subject under discussion, the ones in between, are likely the Spanish born in the Americas (B). When he describes his people as young, he means they are young as a nation, not in terms of chronological age (A).

38. **B** Since Bolívar's complaints are regarding the traditional landholding system and mercantilist policies, one can infer that he favors laissez-faire economics, which eliminates trade restrictions and is, in some ways, the antithesis of mercantilism. By stating that the American provinces are fighting for their freedom, Bolívar implies a resistance to traditional political authority, rather than acceptance (D). By comparing their social position to feudal serfs (which had been abolished in Europe), he similarly critiques the social hierarchies (C). He does not discuss human nature in the passage at all (A).

39. **A** The rural-to-urban population migration that accompanied the Industrial Revolution from 1750 onward worsened conditions that were already dismal. Crowded cities became more crowded, overloading already overloaded existing sanitation resources, and advances in sanitation resources were lacking. Trade was expanding rather than concentrated (B). The rise in the number of rodents followed population increases and density (C), as did an agricultural decline (D).

40. **C** The author refrains from making any judgments (A, B, C) and simply states facts.

41. **C** Raw sewage precedes other elements that act as disease vectors, and removing it from the environment is the obvious first step to limiting or ending other preconditions for the spread of infectious diseases. Isolating or segregating populations (A), curtailing international trade (B), and storing all crops in airtight containers (D) are all impractical, as well as nearly impossible.

42. **C** The impetus to exploration was primarily trade, and from the Silk Roads on in history, and the realization that travel to resources was more easily accomplished by sea than over land, merchants would make up the majority of early travelers. Their creation of maritime empires rested on technological advances like the astrolabe and magnetic compass and more efficient ships and sails. Explorers (D), soldiers (A), and missionaries (B) were, however, quick to follow.

43. **D** Cartography (A), shipbuilding (B), and the magnetic compass (C) all contributed to opening up means of exploration and discovery.

44. **B** Mercantilism, or the economic system based on the belief that wealth—particularly in the form of gold and silver—equaled power and that to accrue wealth and maintain power required a favorable balance of trade (meaning that a country sold more than it bought). By acquiring through any means possible, gold, silver, and raw materials, mercantilists could take "wealth" home, manufacture goods at a

low cost, and sell such goods back to those who were the source of this wealth. The spread of religion (A) often led to antagonisms between the church and mercantilists. Local industry in discovered lands was not just discouraged, it was often legally forbidden, even on a small scale (C). Wars followed after one country had established control over sources of wealth that a rival country desired (D).

45. **B** Inevitably, encounters between different cultures and civilizations led to a kind of acculturation, or the mixing of social, cultural, religious, and even political elements (syncretism). Syncretism involves borrowing and adapting institutional, intellectual, or artistic elements to the mutual benefit and enrichment of those involved. Economic hegemony (A) and growth of local cottage industries (D) were not in the merchant vocabulary. After initial colonization, and thanks to ongoing scientific and technological innovations, populations stabilized and began to grow.

46. **A** The economy of the Soviet Union traditionally relied heavily on central planning. Sometimes called command economies, these systems used a series of social and economic targets and regulations to control ownership of resources, supply chains, distribution, wages, and prices. This is the opposite of the laissez-faire philosophy popularized during the Enlightenment, in which private business operated in a free market with little government regulation (B). Mercantilism is associated with early colonization, in which countries measured their power in terms of wealth. To maximize this, they sought a favorable balance of trade using a mix of tariffs, colonies, and subsidies for domestic production (C). Privatized refers to the idea of selling government-owned economic assets to private interests or contracting with the private sector to provide government functions under the assumption that the private sector is more efficient and productive. While this might apply to the new Soviet economic reforms, it would not apply to the economy before the 1980s (D).

47. **C** The passage makes reference to the economic costs of the arms race with the United States, which intensified in the 1980s under Ronald Reagan's presidency. Many historians have pointed to this as a contributing factor to the fall of communism. Although there have been historical crop failures in Ukraine, most notably in the 1930s, this is not traditionally cited as a cause of the fall of the USSR, except inasmuch as all of its economic sector had inefficiencies (A). The Baltic states did not become independent until after the fall of the USSR, so this cannot be a factor (B). Finally, although Gorbachev's restructuring allowed for some market reforms, including letting workers strike for better wages, the impact of this would have been nominal (D).

48. **B** As glasnost and perestroika progressed, Gorbachev faced an attempted coup from party elites, ultimately leading to his resignation; therefore (A) is incorrect. The perceived weakness of the USSR emboldened satellite countries to openly criticize the USSR and even claim independence (C), while at home people were frustrated that his economic reforms took a long time to show improvement. Finally, while the current government in Russia may appear democratic, in reality, its institutions under Vladimir Putin are more authoritarian in nature (D).

49. **A** Under Deng Xiaoping, China underwent an economic opening. While still politically communist, they gradually allowed privatization of state industries, foreign investment, entrepreneurship, and other market-based reforms. Under Mao Zedong, China's economic was centrally directed, with plans like the Great Leap Forward organizing farms into large communes (C). Kim Il-Sung of North Korea was influenced by Mao's China and implemented similar centralized agricultural policies. Under Fidel Castro, Cuba was also a centrally controlled economy, in that the state owned most sectors, with wages, prices, and jobs subject to government regulation (B).

50. **D** The Mandate System was created by the League of Nations after WWI as a means of dealing with territories ceded by nations who had fought for the Triple Alliance, like the Ottoman Empire. The victors did not want to

appear to be continuing imperialist policies, nor did they want the newly ceded territories to become flash points for new conflicts. Thus provisional administrative control was given to one of the Allies until the territory was "ready" for independence. Although religion was an ongoing issue in the region, the government was secular (A). Though it wasn't strictly democratic, the mandatory power did not control all aspects of life as in a totalitarian system (B). The Mandate System was a political system and did not extend to East Asia (C).

51. C The singling out of Jerusalem to be controlled by an international regime indicates that it was a point of contention between Muslims (Palestinians) and Jews (Israelis), given that it has religious significance for both. Although terrorism (B) and settlement building (D) would later become points of conflict in the region, at the time of the passage, these were not yet issues. Similarly, Israel currently has nuclear capability, but that did not happen until the 1960s, so it would not have been included in the passage (A).

52. A There are many similarities between the partition of Pakistan and the division of Palestine. To begin, both were occupied by Britain, though India was a colonial possession. The division between India and Pakistan was seen as a solution to a religious divide in the territory. Pakistan was created as a Muslim state, and India became a secular state with a predominantly Hindu population. Finally, both continue to have contested territory today. Liberia was created in Africa as a U.S. colony to resettle freed slaves (B). Taiwan had been part of China, was ceded to the Japanese in 1895, but was taken over by Chinese nationalists from the Republic of China after they fled communist forces in mainland China (C). Estonia had been an independent nation after the Russian Revolution, but was annexed by the Soviet Union in 1940 and remained under their control until they declared independence in 1991 (D).

53. C In order to answer this question, you must have a general familiarity with the regions of the world. According to the graph, most

nations in Africa have a life expectancy of between 55 and 70 years, with a few African nations as low as 50 to 55 years (the only continent to have a life expectancy this low). Both North America and Europe (especially Western Europe) have life expectancies generally higher than 70 years, but Asia (especially South Asia) has quite a few countries in the 60- to 70-year range (D). One limitation of this chart is that it only shows life expectancies at a fixed point in time, and thus cannot be used to determine changes over time (A, B).

54. A One pattern that emerges as health care improves life expectancy is that diseases associated with old age, such as Alzheimer's and heart disease, also increase. One cannot make the same times of inferences regarding diseases not as directly associated with age, like asthma (B) or pandemics (D). It is difficult to isolate the role of infant mortality in this chart as any number of variables can influence the life expectancy (violence, for example), which means C is not the best choice.

55. B Certain diseases are much more likely to be correlated with poverty, like malaria, tuberculosis, and cholera; and Africa has many nations with higher poverty rates than other continents. Increased access to family planning might lead to lower birth rates, but this would not impact life expectancy since that is based on live births (A). Desertification may have disrupted agricultural patterns, but the link between that and life expectancy is much more tenuous and indirect, making this a weaker choice (C). Finally, efforts by international organizations like the WHO are more likely to increase life expectancy rather than lower it (D).

Section I, Part B:
Short-Answer Questions

1A. According to the passage, the sources of well-water contamination include nearby "privy pits" containing human waste and piles of garbage from the house. Also manure from the pigsty soaks into the ground and then seeps into the well. Finally, rainwater, though it doesn't contaminate the well itself, becomes the means by which the contaminants flow into the wells.

1B. Florence Nightingale argues that the authorities seem to want unequivocal data before acting and therefore wait and document the connections between sanitation and public health epidemics, rather than acting to prevent them from forming in the first place.

2A. You should mention that Rupert Brooke's poem shows the English idea of superiority along with the ideal of sacrifice. At the beginning of WWI, the men who enlisted did so for a cause: saving English ideals of justice and hope. And they were convinced they would have an effect, even after death. Siegfried Sassoon in his savagely satirical poem written just after WWI makes clear that the sacrifices so many soldiers made were, when all was said and done, neither noble nor shared. From a prewar optimistic, nationalistic fervor, the postwar poetry reflects disillusionment and despair.

2B. Siegfried Sassoon closes his poem by saying that no one will be overly concerned with the dreadful condition of the walking wounded. He uses adjectives like "kind" and "splendid" to contrast the dreadful situation of an injured soldier.

3A. Syncretism, or the borrowing, adapting, and mixing of institutional, intellectual, artistic, and especially religious elements to create something new and unique, is most evident in religion and the arts. In the Eastern Hemisphere the clearest example of syncretism is the blending of Confucianism, Taoism, and Legalism, resulting in a hybrid set of religious beliefs and practices. In the arts, the most obvious syncretism can be seen in statues of the Buddha wearing Greek clothing.

3B. In the Latin American region cultural syncretism is evident in the Rastafarian movement in Jamaica. African-Hebrew and Christian religious practices blend together with Caribbean freed slave culture and a 19th-century Pan African identity to make something new and unique.

4A. Any of the following causes could lead to the collapse of a modern empire: loss of faith in the ideology that allows personal identification with empire; declining economic rewards as a result of the exhaustion of raw materials or natural resources; overexpansion and the inability to control too large an area (contiguous or not); nationalistic or ethnic rebellions or revolutions with differing ideologies or goals; rising expectations, or the desire of those being controlled to have the amenities and power of those doing the controlling.

4B. Using the examples that you did NOT use in **4A**, pick two that cause modern empires to flounder or collapse.

Section II, Part A: Document-Based Question

In order to write a strong response, you should read the directions for the DBQ carefully. Your first task is to be sure you understand the question. Then read the documents. You have 15 minutes to dedicate to this. Having done this, you will be in a position to come up with a thesis statement that answers the entire question, and that uses all the information given in the documents. You will need to take a stand, deciding whether the idea of what constitutes human rights has evolved. Before beginning to write, you might jot down a brief outline that shows the evidence you will use to support your thesis.

This question has two parts. The first requires you to show how the very term "human" decided what rights were sought after. The Magna Carta refers to the rights of "all free men of the kingdom" (Doc. 1), and that is a far cry from a declaration of the "equal and inalienable rights of all members of the human family" (Doc. 5) or from assuring the rights of colonizers, though not necessarily of those being colonized (Doc. 2). You might answer the first part of the question by working off a thesis that refers to human rights as they are defined in historical context, with a specific purpose. The second part of the question allows you to cite specific examples of changes in the definition of human rights. It becomes clear that such rights are relative instead of absolute. Is this an idea that you should incorporate into your thesis statement?

Analysis of the documents shows that elements like citizenship, social status, and gender are addressed at different times in different ways. Further, the audience or those affected by these definitions goes from one class or one gender to all humankind. In short, it becomes universal (Doc. 5). By the mid- to late twentieth century, a new element comes into play: human rights become entangled with national, geopolitical, and religious rights. To answer the question fully, that is, both parts, you must place the documents within their historical context and point out the purpose of ceding or supporting human rights. Each document reveals an obvious purpose: from keeping propertied classes in control of economic wealth and politics, to promoting peace and justice globally, to guaranteeing the supremacy of religion in a given society, to promoting a nationalist agenda.

You may conclude that human rights, those that are inherent (inalienable, natural), cannot be separated from freedoms associated with institutions. Does that show a positive or negative evolution of rights? You may conclude that human rights are never going to be static and that they must respond to contemporary circumstances. You may conclude that cultural, social, religious, and economic differences prevent any universal application of human rights. You may conclude that human rights are one of many political tools used to gain or maintain power; perhaps human rights are an illusion. What is important is that you use the documents to sustain (or refute) your original thesis.

Section II, Part B: Long-Essay Question

To write a strong essay, you need to be direct and to use specific examples. First, you might consider the term "imperialism": the building and maintenance of an empire. All three questions lend themselves to a discussion of the purposes of imperialism and the means used to establish a lasting presence, even if not physical, in colonies or former colonies. You might begin by stating that imperialism was positive in that it allowed economic progress, globalization of science and technology, and establishment of universal values. Or you might think that imperialism, for all its visible and tangible legacies, was inherently a Social Darwinist experiment gone wrong. Once you have a thesis, even one that could be considered controversial, then you can choose your examples that will sustain it.

You have limited time, so you might jot down quick examples of legacies for each question. If you have difficulty coming up with examples for one of the questions, then you might eliminate it from your choice. The first question is more broad than the second and third questions. Still, you might find that quick notes of legacies speak specifically to the second or third questions.

For example, short- and long-term legacies of European imperialism might include the following:

Short-term—depopulation of native peoples due to disease or conquest by force; introduction of social structures (the casta system in Spanish America comes to mind); the destruction of incipient industry (this could also be considered long-term, as it presented severe obstacles to the creation of economic infrastructures following independence).

Long-term—languages spoken; establishment of a dominant religion; implementation of educational systems patterned on those of the imperialist; control of economic and political infrastructures, which, as noted above, left many countries without any operable infrastructures when they achieved independence; adoption of legal systems that reflect laws and values of the imperialist and may ignore or destroy those of native populations; syncretism visible in the arts, architecture, religion; the breaking apart of social units (as in Africa, when Europe divided the continent geographically without taking into account tribal boundaries).

What is most important is your statement of a thesis, evidence to support that thesis, and conclusions based on that evidence.

Scoring: How Did I Do?

As you evaluate how you did on the practice exams, you need to keep several things in mind.

First, look again at the chart from the first chapter of the book. This tells you how much of your score will be determined by each part of the test. The multiple-choice counts the most, but no one part of the exam will determine your final grade. The scoring chart below reflects the same percentages shown here.

Section	Type of Question	Number of Questions	Time	Recommended Time	% of Exam Score
Section I, Part A	Multiple Choice	55	95 Minutes	55 Minutes	40%
Section I, Part B	Short Answer	Answer 3 questions out of 4.		40 Minutes	20%
Section II, Part A	Document-Based Question (DBQ)	1	100 Minutes	60 Minutes	25%
Section II, Part B	Long Essay	Choose 1 of 2 Questions		40 Minutes	15%

An overall score of 3 (out of 5) is considered passing. However, each college or university has different policies as to the score needed and the amount of credit offered. Check the schools you're considering to determine the score you'll need and the credit hours awarded. You can find all this information at https://apstudent .collegeboard.org/creditandplacement/search-credit-policies.

You'll have to grade your own answers for the short-answer questions, the document-based question, and the long essay. Look at the explanations and evaluate how your answers measure up. The apcentral.collegeboard.com website has specific information about rubrics for the questions. Your teacher should also have this information.

abacus An ancient Chinese counting device that used rods on which were mounted movable counters.

absolute monarchy Rule by a king or queen whose power is not limited by a constitution.

Afrikaners South Africans descended from the Dutch who settled in South Africa in the seventeenth century.

age grade An age group into which children were placed in Bantu societies of early sub-Saharan Africa; children within the age grade were given responsibilities and privileges suitable for their age and in this manner were prepared for adult responsibilities.

Agricultural Revolution The transition from foraging to the cultivation of food occurring about 8000–2000 BCE; also known as the Neolithic Revolution.

Allah The god of the Muslims; Arabic word for "god."

Alliance for Progress A program of economic aid for Latin America in exchange for a pledge to establish democratic institutions; part of U.S. President Kennedy's international program.

Allied Powers In World War I, the nations of Great Britain, France, Russia, the United States, and others that fought against the Central Powers; in World War II, the group of nations including Great Britain, France, the Soviet Union, and the United States, that fought against the Axis Powers.

al-Qaeda An international radical Sunni Muslim organization that uses terrorist tactics to oppose Western culture, values, and policy.

animism The belief that spirits inhabit the features of nature.

Anschluss The German annexation of Austria prior to World War II.

apartheid The South African policy of separation of the races.

appeasement Policy of Great Britain and France of making concessions to Hitler in the 1930s.

aristocracy Rule by a privileged hereditary class or nobility.

artifact An object made by human hands.

artisan A craftsman.

astrolabe A navigational instrument used to determine latitude by measuring the position of the stars.

Austronesian A branch of languages originating in Oceania.

ayatollah A traditional Muslim religious ruler.

ayllus In Incan society, a clan or community that worked together on projects required by the ruler.

bakufu A military government established in Japan after the Gempei Wars; the emperor became a figurehead, while real power was concentrated in the military, including the *samurai*.

Bantu-speaking peoples Name given to a group of sub-Saharan African peoples whose migrations altered the society of sub-Saharan Africa.

Battle of Tours The 732 CE battle that halted the advance of Muslim armies into Europe at a point in northern France.

benefice In medieval Europe, a grant of land or other privilege to a vassal.

Berlin Conference (1884 to 1885) Meeting of European imperialist powers to divide Africa among them.

Black Death The European name for the fourteenth-century outbreak of the bubonic plague that spread from Asia, across Europe and North Africa, following land and sea commercial trade routes.

bodhisattvas Buddhist holy men who accumulated spiritual merits during their lifetimes; Buddhists prayed to them in order to receive some of their holiness.

Boer War (1899 to 1902) War between the British and the Dutch over Dutch independence in South Africa; resulted in British victory.

Boers South Africans of Dutch descent.

bourgeoisie In France, the class of merchants and artisans who were members of the Third Estate and initiators of the French Revolution; in Marxist theory, a term referring to factory owners.

Boxer Rebellion (1898) Revolt against foreign residents of China.

boyars Russian nobility.

Brahmin A member of the social class of priests in Aryan society.

brinkmanship The Cold War policy of the Soviet Union and the United States of threatening to go to war at a sign of aggression on the part of either power.

British Commonwealth A political community consisting of the United Kingdom, its dependencies, and former colonies of Great Britain that are now sovereign nations; currently called the Commonwealth of Nations.

bushi Regional military leaders in Japan who ruled small kingdoms from fortresses.

bushido The code of honor of the *samurai* of Japan.

caliph The chief Muslim political and religious leader.

calpulli Aztec clans that supplied labor and warriors to leaders.

capital The money and equipment needed to engage in industrialization.

capitalism An economic system based on private ownership and opportunity for profit-making.

caravel A small, easily steerable ship used by the Portuguese and Spanish in their explorations.

cartels Unions of independent businesses in order to regulate production, prices, and the marketing of goods.

Catholic Reformation (Counter-Reformation) The religious reform movement within the Roman Catholic Church that occurred in response to the Protestant Reformation. It reaffirmed Catholic beliefs and promoted education.

Central Powers In World War I, Germany, Austria-Hungary, Bulgaria, the Ottoman Empire, and other nations who fought with them against the Allies.

chinampas Platforms of twisted vines and mud that served the Aztecs as floating gardens and extended their agricultural land.

chivalry A knight's code of honor in medieval Europe.

civilization A cultural group with advanced cities, complex institutions, skilled workers, advanced technology, and a system of recordkeeping.

climate The pattern of temperature and precipitation over a period of time.

coalition A government based on temporary alliances of several political parties.

Code Napoleon Collection of laws that standardized French law under the rule of Napoleon Bonaparte.

Cold War The tense diplomatic relationship between the United States and the Soviet Union after World War II.

collectivization The combination of several small farms into a large government-controlled farm.

Columbian Exchange The exchange of food crops, livestock, and disease between the Eastern and Western Hemispheres after the voyages of Columbus.

commercial revolution The expansion of trade and commerce in Europe in the sixteenth and seventeenth centuries.

communism An economic system in which property is publicly owned; each member of a classless society works and is paid according to his or her needs and abilities.

conscription Military draft.

conservatism In nineteenth-century Europe, a movement that supported monarchies, aristocracies, and state-established churches.

containment Cold War policy of the United States whose purpose was to prevent the spread of communism.

Cossacks Russians who conquered and settled Siberia in the sixteenth and seventeenth centuries.

covenant Agreement; in the Judeo-Christian heritage, an agreement between God and humankind.

criollos (creoles) A term used in colonial Spanish America to describe a person born in the Americas of European parents.

cubism A school of art in which persons and objects are represented by geometric forms.

cultural diffusion The transmission of ideas and products from one culture to another.

Cultural Revolution A Chinese movement from 1966 to 1976 intended to establish an egalitarian society of peasants and workers.

cuneiform A system of writing originating in Mesopotamia in which a wedge-shaped stylus was used to press symbols into clay.

daimyo A Japanese feudal lord in charge of an army of *samurai*.

Dar al-Islam The House of Islam; a term representing the political and religious unity of the various Islamic groups.

Declaration of the Rights of Man and the Citizen A statement of political rights adopted by the French National Assembly during the French Revolution.

Declaration of the Rights of Woman and the Female Citizen A statement of the rights of women written by Olympe de Gouges in response to the Declaration of the Rights of Man.

Deism The concept of God common to the Scientific Revolution; the deity was believed to have set the world in motion and then allowed it to operate by natural laws.

democracy A political system in which the people rule.

deoxyribonucleic acid (DNA) The blueprint of heredity.

devshirme A practice of the Ottoman Empire to take Christian boys from their home communities to serve as Janissaries.

dharma In the Hindu tradition, duty or obligation.

diaspora The exile of an ethnic or racial group from their homeland.

divine right The belief of absolute rulers that their right to govern is granted by God.

domestic system A manufacturing method in which the stages of the manufacturing process are carried out in private homes rather than a factory setting.

Duma The Russian parliament.

Dutch learning Western learning embraced by some Japanese in the eighteenth century.

dynasty A series of rulers from the same family.

economic imperialism Control of a country's economy by the businesses of another nation.

economic liberalism The economic philosophy that government intervention in and regulation of the economy should be minimal.

Edict of Milan A document that made Christianity one of the religions allowed in the Roman Empire.

empirical research Research based on the collection of data.

enclosure movement The fencing of pasture land in England beginning prior to the Industrial Revolution.

encomienda A practice in the Spanish colonies that granted land and the labor of Native Americans on that land to European colonists.

Enlightenment A philosophical movement in eighteenth-century Europe that was based on reason and the concept that education and training could improve humankind and society.

entrepreneurship The ability to combine the factors of land, labor, and capital to create factory production.

estates The divisions of society in prerevolutionary France.

Estates-General The traditional legislative body of France.

euro The standard currency introduced and adopted by the majority of members of the European Union in January 2002.

European Union An organization designed to reduce trade barriers and promote economic unity in Europe; it was formed in 1993 to replace the European Community.

evangelical Pertaining to preaching the Gospel (the good news) or pertaining to theologically conservative Christians.

excommunication The practice of the Roman Catholic and other Christian churches of prohibiting participation in the sacraments to those who do not comply with Church teachings or practices.

extraterritoriality The right of foreigners to live under the laws of their home country rather than those of the host country.

factor An agent with trade privileges in early Russia.

fascism A political movement that is characterized by extreme nationalism, one-party rule, and the denial of individual rights.

feminism The movement to achieve equal rights for women.

feudalism A political, economic, and social system based on the relationship between lord and vassal in order to provide protection.

fief In medieval Europe, a grant of land given in exchange for military or other services.

filial piety In China, respect for one's parents and other elders.

Five Pillars Five practices required of Muslims: faith, prayer, almsgiving, fasting, and pilgrimage.

Five-Year Plans Plans for industrial production first introduced to the Soviet Union in 1928 by Stalin; they succeeded in making the Soviet Union a major industrial power by the end of the 1930s.

footbinding In China, a method of breaking and binding women's feet; seen as a sign of beauty and social position, footbinding also confined women to the household.

foraging A term for hunting and gathering.

fundamentalism A return to traditional religious beliefs and practices.

Geneva Conference A 1954 conference that divided Vietnam at the seventeenth parallel.

genocide The systematic killing of an entire ethnic group.

geocentric theory The belief held by many before the Scientific Revolution that the earth is the center of the universe.

glasnost The 1985 policy of Mikhail Gorbachev that allowed openness of expression of ideas in the Soviet Union.

Glorious Revolution The bloodless overthrow of English King James I and the placement of William and Mary on the English throne.

gold standard A monetary system in which currency is backed up by a specific amount of gold.

Gothic architecture Architecture of twelfth-century Europe, featuring stained-glass windows, flying buttresses, tall spires, and pointed arches.

Gran Colombia The temporary union of the northern portion of South America after the independence movements led by Simón Bolívar; ended in 1830.

Great Depression The severe economic downturn that began in the late 1920s and continued into the 1930s throughout many regions of the world.

Great Leap Forward The disastrous economic policy introduced by Mao Zedong that proposed the implementation of small-scale industrial projects on individual peasant communes.

Green Revolution A program of improved irrigation methods and the introduction of high-yield seeds and fertilizers and pesticides to improve agricultural production; the Green Revolution was especially successful in Asia but also was used in Latin America.

griots Storytellers of sub-Saharan Africa who carried on oral traditions and histories.

guano Bird droppings used as fertilizer; a major trade item of Peru in the late nineteenth century.

guest workers Workers from North Africa and Asia who migrated to Europe during the late twentieth century in search of employment; some guest workers settled in Europe permanently.

Guomindang China's Nationalist political party founded by Sun Yat-sen in 1912 and based on democratic principles; in 1925, the party was taken over by Jiang Jieshi, who made it into a more authoritarian party.

Hadith A collection of the sayings and deeds of Muhammad.

hajj The pilgrimage to the Ka'aba in Mecca required once of every Muslim who is not limited by health or financial restrictions.

harem A household of wives and concubines in the Middle East, Africa, or Asia.

heliocentric theory The concept that the sun is the center of the universe.

Hellenistic Age The era (c. 323 to 30 BCE) in which Greek culture blended with Persian and other Eastern influences spread throughout the former empire of Alexander the Great.

Helsinki Accords A 1975 political and human rights agreement signed in Helsinki, Finland, by Western European countries and the Soviet Union.

hieroglyphics A system of picture writing used in Egypt.

hijrah The flight of Muhammad from Mecca to Medina; the first year in the Muslim calendar.

Holocaust The Nazi program during World War II that killed 6 million Jews and other groups considered undesirable.

imperialism The establishment of colonial empires.

import substitution industrialization An economic system that attempts to strengthen a country's industrial power by restricting foreign imports.

Inca The ruler of the Quechua people of the west coast of South America; the term is also applied to the Quechua people as a whole.

indentured servitude The practice of contracting with a master to provide labor for a specified period of years in exchange for passage and living expenses.

Indian National Congress Political party that became the leader of the Indian Nationalist movement.

Indo-Europeans A group of seminomadic peoples who, around 2000 BCE, began to migrate from central Asia to India, Europe, and the Middle East.

indulgence A document whose purchase was said to grant the bearer the forgiveness of sins.

Industrial Revolution The transition between the domestic system of manufacturing and the mechanization of production in a factory setting.

International Monetary Fund An international organization founded in 1944 to promote market economies and free trade.

International Space Station A vehicle sponsored by sixteen nations that circles the earth while carrying out experiments.

investiture The authority claimed by monarchs to appoint church officials.

Jacobins Extreme radicals during the French Revolution.

Janissaries Members of the Ottoman army, often slaves, who were taken from Christian lands.

jati One of many subcastes in the Hindu caste system.

Jesuits Members of the Society of Jesus, a Roman Catholic missionary and educational order founded by Ignatius of Loyola in 1534.

jihad Islamic holy war.

junks Large Chinese sailing ships especially designed for long-distance travel during the Tang and Song dynasties.

Ka'aba A black stone or meteorite that became the most revered shrine in Arabia before the introduction of Islam; situated in Mecca, it later was incorporated in the Islamic faith.

Kabuki theater A form of Japanese theater developed in the seventeenth century that features colorful scenery and costumes and an exaggerated style of acting.

kamikaze The "divine wind" credited by the Japanese with preventing the Mongol invasion of Japan during the thirteenth century.

karma In Hindu tradition, the good or evil deeds done by a person that determine reincarnation or reaching nirvana.

Khan A Mongol ruler.

kowtow A ritualistic bow practiced in the Chinese court.

kulaks Russian peasants who became wealthy under Lenin's New Economic Policy.

laissez-faire **economics** An economic concept that holds that the government should not interfere with or regulate businesses and industries.

lateen sail A triangular sail attached to a short mast.

latifundia Large landholdings in the Roman Empire and in Latin America.

League of Nations International organization founded after World War I to promote peace and cooperation among nations.

liberalism An Enlightenment philosophy that favored civil rights, the protection of private property, and representative government.

Liberation Theology A religious belief that emphasizes social justice for victims of poverty and oppression.

limited liability corporation (LLC) A business organization in which the owners have limited personal legal responsibility for debts and actions of the business.

Magna Carta A document written in England in 1215 that granted certain rights to nobles; later these rights came to be extended to all classes.

Malay sailors Southeast Asian sailors who traveled the Indian Ocean; by 500 CE, they had colonized Madagascar, introducing the cultivation of the banana.

Mamluks Turkic military slaves who formed part of the army of the Abbasid Caliphate in the ninth and tenth centuries; they founded their own state in Egypt and Syria from the thirteenth to the early sixteenth centuries.

Manchus Peoples from northeastern Asia who founded China's Qing dynasty.

mandate A type of colony in which the government is overseen by another nation, as in the Middle Eastern mandates placed under European control after World War I.

Mandate of Heaven The concept developed by the Zhou dynasty that the deity granted a dynasty the right to rule and took away that right if the dynasty did not rule wisely.

manorialism The system of self-sufficient estates that arose in medieval Europe.

Maori A member of a Polynesian group that settled in New Zealand about 800 CE.

maroon societies Runaway slaves in the Caribbean who established their own communities to resist slavery and colonial authorities.

Marshall Plan A U.S. plan to support the recovery and reconstruction of Western Europe after World War II.

mass consumerism Trade in products designed to appeal to a global market.

matrilineal Referring to a social system in which descent and inheritance are traced through the mother.

May Fourth Movement A 1919 protest in China against the Treaty of Versailles and foreign influence.

medieval Pertaining to the middle ages of European history.

Meiji Restoration The restoration of the Meiji emperor in Japan in 1868 that began a program of industrialization and centralization of Japan following the end of the Tokugawa Shogunate.

mercantilism A European economic policy of the sixteenth through the eighteenth centuries that held that there was a limited amount of wealth available, and that each country must adopt policies to obtain as much wealth as possible for itself; key to the attainment of wealth was the acquisition of colonies.

mestizos In the Spanish colonies, persons of mixed European and Indian descent.

metropolitan The head of the Eastern Orthodox Church.

Mexica The name given to themselves by the Aztec people.

Middle Ages The period of European history traditionally given as 500 to 1500.

Middle Kingdom Term applied to the rich agricultural lands of the Yangtze River valley under the Zhou dynasty.

Middle Passage The portion of transatlantic trade that involved the passage of Africans from Africa to the Americas.

minaret A tower attached to a mosque from which Muslims are called to worship.

mita A labor system used by Andean societies in which community members shared work owed to rulers and the religious community.

moksha In Hindu belief, the spirit's liberation from the cycle of reincarnation.

Mongol Peace The period from about 1250 to 1350 in which the Mongols ensured the safety of Eurasian trade and travel.

monotheism The belief in one god.

Monroe Doctrine (1823) Policy issued by the United States in which it declared that the Western Hemisphere was off limits to colonization by other powers.

monsoon A seasonal wind that can bring dry or wet weather.

mosque The house of worship of followers of Islam.

Mughal dynasty Rulers who controlled most of India in the sixteenth and seventeenth centuries.

mulato **(mulatto)** In the Spanish and Portuguese colonies, a person of mixed African and European descent.

Muslim "One who submits"; a follower of Islam.

mystery religion During the Hellenistic Age, religions that promised their faithful followers eternity in a state of bliss.

National Organization for Women (NOW) U.S. organization founded in 1969 to campaign for women's rights.

nation-state A sovereign state whose people share a common culture and national identity.

natural laws Principles that govern nature.

natural rights Rights that belong to every person and that no government may take away.

Neo-Confucianism A philosophy that blended Confucianism with Buddhism thought.

New Deal U.S. President Roosevelt's program to relieve the economic problems of the Great Depression; it increased government involvement in the society of the United States.

New Economic Policy (NEP) Lenin's policy that allowed some private ownership and limited foreign investment to revitalize the Soviet economy.

New Testament The portion of the Christian Bible that contains the Gospels that relate the account of the life of Jesus; letters from the followers of Jesus to the early Christian churches and the Book of Revelation, a prophetic text.

nirvana In Buddhism, a state of perfect peace that is the goal of reincarnation.

No theater The classical Japanese drama with music and dances performed on a simple stage by elaborately dressed actors.

nonalignment The policy of some developing nations to refrain from aligning themselves with either the United States or the Soviet Union during the cold war.

North American Free Trade Agreement (NAFTA) An organization that prohibits tariffs and other trade barriers among Mexico, the United States, and Canada.

North Atlantic Treaty Organization (NATO) A defense alliance between nations of Western Europe and North America formed in 1949.

Northern Renaissance An extension of the Italian Renaissance to the nations of northern Europe; the Northern Renaissance took on a more religious nature than the Italian Renaissance.

Northwest Passage A passage through the North American continent that was sought by early explorers to North America as a route to trade with the East.

Opium War (1839 to 1842) War between Great Britain and China began with the Qing dynasty's refusal to allow continued opium importation into China; British victory resulted in the Treaty of Nanking.

oracle bones Animal bones or shells used by Chinese priests to receive messages from the gods.

Organization of Petroleum Exporting Countries (OPEC) Organization formed in 1960 by oil-producing countries to regulate oil supplies and prices.

ozone depletion The thinning of the layer of the gas ozone high in the earth's atmosphere; ozone serves as a protection against the sun's ultraviolet rays.

Pan-Slavic movement A Russian attempt to unite all Slavic nations into a commonwealth relationship under the influence of Russia.

parallel descent In Incan society, descent through both the father and mother.

parliament A representative assembly.

parliamentary monarchy A government with a king or queen whose power is limited by the power of a parliament.

pastoralism The practice of herding.

patriarchal Pertaining to a social system in which the father is the head of the family.

Pax Romana The Roman Peace; the period of prosperity and stability throughout the Roman Empire in the first two centuries CE.

peninsulares In the Spanish colonies, those who were born in Europe.

People of the Book A term applied by Islamic governments to Muslims, Christians, and Jews in reference to the fact that all three religions had a holy book.

perestroika A restructuring of the Soviet economy to allow some local decision making.

Persian Gulf War The 1991 war between Iraq and a U.S.-led coalition to liberate Kuwait from an Iraqi invasion.

perspective An artistic technique commonly used in Renaissance painting that gave a three-dimensional appearance to works of art.

pharaoh An Egyptian monarch.

philosophes French Enlightenment social philosophers.

pogrom Violence against Jews in tsarist Russia.

polis A Greek city-state.

polytheism The belief in many gods.

Pope The head of the Roman Catholic Church.

Potsdam Conference A 1945 meeting of the leaders of Great Britain, the United States, and the Soviet Union in which it was agreed that the Soviet Union would be given control of eastern Europe and that Germany would be divided into zones of occupation.

Prague Spring A 1968 program of reform to soften socialism in Czechoslovakia; it resulted in the Soviet invasion of Czechoslovakia.

predestination The belief of Protestant reformer John Calvin that God had chosen some people for heaven and others for hell.

proletariat In Marxist theory, the class of workers in an industrial society.

Protestant Reformation A religious movement begun by Martin Luther in 1517 that attempted to reform the beliefs and practices of the Roman Catholic Church; it resulted in the formation of new Christian denominations.

purdah The Hindu custom of secluding women.

purges Joseph Stalin's policy of exiling or killing millions of his opponents in the Soviet Union.

Quechua Andean society also known as the Inca.

quipus A system of knotted cords of different sizes and colors used by the Incas for keeping records.

Quran The holy book of Islam. Also called *Koran*.

radicalism Western European political philosophy during the nineteenth century; advocated democracy and reforms favoring lower classes.

Ramadan The holy month of Islam which commemorates the appearance of the angel Gabriel to Muhammad; fasting is required during this month.

Reconquista (Reconquest) The recapture of Muslim-held lands in Spain by Christian forces; it was completed in 1492.

Red Guard A militia of young Chinese people organized to carry out Mao Zedong's Cultural Revolution.

Reign of Terror (1793–1794) The period of most extreme violence during the French Revolution.

reincarnation Rebirth; a belief of both Buddhism and Hinduism.

Renaissance The revival of learning in Europe beginning about 1300 and continuing to about 1600.

reparations The payment of war debts by the losing side.

repartamiento In the Spanish colonies, a replacement for the *encomienda* system that limited the number of working hours for laborers and provided for fair wages.

Revolution of 1905 Strikes by urban workers and peasants in Russia; prompted by shortages of food and by Russia's loss to Japan in 1905.

Revolutions of 1848 Democratic and nationalistic revolutions, most of them unsuccessful, that swept through Europe.

romanticism A literary and artistic movement in nineteenth-century Europe; emphasized emotion over reason.

Russification A tsarist program that required non-Russians to speak only Russian and provided education only for those groups loyal to Russia.

Russo-Japanese War (1904 to 1905) War between Japan and Russia over Manchurian territory; resulted in the defeat of Russia by the Japanese navy.

samurai The military class of feudal Japan.

Sandinistas A left-wing group that overthrew the dictatorship of Nicaraguan Anastacio Somoza in 1979.

sati (also suttee) The custom among the higher castes of Hinduism of a widow throwing herself on the funeral pyre of her husband.

scholar-gentry The Chinese class of well-educated men from whom many of the bureaucrats were chosen.

Scientific Revolution A European intellectual movement in the seventeenth century that established the basis for modern science.

Second Industrial Revolution The phase of the Industrial Revolution beginning about 1850 that applied the use of electricity and steel to the manufacturing process.

self-strengthening movement A late nineteenth-century movement in which the Chinese modernized their army and encouraged Western investment in factories and railways.

separation of powers The division of powers among the legislative, executive, and judicial branches of government.

Sepoy Rebellion (1857) Revolt of Indian soldiers against the British; caused by a military practice in violation of the Muslim and Hindu faiths.

sepoys South Asian soldiers who served in the British army in India.

serf A peasant who is bound to the land he or she works.

service industries Occupations that provided a service rather than a manufactured or agricultural product.

Seven Years' War (1756 to 1763) Conflict fought in Europe and its overseas colonies; in North America, known as the French and Indian War.

shamanism A belief in powerful natural spirits that are influenced by shamans, or priests.

shariah The body of law that governs Muslim society.

Shi'ite The branch of Islam that holds that the leader of Islam must be a descendant of Muhammad's family.

Shinto The traditional Japanese religion based on veneration of ancestors and spirits of nature.

shogun Military leaders under the *bakufu*.

shogunate The rule of the *shoguns*.

Silk Roads Caravan routes and sea lanes between China and the Middle East.

Six-Day War A brief war between Israel and a number of Arab states in 1967; during this conflict, Israel took over Jerusalem, the Golan Heights, the Sinai Peninsula, and the West Bank.

slash-and-burn cultivation An agricultural method in which farmers clear fields by cutting and burning trees, then use the ashes as fertilizer.

social contract Enlightenment concept of the agreement made by the people living in a state of nature to give up some of their rights in order for governments to be established.

Social Darwinism The application of Darwin's philosophy of natural selection to human society.

socialism Political movement originating in nineteenth-century Europe; emphasized community control of the major means of production, distribution, and exchange.

Solidarity A Polish trade union that began the nation's protest against Communist rule.

sovereignty Self-rule.

Spanish-American War (1898) Conflict between the United States and Spain that began the rise of the United States as a world power.

Spanish Civil War A conflict lasting from 1936 to 1939 that resulted in the installation of Fascist dictator Francisco Franco as ruler of Spain; Franco's forces were backed by Germany and Italy, whereas the Soviet Union supported the opposing republican forces.

specialization of labor The division of labor that aids the development of skills in a particular type of work.

spheres of influence Divisions of a country in which a particular foreign nation enjoys economic privileges.

stateless society A society that is based on the authority of kinship groups rather than on a central government.

steppe A dry grassland.

steppe diplomacy The skill of political survival and dominance in the world of steppe nomads; it involved the knowledge of tribal and clan structure and often used assassinations to accomplish its goals.

stock market A market where shares are bought and sold.

Stoicism The most popular Hellenistic philosophy; it involved strict discipline and an emphasis on helping others.

Suez Canal Canal constructed by Egypt across the Isthmus of Suez in 1869.

Sufis Muslims who attempt to reach *Allah* through mysticism.

sultan An Islamic ruler.

Sunni The branch of Islam that believes that the Muslim community should select its leaders; the Sunnis are the largest branch of Islam.

syncretism A blend of two or more cultures or cultural traditions.

system of checks and balances Constitutional system in which each branch of government places limits on the power of the other branches.

Taiping Rebellion (1853 to 1864) Revolt in southern China against the Qing Empire.

Tanzimat reforms Nineteenth-century reforms by Ottoman rulers designed to make the government and military more efficient.

tea ceremony An ancient Shinto ritual still performed in the traditional Japanese capital of Kyoto.

Tehran Conference A 1943 meeting of leaders of the United States, Great Britain, and the Soviet Union; it agreed on the opening of a second front in France.

Ten Commandments The moral law of the Hebrews.

theocracy A government ruled by God or by church leaders.

Tiananmen Square Beijing site of a 1989 student protest in favor of democracy; the Chinese military killed large numbers of protestors.

Torah The first five books of the Jewish scripture.

Treaty of Brest-Litovsk The 1918 treaty ending World War I between Germany and the Soviet Union.

Treaty of Nanking (1842) Treaty ending the Opium War that ceded Hong Kong to the British.

Treaty of Tordesillas The 1494 treaty in which the pope divided unexplored territories between Spain and Portugal.

Treaty of Versailles The 1919 peace treaty between Germany and the Allied nations; it blamed the war on Germany and assessed heavy reparations and large territorial losses on the part of Germany.

triangular trade The eighteenth-century trade network between Europe, Africa, and the Americas.

tribute The payment of a tax in the form of goods and labor by subject peoples.

Truman Doctrine A 1947 statement by U.S. President Truman that pledged aid to any nation resisting communism.

Twelve Tables The codification of Roman law during the republic.

umma The community of all Muslim believers.

United Nations The international organization founded in 1945 to establish peace and cooperation among nations.

universal male suffrage The right of all males within a given society to vote.

untouchables The social division in Hindu society that fell in rank below the caste system; it was occupied by those who carried out undesirable occupations such as undertaking, butchering, and waste collection.

varna A caste in the Hindu caste system.

vassal In medieval Europe, a person who pledged military or other service to a lord in exchange for a gift of land or other privilege.

Vedas The oral hymns to the Aryan deities, later written down, that formed the basis of the Hindu beliefs during the Vedic Age (1500–500 BCE).

viceroyalty A political unit ruled by a viceroy that was the basis of organization of the Spanish colonies.

Wahhabi rebellion An early nineteenth-century attempt to restore Ottoman power through a return to traditional Islam and strict *shariah* law.

Warsaw Pact The 1955 agreement between the Soviet Union and the countries of Eastern Europe in response to NATO.

welfare state A nation in which the government plays an active role in providing services such as social security to its citizens.

World Bank An agency of the United Nations that offers loans to countries to promote trade and economic development.

World Trade Organization (WTO) An international organization begun in 1995 to promote and organize world trade.

xenophobia An intense fear of foreigners.

Yahweh Jehovah, the god of the Jews.

Yalta Conference A meeting of the leaders of the Soviet Union, Great Britain, and the United States in 1945; the Soviet Union agreed to enter the war against Japan in exchange for influence in the Eastern European states. The Yalta Conference also made plans for the establishment of a new international organization.

yin* and *yang In ancient Chinese belief, the opposing forces that bring balance to nature and life.

Young Turks Society founded in 1889 in the Ottoman Empire; its goal was to restore the constitution of 1876 and to reform the empire.

zaibatsu A large industrial organization created in Japan during the industrialization of the late nineteenth century.

ziggurat A multitiered pyramid constructed by Mesopotamians.

Zoroastrianism An ancient Persian religion that emphasized a struggle between good and evil and rewards in the afterlife for those who chose to follow a good life.

BIBLIOGRAPHY

In addition to this manual and your textbook, the following titles may help you in your preparation for the AP World History: Modern examination:

Adams, Paul V. et al. *Experiencing World History*. New York: New York University Press, 2000. ISBN: 0-8147-0691-6.

Diamond, Jared. *Guns, Germs, and Steel: The Fates of Human Societies*. New York: W. W. Norton & Company, 1999. ISBN: 0-393-31755-2.

McNeill, J. R., and William H. McNeill. *The Human Web: A Bird's-Eye View of World History*. New York: W. W. Norton & Company, 2003. ISBN: 0-393-05179-X.

Stearns, Peter N. *Cultures in Motion: Mapping Key Contacts and Their Imprints in World History*. New Haven, CT: Yale University Press, 2001. ISBN: 0-300-08229-0.

WEBSITES

The following websites may help you in your test preparation:

http://www.worldhistorymatters.org

http://www.collegeboard.com

http://www.fordham.edu/halsall/mod/modsbook.html

MAPS OF THE WORLD

The following selection of maps serves several purposes. It is not meant to be a comprehensive atlas. Your textbook contains many more specific and comprehensive maps. The selection does allow you to visualize and to put into context specific events and places and suggests general ways to look at maps. It enables you to see results of actions and changes over time. More important, this selection of maps is designed to teach you how to garner information from visual as opposed to exclusively textual sources. Questions to consider are at the end.

Political Map of the World

AUSTRALIA   Independent state

Bermuda   Dependency or area of special sovereignty

Sicily / AZORES   Island / island group

★   Capital

Scale 1:35,000,000
Robinson Projection
standard parallels 38°N and 38°S

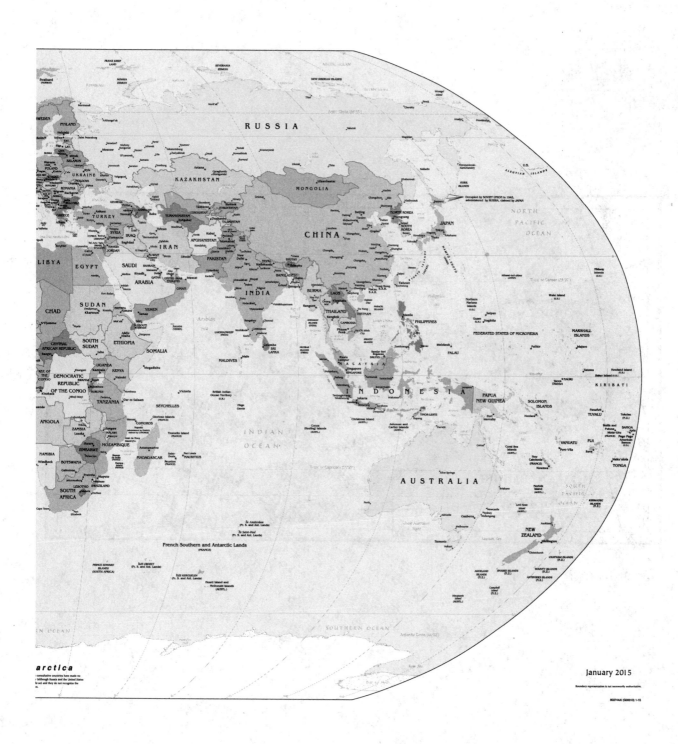

January 2015

The Roman Empire

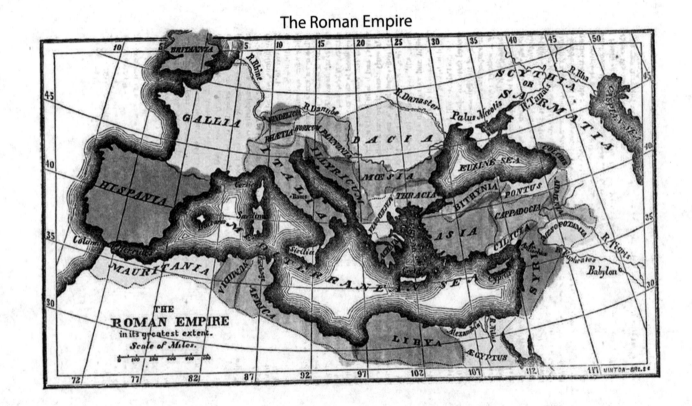

The Han Empire

CHINA
Han Dynasty
206 B.C. - 220 A.D.

- Land under rule
- Great Wall
- Current political boundaries

Kilometers
0 — 500
0 — 500
Miles

LO YANG
CHANG'AN

CHINA

Han Dynasty

THE MINNEAPOLIS INSTITUTE OF ARTS

The Gupta Empire

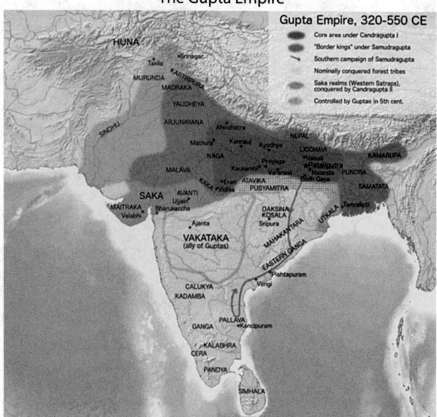

Gupta Empire, 320-550 CE

- Core area under Candragupta I
- "Border kings" under Samudragupta
- Southern campaign of Samudragupta
- Nominally conquered forest tribes
- Saka realms (Western Satraps), conquered by Candragupta II
- Controlled by Guptas in 5th cent.

Mayan Empire

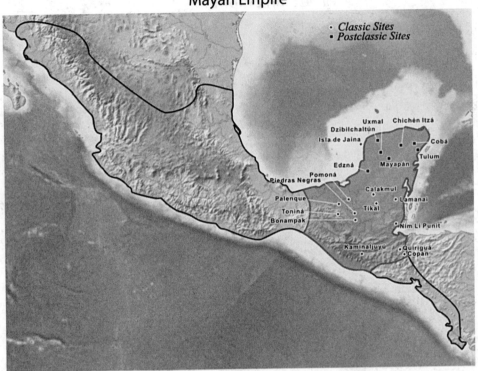

Classic Sites
Postclassic Sites

Uxmal
Dzibilchaltún
Chichén Itzá
Isla de Jaina
Cobá
Edzná
Tulum
Mayapán
Pomoná
Piedras Negras
Calakmul
Palenque
Lamanai
Toniná
Tikal
Bonampak
Nim Li Punit
Kaminaljuyú
Quiriguá
Copán

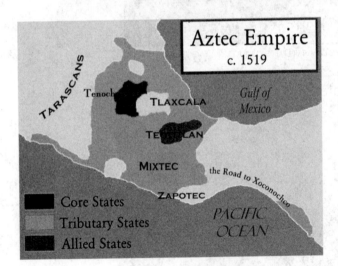

Aztec Empire
c. 1519

TARASCANS
Tenoch
TLAXCALA
Gulf of Mexico
TENOCHTITLAN
MIXTEC
the Road to Xoconochco
ZAPOTEC
PACIFIC OCEAN

Core States
Tributary States
Allied States

Incan Empire

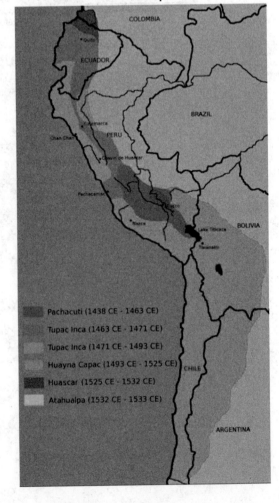

COLOMBIA
Quito
ECUADOR
Cajamarca
BRAZIL
Chan Chan
PERU
Chavín de Huascar
Pachacamac
Cuzco
Nazca
Lake Titicaca
BOLIVIA
Tiwanaku
CHILE
ARGENTINA

Pachacuti (1438 CE - 1463 CE)
Tupac Inca (1463 CE - 1471 CE)
Tupac Inca (1471 CE - 1493 CE)
Huayna Capac (1493 CE - 1525 CE)
Huascar (1525 CE - 1532 CE)
Atahualpa (1532 CE - 1533 CE)

The Mongol Empire

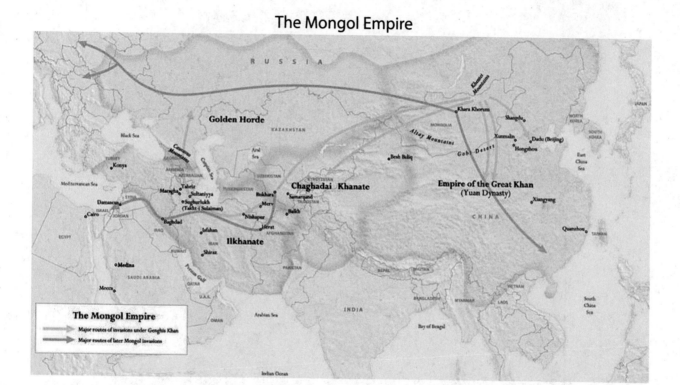

African Empires

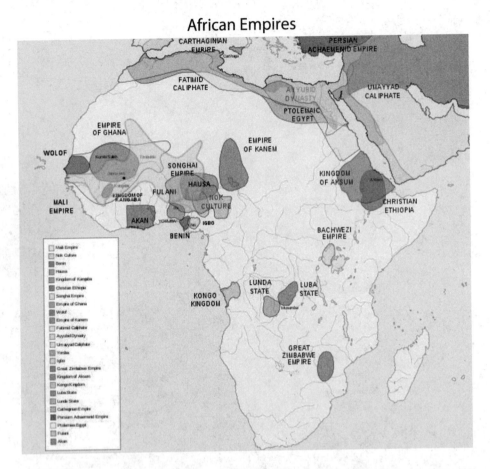

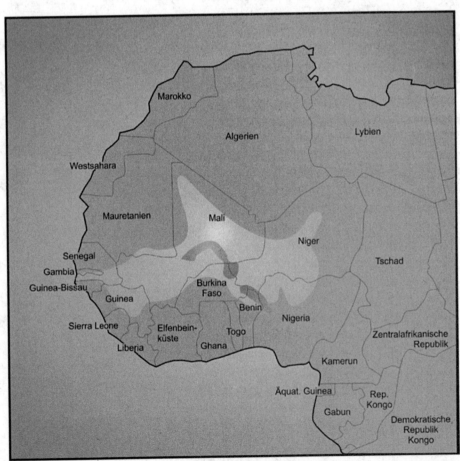

The Umayyad Empire

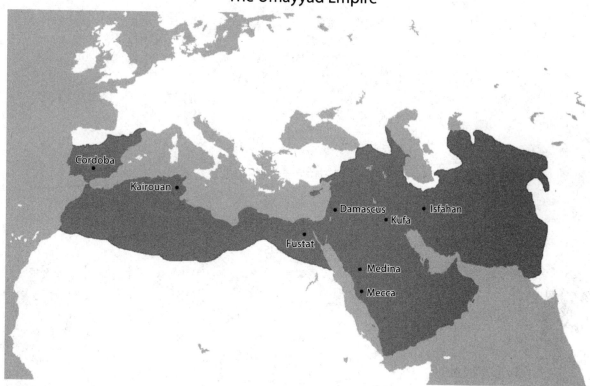

The Ottoman Empire

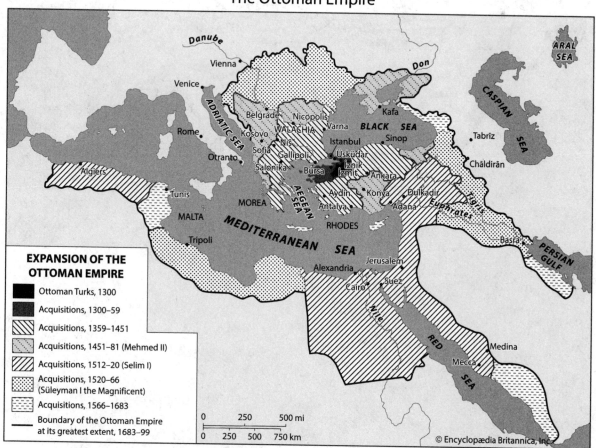

EXPANSION OF THE OTTOMAN EMPIRE

- Ottoman Turks, 1300
- Acquisitions, 1300–59
- Acquisitions, 1359–1451
- Acquisitions, 1451–81 (Mehmed II)
- Acquisitions, 1512–20 (Selim I)
- Acquisitions, 1520–66 (Süleyman I the Magnificent)
- Acquisitions, 1566–1683
- Boundary of the Ottoman Empire at its greatest extent, 1683–99

© Encyclopædia Britannica, Inc.

Silk Roads

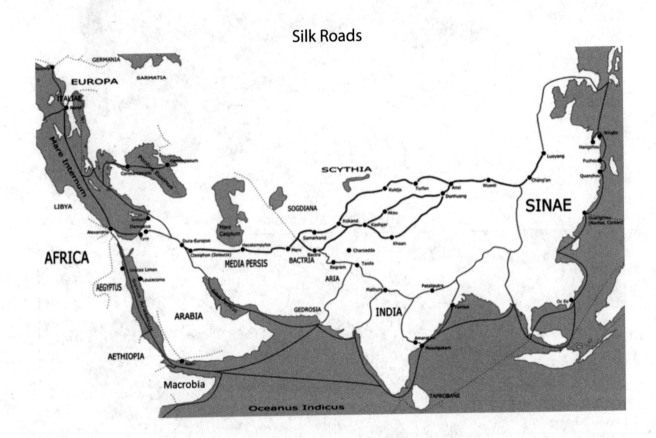

Trade Routes

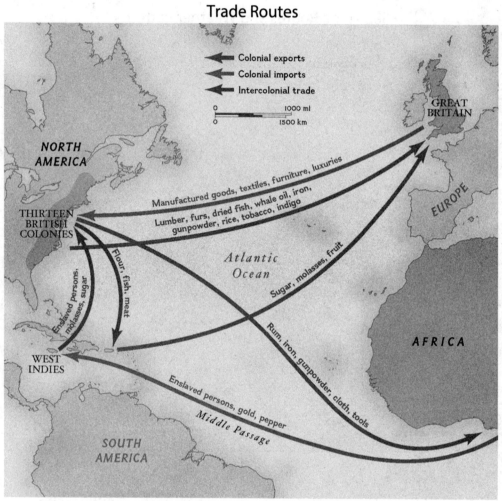

Sea Trade Routes and Weather Patterns

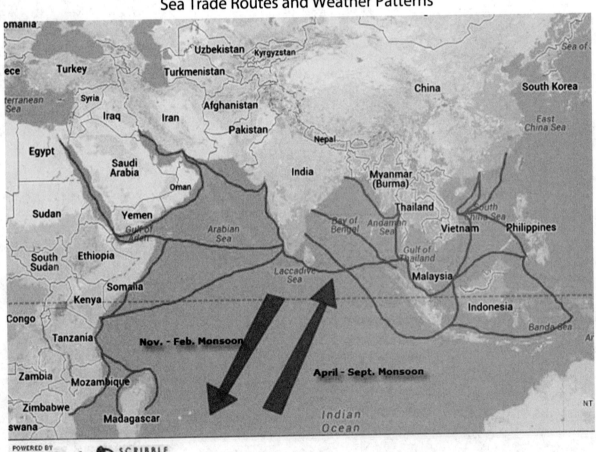

Scramble for Africa
c. 1914

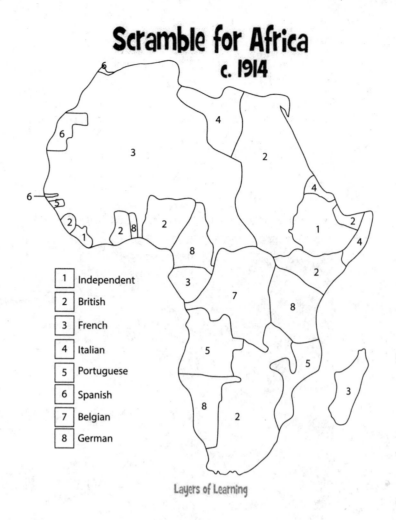

1	Independent
2	British
3	French
4	Italian
5	Portuguese
6	Spanish
7	Belgian
8	German

Layers of Learning

Pre- and Post-WWI Europe

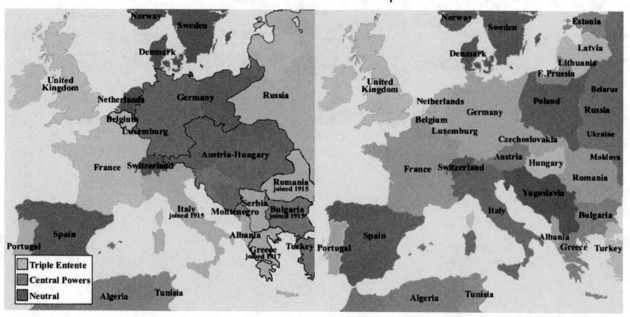

Imperial Possessions in Asia and Oceania

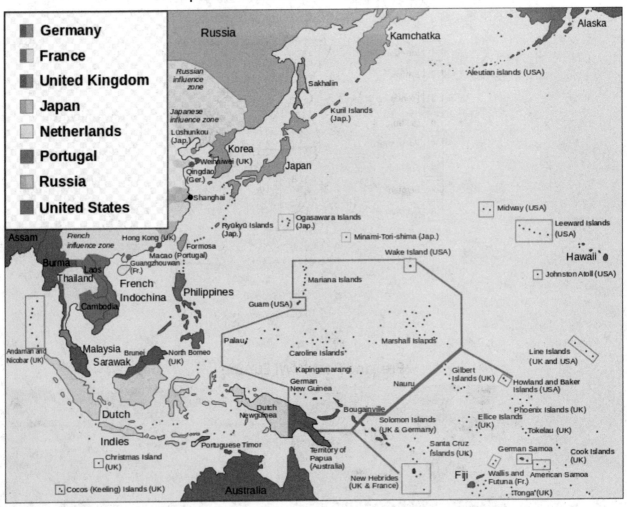

Guiding Questions and Tasks

- Be sure you can identify the seven continents, oceans and seas, major regions or countries, and major landforms (mountains, deserts, rivers) on each continent.
- General information to be gleaned from maps, includes the following, for example:
  - What European nation, bordered by Portugal, suffered a devastating civil war between 1936 and 1939?
  - What country, bordered by India, was brought under communist rule in 1949?
  - What river, the longest in the Eastern Hemisphere, begins in Tibet and flows into the East China Sea?
  - The world's largest ocean, with 46 percent of the world's water, borders the west coast of North and South America and is called…?
  - What is the world's largest continent?
- What modern-day countries fell within the confines of the ancient Roman Empire?
- How did the Romans manage (administer) their empire? Using your knowledge of world history, and considering the maps of empires, discuss shared administrative techniques of empires through history.
- What geographic features distinguished the Gupta Empire from the Han, and how might these features have contributed to its longevity?
- The North American Mayan and Aztec empires were famous for their cities and monumental architecture, while the South American Incan Empire was famous for its roads and bridges. As evidenced by the map, what geographical configurations might account for that difference?
- According to the maps, what was one unifying element of the extensive Mongol Empire? How might the Mongols have integrated the Khanates?
- How does geographic location benefit an empire economically, culturally, and politically?
- How did the exclusion or limited participation of western Europe from the major trade routes affect industrial development?
- How did trade in Russia and China differ from that in India or western Europe?
- Using your knowledge of world history and the information on the maps showing trade routes, consider how trade routes facilitated the spread of religion and the diffusion of ideas and technology.
- Support or refute the proposition that the treaties from World War I laid the foundations for future conflicts.
- Which European countries were the "winners and losers" in the scramble for Africa?
- What strategic purposes did colonial empires fulfill? Political? Economic and in terms of resources? Geopolitical?

KEY INDIVIDUALS

Following you will find the names of some of history's more influential individuals. We suggest that you begin by identifying each person. Then, consider both the reasons for the person's importance within the context of his or her times and that individual's legacies.

For example, Christopher Columbus lived from 1451 to 1506, or during the age of exploration and discovery in both the Eastern and Western Hemispheres, during the Italian Renaissance, and during the flourishing of the Incan and Aztec empires. Think about which scientific or technological advances made possible Columbus's expeditions to the New World, what Renaissance, schools of thought contributed to support for such expeditions, and both the draw of the Incan and Aztec empires as targets of conquest—God, gold, glory—and the results of conquest on the indigenous and the conquering societies. Consider Columbus's contemporaries. Who were they? How did they affect him and how did he affect them?

Abd-al-Rahman III
Albert Einstein
Alexander the Great
Aristotle
Asoka
Atahualpa
Chandragupta
Charlemagne
Charles Darwin
Chinggis Khan (Temujin)
Christopher Columbus
Cleopatra
Confucius (Kong Fuzi, Kung Fu Tzu)
Constantine
Copernicus
Cyrus the Great
Darius the Great
Eleanor of Aquitaine
Elizabeth I (England)
Empress Wu
Ferdinand Magellan
Galileo Galilei
Gautama Buddha
Hammurabi
Hernando Cortés
Hitler

Homer
Ibn Battuta
Isaac Newton
Isabella of Castille
Jesus Christ
Joan of Arc
Johann Gutenberg
Julius Caesar
Justinian
Karl Marx
King David
Kublai Khan
Lady Murasaki
Lao Tsu (Lao-zi)
Leonardo da Vinci
Louis Daguerre
Louis Pasteur
Mahatma Gandhi
Mansa Musa
Mao Zedong
Marco Polo
Martin Luther
Menes (*or* Narmer)
Michelangelo
Moctezuma II
Moses

Muhammad
Napoleon Bonaparte
Nefertiti
Nelson Mandela
Octavian (Augustus)
Pericles
Peter the Great
Saladin

Shakespeare
Simón Bolívar
Stalin
Suleiman the Magnificent
Thomas à Becket
William the Conqueror
Zheng He

The Cross-Platform Prep Course

McGraw Hill's multi-platform course gives you a variety of tools to help you raise your test scores. Whether you're studying at home, in the library, or on-the-go, you can find practice content in the format you need—print, online, or mobile.

Print Book

This print book gives you the tools you need to ace the test. In its pages you'll find smart test-taking strategies, in-depth reviews of key topics, and ample practice questions and tests. See the Welcome section of your book for a step-by-step guide to its features.

Online Platform

The Cross-Platform Prep Course gives you additional study and practice content that you can access *anytime, anywhere.* You can create a personalized study plan based on your test date that sets daily goals to keep you on track. Integrated lessons provide important review of key topics. Practice questions, exams, and flashcards give you the practice you need to build test-taking confidence. The game center is filled with challenging games that allow you to practice your new skills in a fun and engaging way. And, you can even interact with other test-takers in the discussion section and gain valuable peer support.

Getting Started

To get started, open your account on the online platform:

Go to the URL shown on the inside front cover

↓

Enter your access code

↓

Provide your name and e-mail address to open your account and create a password

↓

Click "Start Studying" to enter the platform

It's as simple as that. You're ready to start studying online.

Your Personalized Study Plan

First, select your test date on the calendar, and you'll be on your way to creating your personalized study plan. Your study plan will help you stay organized and on track and will guide you through the course in the most efficient way. It is tailored to *your* schedule and features daily tasks that are broken down into manageable goals. You can adjust your test date at any time and your daily tasks will be reorganized into an updated plan.

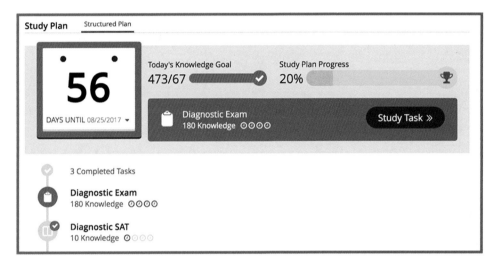

You can track your progress in real time on the Study Plan Dashboard. The "Today's Knowledge Goal" progress bar gives you up-to-the minute feedback on your daily goal. Fulfilling this every time you log on is the most efficient way to work through the entire course. You always get an instant view of where you stand in the entire course with the Study Plan Progress bar.

If you need to exit the program before completing a task, you can return to the Study Plan Dashboard at any time. Just click the Study Task icon and you can automatically pick up where you left off.

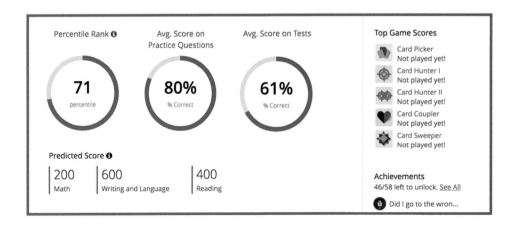

Practice Tests

One of the first tasks in your personalized study plan is to take the Diagnostic Test. At the end of the test, a detailed evaluation of your strengths and weaknesses shows the areas where you need the most focus. You can review your practice test results either by the question category to see broad trends or question-by-question for a more in-depth look.

The full-length tests are designed to simulate the real thing. Try to simulate actual testing conditions and be sure you set aside enough time to complete the full-length test. You'll learn to pace yourself so that you can work toward the best possible score on test day.

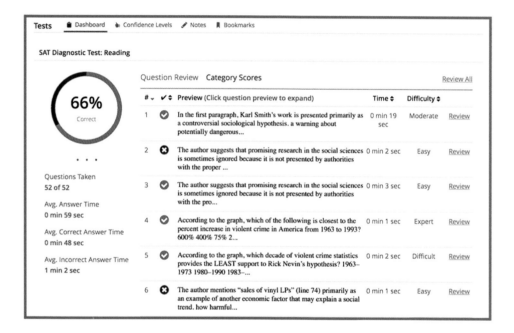

Lessons

The lessons in the online platform are divided into manageable pieces that let you build knowledge and confidence in a progressive way. They cover the full range of topics that you're likely to see on your test.

After you complete a lesson, mark your confidence level. (You must indicate a confidence level in order to count your progress and move on to the next task.) You can also filter the lessons by confidence levels to see the areas you have mastered and those that you might need to revisit.

> *Use the bookmark feature to easily refer back to a concept or leave a note to remember your thoughts or questions about a particular topic.*

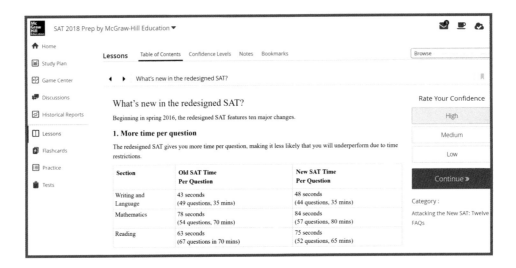

Practice Questions

All of the practice questions are reflective of actual exams and simulate the test-taking experience. The "Review Answer" button gives you immediate feedback on your answer. Each question includes a rationale that explains why the correct answer is right and the others are wrong. To explore any topic further, you can find detailed explanations by clicking the "Help me learn about this topic" link.

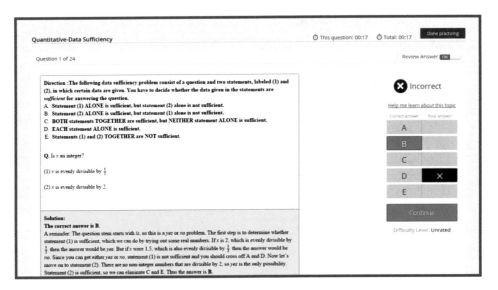

You can go to the Practice Dashboard to find an overview of your performance in the different categories and sub-categories.

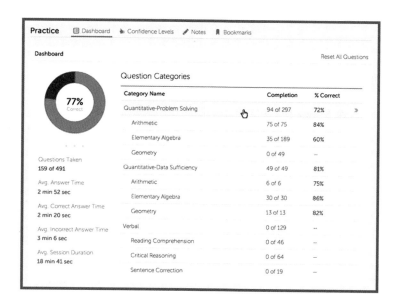

Dashboard

The dashboard is constantly updating to reflect your progress and performance. The Percentile Rank icon shows your position relative to all the other students enrolled in the course. You can also find information on your average scores in practice questions and exams.

A detailed overview of your strengths and weaknesses shows your proficiency in a category based on your answers and difficulty of the questions. By viewing your strengths and weaknesses, you can focus your study on areas where you need the most help.

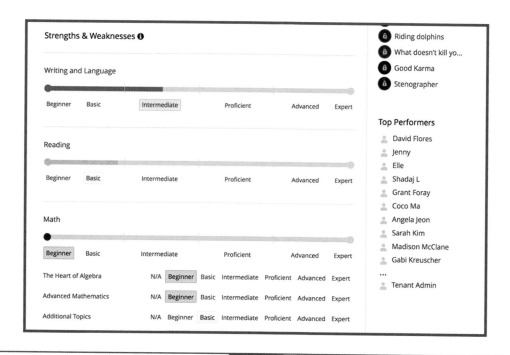

Flashcards

The hundreds of flashcards are perfect for learning key terms quickly, and the interactive format gives you immediate feedback. You can filter the cards by category and confidence level for a more organized approach. Or, you can shuffle them up for a more general challenge.

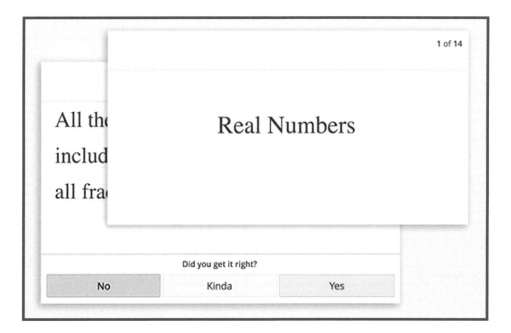

Another way to customize the flashcards is to create your own sets. You can either keep these private or share or them with the public. Subscribe to Community Sets to access sets from other students preparing for the same exam.

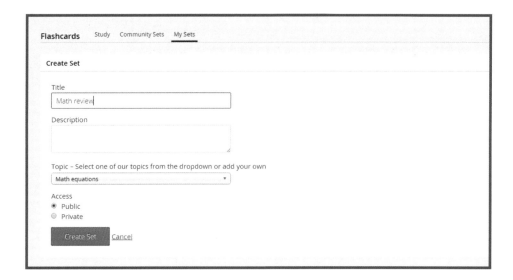

Game Center

Play a game in the Game Center to test your knowledge of key concepts in a challenging but fun environment. Increase the difficulty level and complete the games quickly to build your highest score. Be sure to check the leaderboard to see who's on top!

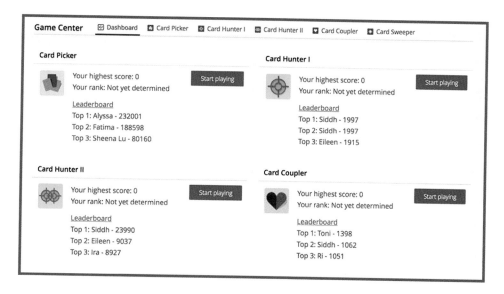

Social Community

Interact with other students who are preparing for the same test. Start a discussion, reply to a post, or even upload files to share. You can search the archives for common topics or start your own private discussion with friends.

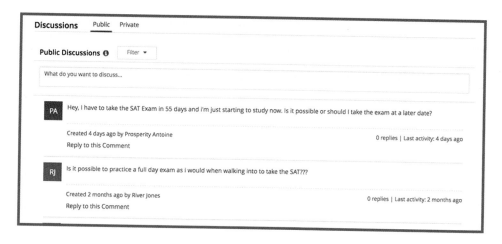

Mobile App

The companion mobile app lets you toggle between the online platform and your mobile device without missing a beat. Whether you access the course online or from your smartphone or tablet, you'll pick up exactly where you left off.

Go to the iTunes or Google Play stores and search "McGraw-Hill Education Cross-Platform App" to download the companion iOS or Android app. Enter your e-mail address and the same password you created for the online platform to open your account.

Now, let's get started!